The Yezidi Oral Tradition in Iraqi Kurdistan

The Yezidi Oral Tradition in Iraqi Kurdistan

Christine Allison

Routledge
Taylor & Francis Group
LONDON AND NEW YORK

First published 2001 by Routledge
Published 2014 by Routledge
2 Park Square, Milton Park, Abingdon, Oxfordshire OX14 4RN
711 Third Avenue, New York, NY 10017

First issued in paperback 2014

Routledge is an imprint of the Taylor & Francis Group, an informa business

Typeset in Sabon by LaserScript Ltd, Mitcham, Surrey

British Library Cataloguing in Publication Data
A catalogue record of this book is available from the British Library

Library of Congress Cataloguing in Publication Data
A catalogue record for this book has been requested

ISBN 978-0-700-71397-4 (hbk)
ISBN 978-1-138-88387-1 (pbk)

To David

Contents

Preface ix
Acknowledgements xiii
Abbreviations xv
Map 1: Areas inhabited by Kurds xvii
Map 2: Yezidi communities in Northern Iraq: Badinan and Sinjar xviii

Part I

1 Interpreting Yezidi Oral Tradition: Orality in Kurmanji and Fieldwork in Kurdistan 3
2 The Yezidis of Northern Iraq and the People of the Book 26
3 Chronological and Generic Frameworks in Yezidi Oral Tradition 53
4 Battles, Heroes and Villains: Portrayals of Conflict 86
5 Representations of Romantic Love 135
6 Death, Loss and Lamentation in Yezidi Verbal Art 167
7 Conclusions 200

Part II: Kurdish Texts and Translations

Introduction 213
Section A: Stories and Songs of Battle 215
Section B: Stories and Songs of Love 259
Section C: Songs of Grief and Lamentation 273

Notes to Chapters 1–6 281
Appendix: Informants and Performers 292
Bibliography 297
Index 304

Preface

This book is an exercise in 'mapping', in a form comprehensible to outsiders, the terrain of the oral tradition of the Yezidis, Kurdistan's misunderstood religious minority. It attempts to identify the major areas and features of this oral tradition, and to note their relationships with one another. Like most initial attempts at mapmaking, it is quite possible that as the territory becomes better known to scholars, many of the contentions and conclusions of this work will be debated. Nevertheless, the first step has to be taken. Scholarly attention has so far focused primarily on traditions associated with the Yezidi religion. Most of the secular material published so far has been in Kurdish, and even where translations into European languages have been made, the meanings of the traditions for the Yezidis have not been explored. They are certainly overdue for academic study; the oral traditions of the Yezidis, and of Kurds in general, are one part of a whole field of 'folklore' which is not only full of variety but also very strong in emotional resonance. Even the discourses of identity of young, urban Kurds make some use of it. Images from oral tradition are found in popular songs, political speeches, paintings and novels; they are employed with great enthusiasm by Kurdish nation-builders. The Yezidis are part of this Kurdish cultural process, but they have their own special concerns.

It is no idle metaphor to use the analogy of cartography for the process of studying the oral traditions of Yezidis and other Kurds. For many peoples who recall much of their past orally, there is an intimate relationship between the topography of the land and the narratives of the people. Oral tradition is the vehicle for the transmission of most Kurdish history and almost all specifically Yezidi history. The events recalled in that tradition are very closely associated with particular locations in the homeland. In Kurdish discourses, the process of remembering the land also recalls its history, including both conventionally 'historical' and more 'legendary' events. For the Yezidis in particular, whose whole way of life is integrated into their religion, past and present events are closely linked to each other and to their environment. Locations are not only associated with past events, but may also be imbued with strong religious meanings. History, especially religious history, finds expression in current social structures; Yezidi identity is expressed in terms of religious purity and of difference from other groups. At such an early stage in Kurdish oral studies, this book will not venture to consider the religious dimensions of Yezidi oral culture in detail, but it will consider some of the most popular kinds of secular oral tradition, set them in the context of Yezidi discourse, and consider their position in Yezidi life in Iraqi Kurdistan at the close of the twentieth century.

I have tried to understand some of the most important meanings which the Yezidis ascribe to their oral traditions by collecting some traditions myself, comparing them to the relatively few examples already published, and asking numerous Yezidis, in Northern Iraq and in Europe, about the meaning and significance of oral traditions in general and specific examples in particular. I have tried to avoid limiting individual Yezidi voices as Orientalists have been so wont to do in the past, though some factors have complicated this. Given the volatility of politics in Iraq, where association with Westerners can sometimes bring reprisals, acquaintances and friends still living there will remain anonymous in this book. Even for those Iraqis now living outside Iraq I think it best to use names sparingly. Thus I have sometimes referred to 'informants', though I have also tried to give some sense of individual identity and integrity by using such shorthand as 'Mr H.' etc. The reader can then gain some idea of the help given by each of these individuals, and I hope it will be clear that some gave a great deal of their time and patience. It will certainly be abundantly clear that this book has been written by an outsider, a non-native speaker, conditioned to think in Western academic terms, who has had to start from first principles in attempting to understand very complex forms of communication.

In trying to find a framework in which Yezidi oral traditions could be analysed and discussed, I discovered that the three broad themes of war, love and death, apart from being readily understandable to outsiders, were also used by Yezidi performers themselves to categorise the lyrical songs which they sing. Analysis of the treatment of these three themes is the core of this book. However, thematic analysis is not enough without an understanding of genre and context. Thus a number of introductory chapters are also necessary; Chapter One sets the current work in its academic context, of studies of Kurdish 'folklore' and of orality and literacy. Chapter Two describes the fieldwork environment of the Northern Iraqi Yezidi community, including some important aspects of Yezidi identity. Chapter Three gives an overview of the most important generic and historical frameworks of the oral traditions. In Chapters Four, Five and Six, a number of Kurdish texts and translations are discussed; some of these are quite long and, if placed within the main part of the book, they would break up the argument. Instead I have opted to put them together at the end, though this admittedly incurs the risk that they will be 'lost', or that the reader will endlessly be trying to move between text and discussion. I have attempted to minimise this annoyance by quoting substantially from the texts during the discussion chapters, so that the argument can be followed, but the reader will have a much fuller impression of these compositions if each is read at the point at which it is summarised in the main part of the book, before the discussion begins. Chapter Seven briefly brings together some of the conclusions of the preceding chapters and considers their implications.

I have used the term 'Iraqi Kurdistan' in the full knowledge that it is unacceptable to many; however, despite this, and despite the many debates over the exact extent of the territory of Kurdistan, it still seems to me the most widely understandable term referring to that part of the modern state of Iraq which is predominantly inhabited by Kurds. Iraqi Kurdistan, in its traditional sense, comprises the Kurdish provinces of Badinan, north-west of the Great Zab river, where the northern Kurdish dialect of Kurmanji (the language of the Yezidis) is spoken, and Soran, to the south, where the other major dialect, Sorani, is spoken. Since 1991, when much of Iraqi Kurdistan came under Kurdish control, the term has been used to denote the area under Kurdish administration (the modern governorates of Dihok, Erbil and Suleymaniye); however, this 'Kurdish autonomous zone' or 'Kurdish zone' is smaller than the true extent of Iraqi Kurdistan. This zone stretches beyond the so-called 'safe havens' originally set up by the Allied military, extending from Pêsh Khabûr in the west to the Iranian frontier in the east; its border follows a line through the 'Saddam Lake', Fayde (near Dihok), to the south of Ba'drê, north of 'Eyn Sifni, west of 'Aqra, southwards to the Kelek Bridge (south-west of Erbil), and west of Chemchemal; thus it covers the large towns of Dihok, Erbil, Suleymaniye and Halabja. It includes some, but not all, of the sizeable Yezidi settlements of Northern Iraq. The frontier between Kurdish and Iraqi government-held areas passes through the Yezidi region of Sheykhan.

Kurdish is usually written in Arabic script in Iraq and Iran and often in Cyrillic in the former Soviet Union. The transcription system which has been used for the texts in this work broadly follows the scheme developed by Bedir Khan for writing Kurmanji in Roman script. The system has been well explained elsewhere, and it would be superfluous to list it in detail here. Letters are pronounced as in UK English, with the following exceptions: a is long as in f*a*rmer, c as in *j*elly, ç as in *ch*ip, e is close (in Badinan) to the English short a of c*a*t, ê as in French m*è*re, i either as Turkish ı or as in English f*i*sh, î as in f*ee*l, j as in English plea*s*ure, q as pronounced in Arabic, ṛ as a strongly rolled 'Italian' r, ş as in *sh*ip, û as in f*oo*l, x as in lo*ch*. Among Iraqi Kurds, letters such as ḥ (as in the name Ḥasan), '('ain, glottal stop) and ẍ (ghain) are given the Arabic pronunciation. The difference between î and ê, and e and a at the end of words, is often very difficult to hear in Badinani Kurmanji. Double consonants are usually not used by Kurdish authors, and their convention has been followed here.

The texts are taken from various sources, with slightly differing transcription systems; for the sake of consistency, slight modifications have been made to the way some texts transcribe certain sounds. However, in those texts which I transcribed myself, I have tried to remain faithful to the performance by preserving the pronunciation of the speaker; thus some slight inconsistencies may be detectable in words which are used many times, and at some points where the words do not seem to conform to 'standard' Kurdish grammar. All the translations, except that of the love song *Kherabo*, which is based on an existing French translation by Roger Lescot, are my own.

For Kurdish words and the proper names in Part I, it is difficult to achieve consistency. Arabic and Persian names have different transcription conventions, and the Turkish alphabet is different again. There are certain very well-known placenames, such as Erbil or Halabja, and words, such as *sheykh*, where deviation from norms would simply be distracting, so I have kept to common English norms. In general, I have attempted to make the main body of text easily readable by avoiding excessive use of diacritical marks. For the less familiar Kurdish names, I have used a transcription system as close to English as possible when they are presented in their Kurdish context. Thus I have used sh for Kurdish *ş*, ch for Kurdish *ç*, kh for Kurdish *x*, and zh for Kurdish *j* (as in English vision). For the vowels, the Kurdish system, with its circumflexes, is not counter-intuitive for English speakers, and I have adopted it. However, there are certain key Kurdish terms where Kurdish transcription has been retained throughout, such as *stranbêj*; these are italicised. In general I have avoided the use of the *ezafet* in Kurdish names; however some individuals, usually poets or heroes of oral traditions, are invariably referred to by at least two names, such as Ehmedê Khanî or Derwêshê 'Evdi, and I have retained it in these cases. For certain Kurdish tribal and village names I have used standardised Kurdish forms such as Bekiran, where local usage is more often Bekira. For names which are well known or are common in this book, such as Tur Abdin, Sheykh Adi, and Kurmanji, simplified forms are used. Where Kurdish authors or informants have themselves chosen to transcribe their names in a specific way, it seems courteous to keep to their preferences.

Many of the conclusions of this book are rather tentative; the 'map' I have drawn still has many sections marked 'Here be Dragons' or similar. Certainly the meaning and significance of certain images and concepts could be explored much further; this will require a detailed consideration of a wider range of oral traditions. Even those relatively few texts I have selected for analysis are considered primarily from the standpoint of the subject-matter, the imagery and the broader patterns of construction. Much more could be done on the analysis of technical formal details. I hope that such work will be done in the future, and that the terrain of Kurdish oral tradition will become much more familiar to scholars.

Acknowledgements

Many people have helped and advised me during the preparation of this book, though its weaknesses and errors are all my own. Professor Philip Kreyenbroek, who supervised the original doctoral thesis and read the final drafts, has always managed to combine acute criticism with steadfast support. Dr Khelîl Jindî Rashow supplied a great deal of information and some hitherto unpublished traditions; he also painstakingly read and advised on the translations. Professor Jelîlê Jelîl gave permission to reproduce material from his previous publications. I am particularly grateful for Mrs Catherine Lawrence's maps, which are not only clear, but the map of western Badinan is the most up-to-date I have yet seen. Its basis, which needed many updates, came from Edmonds 1967, with the kind permission of the Royal Asiatic Society. I would also like to thank Professor Joyce Blau, Dr Stuart Blackburn, Professor Martin van Bruinessen, Mr Peter Colvin, Dr Ken Emond, Dr Nelida Fuccaro, Professor Graham Furniss, the late Mr John Guest, Mr Ḥeso Nermo, Mrs Mieke Kreyenbroek, Dr Oric L'vov Basirov, Dr Maria T. O'Shea, Mr Abdilaḥad Hormuz Khoshaba, Mrs Fawziya Rahman, Mr Ibrahim Sheykh Rashow, Mrs Hayat Rashow, Dr Shukriya Rasul, Mr Baran Rizgar, the late Mr Kurt Schork, Pîr Khidir Silêman, Mr Qasim Shesho.

Acknowledgements are also due to the British Academy, the Harold Hyam Wingate Foundation, the School of Oriental and African Studies, and the University of London Central Research Fund, for generous financial support. For help during the fieldwork in the 'Safe Haven' I would like to express my gratitude to both KDP and PUK, and to members of the other parties, for general encouragement and practical help, and also to MCC personnel; among the Yezidis, to the family of Mîr Teḥsin Beg, and to those private individuals who helped organise transport, accommodation and contacts. In particular, I wish to thank the many local people, Yezidi, Muslim and Christian, who welcomed me generously as a guest and gave their time and expertise to my research. They must remain anonymous here but their help is certainly not forgotten. Finally, and most importantly of all, I would like to thank my husband, David Taylor, to whom I dedicate this book.

Abbreviations

JOURNALS

AION	*Annali dell'Instituto Orientale di Napoli*
ARA	*Annual Review of Anthropology*
BMGS	*Byzantine and Modern Greek Studies*
BSOAS	*Bulletin of the School of Oriental and African Studies*
BSOS	*Bulletin of the School of Oriental Studies*
JA	*Journal Asiatique*
JAF	*Journal of American Folklore*
JRAS	*Journal of the Royal Asiatic Society*
IJMES	*International Journal of Middle East Studies*
JMMA	*Journal of Muslim Minority Affairs*
JFR	*Journal of Folklore Research*
REMMM	*Revue du Monde Musulman et de la Mediterrannée*
ROC	*Revue de l'Orient Chrétien*
RSO	*Rivista degli Studi Orientali*
StIr	*Studia Iranica*

INFORMANTS AND SOURCES

BR	*Kurdish-English English-Kurdish Dictionary* (Rizgar 1993)
KJR	Dr. Khelîl Jindî Rashow
PKS	Pîr Khidir Silêman
ZK	*Zargotina K'urda* (Jelîl 1978)

OTHER

Ar.	Arabic
Kd.	Kurdish
Kurm.	Kurmanji
Ps.	Persian
Sor.	Sorani
Tk.	Turkish

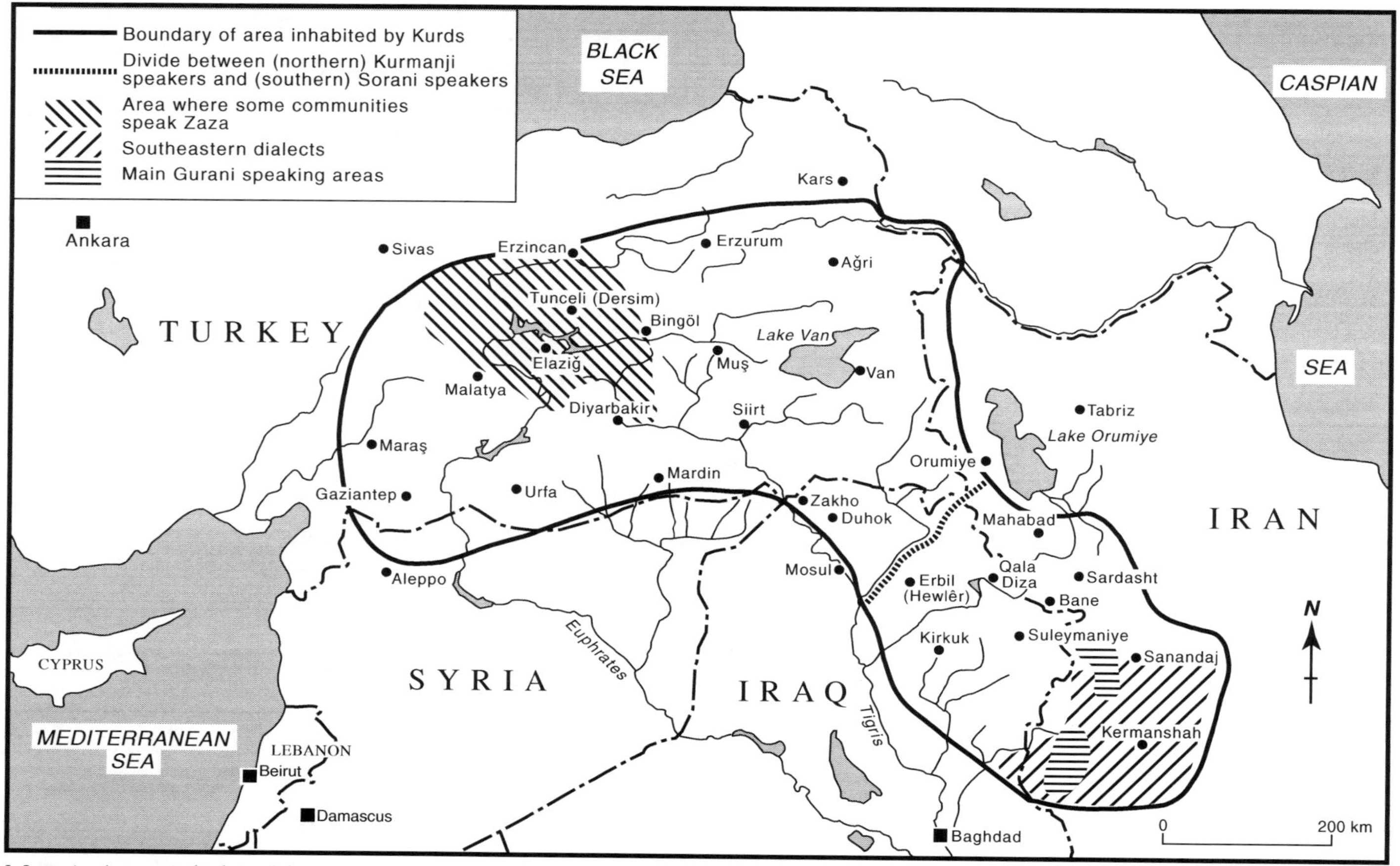

Map 1: Areas inhabited by Kurds

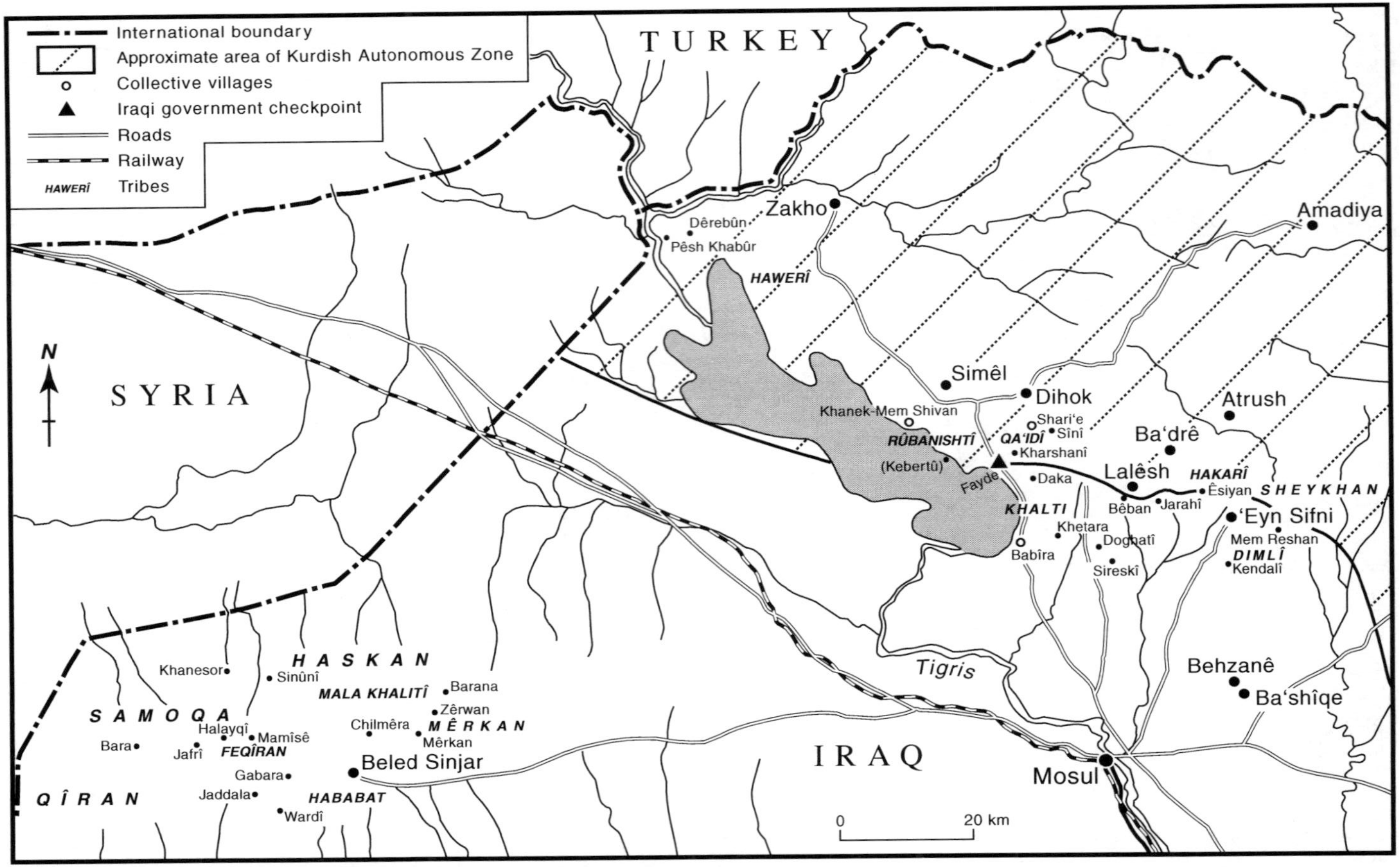

Map 2: Yezidi communities in Northern Iraq: Badinan and Sinjar

Part I

CHAPTER ONE

Interpreting Yezidi Oral Tradition: Orality in Kurmanji and Fieldwork in Kurdistan

INTRODUCTION

For centuries Orientalists have been fascinated by the Yezidis of Kurdistan and their curious religion. A great deal has been written, much of it speculative, about their origins, their beliefs and their more arcane practices. Both Oriental and Western scholars and travellers of the past, conditioned by contact with 'religions of the Book', usually came to the Yezidis with a preconceived scheme of religious categories in their minds, into which they sought to fit the Yezidis. The Yezidis' answers were determined by the researchers' questions, and where entire Yezidi accounts of events or beliefs were collected, these were not interpreted in the light of the Yezidis' world-view, but according to the researchers' own preconceptions. Until the recent emergence of an educated younger generation, they only reached a reading public at second hand, via others' descriptions. As a result, the Yezidis became one of the more misunderstood groups of the Middle East, the exotic 'devil-worshippers of Kurdistan'.

Within the last generation there has been a move towards a fuller study of the Yezidis' own discourses. This has partly been done through ethnography (al-Jabiri 1981, Murad 1993, Ahmad 1975) but also by means of considering their religious 'texts' as examples of oral tradition (Kreyenbroek 1995). Oral tradition is crucially important for the Yezidis, as amongst their many religious taboos was a traditional ban on literacy. They communicated with their neighbours, and passed on their community history, literature, wisdom and religious texts to their descendants, orally. There is an intimate relationship between the spoken forms and methods of transmission of this oral material and its content. This book seeks to analyse the way this community, so often described by outsiders, describes the key subjects of war, love and death through oral tradition, the only form of literature available to the entire community. These traditions are intimately related to the Yezidis' perception of their own identity.

This is not the first study of Yezidi oral 'texts'; academic understanding of the religion has advanced considerably through recent publications on Yezidi cosmogonies, and on the orally transmitted sacred hymns or *qewl*s and their place in the religion (Kreyenbroek 1992, 1995). However, it is the first study of Yezidi, and indeed of Kurdish, secular oral traditions within their social context. Although this book concentrates on secular oral tradition, it should be emphasised that, since Yezidism is a religion of orthopraxy, practising Yezidis are living out their religion in their everyday life; every aspect of the traditional life is associated with taboos, observances or devotions. Thus even those secular oral traditions which will be discussed here contain many allusions to Yezidi religious themes, and should not be divorced from their religious context. The traditions under consideration in this book are historical, that is, they are generally believed to be about real individuals who lived in the past. The performances of oral literature in which they are couched are not only a major source of factual knowledge of the past for Yezidis, but for the outsider their analysis can also yield a great deal of information, not only about Yezidi aesthetics and poetics, but also about their current preoccupations. What the Yezidis choose to tell, or to withhold, about the past, reveals much about their present attitudes.

This study, then, hopes to come closer to the Yezidis' identity than the approaches of the older Orientalists, though, as the work of an outsider, it cannot claim to understand the community's comment on itself at every level. It is fully appreciated that the concept of 'social context' is itself ethnocentric; which social and cultural elements are emphasised and which ignored are at the discretion of the researcher. For reasons of space, this study cannot discuss every single form of oral tradition used by the Yezidis, and it is a matter of particular regret that the music of the traditions will not be analysed. Nevertheless, the material presented here has never before been the subject of academic study, and those few traditions which I will discuss in detail are certainly considered by the Yezidis to be important. Since not only the content of the traditions, but also the forms used, the modes of transmission and, wherever possible, the styles of performance will be considered, it is hoped that this work will be a starting-point for new methodologies in Kurdish studies. No study can be fully objective; later in this chapter I shall declare my own preconceptions as far as possible by outlining the methodologies to be used.

The Yezidi community in Northern Iraq lends itself particularly to this type of study. They are a discrete community among other groups, but their religious and social structure ensures a degree of social and cultural uniformity which, given the variety of cultures found in Kurdistan, is greater than might be expected from a group spread over an area stretching from Jebel Sinjar to ʿAqra in Iraq. During fieldwork, done between March and mid-October 1992 in the area of Northern Iraq controlled by the

Kurds, Yezidi informants claimed that the important stories were uniform throughout the community as they represented the 'true' and distinctive Yezidi history. However, this book will not only present material collected during fieldwork. Published collections of Kurdish 'folklore' have included Yezidi material collected in Armenia and Syria earlier this century and in Badinan and Jezîre Botan at the end of the nineteenth century; these offer opportunity for comparative study, and have been used accordingly.

The Yezidis of Northern Iraq, with the exception of a few Arabic-speaking villages, have Kurmanji Kurdish as their mother-tongue, and their oral traditions include a great deal of material describing past events in what is now Eastern Turkey. Despite their notions of separateness, they have never been a community in isolation from the rest of Kurdish tribal politics. Some of the observations one can make about Yezidi discourses also hold good for those of other Kurdish groups, and before we can describe the special nature of Yezidi orality (which will be discussed in the next chapter), we must place the Yezidis in sociolinguistic context, by discussing what 'orality' and 'literacy' mean, and how they apply, in the context of Kurmanji. It will then be necessary to contextualise this work, by outlining its relationship to past studies of Kurmanji material, its theoretical stance within the multidisciplinary field of oral studies, and the fieldwork environment which influenced the methodologies used.

THE KURMANJI CONTEXT

It is unfortunate that despite a number of very useful studies of Near and Middle Eastern oral poetry and folktales (e.g. Slyomovics 1987, Muhawi 1989, Reynolds 1995), and a few outstanding accounts of the role of oral traditions within certain groups (e.g. Abu Lughod 1988, Grima 1992, Mills 1990, Shryock 1997), oral traditions remain irrevocably associated in many academic minds with 'folklore' in its most pejorative sense, with picturesque but obsolete customs and spurious accounts of the past. This is a narrow and outmoded view of both oral tradition and folklore, of which oral tradition forms a part. With some honourable exceptions, scholars of the Near and Middle East lag behind those working on other regions, notably Africa, in their appreciation of the political dimensions of oral tradition. Orientalists in general seem to show a reluctance to move on from their perception of 'folklore studies' as merely a matter of classically inspired oral-formulaic analyses of reassuringly obscure and irrelevant genres. Yet in the authoritarian states of the Near and Middle East, where written material is rigorously censored, points of view which contradict the government are usually by necessity expressed orally. Oral communication is often the vehicle of minority discourses, of tendencies deemed to be subversive; oral tradition, with its hallowed accounts of the people's past, provides a whole fund of folkloric examples which can be used to justify political courses of action, to rouse a rabble, or to fuel a revolution. During the 1990s, the Newroz myth of the Iranian New Year (as told in Kurdish tradition rather than the Persian version of the *Shah-name*) was used as a symbol of Kurdish liberation in Turkey, sparking widespread unrest in towns and cities every March. Governments also use folklore in their own propaganda; Turkey, for instance, claims Nasruddin Hoca as its own, though he is found in the traditions of many countries in the region (Marzolph 1998). Oral tradition, along with other aspects of folklore, is an important element in discourses of nationalism and of identity all over the modern Middle East; Kurdistan is not exceptional in this respect, though circumstances have conspired to make Kurmanji in particular more 'oral' and less 'literary' than many other languages of the region.

Despite the long tradition of Kurdish scholars and authors, many of whom used Arabic, Persian or Turkish as well as Kurdish in their writings, the great majority of Kurds in the past have not been literate enough to be able to read 'literature'. Kurmanji, the northern dialect of Kurdish, is spoken by Kurds living in Eastern Turkey, Northern Iraq, Northern Syria, Iran, and Transcaucasia. It is the dialect of the first Kurdish written literature, the works of Melayê Jezîrî and Ehmedê Khanî,[1] and is spoken by more people than the other major dialect, Sorani. However, its influence has been lessened in the twentieth century by government repression of the language in those states where Kurds live. In the last years of the Ottoman empire, literacy overall must have been relatively low among the Kurmanji speakers of Eastern Anatolia by comparison with other provinces.[2] Kurdish had not hitherto been proscribed, but in the new Republic of Turkey it was outlawed in the 1920s, beginning with its prohibition for all official purposes in 1924. Even education in Turkish was out of the question for most Kurds at this time; only 215 of the 4,875 schools in Turkey were located in Kurdish areas (MacDowall 1996: 192). Educational opportunities in Eastern Anatolia grew far more slowly than those elsewhere in Turkey as the century passed, but what State education was available was in Turkish. Education in Kurmanji was never officially permitted; this situation continues today. Not only were publication and broadcast in Kurmanji forbidden for most of the twentieth century, but at times of greatest repression Kurds could be fined, or otherwise punished, for speaking the language. Along with the renaming of Kurds as 'mountain Turks' came spurious classification of Kurmanji as a deviant Turkish language (e.g. Firat 1961). With the exception of a few years during the 1960s, and the years since 1991 when Kurmanji was once more legalised, no Kurdish publications have been produced at all in Turkey. Social mobility and progress required Turkish, usually learned at school or during military service. Men, of course, had more access to these forms of education than women. The development of Kurmanji suffered enormously during the whole period; by the 1970s it was a household language only, and could hardly be used for serious political debate. Since then, the efforts of Kurdish intellectuals, politicians, journalists and broadcasters, mainly based in the diaspora, have improved the situation to some extent (van Bruinessen 1998: 46), but Kurmanji remains at a serious disadvantage, with many Kurds from Turkey still perceiving it as primitive. The position in Syria, where Kurmanji has no official status, has been little better (e.g. Nazdar 1980). The situation in Iraq was rather different; when the *vilayet* of Mosul was awarded to the new state, the League of Nations stipulated that Kurdish should be the official language of administration, justice and education in the Kurdish areas (MacDowall 1996: 145–6). However, it was the southern dialect of Kurdish, Sorani, the majority language of the Iraqi Kurds, which received sanction as an official language of Iraq. The Kurmanji speakers of Badinan province, north of the Great Zab, amongst whom were many Yezidis, did not receive the same range of language rights. Nevertheless, publication and broadcasting of Kurmanji was permitted (though censored), and Kurmanji literature could be studied at university level. But Sorani, with its burgeoning written literature, became culturally dominant over Kurmanji. In Iran, where, as in Iraq, Kurmanji is a minority dialect, the Kurdish language was banned at times during the twentieth century. Only within the Soviet Union, and in the Kurdish diaspora, did extensive study and development of Kurmanji take place. In Soviet Georgia and Armenia, though subject to political censorship, Kurds have been able to publish and broadcast in Kurmanji throughout this century.

Native speakers of Kurmanji living in Turkey, Iraq, Iran and Syria did not receive their education in Kurmanji but in Turkish, Arabic or Persian, and consequently, though some living in Southern Iraqi Kurdistan might have learned to read Sorani, few learned to read Kurmanji. The scope for literary contact between Iraq and Turkey has been lessened by the fact that in Iraq (as in Iran) a modified Arabic script has been used to write Kurdish, whereas the Kurds of Turkey who published clandestinely or in the diaspora used a modified Roman alphabet similar to that used for Turkish. In the rural Kurmanji-speaking areas of both Turkey and Iraq the lack of access to state schooling has meant that, despite the growth of mass literacy in these countries during the twentieth century, Kurmanji in the homeland remains a language used primarily for speaking rather than writing.

Definitions: 'Oralities' and 'Literacies' in Kurmanji

It is legitimate to say that Kurmanji is a primarily 'oral' as opposed to literary language, notwithstanding the considerable number of new writers and works (Blau 1996); to investigate what this implies for Kurdish culture, we must consider our terms carefully. Although the term 'oral' can be liberating, opening up whole new areas of literature for academic consideration, it can also be problematic; by applying it to a whole people or culture one may imply that some uniform 'oral' world-view prevails in all areas, over all those who lack sophisticated reading skills. Even in Turkey where Kurmanji is least developed, many Kurds read Turkish, and some older people read some Arabic, learned in the village *medrese* or Koranic school. (Such schools were outlawed by the secularist Turkish state but some continued to exist clandestinely.)[3] Worse still, the universalist view of 'orality' or 'preliteracy' as a general condition, a stage through which all societies must pass on their way to literacy and consequent civilisation, has become influential in the studies of Middle Eastern literatures, as a result of the work of Ong (1982) in particular, which draws heavily on the work of Eric Havelock and Albert Lord. These somewhat romantic views can encourage the idea that oral genres are unsophisticated because of their contention that literacy is necessary for higher cultural forms.[4] Trenchant and convincing criticism of such work has been made by Finnegan (1990: 143–6) and Thomas, whose summing up of the issues is particularly clear and perceptive (1992: 15–20); it is unnecessary to reproduce the arguments here. However, outdated ideas are often taken up in propaganda wars; Kurmanji is sometimes portrayed in the Turkish context as pre-literate and therefore primitive, just as its marvellously rich range of subdialects and lack of a standardised form are said to prevent it from being a 'proper language'. Such ideas do not stand up to scrutiny and would be laughable if they were not believed by some Kurds.

Because of the universalist associations of 'orality' as a term, some scholars are justifiably reluctant to use it; however, it seems to me to be permissible if its meaning is carefully qualified, because it implies a legitimate range of modes of communication; it dignifies and assigns a status to non-literate messages, and, by extension, to the study of these messages. Orality is not just a negative, a lack of literacy, nor is it such a dominant characteristic that it determines all the features of a group's oral culture and cognitive processes. It is only one of a number of important factors, and it is culture-specific. To describe a group's orality in a meaningful way one must understand its uses of language and the major genres used for communication. Certain features, such as repetition and the use of mnemonics, are found in most types of oral tradition throughout the world, but one cannot generalise about the nature of 'oral' forms of communication or the thought processes of those who produce and listen to them. One can merely identify common tendencies.

The question of 'literacy', a term whose meaning is questioned far less often than that of orality, is similarly complex. The work of Scribner and Cole among the Vai of Liberia is illuminating, as, like Kurdistan, their fieldwork area was a milieu where various languages were used; they compared the literacy of the Qur'anic schools with that of the state schools teaching English and that of the Vai syllabic script, taught outside these institutional environments. Their definition of literacy was as a 'recurrent, goal-directed sequence of activities using a particular technology and particular systems of knowledge' (1981: 237). Street (1984) has convincingly argued for an 'ideological' rather than an 'autonomous' definition of literacy – for him, as for Scribner and Cole, literacy is not a neutral, easily defined skill, but there are many types of literacy, and its impact on those who learn it will vary considerably according to its usages in that society. He demonstrates that notions of 'functional literacy' are often flawed because they take no account of this ideological dimension of literacy teaching. It is extremely difficult to separate 'literacy' from the ideological dimension. It follows from this that such experiments as those of Luria in the Soviet Union (1976, discussed in Ong 1982: 49–57) which purported to find general cognitive change in peasants who had been taught to read, become less convincing as a general paradigm of the result of literacy, because it is very difficult to prove that it was in fact the literacy, not the ideology of the education received, which made the changes. Literacy has undoubted effects on human communication, but it is more reasonable to see it as one of several major factors in the development of a society rather than a defining condition. If Lord was right in ascribing the decline in educated Yugoslav bards' abilities to literacy itself rather than to the ideology of the education they received (Lord 1960: 20), it is not at all clear whether one can apply this elsewhere. Literacy *per se* cannot be safely regarded as the primary factor in the decline of 'folkloric' oral traditions among the educated in Kurmanji-speaking areas, given that in all these areas the official forms of education place a higher value on concepts of 'modernity' and 'science' than on 'folklore'. There are also other obvious factors in the decline of Kurmanji oral tradition, such as population movements (both forced and voluntary), the clearing of villages, and modern forms of broadcasting, particularly television.

Thus the term 'literacy' proves as elusive as the term 'orality'. Although it would be methodologically tidy if the two could be used as simple opposites, this is not really possible – societies tend to be oral, whether or not they are literate as well. Nevertheless, we should have working definitions of both terms. Although the two terms are not true parallels, 'orality' when applied to a group such as the Yezidis may be defined as the extent and nature of the use of spoken communications, and 'literacy' the extent and nature of the use of writing. Clearly there are a great many variables which must be known before one can make a meaningful statement about a group's 'orality' or 'literacy.'

An important dimension of the orality or literacy of any group is the relationship between oral or literate forms of communication, and power. Oral traditions, particularly those which are seen as embodying ancient religious or historical knowledge, may well confer religious status or political power, and access to such traditions may be strictly controlled or kept within an élite group. In the Kurdish context, examples of this include traditions retained by sheykhs and passed on to disciples (van Bruinessen 1992: 205–259), or the learning and recitation of genealogies to confer legitimacy. However, not all oral traditions are prestigious enough to give power to those who know them. Literacy also confers status, but again this is complex and depends on the type of literacy. Street's fieldwork in a village in North-East Iran may have parallels in Kurdistan: young people often opted for (city-based) continued education, at secondary school level and beyond, in contrast to the *maktab* (village school) literacy of their village elders, who, for their part, were ambivalent about state education; they respected their children's ability to read advanced texts which they themselves could not understand, and regarded them as progressive and modern, but they also made clear their reservations about the ideology on which the state education was based (1984: 174–177). This dimension of power is essential for understanding Kurdish 'orality' and 'literacy'.

Kurdistan has not been what Goody defines as a truly 'oral' society (1996: 14), that is, a society where writing is unknown, for many centuries; like the rest of the Near and Middle East, it is dominated by the three 'religions of the Book', namely, Judaism, Christianity and Islam. Throughout the entire region there has been a long-standing complex relationship between the oralities of the masses and the literacies of religious and political élites. It is important to note that even in the scriptural religions, where holy texts are fixed and their recitations governed by strict rules, oral tradition, often in the form of interpretation and teaching, goes hand in hand with studies of holy writ. Learning was controlled by this combination; in many religious traditions of the region, aspiring scholars had to study with a known and accepted teacher and hear and learn his oral teachings as well as learning written texts (Nasr 1995). The scriptural nature of the three religions, all of which were present in Kurdistan until the second half of the twentieth century, also affected the illiterate. Members of most communities would have had some degree of access, even at a distance, to someone, often a mullah, who had some reading and writing skills; the prestige of religious literacy was and still is considerable, with the clergy and other literate holy men in some demand for the writing of amulets and other apotropaic texts, signs and symbols, and also for divination.[5]

Apart from its association with religion, the existence of literacy for the purpose of what might be termed 'written literature' was well known amongst the Kurds, a people in contact with Persians, Arabs and Turks, whose nobility occasionally received a cosmopolitan education in Persian or Arabic. Many of the Kurdish emirs, who flourished up to the mid-nineteenth century, were patrons of the arts, whose courts hosted performances of both literary and oral material, and it is possible that many of the performers of oral traditions were literate and multi-lingual.[6] Tribal leaders, both settled and nomadic, also provided venues for performance and had their own court poets to sing their praises, as befitted their status.[7] Thus one would expect episodes or characters originating in written Persian and Arabic literature in particular to influence oral material. The Yezidis, less literate than other Kurdish groups, shared many legends with other Kurds which had their origins in written literature. Much of the variety of Kurdistan's oral traditions comes, not only from the free exchange of stories and songs and their components between Kurds and their neighbours, but also from the influence of literary tradition. It is also now more than a century since Kurdish oral traditions began to be collected and published, becoming written texts, which in turn now influence audience conceptions of folklore and the small but increasing number of literate performers who learn some of their material from books. Thus the relationship between the written and the oral becomes ever more complex.

The Kurmanji-speaking part of Kurdistan, of course, is not only inhabited by Kurds; many other languages are spoken there in addition to the major state languages of Turkish, Persian and Arabic. Some communities in the North speak Caucasian languages; there are also groups of Turkomen speaking minority Turkic dialects. The Iranian language Dimli, or Zaza, though linguistically not a form of Kurmanji, is spoken by people who claim Kurdish identity; thus it may be described as Kurdish in a social and political sense.[8] Even after the massacres and deportations of Armenians and other Christians, communities of Christian Neo-Aramaic speakers remain, notably the Syrian Orthodox (so-called 'Jacobites') living in the Tur Abdin area around Mardin and Midyat in Turkey, and 'Assyrians' of the Church of the East (so-called 'Nestorians'), as well as their Catholic counterparts, the Chaldaeans, in Hakkari province in Turkey and in various communities in Badinan. The Jews of Kurdistan also spoke Aramaic, but few if any remain; most live in Israel. Members of other religious communities in rural areas often shared important features of material culture with Muslim and Yezidi Kurds, and there is anecdotal evidence for a number of common religious practices, such as the veneration of local saints. Not only did these languages share many oral traditions with Kurdish, but many members of minority groups speak impeccable Kurdish; some have contributed to collections of Kurdish oral traditions.[9]

The proportion of Kurds living in traditional villages is constantly declining. More and more Kurds live in cities, either the predominantly Kurdish cities such as Diyarbakir, Erbil or Suleymaniye, or larger multicultural cities, such as Istanbul, Baghdad and Tehran. Kurdish culture and forms of communication are so diverse that it is more accurate to speak of 'oralities' in Kurmanji than one single 'orality'; for instance, an urban Muslim Kurd who can read Turkish novels is likely to have very different attitudes to history, the supernatural and aesthetics from, say, a Yezidi villager in Northern Iraq who has never been to school. Kurmanji may be an oral language for both, and they may both make use of Kurdish oral tradition, by listening to it or performing it themselves, but their interpretations of the traditions are likely to be very different.

Thus there is a complex interplay of oral and literate forms of communication in Kurmanji. Although there has been, and continues to be, some fascinating research on language contact and its effects (e.g. Dorleijn 1996), language use and meaning have been little studied, and it is difficult to venture beyond preliminary remarks on general oralities in Kurmanji. The sheer variety of language, religion, and social structure in Kurdistan should prompt us to avoid thinking in terms of one type of 'oral' mind-set existing over the whole area. The Kurmanji-speaking area contains many speech communities, or groups which share 'both linguistic resources and rules for interaction and interpretation' (Coulthard 1985: 35). To delineate the effects of orality on Kurdish culture, more detailed work focusing on specific areas and communities is needed.

Oral Traditions in Kurmanji

Defining a text as 'oral' may not always be straightforward; this broad term may mean either a 'spoken' (as opposed to written) or 'verbal' (as opposed to non-verbal) means of communication (Finnegan 1992: 5). For oral literature, sometimes called verbal art, the shadows of Parry and Lord loom large over the study of oral traditions in the Near and Middle East. This is reasonable in many cases, since Parry (1971) showed brilliantly the oral nature of the Homeric poems, and Lord (1960) demonstrated the application of oral formulaic analysis to Yugoslav poetry and to Homer. This form of analysis has also been applied, with positive results, to poetry from many other periods and regions. However, it has also led to difficulties in terminology, and debate as to whether *all* truly 'oral' poetry involves constant improvisation during the performance, and constant composition without any writing at all. Finnegan (1976, 1977) cited examples of African oral literature which did not fit this description. Similarly, the approach is of little use in studying many Kurmanji genres, including much of the secular prose and poetry of the Yezidis, since the structure of the material does not suit rigid metrical and formulaic analysis. For instance, the Kurmanji lyrical song, which is called *stran* or *lawik* and is one of the most popular forms of Yezidi oral tradition, is not composed in performance but sung from memory. Given the composition of the material and its transmission and performance by illiterate singers, its 'oral' status can hardly be in doubt.

A song, or story, or poem, may be composed, or transmitted, or performed, or all three, without the use of writing. To understand the development of a given oral tradition, rather than aiming for a purely 'oral' text, which can only be said to be oral in that a written literary element cannot be decisively proved, it is surely justifiable to include such elements of demonstrably literary origin as have found their way into orally transmitted stories. During my own fieldwork, many performers of traditions had never encountered the literary versions of their stories, and may even have been unaware of them, but had learned them orally.

The term 'tradition' implies something which is handed down from one person to another, either old, or believed to be old. Kurmanji has vast amounts of such material, a 'hypertrophe of folklore'[10] in the words of one Russian scholar. Most of the material which has been collected by folklorists is 'traditional' in the sense that its exponents claim to have received it *in toto* from someone else. They have also denied any contribution to composition. A notable exception to this is the women's lament, found all over Kurdistan, which is composed *extempore*, but which is traditional in that it follows long-established conventions of form and motif. In this case, it is the process of lamentation rather than the product which is traditional, though the content itself often includes well-known and well-used images and vocabulary. An entire tradition can last for many hundreds of years; certain elements or 'motifemes' within a narrative may be replaced with others which better serve the social context within which the tale is told, and these elements may also be very ancient (Allison 1996: 30–31). This is also true of much of the material presented here.

It is not the aim of this chapter to describe Kurmanji oral tradition in full, but it is worth characterising some of the major themes and forms very briefly. They form part of the Iranophone pool of common traditions; thus such narratives as *Yusif and Zuleikha*, *Leyla and Majnun*, and *Koroğlî*, are widely attested. These are found in the form of long narrative poems, spoken prose alternating with sung verse, and prose narratives. Naturally the Kurds place their own emphases on the material, often placing alien stories in the setting of Kurdish society, or stressing the role of local characters. There are also long Kurdish narratives, such as *Mem and Zin/Memê Alan*, *Dimdim/Khanê Lepzêrîn*, and *Khej and Siyabend*. Folktales include many common Iranian, Turkic and Islamic elements, such as the *dîv* or demon, the mythical bird the *Sîmurg*, the *jinn* and immortals such as *Khidir Elias*. Kurmanji has a wealth of fables about animals, proverbs (called 'the sayings of the ancestors' and considered a repository of folk wisdom), amusing stories of the Mullah Nasruddin type, and riddles. The figure of Alexander has accumulated a large volume of tales, as has Shah ʿAbbas; most of these owe little to written histories. Rustam is particularly popular, and many Kurdish tribes believed that Rustam was a Kurd (e.g. Jelîl 1978 II: 108–10). Stories about the Prophets, not only Muhammad but also Solomon, Abraham, and others, are common. Diverse elements from various sources, some ancient and others modern, can often be found in a single narrative. There are also many prose narratives and lyrical songs about historical events and people.

Studies of Kurmanji Oral Tradition

The early collectors of Kurdish oral traditions were primarily interested in language, though some also sought to give information on other aspects of Kurdish culture. Jaba, a former Russian consul at Erzurum, presented his collection in 1860 as 'servant à la connaissance de la langue, de la littérature et des tribus du Kourdistan,' and the collection accordingly not only includes résumés of the great Kurdish romances such as *Dimdim*, but also humorous anecdotes and accounts of tribal feuds. Other important linguistic collections include those of Oskar Mann (1906, 1909), on the dialect of the Mukri Kurds of Persia,[11] Piyotr Lerch (1857–8), who used prisoners from the Crimean war as sources, and Hugo Makas (1926). Naturally, many of these early collections lacked detailed performance data or accounts of the role of the individual traditions and their performances in community life.

The development of folklore as a field of study had a profound influence on Kurdish scholarship. Early Kurdish journals such as *Hawar*[12] published many oral traditions as examples of folklore, sometimes with explanatory notes for non-Kurds. Oral literature was perceived as an important part of Kurdish folklore, which is also considered to include many other items of material culture, music, etc. The pervasive idea that folklore reflects the 'national character' of the people producing it in a uniquely intimate way has found expression amongst both Kurdish and foreign folklorists.[13] Kurdish scholars in particular have seen folklore as a fund of information about the past, an expression of the people's feelings, and a repository of popular wisdom – a national treasure, in fact.[14] In the second half of the twentieth century it became clear that Kurdish oral traditions were in decline, as a result of general modernising processes found in many developing societies, of conflicts between government forces and nationalists, and of the specific proscription of Kurdish culture in Turkey and Iran. As one eminent scholar has written 'not a day goes by but Kurdish oral tradition loses something of value' (Jelîl 1985: 9), and Kurds have responded to this crisis by making collections and publishing them. These initiatives range from the large-scale works, such as *Zargotina K'urda* 'Kurdish Oral Tradition' of the Jelîl brothers (1978) in the former Soviet Union, to the valuable smaller collections made by teachers, writers and other interested parties who devoted their spare time to visiting villages and recording folklore.[15] For obvious reasons, most collections were made in Iraq and the former Soviet Union, with some in Iran, Syria and the diaspora and very few indeed in Turkey, though some Turkish collections of folklore apparently include translated Kurdish material. Since Iraqi collections focused mainly on Sorani material, it was the Soviet folklorists who kept Kurmanji folklore studies alive through the twentieth century. Academics based in Yerevan, Leningrad and Moscow, most of them Kurds, were able to travel to Kurdish communities (mainly in the USSR) and record a variety of oral traditions. These scholars, notably the Jelîl brothers and Hejiyê Jindî, have collected the material as 'folklore'; they list the sources of their items, the time and place of their recordings, and most usefully of all, they give biographical details of their informants. They also indicate whether they were literate or not, though it is unclear exactly what they mean by 'literate' and semi-literate'. This indication of provenance is invaluable for the analysis of the origins and histories of given traditions, but the necessary contextual data on the relationship between a given performance and its environment, the purpose it serves within the community, the status of the performer, and so on, is still omitted. In general, the published collections of Kurdish folksongs and stories make no attempt to relate given texts to their social context, though it is, admittedly, unfair to expect this from those collectors whose interests were primarily linguistic.[16] The value of the collections made so far lies not only in the indication they give of the rich variety of traditional material existing in Kurdish, but also in their attestation of various beliefs and stories; their evidence makes it possible to compare variants and trace the development of individual oral traditions, and to test how far local perception of the inviolability of traditions older than living memory applies to the material.

Secondary literature on Kurmanji oral traditions is not plentiful. Most of the works by Kurdish folklorists are collections rather than studies of the material, though there are exceptions to this (e.g. Jelîl 1960), Although they provide important records of oral traditions, they were mostly produced for a public which was already familiar with local genres and performance trends, and much remains unexplained for the outsider. As with the linguistic works, performances are rarely contextualised. Although some noted Kurdologists have given broad outlines of the role played by oral literature in Kurdish life (Bois 1946: *passim*, Nikitine 1956: 255–281), outsiders wishing to understand this on a detailed localised basis have needed to do fieldwork, which recent history has made difficult. There have been some important studies of Kurdish music (e.g. Christensen 1963, 1975, Jemîla Jelîl 1973–86, Tatsumura 1980, Blum and Hassanpour 1996), which is, of course, a vital accompaniment to much oral literature and some of these include description of social context, but unless extensive fieldwork could be done, scholars have had to undertake the type of analysis which can be based mostly on collected texts, such as Chyet's detailed folkloric study of *Mem and Zîn* (Chyet 1991). Such studies are also scanty; for instance, no comprehensive typology of narratives has yet been made for Kurdish.[17] Comparison with better-documented traditions, such as Arabic, Turkish, Aramaic and Armenian, can be fruitful, and the studies of the folklore of the Kurdish Jews now living in Israel are particularly useful for the Kurdologist (Sabar 1982, Brauer and Patai 1993).

Of the studies made in the past, a few are especially relevant to the Yezidis in Northern Iraq. Badinani traditions were attested by the collection of Prym and Socin (1887, 1890), which includes much material still circulating in Badinan one hundred years later, and Makas (1900, 1926) includes some Yezidi material from Turkey. Of the more modern studies of the dialects of Iraqi Kurdistan, that of Blau is particularly useful for its engaging description of a storytelling performance among Sinjari Yezidis (Blau 1975: 6–8). Important Yezidi religious oral traditions can be found in Layard 1849, Badger 1852, Lescot 1938, Guest 1993; the 'sacred books of the Yezidis' (Bittner 1913) may also have oral origins, but the most substantial collections are in Silêman and Jindî 1979 and Kreyenbroek 1995. For secular oral traditions, Ritter 1976 is a selection of anecdotes; this type of material can also be found in Jelîl 1978, 1985, along with much Yezidi historical narrative and lyric.

Kurmanji Oral Traditions at the end of the Twentieth Century

It is true that, as the Kurdish folklorists fear, many Kurmanji oral traditions are dying out. Population movements and changes in the Kurdish way of life have meant that traditions associated with tasks no longer performed, or places no longer visited, are in decline. Nevertheless, oral traditions retain a strong symbolic value even for urban Kurds. Old types of narrative, once oral, are being turned into literary products and plays (e.g. Shemo 1983). The 'literary landscape', as it were, of Kurmanji oral tradition, with its lyrical descriptions of the mountains, rivers, plants and animals, and its declarations of passionate emotion, provides much of the most powerful imagery of Kurdish nationalism. Such images are used in the Kurdish print and broadcast media, including, most recently, satellite television.[18] The most popular nationalistic Kurdish singers, such as Şivan Perwer, use the imagery of Kurdish oral tradition, and the various Kurdish satellite channels see Kurdish folk music as an important part of Kurdish cultural heritage and feature performances from many parts of the homeland. Such enterprises have in turn had an effect on the oral traditions, as a concept of 'the correct version' grows among the audience, and young performers sometimes learn material from books or broadcasts. There is an ambivalence about 'folklore' – it is seen by many urban Kurds as outmoded and primitive, but also as picturesque and valuable. Kurdish oral tradition seems to be more accessible to modern, urban Kurds when recontextualised, when presented (often in more concise, glossy form than in the villages) by the Kurdish media or by novelists. The Kurmanji oral traditions are not dying out altogether; they are changing in form, and becoming less varied, but they remain powerful and emotive.

STUDYING YEZIDI ORAL TRADITIONS

The oral traditions presented in this book were collected in a war zone, from a people traumatised by conflict and insecurity. Fieldwork conditions must always have a bearing on the way work is done, and in many ways the circumstances were less than ideal, though there were some unexpected advantages. The special situation pertaining in the Kurdish autonomous zone of Northern Iraq in 1992 (MacDowall 1996: 368–388) had an influence both on the choice of material studied, and the way it was collected. This in turn had an obvious effect on the methodologies used in analysing the oral traditions and their role in Yezidi society.

Choice of Fieldwork Area

Although the cultural expression of Yezidis in the diaspora is no less valid than that found in areas where Yezidis have been settled for centuries, I felt that the ideal fieldwork area should include a long-established Yezidi community; in such a society it might be a more straightforward task to understand the relationship between oral traditions and their context. At first, Armenia and Georgia seemed the best sites for fieldwork; Yerevan and Tbilisi are important centres for Kurdish cultural studies, and much of the Kurdish-speaking population in these republics is Yezidi. However, during the time I was planning fieldwork, in 1990–91, there was considerable unrest in both republics. In 1991, however, after the Kurdish uprising and the creation of the so-called 'safe havens', an area of Northern Iraq, which includes the most important Yezidi centre of Lalêsh, came under Kurdish control and Europeans were welcomed. Within the area, problems of access were logistical rather than ideological. Although it was often difficult to find resources, such as a car, to reach particular sites, there were no overt attempts to block my research, and no obvious checks were made by the Kurdish authorities on whether it was conforming to an accepted Kurdish ideology. In fact, foreign interest in Kurdish culture was encouraged.

Local Expressions of Kurdish Identity

After the 1991 uprising and its aftermath, the inhabitants of the Kurdish-held zone took advantage of their freedom to express their nationalist sentiments; such discourses were being developed by intellectuals and political leaders to reinforce community cohesion. The political climate of previous years had been very divisive, with many Kurdish individuals and groups known to be supporting the Iraqi government. Amnesties had been issued to many of these, and the leaders of the two major Kurdish parties, Mesʿud Barzani of the Kurdish Democratic Party (KDP), and Jalal Talabani of the Patriotic Union of Kurdistan (PUK), were attempting to preserve alliances with powerful hostile leaders who had previously been aligned with the government. Barzani and Talabani were also trying to reconcile their own differences; this task eventually proved too much, with civil war openly breaking out, amid rampant corruption and abuse of human rights, in 1994. However, in 1992, there was some fragile optimism; the Kurds had a degree of autonomy, international aid was being given, and many wanted to try the experiment of self-rule. I shall never forget the sight of hundreds of people, old and young, rich and poor, queueing for hours outside polling stations in order to vote in their first democratic election.

The political restructuring of Iraqi Kurdistan, as epitomised by the 1992 elections, was an important element in the forging of the national consciousness, but equally significant was the emphasis on common elements of culture and aspects of heritage. Kurdish-language television stations showed Kurdish dances and songs, both traditional and modern, performed in traditional dress; documentaries were made about individual villages, many destroyed and only resettled since 1991, where elders gave accounts of village life and sang traditional songs remembered from their youth. As in many other nationalist movements, intellectuals and politicians who wished to modernise their society also wished to empower their people by emphasising their special Kurdish identity. People living in towns recalled their youth in villages with fondness; this was not mere nostalgia, forgetting the harshness of the conditions of rural life, but rather the result of a feeling, expressed by Kurds of all classes in Iraqi Kurdistan, that the authentic Kurdish life was village life, and that the villages were the repository of Kurdish culture. Town life and its comforts might have become the norm, but emotional and social considerations, as much as any economic factor, were elements in the drive towards reconstruction of the destroyed villages of Iraqi Kurdistan.

Local Perceptions of 'Folklore'

Since folklore studies are of course well established in Iraq, people were quite familiar with the process of collecting oral traditions. However local attitudes towards the material collected did not always accord with my own approach. I was interested in various sorts of verbal art which fell outside the range of Yezidi material I had come to study, and was very interested in, for example, an impromptu lament for those lost in the camps during the exodus of 1991, which I heard performed spontaneously in a modern style by a KDP *pêşmerge* (guerilla fighter), in Dihok in March 1992. However, local opinion placed a higher value on what it calls *folklor*, 'folklore', which is traditional in style and is, or appears to be, old. 'Folklore' could be traditional Kurdish dress, carpets, music, agricultural implements or any other old-fashioned attribute of Kurdish life. The term was used in Kurdish broadcasts and other discussions in the media of traditional elements of

Kurdish culture. Songs and stories dating from before living memory were felt to be ancient, and this status was inviolable. Innovation was not admitted; variant forms of 'historical' material seemed to be tolerated provided they were sufficiently old in themselves. Many educated people knew the work of the Jelîl brothers, who collected numerous variants of popular stories such as the Yezidis' *Derwêshê 'Evdî* and also the generally known *Dimdim*, but there was always a tendency to interpret one variant as correct and reject others.[19] This is hardly surprising in the case of historical material, if truth is felt to be at stake, but it even applied in the case of stories containing fantasy elements. The concept that a 'correct' version of a given tradition does not exist, that there are merely variant forms performed in different ways according to the purposes and limitations of the performer, did not conform at all to local opinion; the influence of literacy and broadcast was such that people would say that a particular retelling of a story was 'wrong' because it differed from a version read in a published collection of folklore, or a radio or television programme.

Certain types of material were felt to be more prestigious than others. Songs dealing with tribal history, and epic songs, were felt to merit a researcher's attention; however, bewilderment was often expressed, both in villages and in urban educated circles, at my interest in, for example, women's work songs. Material associated with certain members of the community reflected the status of those members.

This choice of fieldwork area had its disadvantages. Significant proportions of the general population had been displaced from their homes, and the effects of the last traumatic thirty years or so on data gathered had to be taken into account. The ethical aspect of the fieldwork was complicated by high poverty and unemployment levels. The lack of basic resources, especially fuel, meant that travel within the region was not easy, and the security situation made it impossible for a lone European to live permanently in a village. Yezidi communities in particular were situated near Iraqi army lines. This meant that I had to be based in the town of Dihok, making as frequent visits to Yezidi communities as possible.

I had originally come to Iraq hoping to study Yezidi women's oral traditions, but I soon encountered considerable difficulty in studying questions relating to oral traditions and gender. For all interviews it was necessary for a member of the community to be present, partly to translate (my university Kurdish was not easy for rural Yezidis to understand at first acquaintance, though time brought better mutual understanding) and partly to provide introductions. This had to be a Yezidi as interviewees did not feel at ease with Muslims; in the one interview I conducted with a Muslim interpreter, the (male) interviewee was extremely polite but utterly uninformative. For interviewing women, a female Yezidi with fluent English was required, and there were very few such women in Badinan province. One kindly arranged some very productive interviews, but was not available very often. Realising that there would be a relative lack of data on Yezidi women's practice of oral tradition, I broadened my focus to Yezidi oral tradition in general. The under-representation of women in this study is unfortunate but inevitable given the fieldwork circumstances.

Questionnaires as a means of assessing attitudes to oral traditions were rejected for various reasons, specifically the high level of illiteracy amongst rural Yezidis, their fears that information taken in writing might somehow find its way into Government hands, and the novelty of many of the concepts under discussion. Longer interviews with fewer informants proved more rewarding – opinions were (in most cases) apparently expressed freely. This may have been because interviewees had little fear that I was a spy (a very real possibility to them) but it is also likely that the information I requested, very little of which referred to the recent past, could safely be defined as *folklor* rather than 'live' politics. Many also allowed themselves to criticise the Kurdish leaders freely, though they would certainly not have done this if Kurdish Muslims were present. Although it was not possible to survey village communities in as much detail as an ethnographic study would require, I was able to live in Dihok, a short distance from the major Yezidi settlements, and to maintain a variety of Yezidi, Muslim and Christian contacts locally without exclusive reliance on any one of them. Numerous trips of one day were made to the nearby collective villages of Khanek and Shari'e (see below) and of several days at a time to sites further away such as Ba'drê and Lalêsh.

A great disadvantage of being confined to the Kurdish-held zone was the impossibility of visiting the Jebel Sinjar, which was under the control of the Iraqi government. Sinjari Yezidis were perceived as less urbanised than others; they dress differently and were felt by other Yezidis to adhere more closely to Yezidi cultural customs. There is a history of political conflict between the Sinjaris and the Sheykhani Yezidis, though the community presents a united front to outsiders. The Sinjar was the most important centre of Yezidi *stranbêj*, the semi-professional singers who perform 'the old songs'. Fortunately I was able to meet several *stranbêj* during 1992, and one well-known one in Germany in 1998. I recorded as many performances of songs and spoken narratives as I could, but most of my recordings of Sinjari singers were by necessity purchased in Dihok.

I bought some 120 hours of recordings, which apparently constituted all of the 'traditional Yezidi folklore' available in Dihok at the time. The performers were known semi-professional *stranbêj* whose songs had instrumental accompaniment. Yezidi contacts spent some weeks inquiring after and tracing rare recordings, and on checking with various informants, in particular Pîr Khidir Silêman and 'Eydo Baba Sheykh, both authorities on Yezidi culture, it was discovered that almost all the most famous living *stranbêj* and popular traditions were represented in the collection. Due to the somewhat haphazard way the recordings had been made and distributed, no comprehensive lists of performers and recordings were available. My own recordings consist mostly of stories told by individuals, mainly the elderly, and interviews on the subject of Yezidi customs, how traditions are learned, circumstances of performance, etc. The local concept of 'folklore' meant that informants had a clear idea of what I was asking for, and of which members of the community knew most and should be approached; the focus on older material ensured goodwill, as it was felt to be a fitting subject of study.

THEORETICAL PERSPECTIVES AND FIELDWORK METHODOLOGIES

The stated aim of this work is to study Yezidi oral traditions within their social context. Oral traditions may be narrative or lyrical, or even gnomic (e.g. proverbs), and have been passed on from one person to another. The examples which will be considered here are believed to be of a certain age, and have a known place in the life of the community. The oral traditions which will be examined in detail here are all examples of performed oral literature, or verbal art, but other forms of communication which are not, strictly speaking, 'oral traditions' are also used here. These include life-stories and eyewitness accounts, and are primarily used to give background information on Yezidi attitudes to their history and social environment, and to their traditional songs and stories.

We should also define 'social context.' Dundes' definition of the context of an item of folklore as 'the specific social situation in which that particular item is actually employed' (Dundes 1964: 274) is not adequate if one is reflecting on general meanings ascribed to that tradition outside the immediate performance environment. Bauman proposes a much more complex view of context, which does more justice to the multidimensional nature of communication; it comprises six different categories – 'context of meaning', 'institutional context', 'context of communicative system', 'social base', 'individual context', and 'context of situation' (Bauman 1983). However, one then runs into the danger of overcontextualising, by describing context *ad infinitum*. Bauman and Briggs (1990: 68) warn of the dangers of 'reifying' context and advocate an emphasis on the process of contextualisation, largely to avoid dangers of false objectivity, of claiming to give an 'objective' description of a social environment. Whilst an effort has been made to discover how the Yezidis contextualise their oral traditions, this information has not always been available. I have described individual performances where I have witnessed them and as far as possible have tried to use local comment to evaluate it; I have also attempted to discover the place of the performances in the life of the community.

This work is not an ethnographic study of the Yezidi community, though it makes use of past ethnographic work; it aims to be multidisciplinary. Though it takes account of social institutions, it does not focus on them at the expense of the traditions themselves, which cannot be understood without clarification of their idioms and underlying aesthetics – in other words, without approaching them as literature. The methodology of this work has elements of a functionalist approach, in that I have assumed at the outset that the material collected must be useful to the community or it would not have survived. However, I have taken a very broad view of what its 'function' might be. It could be 'useful' in a variety of ways – a tradition might survive because of its aesthetic merits, for instance. Nevertheless, it is appreciated that not every function of a given tradition in its society can be isolated, and that not every element of a given tradition can be accounted for. The links between oral traditions and social institutions are invariably complex; this book will include some traditions which purport to uphold social norms and others which are apparently critical, and will attempt to account for these stances. Moreover, stories which have been told for generations may often include random elements introduced in the past, which are not felt to add anything significant to contemporary performance and may not even be understood, but which are retained purely through conservatism. Where this is the case, I will consider the nature of and reasons for that conservatism.

In some respects this work has also been influenced by the 'ethnography of speaking' with its stress on language, local values and ethnopoetics. However, studies in Kurdish language are still in their infancy; adequate dictionaries are few, and dialects are still being described; we are far from being able to make confident assertions about such subtleties as registers of language, or to give accounts of the full range of 'speech acts' and 'speech events' used in Kurmanji. During fieldwork it was not always easy to question informants on nuances of meaning, and informants' evaluations of traditions and performances were sometimes difficult to interpret. It is all too easy to attempt a critique of foreign language material with the aim of applying the 'ethnography of speaking' to it, and fall into the trap of carrying out traditional Western literary criticism on it. The application of Western literary theory to alien literatures, of course, is not necessarily wrong in itself, but is inappropriate if the avowed aim is to discover more about the aesthetic system of the group which created the literature. During discussions of the artistry of the oral traditions, I have attempted to focus on what the community finds artistically valuable in them (as explained to me, of course) rather than their literary merit for Westerners. It is important to map out the artistic and emotional language of Kurdish oral tradition. However, given the difficulties of discussing the material with informants as 'literature', the conclusions as to the significance of traditions or of images are inevitably sometimes based on deduction.

There were also occasions where the purity of an approach such as 'ethnography of speaking' was compromised by my own wish to argue that these traditions also meet Western criteria for 'literature'. I make no apologies for this, given the regrettable tendency among some Kurds to belittle the artistic merits of their oral tradition in favour of the apparent sophistication of the new and lively Kurdish literary tradition.

Performance and Text

The artistry of 'oral literature' or verbal art, which may give it a privileged and influential position in society, is not confined to choice of words. The performance is an integral part of it. Unlike a written text, an oral 'text' is never the same twice. Ruth Finnegan (1990: 134) articulated a common feeling among those who have done fieldwork on oral traditions:

> When I came back and typed up my transcriptions I could not understand why they seemed so lifeless. All the wisdom and art that I thought I had seen seemed to be gone.

Not only does the performance breathe life into the form of words, but, if the tradition is performed within the community, the performance is a vital dimension which must be understood before the role of the tradition in context can be understood. Of course, the performance is a multi-dimensional speech act, with links not only to its specific environment, but also to past and future performances, and possibly many other communicative acts as well. This is certainly the case for Yezidi lyrical songs in particular, where performances are carefully evaluated and compared with those of the past and those of different singers.

Bauman's definition of performance (1977: 11) proved particularly useful in the context of Yezidi oral traditions:

> Performance involves on the part of the performer an assumption of accountability to an audience for the way in which communication is carried out, above and beyond its referential content.

The key characteristic of performance here is the fact that it is socially appropriate. The breadth of Bauman's definition proved well suited to the variety of performances encountered in the Yezidi material, which ranged from prose tales to sung lyric and ritual lamentation. Each was performed appropriately, within an appropriate context.

As Finnegan observed, performance can not be adequately described by the isolated transcription of words on the page; a reader from another culture needs more information on the following points:

i) Genre: is this well-defined? Is the audience aware of its rules? How a performance conforms to the perceived rules of its genre may give the best indication of local perceptions of success and failure.
ii) Non-verbal elements: the performance may be accompanied by music, or an elaborate language of gesture and body posture by the performer(s).

iii) The performer(s): does he or she have a well-defined social status, and does this affect perceptions of the performance?
iv) The audience: its participation in and reaction to the performance.
v) The context: is the performance formally sanctioned? Is it taking place at a time and place considered to be appropriate?

I will attempt to answer the above points in relation to the material considered. However, since I was not present at the recorded performances of many of the songs I will discuss, it will not be possible to supply this information in all cases; the best that I can offer is information about the *type* of performance gained from questioning people who have seen such performances and who listen to the cassettes. Where information was lacking, this will be indicated.

Working on prerecorded material has various methodological implications, and was not undertaken lightly. It was the only realistic way of gaining access to the work of the Sinjari *stranbêj* without being able to visit their locality, and despite its inferior sound quality, it did have the advantage of representing a performance requested by the community at a time and place of local choice, with audience attention on performer and performance rather than on the odd-looking foreigner with the tape-recorder. I must acknowledge that in many cases I knew little about the individual performances; I could not even analyse some recordings as entire 'performances' since I could not be sure whether it constituted the whole performance or even if all the material was recorded during one performance. The relative lack of information about immediate performance context and the disproportionate reliance on information about the wider context will inevitably cause some distortion. It will also, unfortunately, prevent any meaningful consideration of possible covert political and rhetorical messages, dependent on context, underlying the words of the performances, such as those considered in Afghan storytelling performances in Mills 1991.

A more important consequence of having to use prerecorded material is that the focus shifts from 'context' back towards 'texts'; the material is presented as a set of texts, with such comments on context as can be gleaned from the information available. Some scholars have argued for a strong emphasis on text and content (Blackburn 1988: xviii), though it is also possible to argue that, since no two performances are the same, there is no such thing as 'text', only performance. However, there is a methodological virtue to be made out of this necessity. The prerecorded material used consists of lyrical songs on historical subjects; there is good reason for thinking that considering them as 'texts' parallels their use in the Yezidi community. Not only do the Yezidis conceive of them as compositions which are to be passed from singer to apprentice without change – to the extent to which audiences will query obvious changes in wording made to the songs they know – but they also discuss them as entities with an objective existence; the singer's rendition of the song is, for the Yezidis, a separate matter from the existence of the song itself. This way of thinking about the songs 'entextualises' them, to use Bauman and Briggs' term (1990: 73). It is very different from the way the Yezidis talk about the extemporised lament, for instance, where it is the process, not the product, which is the 'thing' under discussion. Thus these lyrics can be seen as text, and it is clear that the process of recording and replaying decontextualises and recontextualises them. The cassette, with its lack of peripheral data (for sleeve notes are not a part of this type of production) is a very different frame for the material from the conditions of the performance, and the context of an audience listening to a famous singer playing live at a party is very unlike that of people in a car, conversing amongst themselves whilst the songs play in the background – the more common scenario now. Whilst one must not lose sight of context, it is crucial to consider text.

Some of the other texts discussed here come from other collections of Kurdish 'folklore', particularly those of the Jelîl brothers, which have more information on performers and performance than many others, though admittedly not as much as one would desire. Few if any of these other texts were collected in Northern Iraq, and their purpose is twofold. Some are included for comparative purposes, as in the case of the *Dawûdê Dawûd* collected in Syria, which is clearly part of the same tradition as that performed in Sinjar. Others are to supplement information which was not collected during the fieldwork, for various reasons. One example of this is the group of short songs of semi-professional lamentation which come from the Jelîls' collection; their recordings were made in Tbilisi. I did not have the privilege of attending a *taziye* for a recently deceased person in Northern Iraq, though I did interview a semi-professional performer of laments there. I am assured by knowledgeable Yezidis that the Jelîl group of laments is typical of the tradition, so I consider it legitimate to include them here.

This book will consider a number of secular oral traditions acknowledged by the Yezidis to be important, and examine how the community in Northern Iraq perceives and uses them. They will be considered from the viewpoint of both text and context. This will be the first such attempt to study oral traditions in Kurmanji, a language which has a complex pattern of literacies and oralities across different areas and communities, and whose written literature is underdeveloped by comparison with Turkish, Arabic and Persian. Before describing these Yezidi traditions in detail, I will move from the general cultural environment of the Kurmanji-speaking areas to the specific setting of the Yezidi community, whose orality has a number of special features, and whose religiosity is so different from the more 'orthodox' forms of Islam, Christianity and Judaism that outsiders have consistently misjudged them, often with tragic consequences.

CHAPTER TWO

The Yezidis of Northern Iraq and the People of the Book

INTRODUCTION

The Yezidis are a religious minority with many taboos and a strict caste system. They constitute a sizeable community in the Kurdish-held zone of Northern Iraq, though there are no reliable statistics. Estimates for Iraq as a whole vary between 100,000 and 250,000 (Kreyenbroek 1995: vii). The Yezidis are neither Muslim, Christian nor Jewish and therefore not 'People of the Book'. This has had important implications in the past for their legal status, and is still a factor in their relationships with their neighbours and with authority. Their religion contains elements originating in various majority religions, but cannot be defined as purely, or even principally, Christian, Islamic or Zoroastrian; it appears to be truly syncretistic. In the past they were described as 'devil-worshippers' by adherents of the majority religions, and by European travellers. Their status as a piece of 'living folklore' has been a mixed blessing for them. Contrary to their popular image as an isolated, unchanging group, they did not (and do not) exist in isolation from their neighbours in Kurdistan; many of the great Kurdish tribal confederations, such as the Milan and the Heverkan, had large Yezidi sections. Yezidis sometimes lived in mixed villages, alongside Christians in particular. They never stood outside the political and economic systems of the regions in which they lived. Nevertheless, the borders between Yezidi and non-Yezidi are clearly defined. Birth of Yezidi parents is the criterion for membership of the Yezidi community, and Yezidi custom in Northern Iraq dictates that if one marries a non-Yezidi one forfeits one's right to membership of the community.[1]

THE YEZIDI COMMUNITIES OF NORTHERN IRAQ

The Yezidis of Northern Iraq, that is the communities of Sheykhan and Sinjar, are the focus of this book, and indeed of most Yezidi studies. Over the last century and a half, the Yezidis of these areas have given a great deal of information about themselves and their religion to interested parties from outside their community, and a whole field of 'Yezidi studies' has grown up. Almost all the information we have about Yezidi belief and attitudes has been provided by the communities of Sheykhan,[2] whose élite controls the sacred shrine of Lalêsh, north-east of Mosul, and attempts to control the religious life of Yezidi society as a whole. Yet Yezidis do not live only in Iraq. They were once found in many parts of what is now Turkey; however, most of the Yezidis of Turkey fled persecution, either to Transcaucasia during the last decades of the Ottoman Empire (Guest 1993: 193–203), to Iraq after the First World War, or to Europe, particularly Germany, later in the twentieth century. There are also significant and long-established communities in Syria. Some of these communities have been isolated from each other for long periods; for instance, there was little contact between the Transcaucasian and the Iraqi Yezidis during the Soviet period. In terms of temporal authority, it is clear that the Yezidi tribes of the Heverkan and Milli federations at the end of the nineteenth century cannot have taken orders from the Mîr of Ba'drê, despite his seniority in the sheykhly hierarchy. Even the methods of religious control exerted by the ruling castes of Sheykhan were limited over long distances, and it is likely that there were significant differences in practice between all these areas. Yezidism[3] is an extremely adaptable religion, and people were more likely to follow the rules imposed by local religious authorities than by distant ones. Even within Iraq, outsiders have found substantial differences in accounts of important holy beings and events; it cannot be assumed that the 'Yezidism' of, say, the Tur Abdin communities near Mardin in Turkey and the Transcaucasian groups are one and the same, nor that it remained the same for long periods in any one area. Sources are limited, but a brief seventeenth century description of Yezidis in Syria gives an indication of a rather different religious hierarchy from that of modern Sheykhan (Fuccaro 1993, 1999: 11). The cult of the holy being Sheykh Adi seems to have been less important in the Tur Abdin than in Sheykhan. Instances in Transcaucasia[4] and Turkey[5] are also reported of the tolerance of violations of taboo, such as marrying out, which would risk ostracism in Iraq.

Geographical Location in Iraq

Much of the Sheykhan region, including its principal town, 'Eyn Sifni, and the entire Jebel Sinjar, was under Iraqi government control throughout 1992. Within the Kurdish autonomous zone of Northern Iraq, Yezidis were living mainly in the collective villages (settlements built by the Iraqi government) of Khanek and Shari'e near Dihok, Dêrebûn near Zakho, and the small town of Ba'drê at the edge of Sheykhan. A small number of families lived in Dihok town, a few in Zakho, and fewer still in Erbil. The village of Lalêsh, also known as the shrine of Sheykh Adi, which is the Yezidis' holiest site overall, was also located in the Kurdish-held zone, though only a few kilometres from 'Eyn Sifni. Although very few people live there all year round, it is a centre for Yezidi pilgrimage at festival seasons. In 1992 even the most important festivals were very sparsely attended, as most of the Yezidis living in the Iraqi government-held zone were reluctant to incur government opprobrium, and suffer intrusive searches at checkpoints on the road, by crossing into the Kurdish-held zone. Yezidis in Iraq all know each other, by clan if not by name, and becoming isolated from the community is considered undesirable. Mass gatherings at festivals serve important social as well as religious purposes. News is exchanged, business is transacted, possible marriage partners are surveyed by young people and their families. In subsequent years the great festivals have been better attended, though it is unclear whether they have reached levels which would previously have been seen as normal. Such long-term undermining of this opportunity to assemble is likely to have negative consequences for the community.

Although the communities of Sheykhan (including those of the Dihok area) and Sinjar trace a common Yezidi heritage and stress their unity to outsiders, there are important differences between them. The Mîr's family has exerted religious control over both areas (and more widely) for at least three centuries, but there have been periods, notably that at the end of the nineteenth and beginning of the twentieth century, when Sinjar challenged Sheykhan for religious dominance. During the massacres perpetrated by the Ottoman official 'Umar Wahbī Pasha, known as 'Ferîq Pasha,' in 1893, which will be described more fully in Chapter Four, the Mîr was ignominiously forced to convert to Islam and the shrine of Sheykh Adi taken from Yezidi control. After these calamities, there was a religious revival in Sinjar, led by figures such as Ḥemo Shêro, which lasted some time, and was a serious challenge to the supremacy of Sheykhan.[6] Moreover, there are important differences in political and social structures. In some ways, Sinjari society has been more volatile, with political influences waxing and waning; the allegiances of a tribe might differ within its constituent clans, the *mal* or *bav*. Although membership of the Yezidi community was fixed by birth, membership of tribes was apparently not; the Sinjari tribes seem to have been more open and fluid than the Sheykhani, and some tribes, such as Ḥemo Shêro's Feqîran, grew very quickly in both influence and number. There was also a degree of autonomy for agricultural production; semi-nomadic Yezidi tribes pastured the flocks of the sedentary villagers, who cultivated a variety of crops and fruits. The mountainous terrain offered possibilities of defence and resistance against outside forces; the history of Mount Sinjar is punctuated by successive governments' punitive expeditions, few of which were successful until air attacks were developed. The Sinjari Yezidis also used their strategic position to offer sanctuary to persecuted Christians from 1915 onwards. (Fuccaro 1999: 44–70). In Sheykhan, however, the situation was different; the Yezidi Mîr owned a substantial amount of land in the area around Ba'drê, which was worked by landless peasants, not all of them Yezidis. In general, the Sheykhani religious élite exerted economic and political control as well as religious control over their area. In Sinjar, religious phenomena such as the cult of Kochek Mîrza, a charismatic figure mentioned in oral tradition, were more likely to develop than in Sheykhan. However, the established religious élites did not automatically control the political and economic domains there (Fuccaro 1999: 19).

Collectivisation

After the Kurdish rebellion of the early 1970s and the Iran-Iraq war, the policy of demolishing villages and resettling populations into those larger settlements known as *mujama'at* 'collective villages' was pursued vigorously by the Iraqi government. The first villages to be destroyed were in the border area, and the reason given for their clearance was the creation of a border security zone, though later on villages much further inside Iraq were cleared. The collectivisation of Yezidi villages began after 1975. The villages, both Sinjari and Sheykhani, which are mentioned in the songs which will be discussed later in this book are almost all now destroyed. Few if any of the Yezidi villages in the Kurdish-held zone which existed before the 1960s now remain extant, although some have had collective villages built on their sites. An exception is Ba'drê, at the edge of the Kurdish zone, a large village containing many properties belonging to the Mîr's family; however, the original settlement, built in the traditional style, has been supplemented by a collective village housing Yezidis from the Jebel Sinjar who were suspected by the Government of complicity in the Kurdish rebellion of the 1970s.

Some, though not all, of the Yezidi land was redistributed under 'Arabisation' policies. The lands formerly belonging to the inhabitants of Shari'e and Khanek had been settled by Arabs until 1991, but after the Kurdish uprising and the establishment of the autonomous zone, many Arabs left the area.[7]

Pro-government informants have stressed the modernising effect of collectivisation, and the improvement in access to medical care and education; in the Kurdish zone, inhabitants of collective villages in general have complained bitterly and justifiably of lack of essential supplies, poverty, and lack of opportunity. During the period of the Anfal campaign (1988) waged by the Iraqi government against Kurdish civilians, the authorities constructed prison camps whose inhabitants had lost their livelihoods and were forced to rely on state hand-outs for survival; many were executed (Middle East Watch 1993: 209–237). Most Yezidi collectivisations were not part of this, though some Yezidis did lose their lives in the Anfal. Unlike some Kurdish village communities, such as the Barzanis, who were often scattered or deported to areas in the South of Iraq, Yezidis tended to be settled together, usually in areas near their former village sites. The Khanek/Mem Shivan collective near Simêl, a few miles from Dihok, is one of the largest examples. It was built when a hydro-electric dam flooded Yezidi villages in the area.

Internal Social Structure: the Caste System

Perhaps the most striking aspect of Yezidi society is its caste system. Membership of a Yezidi caste comes from both parents and cannot be changed. Most Yezidis belong to the *murîd* or 'lay' class; each murîd owes allegiance to a particular *sheykh*, 'lord', and a particular *pîr* or 'elder'. Sheykhs have greater spiritual authority than pîrs; the highest secular Yezidi authority is the Mîr 'emir', who can pronounce the ultimate sentence of ostracism on one who violates Yezidi laws; the highest ranking religious leaders are the Baba Sheykh and the Pêsh Imam. All three are of the Sheykh class. A man has the same sheykh and pîr as his father; a woman inherits female sheykh and pîr from the families of her father's sheykh and pîr until her marriage, whereupon she receives her husband's. Every Yezidi must have a pîr and a sheykh; pîrs have a pîr from a higher ranking family, and sheykhs have a sheykh from a higher ranking family; the Mîr's family is the highest. Sheykhs and pîrs perform various religious functions during a murîd's life and at death; they are often associated with the shrines of revered saints, and receive respect and cash donations from the faithful, especially their own murîds. The differences in function between sheykhs and pîrs has never been clearly explained, but most commentators and informants agree that sheykhs outrank pîrs.[8] Both are entitled to alms from their murîd families, and senior sheykhly families in particular can make wide-ranging collections throughout the community. Younger murîds sometimes profess distaste for the expressions of veneration of their sheykhs and pîrs, particularly the custom of hand-kissing. Although each caste has its role in the community, there is no restriction on social mixing, physical contact (between members of the same sex) or communal eating, between castes. Nevertheless, despite the decline in respect for the caste system among murîds, all Yezidis questioned in 1992 professed complete support for the Yezidi ban on intermarriage between castes.

The Yezidi structure also accommodates certain special groups. The *feqîrs*, whose name literally means 'poor ones', were once a religious order open to all but seem to have become in effect a hereditary caste, with members drawn from a few families within the sheykh, pîr and murîd groups (Kreyenbroek 1995: 133). In Sinjar the influence of a group of feqîrs grew so quickly towards the end of the nineteenth century that a tribe of that name, the Feqîran, came into being. After initiation into the order, feqîrs traditionally led a life of fasting and abstinence, and their persons were considered sacred. The *qewwals*, meaning 'chanters', are also drawn from certain families, particularly the Kurmanji-speaking Dimlî and the Arabic-speaking Tazhî. They play the sacred music at religious occasions, and are specially trained in the recitation of the religious traditions. Most of both these groups are murîd; they enjoy considerable prestige. Their status is not automatically bequeathed to their sons, and they must marry within their caste (sheykh, pîr or murîd) rather than within the families of members of their order (feqîr or qewwal). A very small group, in 1992 only three individuals, dedicate themselves to celibacy and service at the holiest shrine of Lalêsh. The Baba Chawûsh, guardian of the shrine, from the pîr caste, was also a eunuch;[9] he was assisted in his religious duties by two celibate women. All three have made a conscious decision, regardless of their original caste, to embrace the religious life. Another non-hereditary group is the *kocheks* or 'little ones' who undertake tasks associated with the shrine, such as collecting wood and fetching water for specific occasions. Some are also visionaries, diviners, and miracle-workers (Kreyenbroek 1995: 134–5), and certain kocheks have become influential; Kochek Mîrza, for instance, who came to Sinjar in the early 1890s, at a time of great religious tension, predicted the imminent demise of Islam and attracted many followers, who drifted away when the events he foretold failed to materialise. However, he had amassed a considerable sum before being forcibly returned to Sheykhan (Lescot 1938: 183, Guest 1993: 140). There are similarities between feqîrs and kocheks in terms of dress and code of conduct, and earlier sources make a connection between the two (Kreyenbroek 1995: 142).

Certain Yezidi sheykhly families have been wealthy for centuries, especially land owners such as the Mîr's family and those who could make wide-ranging collections of alms. In the twentieth century Yezidi murîds became financially successful, often by using their status as non-Muslims to advantage and keeping hotels and bars. In the Kurdish-held zone in 1992, it was not uncommon to see people of the murîd class, technically the lowest Yezidi caste, living in prosperity whilst those of sheykhly rank, technically the highest, were impoverished. Many murîds who had been to university and were working as teachers or engineers considered themselves a much more progressive class than the sheykhs, who often still made their money from land ownership or contributions due to their religious rank.

Endogamy

The Yezidis' consciousness of uniqueness is nowhere seen more clearly than in their refusal to intermarry with other social groups. Converts to their religion are not accepted. This strict endogamy, which is even professed (openly, at any rate) by young, educated, secular Yezidis in Iraq, is often justified on the grounds of racial purity, which are clearly spurious; informants who claim that Yezidis are Kurds will not countenance intermarriage with other Kurds, whose great-grandfathers may have been forcibly converted from Yezidism to Islam. Ritual or religious purity, the maintaining of Yezidi separateness, seems to be the point at issue. An example of a Yezidi woman who married a Christian was mentioned by one informant; as is the rule in such cases, she forfeited her right to be a member of the Yezidi community and went to live with her husband some distance away. Old and young men declared in all seriousness that they would kill their daughters and sisters if they attempted elopement with a Muslim.[10] Rules of intermarriage are strict even within the Yezidi community; as Yezidi society becomes more secularised, it is here that the outsider sees the caste system most obviously at work. A murîd can marry any other murîd, but the sheykh and pîr castes are divided into groups; each sheykh or pîr must marry within his or her own group. The strictest rules apply to the highest ranking groups – members of the Mîr's family may only intermarry with members of their own clan or with members of one other sheykhly clan.

It is perhaps worth remarking that Yezidis traditionally practised polygamy; there was no limit to the number of wives permitted, and the Mîr's family in particular was noted for its large number of wives.[11] Polygamy has declined dramatically in recent years; it is more common in Sinjar than Sheykhan. Younger Yezidis who discussed polygamy with me cited the difficulties which can arise between wives, and the economic advantages of monogamy. More outspoken young women declared they would not tolerate a husband who wanted a second wife, and viewed polygamy as oppressive. It was clear that monogamy is perceived as more progressive, and polygamy associated with peasant communities. Polygamy was cited as grounds for criticism of the Sinjaris and of the Mîr's family. A few recent examples were mentioned during the course of the fieldwork of married men who had decided to take another wife; however, the first wife had returned to her family (whether voluntarily or not was not always clear), in all these cases. It is uncertain whether this was now the norm.

The importance of endogamy to the identity of the Yezidis of Northern Iraq is clearly enormous; the strictness of the taboos surrounding the subject and the enormity of the punishments for those who offend by marrying inappropriately are described in detail to any interested outsider. However, infringements of these rules have been tolerated. Members of the community who have literally no-one to marry may apply to the appropriate religious authorities who can consider the case and grant an exemption; one hears anecdotal evidence of Yezidi men who have married Christians and remained part of the community, albeit with a changed role. As with many other areas of Yezidi life, matters are strongly regulated, but one of the key functions of the religious hierarchy is the resolution of cases where the circumstances of real life conflict with the ideal order imposed by Yezidism.

YEZIDISM AND NON-YEZIDI VIEWS OF IT

Even seventeenth century Oriental sources, such as the *Sheref-name* of Sheref Khan Bitlisi and the *Seyahat-name* of Evliya Çelebi, present Yezidism as exotic and strongly differentiated from the religion of neighbouring groups. Sheref Khan's description is hostile:

> The Yezidis who inhabit Mount Sinjar are a barbarous people who know neither prayers nor feasts, fasts, customs or laws, and who, without being subject to any established police authority, devote themselves to agriculture, while in fact living from robbery ... They obey some Sheykhs and have the horrible and barbarous custom of selling their children in the towns ... They are not circumcised ... and they detest the Turks, but seem to esteem the Christians. (Charmoy 1868: 69–70, tr. Kreyenbroek).

In his descriptions of his expedition to Sinjar and of the revolt of Abdal Khan of Bitlis, who is said to be of Yezidi extraction and who was supported by Yezidi warriors of various[12] tribes (1655–6), Evliya Çelebi consistently describes Yezidi fighters as wild, bloodthirsty, insanely brave, and loyal to their comrades. His account of a visit to Yezidis near 'Aqra recounts a discussion of religion, describes the shrine of Sheykh Adi at Lalêsh as much more splendid than any Sunni Kurdish shrine, and refers to some picturesque taboos.

The Yezidis' exotic reputation persisted, though the details of their religion remained little known. When, in the mid-nineteenth century, Austen Henry Layard wrote (1849 I: 271) of his curiosity about Yezidism:

> '...[the Yezidis'] worship, their tenets, and their origin were alike a subject of mystery which I felt anxious to clear up as far as I was able.'

he was emphasising precisely those elements which make Yezidism difficult to comprehend for 'people of the Book', whether local or foreign, Muslim, Christian or Jew, by using the words 'worship' and 'tenets.' Yezidi accounts of their religion, including not only the publications by Yezidi scholars of their sacred texts and collections of their folklore, but also those descriptions given to anthropologists and researchers of religion, make it clear that Yezidi religion is qualitatively different from Christianity, Islam and Judaism, and concepts of 'worship' and 'tenets,' as 'people of the book' would understand them, do not apply. The 'religions of the Book', in their 'mainstream' forms at any rate, have official forms of worship – regular, formal rituals and prayers with fixed words, as well as 'tenets' – formal beliefs which all members can be expected to profess. This is not the case with Yezidism, and the lack of these elements has sometimes caused non-Yezidis to think either that the Yezidis once had these things, but that they are now lost, or that there is no inner life in Yezidism. Typical of this attitude was the Christian of the Tur Abdin who said of the Yezidis, 'They have nothing.'[13]

Yet the Yezidis do worship and have beliefs. They have a strong veneration for holy places and objects, which are associated with holy beings, and their belief in the role of the spiritual in everyday life has been documented by writers such as Layard and Drower. Their solemn rites for the great occasions of human life, and their religious festivals, are mentioned by many writers. Yezidis do not have liturgy as Christians understand it, and the form of prayer (word or gesture) and even the time of day when prayer is made, often seems a matter of great variation, and perhaps of individual choice. Traditionally, there has been no one statement or creed on which all Yezidis would agree as the fundamental statement of Yezidism, and though there are agreed to be seven angels or holy beings, the most important of whom is the Peacock Angel, Melek Tawus, there is not universal agreement on who all the others are.[14] Even the cult of Sheykh Adi, who founded what is now the Yezidi sect, seems to be stronger in some areas than others. As for core 'texts', there are various holy texts or *qewls*, but recent collection of new *qewls* among the diaspora Yezidis shows that the 'canon' of texts is not universal – many are better known in some areas than others. They are still performed, but their meaning is often obscure and known only to a few people with religious authority. There are also the sermons or *meshabet* which are preached to larger groups by the qewwals, when they carry the *senjaq*s, or sacred effigies representing Melek Tawus, round outlying communities, a practice called *ṭawûsgeṛan.* This, like the large gatherings such as the annual autumn festival, is a force for religious standardisation, as well as for Sheykhani influence; a proportion of the revenues thus collected accrue to the Mîr's family (Fuccaro 1999: 21). Such forces, whilst consolidating Sheykhani influence and prosperity, could not hope to produce standard, universal beliefs and practices.

Yezidism does have a common conceptual framework in that the Holy Beings are considered to have taken human form at various points in the past, and their descendants receive appropriate respect. Places associated with them are also venerated. It may be very loosely termed a 'belief-system', and it is capable of borrowing many elements, including holy figures, rituals and symbols, from other religions. However, it is largely a matter of orthopraxy rather than orthodoxy – one is a good Yezidi by being virtuous, avoiding bad behaviour, and following the rules or taboos applicable to one's own status. A key principle underpinning many of the regulations is order – purity is preserved by not allowing inappropriate things to mix. Living within the Yezidi community was in the past seen as essential for maintaining one's status as a Yezidi, though more recently political and economic forces, which have driven Yezidis into large cities and even abroad, have relaxed this rule. Yezidis tend to socialise primarily with each other, whilst expressing affection for Christians and antagonism towards Muslims. This is hardly surprising, given the number of massacres suffered in the past (al-Jabiri 1991: Appendix). European travellers of the nineteenth century commented on their reluctance to give any information about themselves; their practice of concealment of their religion seems to have been institutionalised and no doubt stemmed from a fear of religious persecution. This wish to conceal important aspects of their religion resulted in the telling of some notable lies to outsiders, visible in some of the wilder claims in the literature of 'Yezidology', and the withholding of fundamental pieces of information; Layard, for instance, attended a festival at the holy shrine of Lalêsh without being aware of the location, or even the existence, of the sacred cave, focus of the devotions (Layard 1849: 270–308).

Many taboos reflect the desire for purity; thus, for example, behaviour which is perceived to pollute the earth, such as spitting, is forbidden. Certain words should not be said, particularly 'Sheytan' which shows disrespect to Melek Tawus because it is used by non-Yezidis to slander him.[15] The concern for purity is particularly obvious in social terms, shown by the caste system and the rules on marriage, and also in the Yezidis' interactions with other groups – in the past they have considered it polluting to mix with Muslims, and have cited religious purity as grounds for claiming exemption from military service.[16] At present, this reluctance to associate with Muslims is usually presented as a fear of forcible conversion. However, many tribes, such as the Heverkan, had both Yezidi and Muslim members, and even if the two groups did not marry, they must have associated; it seems likely that there was a difference in Yezidi attitudes to local Muslims who were bound to them by ties of kinship and the *kerafet*,[17] and other Muslims. Yezidis have usually been willing to live alongside Christians, who are also non-Yezidi; it is clear that the religious regulations are tempered by pragmatism. The religious authorities' rulings are probably the source of many of the Yezidis' more striking taboos, though it is rarely remembered who issued the rulings and why. Sometimes aetiological tales arise to support the taboos, such as the tale of an otherwise unknown prophetess Khasse to account for the taboo on eating *khas* or lettuce.[18] However, custom and precedent are powerful enough in themselves to justify many practices as religiously correct.

Thus Yezidism is truly a 'way of life' rather than an internalised dogma, but its elusive religiosity is very difficult for outsiders to comprehend. The problem of the lack of 'worship' and 'tenets' so fundamental to religions of the Book, was compounded by the Yezidis' inability to expound their doctrines in ways comprehensible to educated outsiders. Such Yezidi traditions as became known outside the community often took the form of religious myth or lyric, and were certainly not couched in the forms familiar to scriptural scholars. Westerners of the nineteenth and early twentieth centuries tended to dismiss these as inadequate religious texts, because they were attempting to read and understand them as if they were attempts at scholarly theology. Little sensitivity to the conventions of the genres in which these texts were composed was shown.[19] The myth of Adam, Eve and the Child of the Jar, for instance, was described as 'patchy and puerile';[20] the English missionary Badger quotes an Arabic Hymn of Sheykh Adi which he calls largely 'confused and unintelligible' (1852: 115). Little attention was paid to the ways in which the Yezidis understood, interpreted and used these traditions.

The perceived 'gap' or 'lack' in the Yezidi religion had its consequences for the way outsiders, both local and Western, perceived and presented the Yezidis themselves. Yezidis were assumed by many Westerners to be either mentally or spiritually deficient. The eminent Kurdologist Roger Lescot diagnosed 'an unbelievable slowness of mind' (1938: 6–7, tr. Kreyenbroek (1995: 17)). Badger described them as 'heathen' (1852: 134). There was a common assumption that they must be hiding some Secret, either of an esoteric kind, as in Layard's romantic idea that they could be worshippers of Semiramis (1849: 271), or of a sordid kind. Badger attested that 'great lewdness is said to prevail within their own community' (1852: 132–3). Such remarks are often a reflection of local prejudices about the Yezidis, but they have in turn influenced modern local discourses. Because of the dynamics of Orientalism, the writings of Western scholars, diplomats and travellers of the past two centuries have had a disproportionate influence on discourses of identity in the Middle East, providing both minorities and governments with some of their most powerful images. For instance, Christians of the Church of the East claim Assyrian origin, drawing inspiration for their nationalism from the spectacular products of Layard's excavations. The status of Nineveh and Babylon in Iraqi national discourses is enormous. The exotic past descriptions of Yezidis, by early writers and then by Orientalists, have ensured them a special status.

The Position of the Yezidis in Kurdish Society

Despite their sufferings, the Yezidis in Ottoman times were not always a powerless minority, forced to endure the depradations of Muslim aghas without any chance of retaliation. They had various links with Muslim tribes and, long after the time of Evliya Çelebi, eighteenth, nineteenth and early twentieth century accounts attest to their reputation as fighters and robbers, particularly in the Jebel Sinjar, where the Ottoman authorities tried on several occasions to curb their interference with traffic by punitive raids (Guest 1993: 86–140). From the British mandate onwards, the Jebel Sinjar formed a base for several uprisings until the population was brought under control by the Ba'ath government. After the establishment of the states of Turkey, Iraq and Syria, the location of Yezidi territory provided them with a lucrative business in cross-border smuggling. This was still an important activity after the creation of the 'safe haven', and was carried out over internal Iraqi borders as well as the international frontiers; petrol, kerosene, and other goods in short supply due to an Iraqi government embargo, came into the northern part of the Kurdish zone by two major routes (among others): by boat across the Saddam lake to Khanek and thence Dihok, and by tractor along the dirt tracks from Ba'drê.

There is no doubt that during my own fieldwork, prejudice against Yezidis still existed in both Muslim and Christian communities in Badinan. Neighbours of the Yezidis in Badinan held various beliefs about them; in fact there was a rather distasteful discourse of mutual insults between Muslim, Christian and Yezidi communities. One of these, firmly held by many Christians and Muslims, was that the Yezidis never washed, because their religion forbade it. Not surprisingly, I saw evidence to the contrary innumerable times, but non-Yezidis refused to be swayed by what I had seen, on the grounds that they knew the Yezidis better, having been their neighbours for so long. The Yezidi viewpoint was (predictably) that the Muslims must be dirty people if they needed to be told to wash by their religion; it was clear that they also considered Muslims literally as well as ritually unclean. Non-Yezidis' belief that Yezidis ate dirt can perhaps be accounted for by the Yezidi view that the earth of a shrine is sacred. (Earth in general is an element to be respected). Balls of dust from the shrine of Sheykh Adi are kept as holy objects and sometimes kissed, and holy earth is sometimes crumbled into water or food as medicine. However, the Christians of the area also use the earth of saints' tombs for such purposes, though this did not seem to find its way into the arguments. Rumours that the Yezidis indulged in mass orgies during their religious festivals still circulate. It is probable that this belief grew out of local disapproval of the fact that men and women mixed relatively freely, talking and dancing together at religious festivals.[21] Such beliefs are held elsewhere about other minorities, such as the Alevis, who also have mixed assemblies, and merit attention not for their own sake but rather for the underlying attitudes and tensions that they reveal. The popular fallacies that Yezidis have no form of prayer and that they worship the devil were also still believed.[22]

However, the Kurdish government was making every effort to incorporate them into the community. There was a political point at stake over the Yezidis' identity – official Ba'ath orthodoxy, partly prompted by Yezidi involvement in the Kurdish uprising of the 1970s, declared them to be Arabs. Both major Kurdish parties, KDP and PUK, could boast famous Yezidi martyrs, and in 1992 they and the smaller political parties had a number of Yezidi cadres active within their ranks. The electoral power of the substantial Yezidi community, the economic power of certain of its members, and the strategic location of its settlements on both sides of the Kurdish-Iraqi front line, along with the need to avoid discord between communities in the Kurdish-held zone, prompted the Kurdish government to make public gestures emphasising their acceptance into the wider community. Their religion, privately ridiculed by members of other groups, was publicly given respect by politicians. Newspapers and television issued congratulations to Yezidis on their festival days, Party officials attended Yezidi celebrations, and in summer 1992 KDP leader Mes'ûd Barzani paid an official visit to the acting Yezidi Mîr, a KDP member of Parliament, at Lalêsh. The Yezidis were also useful to the Kurdish government in their construction of the nationalist myth – as their religion appeared to contain pre-Islamic Iranian elements, it was promoted as the authentic Kurdish religion, and both Mes'ûd Barzani and PUK leader Jalal Talabani declared the Yezidis to be 'the original Kurds'.[23] Naturally there could be no proselytising of the Yezidi faith; it was highly unlikely that any Kurdish Muslim would wish to join a community which had still not altogether shaken off its pariah status, and in any case the Yezidis' own religious laws would not permit it. The Kurdish government, which took a secular stance, was simply using the Yezidis to enhance a Kurdish ancient history which owed nothing to the Arabs, and which formed an important part of the Kurdish identity which the Kurdish government was promoting (see below).

Generally the Yezidis were portrayed by their neighbours as picturesque (wearing traditional clothes and speaking 'pure' Kurdish) but backward, part of the region's folklore. Many Muslims in the area were well aware that their family or tribe had previously been Yezidi, and some seemed to take a pride in this, though one in particular expressed relief that his family was now Muslim. The Yezidis' association with old religions gave them a symbolic importance but at the same time confined them to the realms of ancient history. This dismissal of a people as quaint, unchanging and left behind by modernity is very similar to the attitudes of some of the most notorious 'Orientalists.' The Yezidis' status as a piece of Iraqi folklore, and the fact that they were internationally known, may have helped their overall survival in Iraq, but it also belittled them by stereotyping them.

YEZIDI DISCOURSES OF IDENTITY

The term 'discourse' is used here in the sense of 'all kinds of active verbal communication', in other words, what has been written and said about the Yezidis' identity. The issue is complex; attempts by non-Yezidis to label them, and attempts by the Yezidis themselves to claim specific ethnic and religious identities, can usually be linked with contemporary political factors. They have been described as Kurdish from a very early date; in the fourteenth century seven of the most important Kurdish tribes were Yezidi, and Yezidism was the religion of the Kurdish principality of Jezîre (Fuccaro 1999: 10). In the seventeenth century, Evliya Çelebi describes the soldiers of Abdal Khan Bitlisi as 'Yezidi Kurds' (Dankoff 1990: 174). As far as language is concerned, it is worth noting that the great majority speak Kurmanji as their mother tongue, and have done for centuries (Millingen 1870: 274). However, in the twelfth century their religion was profoundly influenced and reformed by an Arab Sufi, Sheykh 'Adī b. Musāfir,[24] and certain influential sheykhly clans trace their descent back to him and his followers; moreover, the inhabitants of Bashika and Beḥzan, the two villages in Sheykhan which are the home of many qewwals or religious chanters, are native Arabic speakers. The dialect of Kurmanji spoken by the Yezidis in the large collectives near Dihok differs from that of the town; Dihok's distinctive *î* where other Kurmanji subdialects have *û* (as in the verb *şû kirin* 'to get married' (for women), which becomes *şî kirin* in Dihok) is not found in the Yezidi communities. According to Dihok townspeople, these local Yezidis use fewer borrowings from Arabic than Dihokis, though this may simply reflect a general lack of formal education, since Badinani Kurmanji borrows most of its technical and elevated vocabulary from Arabic. In my own experience, educated Yezidis did not seem to use less Arabic vocabulary than educated Muslims. There are also distinctive 'Yezidi' turns of phrase, some of which are used in connection with the taboo on pronouncing the word *Sheytan* 'Satan' or words sounding like it (Kreyenbroek 1995: 149–50). For instance, Yezidis prefer to use the verb *karîn* 'to be able' rather than *şîyan* which is more normal locally.

With regard to material culture, there are many similarities between food eaten, crops grown, farming techniques and other items of everyday life in Yezidi and Muslim Kurdish villages. This hardly proves a common ethnic identity, however, since similar observations have been made of the Jews and Christians of Kurdistan, few of whom would claim Kurdish identity (Feitelson 1959). Yezidi costume is often distinctive. When the 'safe haven' had been created there was a resurgence in the wearing of Kurdish traditional costume (O'Shea 1996); Yezidi men often wore traditional Kurdish *şal û şepik*, a baggy trousers and jacket, with a broad and often brightly-coloured sash, but their patterned turbans were always red, never black. The undershirt was white, with a rounded neck for religious reasons (Kreyenbroek 1995: 66). Some men from Sheykhan, particularly the qewwals and some members of sheykhly families, wore more obviously 'Arab' costume, with a long robe and the headdress worn loose, not tied around the head as in Kurdish dress. Some older Yezidis followed the law which forbids the shaving or cutting of the moustache. Younger women usually wore long, full skirts, tops and headscarves – a costume adopted within the last generation, according to informants, in contrast with Kurdish Muslim women who wore either Western-style tailored skirts (in the towns) or full-length Kurdish dresses, usually with trousers. Older women often wore long white dresses and undertrousers with a patterned plaid draped over, a broad sash in which, like the men, they stored small but useful items, and a turban. Sinjari dress differed from these Sheykhani norms, but was rarely seen.[25]

Yezidi identity politics are closely tied to their discourses of origin. A perceived past identity is a key part of present identity, and by claiming descent from powerful groups of the past one can increase one's present power. Throughout the Near and Middle East the claiming of specific origins has been practised for many centuries, for various purposes such as legitimising political power (by claiming descent from past kings, for example) or conferring religious status (as with descendants of the Prophet, or of venerated sheykhs in Islam). The Yezidis' accounts of their origins have incorporated the work of outsiders as they developed. Even early witnesses, such as Sheref Khan Bitlisi, showed an interest in Yezidi origins; Bitlisi suggested Manichaeism (Charmoy 1868: 69–70). This fascination grew with the work of Layard, Badger and their scholarly successors; Layard opted for a Sabian or Chaldaean origin in Southern Iraq, and Badger for a form of dualism associated with Zoroastrianism. Later writers developed these themes, and posited ancient pre-Sabian, non-Indo-European religions, Tammuz-worship, and others (Kreyenbroek 1995: 4–5).

The Yezidis' social and religious institutions are of course founded on genealogy, but the crucial time for them was the foundation of their sect by the holy man Sheykh Adi, as their leading families claim descent from his companions. Their traditions which recounted earlier periods and their myths of the early stages of the world do not dwell on ethnicity, with the possible exception of the traditions telling that the Yezidis were the children of Adam alone and not of Eve, and thus separate from the rest of humanity. With the development of modern concepts of nationalism and racial identity in the 19th and 20th century the question of the Yezidis' ethnic origins was ripe for exploitation by those within and without the community. A witness during the last years of the Ottoman empire found Yezidis who claimed to be descended from the ancient Assyrians 'like the Nestorians' (Sykes 1915: 93). By this time, Ottoman government policies had resulted in religion becoming a prime element in identity, and Yezidis and Christians had both suffered persecution at the hands of Muslim Kurds and Turks (Guest 1993: 96–7). The development of another interpretation of Yezidi identity was set in motion in the mid-1880s, when the French consul in Mosul, Siouffi, identified the Sheykh Adi remembered in Yezidi oral tradition as the Sufi saint 'Adī b. Musāfir (Siouffi 1885; Frank 1911). This identification of Sheykh Adi as a Sunni Muslim enabled the formulation of views such as that of Guidi (1932a, b) and Lescot (1936, 1938) who saw a totally Islamic origin for the Yezidis. It was also useful in the 1960s and 1970s to those Yezidis such as Bayezîd Beg, cousin of the present Mîr, Teḥsîn Beg, who wished to emphasise points of similarity with

Islam, and, since Sheykh Adi himself was of Ummayyad descent, claim an Ummayyad identity. This view was also in line with Iraqi government promotion of Arab identity for the Yezidis.

An opposing discourse is associated with Kurdish nationalism, in the diaspora and the homeland, since the 1970s, and claims descent from the Medes for the Kurds. This eagerness to embrace an ancient Iranian cultural heritage in part reflects a resistance to attempts, by pan-Turkists in particular, to deny a separate Kurdish identity (Nezan 1980: 68–72.). The Medes offer a non-Islamic origin distinguishing Kurds from Turks and Arabs. The claim of descent from a people who were not only ancient, but powerful enough to have an empire, may be seen as a claim for power in the contemporary world.[26] Exponents of these views tended to see Yezidism as a form of Zoroastrianism. Perhaps the most dramatic example of such exploration by a member of the community was *To us Spoke Zarathustra*, by Prince Mu'āwiya, cousin of the present Mîr (Chol 1983).[27] This book, which claimed that not only Yezidis but all Kurds were Zoroastrians, certainly does not embody the views of the community as a whole but reflects the terms of discourse current at the time. In Northern Iraq in 1992 the official view expressed by Barzani that the Yezidi religion was the 'original' Kurdish religion appeared to be shared by most Yezidis, in public, at any rate.[28] Almost every Yezidi man I encountered, and many of the women, volunteered the information that the Yezidis were 'the original Kurds' on first acquaintance. The religion was often referred to as 'Zoroastrianism', not only because it was known that great Iranian empires had been Zoroastrian, but also because there was not much knowledge of ancient Iranian alternatives.[29] However, few if any informants in the field had a clear idea of the beliefs and practices of Zoroastrianism.

This interest in the 'original' religion brought with it a distinct ambiguity about Sheykh Adi. Yezidi advocates of a non-Islamic origin see the pre-Sheykh Adi period as purer – one prominent Yezidi even went so far as to say 'Sheykh Adi ruined our religion.' Some Yezidis described the sheykhly caste (the highest caste) as an Arab imposition on the community by Sheykh Adi. However, the differences between Yezidism and the religion of the Iranian Zoroastrians and the Parsees were obvious to educated Yezidis, and there was considerable debate on the subject. Concern with this issue persists, and there has also been some resentment at being incorporated into Kurdish nationalist discourses. Since the PKK declared the Yezidis to be Zoroastrians, and since documentaries to this effect were broadcast on MED-TV, many non-PKK supporters among the Iraqi Yezidis have been unwilling to be classified in this way, and some are exploring other origins, notably Sumerian.[30] It should be emphasised that this outline applies to the Yezidis of Iraq, both in the homeland and the diaspora; the politics of Yezidi identity are very different in the Caucasus, where dominant discourses do not consider them to be Kurds.

The Yezidis have a complex relationship with their reputation. On the one hand they are aware of their exotic image and exploit it, sometimes telling outrageous lies to gullible foreigners; on the other hand, they resent being viewed as primitive. Despite their pride in being Yezidi and their avowed distaste for belonging to any other group, informants, particularly young adults, showed a drive towards secularism, although the most important factor differentiating Yezidis from other groups in society is their religion. Many people professed contempt for the sometimes arcane customs of their society, such as the compulsory growth of the moustache, and prohibition of wearing the colour blue, or of eating lettuce. This urge towards modernism was tempered by admiration of those, usually of the older generation, who observed religious customs and lived a virtuous life. The Sinjari Yezidis were particularly admired for this in the community; they were felt to be the guardians of true Yezidi traditions. Most of the noted singers of traditional Yezidi material come from the Sinjar.

Village and tribal identity remained strong in the community, even after collectivisation policies had placed them in larger settlements. Whenever a visit was made to a Yezidi collective, local people would point out the sites of the former villages which had been demolished. This concern was general throughout the zone; during 1992 an initiative to rebuild destroyed Kurdish villages was a key policy of the Kurdish authorities. This feeling was noticeable even when the village was not particularly ancient in absolute terms; for example, communities such as the Yezidi Hawerî tribe of Dêrebûn and Khanek, who only migrated to Iraq from Turkey after the First World War, still viewed the village lands of Iraq as their historical tribal territory even when there was a communal memory of previous territory. The territory which had been theirs in Turkey was seen as ancient.

The ancestral villages demolished during collectivisation still lived on in the community's interactions. Not only did people socialise extensively with networks who had lived in their previous villages, but the shrines with their distinctive spires called *qub*, which had belonged to the old villages and had been destroyed, were rebuilt on new sites in collective villages, and continued to play their part in the life of the community. During the spring, Yezidis traditionally hold festivals called *ṭiwaf*. Despite its name, this festival seems to have little in common with the Islamic ritual of circumambulation. The inhabitants of a village would be joined by guests from other villages to visit the *qub* of the village's saint, give an offering to the guardian of the shrine, eat a ritual meal, and dance to the music of drum and the *zuṛne*, a type of shawm. In collectives, the inhabitants performed this ritual for destroyed villages individually in Spring 1992. However, not all aspects of village life survived. Some roles were made obsolete by the collective – one village midwife, for instance, no longer needed because the larger community of the collective had easier access to professional healthcare, expressed regret for the loss of this role and her subsequent loss of status.

YEZIDI HISTORICAL DISCOURSES

The next chapter will discuss the ways in which Yezidi constructs of history are structured and transmitted, but since discourses of history are so closely linked to discourses of identity, it is worth outlining some general features of the Yezidi historical discourse. Given the complexities of the politics of the region in which Yezidis live, and the variety of stances taken over the years by prominent Yezidi individuals, one is justified in asking whether 'Yezidi history' and indeed 'Yezidi identity' are coherent concepts in Northern Iraq. Certainly the Yezidis have never constituted a totally united political force; there have always been differences of opinion and perspective among different tribes and clans in different locations. However, despite their internal differences, the Yezidis have a strong sense that they are separate from the other communities in the area, and informants always showed an understanding of the term 'history of the Yezidis' as distinct from that of the Kurds. There was a strong consensus as to which stories from history were important, and certain broad themes were raised constantly by Yezidis from many different backgrounds. These distinguished their discourse from that of the Muslim Kurds or of the Aramaic-speaking Christians of the region. Three of the most important of these areas of concern, as observed in the community, are: the past influence of the Yezidis, their precarious status as a minority, and their attitude to outside authorities.

Alongside the generally expressed view that the Yezidis were 'the original Kurds' went a feeling of disinheritance. Yezidis used to control much larger areas of Kurdistan than they now do; this was still common knowledge. Most of the Yezidi population of Turkey now lives in Germany because of persecution in their homeland; contacts between them and the Iraqi Yezidis were frequent, and the diaspora Yezidis had funded the refurbishment of the holy shrine at Lalêsh. There were also, less frequently, contacts with Yezidis from Transcaucasia. The following, which is not a formal historical narrative but a piece of ordinary conversation, is typical of the type of remarks made on first acquaintance. It was said by Mr P., a middle-aged murîd in Shari'e, who welcomed me into his house and told me something about the area; I have retained the wording he used, to give an impression of the terms in which these ideas are expressed:

> As we know, this Kurdistan of ours used to be completely Yezidi. Dihok of the Dasenî [a Yezidi tribe], now they also call it Dasenî Dihok, that is ... Yezidi Dihok. Simêl ... was the site of the fortresses of the Yezidi Dina agha, the property of the agha and his court of Dina people were at Simêl. We know all this very well. But all that stuff, those persecutions, came, and the religion of Mohammed brought persecutions on us and plundered us and did this and that,

> they scattered us; people went to Sinjar, they went to Iran, they went to Syria and ... that was a violation against us. Now the Kurds know their origin is Yezidi.

Like their Muslim neighbours, the Yezidis felt the loss of their villages during collectivisation keenly, but their overall perception was that they had been losing settlements and territory not just during the rule of Saddam but for hundreds of years.

Another element of this broad theme in Yezidi historical discourse was the implication that the Yezidis had known for a long time a fundamental truth about Kurdish origin which the Muslim Kurds had only just realised. Mr. P. drew a contrast between what the Yezidis knew of Kurdistan being Yezidi and what the Kurds now knew. Besides this knowledge there was an implication that the Yezidis, in adhering to their caste system and strict taboos, had retained a purity which other Kurds had lost by embracing Islam.[31] There was never any hint of suggestion from any member of the community that if Muslim Kurds had once been Yezidis, then they might return to the Yezidi community.

The Yezidis' awareness of their vulnerability also influenced their tellings of history. Kurdistan in 1992 was a place filled with tension and fear. After generations of uprising and repression, a relative degree of self-determination had been bought at the price of considerable poverty and deprivation. However, nobody knew when the Iraqi army might arrive and take control again. All these tensions were felt by the Yezidis, some of whom had participated in uprisings, whilst others had worked for the government. However, in addition to the Iraqi government, with whom they had a complex relationship, the Yezidis feared their Muslim neighbours.

Unprotected by the status of 'people of the Book' the Yezidis had had no rights under Islamic law until 1849 (Guest 1993: 104). Thus for most of their history they have been vulnerable to depredations and persecutions with little or no right of redress. Some of the Yezidis I met expressed their history as a series of *ferman* or persecutions against them.[32] According to Edmonds (1967: 59):

> The situation of the Yazidis in an Islamic state differed fundamentally from that of the Christians of the various denominations and of the Jews, whose presence as religious minorities entitled to certain privileges was recognised by law. They tended to be regarded ... as apostates and were thus always exposed to the danger that persons in authority, high or low ... might think it not only legitimate but even meritorious to maltreat them.

In Khanek, Sheykh K. said that of seventy-three persecutions of Yezidis, one had been carried out by Arabs and the rest by Kurds. The Kurdish leadership was welcomed, but with caution; during the few visits I made to

Yezidis with Kurdish Muslim companions, the Yezidis treated the Muslim visitor politely but were much more forthcoming when Muslims were not present. During 1992 there was a great deal of anxiety and fear in a suburb of Dihok with a majority Yezidi population, as the town authorities had decided to build a mosque there. The Yezidis found this both oppressive and insulting.

Knowledge of the persecutions in the community seemed fairly detailed. Almost all the older people questioned, and many of the younger ones, could differentiate, for example, between the massacre of the Sheykhanis at Mosul in 1932 and the campaigns of 'Ferîq Pasha' in 1892–93, even though many could not date them accurately (Guest 1993: 68–9, 134–40). However, although accounts of the persecutions constitute a large and pervasive element of the Yezidi historical discourse, the oral traditions often reflect the complexity of relations between the communities. Many of the lyrical songs performed by Yezidis extol the deeds of Muslim Kurds, and do not omit the fact, which is sometimes glossed over by contemporary Yezidi discourse, that there have been many occasions when Yezidis have fought alongside Muslims against other Yezidis. One particularly striking example is a song glorifying Silêmanê Mistê (sometimes called Selîmê Mistê), an outlaw who became famous for killing a Western missionary who lived in Dihok during the 1950s.[33] The song opens with a wish that God should destroy the house of the missionary who was trying to harm Islam. This sentiment, which seems rather bizarre in such a recent song performed by Yezidi singers, is explained by the relationship of *kerafet* between the Yezidis and Silêmanê Mistê's tribe, the Doskî Kurds of Dihok. Such links were not usually emphasised in Yezidi accounts to me of their relationship with Muslims. Although the style of these lyrical songs is associated in Badinan with Yezidis, some singers are Muslim, and the context of the composition of many of them, particularly those of Ottoman times, was mixed. The Milan, one of the larger Kurdish tribal confederations, included some Yezidi tribes, and its paramount chieftain at the end of the nineteenth century, Ibrahim Pasha Millî, had at his court a Yezidi singer, Biroyê Sherqî, who is now considered to be the source of most of the popular Sinjari songs. My own collection contains a significant group of songs, mainly love songs, which are performed by both Yezidi and Muslim singers; some of the Muslim singers represented belong to tribes which include both Muslim and Yezidi clans.

Resistance to outside authority is an important theme in the historical discourse of the Yezidis and, more widely, of the Kurds. Much of the discourse, including many of the historical traditions, refers to conflict between Yezidis or Muslim Kurds and the central government. In most of the historical traditions this was the Ottoman Empire, usually referred to as *Rûm*. Like many other Kurds, the Yezidis had a reputation for brigandage and resistance to outside authority (Kreyenbroek 1995: 1–3). The government is usually portrayed in Kurdish oral tradition as a distant but oppressive entity, whose reasoning is not easy to understand. In general Yezidis, who were less educated than members of other communities, have played little part in official Government structures, even at local level; the notable exceptions such as Êzdî Mîrza are few and far between. This certainly remained true during the Mandatory period (Fuccaro 1999: 91–2) and has been slow to change. The relationships of patronage which prevail in Iraqi politics generally have not encouraged ordinary, non-élite citizens to think of those in positions of power and influence as behaving in logical ways; the accounts I heard of villagers' petitions to senior figures (including Saddam himself) presented an image of authority as capricious. It was clear that people had been encouraged to perceive the government as omnipotent, to become dependent on it and its favours.

An important aspect of the historical discourse, as presented to me during interviews, is the way that Yezidi informants neutralised recent history, omitting details of divisions within their community. It was only on closer acquaintance that people began to discuss these divisions; one important topic of conversation, for instance, was the often fraught relationship between the Mîr's family and the other castes. Details of rivalries and feuds between families were not volunteered. The issue of former *jash*, 'collaborators', was particularly uncomfortable in the Kurdish zone; everyone knew who had been 'with' the government, and said so, but the implications of this were not discussed. Some former government supporters had had links with Kurdish nationalists, and others had not; their role had been varied (van Bruinessen 2000: 20–22). Even in private, most Yezidis were loth to give accounts of what had happened amongst themselves during the years preceding the Gulf War, though they were quite ready to accuse both the government and their Muslim neighbours of persecution. It was clear that a united front was being presented.

YEZIDI ORALITIES AND LITERACIES

The Yezidis have traditionally been not only illiterate but antiliterate. Religious authorities condemned literacy for all but the members of the Adani clan of sheykhs, who trace descent from the saint Sheykh Hesen, and who seem to be more closely associated with the Islamic elements of the religion. Some analysts ascribe this prohibition to a simple desire to control the population. Although it undoubtedly served as one mechanism of control, as did the interplay between the written and the oral in the transmission of Islam (Nasr 1995), other factors must also have been at work. In latter centuries in particular, a lack of books would have helped preserve the secrecy of the religion from outsiders. An oral tradition of revelation can be regulated by strict control of the occasions on which traditions are divulged, and the people who give and receive them. If we are to accept Kreyenbroek's analysis of the evolution of Yezidism as ancient Iranian beliefs and practices profoundly influenced by contact with an Islamic Sufi order (1995: 27–68) – and this hypothesis best explains the limited evidence available – then oral transmission of religious traditions would have been the norm long before the time of Sheykh Adi, and the oral medium may well have been considered the most appropriate vehicle for religious tradition.

We know little about the date of the Yezidi taboo on literacy, or about the circumstances under which it was made. Yezidi tradition has apparently not preserved an account of it. In fact it is not at all clear that a particular senior figure issued a formal declaration against literacy; it is quite likely that Yezidis were generally illiterate and that since this was customary it gained religious sanction as part of Yezidi life. It is also unclear whether the taboo is against literacy or merely against formal education. The current discourse, as with many other aspects of Yezidi life, uses the literacy taboo as a way of differentiating Yezidis from Muslims. One Yezidi folklorist[34] suggests that it is in these terms that the taboo should be understood; the Yezidis were reluctant to attend school with Muslims, study their texts, and run the risk both of conversion and of hearing profanities from them. Even the Adani sheykhs, for whom literacy was permitted, did not learn at school, but at home. It is likely that lack of formal education was the norm and that perceived threats from Islam politicised this norm into a religious regulation.

Despite the lack of formal education, Yezidis have made use of written materials in the past; their literacy, like other aspects of their lives, has evolved over the years to meet the needs of the communities. The story of the 'Sacred Books' of the Yezidis is a case in point. During the nineteenth century many individuals in the Middle East made substantial amounts of money from selling both genuine and fake manuscripts to Westerners. Rumours of Yezidi 'sacred books' abounded, and in 1913 the 'Yezidi sacred books', *Meshefa Resh* (the 'Black Book) and *Kitêba Jilwe* (the 'Book of Revelation') were published, having been purchased by a Christian priest from a Yezidi convert who claimed to have copied them in secret (Anastase Marie 1911; Guest 1993: 146–63). The authenticity of these has been rightly disputed; indeed the Kurdish in which they are written is not credible Kurmanji at all. Nevertheless their contents strongly resemble oral traditions still circulating in the community (Kreyenbroek 1995: 10–16). It is unlikely that they have entered the community from the published books, and very few Yezidis seem to be aware of the contents of these literary publications, so the origins of the 'sacred books' may well be authentic, though they themselves are almost certainly forgeries. It is probable that, by the end of the nineteenth century, some Yezidis felt a need for a 'sacred book' to be identifiable to outsiders, if only to enhance the status of their faith *vis à vis* the scriptural religions.[35]

Within the community, the disapproving view of formal education prevailed until the 1950s at least, but the literacy sanctioned by religious rules enjoyed considerable prestige. Use has been made of 'Sacred Books' at least over the last century or so, known by the same names as the published versions, but it seems unlikely that the contents were the same. Various Adani sheykhs kept copies of a holy book, called the Jilwe, which they used to diagnose sickness and injury, and to prepare healing prayers and amulets for those who visited them. Of course these copies may not all have been uniform, but some at least contained lists of prophets, from the earliest, such as Adam, Abraham and Noah, and then lists of words, with definitions and explanations following each. A troubled person would go to the sheykh's house, ask the sheykh to open the book, and would point to a word, which the sheykh would then read, explain what the problem was, and prescribe a remedy.[36] Other observers have heard references to a book whose contents were unknown and rarely if ever consulted; indeed, in the 1960s, Professor Joyce Blau was shown a blank exercise book and told it was the *Meshefa Resh*, and was given an oral recitation bearing the same name, which is very different from the published version (Kreyenbroek 1995: 14). The two titles seem to be associated with the process of writing down of oral traditions rather than with fixed texts. They apparently carried prestige in the community, but if their use was confined to certain families then the majority of Yezidis cannot have had easy local access to them. The existence of the book seems to have been more important than universal experience of it. In 1990 a religious elder claimed, in a video aimed at the Yezidi community, that the Yezidis had once had many books, but these had been destroyed in persecutions, though the knowledge within them still existed (Guest 1990: 226).[37]

It is tempting to speculate about the literacy prevailing among the formally uneducated Adani sheykhs of the period before mass education. Would many of them be able to read material other than their sacred books? Were the contents of their books traditions which they already knew well and recognised by such elements as layout on the pages, or were they also able to read unfamiliar material fluently? There must have been differences in the skills and training of different individuals, and there may well have been differences in the way they interpreted the material and used it.

In recent years the Yezidis' need for core written texts, available not just to a tiny minority but more generally, has grown as their own community has changed. Several religious statements have emanated from the community itself. The 1872 Petition, despite one scholar's declaration of it as 'the *locus classicus* on the subject of the Yezidi religion' (Driver 1922: 210), does not expound religion but states rules and taboos precluding military service. However, the 1908 statement sent out by Isma'îl Beg Chol to Transcaucasian Yezidis, which is mostly concerned with social rules, begins with three statements of belief. This member of the Sheykhani Mîr's family attempted to assert his own authority by building a power-base in Sinjar; the document should be seen in this context. Its first precepts, as given below (Dirr 1917–18; Furlani 1930: 109, tr. Kreyenbroek (1995: 8)), clearly show influence of contact with 'people of the book' in the way Yezidism is framed:

i) We believe in one God, the Creator of Heaven, Earth, and of all that is alive.
ii) Our Prophet is Ezid.
iii) The Yezidis have no scripture; God's Word is handed down from father to son.

By the 1970s the first generation of literate, University-educated Yezidis in Northern Iraq had reached maturity. It was at this point that they felt the need to consolidate their 'scripture'. Silêman and Jindî's ground-breaking collection and publication of the *qewls* (1979) provoked controversy among some older traditionalists but was motivated by a desire, not to harm Yezidi tradition, but to preserve it. At about the same time, Ordikhan and Jelîlê Jelîl were collecting and publishing *qewls* along with other 'folklore' in the Soviet Republics; Jelîl 1978 contains several. Since then various Yezidi folklorists have published articles, mainly in Kurdish and Arabic, and Yezidis have been among the membership of literary societies in Iraq. The diaspora community produces several periodicals, including *Dengê Êzîdiya* 'Voice of the Yezidis', *Lalêsh*, and *Roj*, 'Sun' or 'Day'.

With the drive to make religious traditions available to a Yezidi reading public has come a need to interpret them. In the diaspora, where children are being brought up in the European education system, far from the values of the homeland, the situation is particularly urgent; Yezidis have needed to 'understand' their religion in a more cerebral way, and formulate that understanding in ways that had not been necessary before. Orthopraxy, with its food and clothing taboos, and the rigid rules on marriage partners, was not enough for them, and young people expressed frustration at the lack of teaching of their religion in terms they could understand. The 'six points' given to Yezidis by Mîr Teḥsîn Beg at a conference in Oldenburg in early 1997 (as reported in *Dengê Êzidiya*), are very revealing of Yezidi concerns, and of Sheykhani agendas in continuing control of the global community. His first two points focus on social problems; he enjoins Yezidis not to marry their sons and daughters to partners they do not love and forbids the taking of bride-price. His third point turns to religion: 'I know that you want to get to know[38] the foundations of your religion. For this to happen, we must all support our students, intellectuals and researchers.' He then stresses the importance of the collection, transcription and publication of the *qewls*, and promises that he will work on this as a priority. The fourth and fifth points stress the need to respect the Yezidi religious officials and castes, and to teach Yezidi children their language and their religion. The final point is aimed at the wider Kurdish community, declaring that the Yezidis as a group are not aligned with any political party and are in general well-disposed to all, but will repay hostility in kind.

Thus Yezidism, because of exposure to the intellectual systems of outsiders, is moving from a religion of orthopraxy to one of orthodoxy. This will change Yezidi religiosity fundamentally, but the change will not be a betrayal of its past. The religion has always evolved to suit its environment, and its belief system is extremely flexible, incorporating whatever ideas or practices it needs. The Yezidi elders and intellectuals who are currently redefining Yezidism are predominantly Sheykhani. There are good historical reasons for this – control of the leading shrine, control of much of the revenues, and control of the qewwals. However, there is some resentment in the diaspora community of the prominent role being played by the Iraqi Yezidis, many of whom are recent arrivals in Europe. If their agendas for change are to be followed and the community is to retain its cohesion, they will need to be sensitive to these tensions.

The Position of Secular Oral Traditions in Yezidi Society

In Northern Iraq, the vast majority of young male adults, and a growing proportion of female adults, are now educated, with different desires and aspirations from those of their parents and grandparents. Among the older generation, education is still seen as dangerous, particularly for girls, as it involves mixing with the corrupting influences of non-Yezidis, especially Muslims. One typical example of such attitudes was Sheykh K. a Hawerî living in Khanek, who justified his refusal to send his daughters to school on these grounds, though his sons were educated, and one ran a business in Baghdad. The educated members of the younger generation whom I met were eager to emancipate their people further by increasing the presently small number of Yezidi engineers, doctors, lawyers and teachers. Women felt this particularly strongly, as the number of Yezidi women educated to university level remained very low.

The younger, literate generation of Yezidis, like most Kurds, has been educated in schools controlled by the central government and thus receives two separate bodies of tradition regarding its own history, namely, the 'official' version emanating from the government, and the predominantly oral version heard from their elders in the community. In Ba'athist Iraq a strong Arab nationalist element was present in the education system which must have been at odds with local accounts of uprisings. Even after the creation of the 'safe haven', the Kurdish authorities, unwilling to lose all government recognition of schools, were approaching educational reform with care; in Sinjar and Sheykhan government control of schools had never been lost. It would be over-simplistic to say that 'official', State-endorsed versions of history are written, and stand in clear opposition to an oral 'Yezidi' history. Some of the 'official' discourse must have been oral; over the past few decades, the central government would have used all forms of communication possible to control unruly groups. In any case, written propaganda would not reach much of the Yezidi population directly. Nevertheless, it remains true that the vast majority of Yezidi accounts of historical events remain oral rather than written.

Younger Yezidis I met in 1992 professed belief in their parents' historical traditions rather than those of the government. Although many young adults educated as far as the end of secondary school professed contempt for Yezidi laws which they considered absurd because they could see no reason for them, there was no indication that they applied the techniques of logical analysis learned at school to the historical songs and stories. Similarly, many professed a lack of belief in God and in Melek Tawus, but none questioned the veracity of the Yezidi presentations of history.

Traditional songs were felt to be part of the Yezidis' true heritage and wisdom, and were respected as such. Love songs in particular, many of which featured historical protagonists, enjoyed great popularity, as in Kurdistan generally, and the cassettes of celebrations and concerts contain numerous audience requests for them. Most of all, the historical tales of Yezidi heroes seemed to inspire great pride – Derwêshê 'Evdî, the star-crossed lover who was also a great warrior of Ottoman times, was particularly favoured, and amongst Sinjari informants, the songs glorifying Dawûdê Dawûd, a Sinjari Yezidi leader of rebellions in the early twentieth century, aroused strong emotions of pride and patriotism. These specific traditions will be considered in later chapters. The continuing power of the oral traditions in the community could be illustrated by one incident – an illiterate octogenarian in Shari'e, Mr. H., refused to finish telling the story of Êzdi Mîrza in which the hero, a Yezidi, took gruesome revenge on Muslims who had wronged him, for fear that Muslims would hear the story, and there would be reprisals against his community. Given that Êzdî Mîrza was appointed governor of Mosul and awarded the rank of Pasha in 1649, it seemed unlikely that this alone would be sufficient motivation for Kurdish Muslims to attack Yezidis in 1992. This served as a rather poignant reminder of the faith of older Yezidis in the veracity of their traditions, and their constant fear of further persecution.

The younger, more educated generation took a slightly different attitude. The affection they felt for the old customs, such as the gatherings at Lalêsh, was evident, as was their enjoyment of traditional songs and dances. Several of the *stranbêj*, 'singers', represented in my collection were educated men in their twenties and thirties. Mostly their songs were learned in the traditional way, by listening and repetition, but for them literacy played a part too. One young singer had learned some of his material from a published collection made by Soviet scholars from recordings of Yezidis in

Armenia (Jelîl 1977). However, there is an ambiguity among the young about oral tradition, which parallels the ambivalence operating in the wider Kurdish context. The oral traditions, as part of folklore, are very strongly associated with the community's history and thus with Yezidi identity. At the same time they are considered old-fashioned and not progressive.

Fewer of the younger generation learn old songs and stories at their parents' or grandparents' knee, and many claim to have no knowledge at all of their *folklor.* This is partly due to a reduction in performances of many types of oral tradition. The environment of the small village, and with it many occasions for performance, has been lost in collectivisation. Every informant questioned in Khanek, Shari'e and Ba'drê expressed regret for his or her previous life in the small villages, even though many, women in particular, spent some time describing the volume of their work there. The middle-aged and elderly found it difficult to sing the work-songs and tell the stories of their youth. This was partly ascribed to the effect of television – 'we don't tell stories any more, we only watch television', a comment made by Mrs. S., an elderly murîd, was typical – but also to the effect of collectivisation and other misfortunes, such as the Iran-Iraq war. The strict Government controls on communities in Kurdistan in general since the 1960s was also highlighted by Mr. B., a Sinjari singer, as limiting the opportunities for large gatherings in which performances could take place. In 1992, the troubled times meant that much conversation naturally revolved around current events and immediate concerns. Some informants also articulated the idea that dancing, singing (with the exception of laments) and telling stories except on special occasions, were inappropriate in such times. However, performances of certain types of oral tradition did take place on some occasions.

Despite their growing rates of literacy and formal education, which are changing the very nature of their religion, the Yezidis value their traditional historical discourse in general very highly. Nevertheless, certain parts of that discourse are felt to be less prestigious and less 'historical'; to elucidate this complex picture, the next chapter will examine the part played in the community by certain important genres, and the complex relationship between these genres and Yezidi constructs of history.

CHAPTER THREE

Chronological and Generic Frameworks in Yezidi Oral Tradition

INTRODUCTION

It is now clear that many Yezidi religious traditions were misinterpreted by the early Orientalists who approached them as if they were examples of scriptural religious traditions, and did not take into account their uses in the Yezidi community. The shortcomings of such approaches are obvious with hindsight. However, there may be similar pitfalls in the study of the secular traditions, and the role in the community of their various tellings must be understood before any interpretation of the treatment of important themes is ventured upon. Many oral traditions fulfil the functions of both 'literature' and 'history' in the community, and any dividing line between these uses may not be at all clear to an outsider, and difficult to enunciate for a Yezidi. It is obvious that different groups conceptualise and tell their past in different ways; moreover, the form in which a tradition is told, its circumstances of performance and its status, are intimately related to the mechanisms of its transmission, and thus to its very survival. Chronological perspective varies considerably across cultures; for instance, in some Middle Eastern groups, accounts of history are structured by family and lineage; there are noticeable lacunae in these accounts, where universal upheavals, which those educated in Western historical traditions might expect to be commemorated, are omitted (e.g. Shryock 1997; Dakhlia 1990: 101–41).

The issue of genre is crucial and often complex; some, but by no means all, traditions are told in various forms. The form used for each telling of a tradition may have a strong bearing on its meaning for its audience, but the performance of a tradition in one form may also draw on the audience's knowledge of that tradition as told in other forms. For audiences, performances are linked both to other performances of the same form, and to performances of the same tradition in different forms. In some contexts there may be a close relationship between genre and chronology, with certain genres closely associated with certain periods or temporal frameworks. It has been argued persuasively that we cannot be sure which genres are more 'historical', until we have a good understanding of their purpose and uses in their social context (Fentress and Wickham 1992: 80). Thus a degree of understanding of both chronological and generic frameworks operating in the Yezidi context is essential before discussing powerful themes and their treatment within the traditions. This chapter will give an account of the ways in which the Yezidis order the events described in their oral traditions, and of some of the principal genres used. Performance in general of the genres will be discussed, but the artistry and poetics of individual performances will be described in later chapters, which will focus on the treatment of key themes in specific oral traditions.

YEZIDI CHRONOLOGY

It is legitimate to ask whether such a thing as a coherent 'Yezidi chronology' exists at all. During my fieldwork, it was certainly not easy to discuss hypothetical chronological 'systems' with informants, for whom such conceptual frameworks, whether systematic or not, were so self-evident as to be pretty much imperceptible in the abstract. One could ask when certain individuals lived, or whether one particular event had happened before another, but it was not easy to frame questions about generalities such as epochs. Answers to questions about the chronology of specific traditions also varied a great deal. The events of *Derwêshê 'Evdî,* for example, were dated to the mid-nineteenth century by a University-educated Yezidi folklorist and to the seventeenth century by the elderly Mr H., in Shari'e; it was clear that not all Yezidis shared the same chronological perspective. Nevertheless, from comparison of the answers to many questions about a variety of traditions, a picture did emerge of relatively consistent patterns of opinion as to when events of different types happened, and how they related to each other. There was no neat chronological system to be observed; indeed, in many cases there seemed to be two or more chronological 'systems' operating in people's conceptualisation of the past. The Yezidi view of the passing of time has some rather special features, apparently not shared by other groups in the area.

'Ages' and Epochs in Yezidi History

Many societies divide their history into periods of time. If these are called 'ages' they are often characterised by a descriptive term; thus people may speak of a 'heroic age' or a 'golden age', as in Hesiod's *Works and Days.* The duration of an 'age' is not fixed; it may last for hundreds or thousands of years. It is a qualitative rather than a quantitative concept. The word 'epoch' as used in the study of oral history often implies a fixed period of time; this is relevant for societies which keep long lists of kings, or of those who have passed through certain key stages, such as initiations. Many such societies have been studied in Africa (e.g. Vansina 1985: 24), but such fixed units of duration cannot be used for Yezidi lists of ancestors, which are qualitatively different, as will be described below.

It seems that the concept of successive ages is part of the traditional Yezidi cosmology. It is certainly used in the published 'Sacred Books' which, though forgeries, seem to have their origins in authentic oral tradition. The *Meshefa Resh* or 'Black Book', an account of the Yezidi creation myth, divides its story into periods of time; God made different angels on different days and created a Pearl out of his divine essence, on which he rested for forty thousand years; later the text states that he ruled over the Pearl for forty years. The *Kitêba Jilwe* or 'Book of Revelation', which purports to be the words of Melek Tawus, speaks of his appointment of a Regent for every age (Guest 1993: 208–12; Kreyenbroek 1995: 55–6). Kreyenbroek notes elements of a cyclical view of history in Yezidism (*ibid.*: 52), citing earlier sources who say that, according to the Yezidis, there are seven divinities, each of which rules the universe for ten thousand years, and that the current epoch is that of Melek Tawus, who will be succeeded by another regent at the end of his ten thousand years. Periods of one thousand years are also mentioned in some sources (Nau and Tfinkdji 1915–17: 271–2; Empson 1928: 89). However, it is not at all clear how prevalent this concept of successive ages of the world is in the modern community. Clearly, as Kreyenbroek comments, the allusive style of the Yezidi *qewls* or hymns, some of which refer to the cosmogony myths, indicates that knowledge of the myths was assumed among listeners. Such knowledge may have been present when the *qewls* first took shape, but detailed knowledge of the *qewls* is now the province of a privileged few in the contemporary Yezidi community and it is quite possible that knowledge of these myths has also declined. Many of my own informants had heard of the *Kitêba Jilwe* and the *Meshefa Resh*, but even the small minority who were literate are unlikely to have had access either to the academic publications or to the sacred books in the control of the Adani sheykhs. It was clear that few knew anything about their contents and only one or two claimed to have seen them.

Other generally agreed 'ages' were used to date modern and secular events. For instance, the 'time of the emirs' was a somewhat nebulous period which ended in the mid- to late nineteenth century, when the relative autonomy of the various Kurdish emirs, whose powers had waxed and waned for centuries, was finally curbed by the Ottoman state. The 'time of the British' referred to the mandatory period and the years immediately following, until Iraq became a republic.

Religious History

Written sources tell that in the early years of the twelfth century, the founder of the 'Adawiyya Sufi order, Sheykh 'Adī b. Musāfir, came to live in the Hakkari mountains. The branch of the order he established there found an enthusiastic following among local people. The extent to which this order was influenced by other beliefs prevalent in the area has been much discussed but it is generally believed, by scholars and Yezidis alike, that Yezidism developed from it. However it is almost certain that Yezidism as it later became would not have been recognised or approved by Sheykh 'Adī (Lescot 1938: 19–44: Guest 1993: 15–43; Kreyenbroek 1995: 1–27).

Sheykh 'Adī's status as prime mover in Yezidi history is acknowledged in the community. The Yezidis have traditionally believed that their social structure has its origins in the personalities of his inner circle and that of his immediate successors. Various institutions are explained in terms of his actions or those of his associates or successors.[1] Contemporary (written) sources indicate that Sheykh 'Adī, who died childless, was succeeded by his nephew, Ṣakhr Abū 'l-Barakāt, whose son, also called 'Adī, succeeded him. The son and successor of the second 'Adī, Sheykh Ḥasan, was executed in 1254CE,[2] and was probably succeeded by his son Sharaf al-Dīn, who died in battle in 1257–8. Sharaf al-Dīn was succeeded not by his son Zayn al-Dīn but by the brother of Sheykh Ḥasan, Fakhr al-Dīn. Most of these individuals are important figures in Yezidi tradition, and are featured in a number of stories.

Yezidi traditions say that Sheykh Adi came to the valley of Lalêsh[3] and describe his encounters with the sons of an Êzdîna Mîr, who were called Sheykh Shems el-Dîn, Sheykh Fekhr el-Dîn and (by another wife) Sheykh Sejadîn and Sheykh Naṣr el-Dîn, of whom little is known. The oral tradition transformed a number of Sheykh Adi's successors into his contemporaries, and the figures are made to conform to a pattern suiting Yezidi religious belief (Kreyenbroek 1995: 39).

The Yezidi religion includes not only a belief in reincarnation, but also a belief that a divine being may be incarnated in human form, and the human figure is worshipped as such. Thus for Yezidi believers Sheykh Adi and his followers are, in a very real sense, the Seven Angels who preside over creation; Sheykh Ḥesen who was executed in 1254 is also Ḥasan al-Basrī, the great seventh-century Sufi.[4] There is a significant difference in the chronological treatment of traditions about holy beings, or *khas*, and those about ordinary human beings. When illiterate informants were questioned during the fieldwork about secular events of history, they would usually place it by saying 'It happened before such-and-such', citing a well-known event such as the First World War. However, Yezidis do not usually locate a specific incarnation of the *khas* in chronological terms; if talking about Sheykh Ḥesen, for instance, they would not necessarily differentiate between Ḥasan al-Basri and Ḥasan the successor of Sheykh Adi. Questions such as 'Did this happen before that?' or 'When did X live?' lose their meaning when applied to these figures, who fit into a pattern which is coherent in terms of Yezidi religious belief, but not in terms of linear chronology. The belief in the *khas* has also assisted the eclecticism of Yezidi religious belief. Yezidi traditions exist about many holy figures of Christianity and Islam, some of whom are identified with *khas*, as are certain historical figures.[5]

'Gaps' in History

A number of oral traditions exist about the advent and succession of Sheykh Adi, which are believed to be true by many modern Yezidis. Many oral traditions were also current during my fieldwork which dealt with events of the last two centuries or so, beginning, for most informants, with the killing of the Yezidi Mîr 'Elî Beg, near the gorge which still bears his name, by the 'Blind' (in fact one-eyed) Mîr of Rawanduz, who tried in vain to force him to convert to Islam, and the subsequent massacre of the fleeing Yezidis of Sheykhan on the banks of the Tigris.[6] These events took place in 1832, and seemed to be the earliest events of 'modern history', as it were, to be generally known.

The situation for accounts of history in general was 'telescoped'; there was a large number of traditions current about the beginnings of Yezidism and also about its recent past, with very little in between. The Yezidis do not recount the past in annalistic terms as a continuous stream of events; they tell and sing about specific events and individuals. The gap between the community's beginnings and its recent history is not total; isolated traditions, such as that of Êzdî Mîrza (d.1650 CE) have remained popular enough to be remembered in song and prose narratives. It remains to be seen whether the temporal gap will be perceived as disadvantageous by the current educated generation, and whether attempts will be made to fill it. Certainly the older illiterate generation do not perceive a 'gap'; they do not see the secular traditions as mostly clustered around the last two centuries or so, but as extending back into the past as far back as 'a thousand years', to use the terms of Mr B., a senior singer. There is not necessarily felt to be a great temporal difference between an event which written sources date at one hundred and fifty years ago and one which happened almost three hundred and fifty years ago.[7] Whether informants during the fieldwork perceived events as distant or immediate seemed to be as much a matter of the nature of the traditions as of timing; the events of *Êzdî Mîrza* are distant in time, but as described in Chapter Two, Mr H. refused to finish the story because he feared Muslim reprisals. Chronology was irrelevant to his perception of the story's importance.

The chronology of events within living memory, on the other hand, was of course much clearer. Informants usually placed remembered events in chronological context by giving their age at the time they took place, or by generally known outside events, such as the creation of the Iraqi republic, or the accession to power of the Ba'ath party. The illiterate informants seldom used year numbering to date events they described. However, most of the oral traditions described to me and cited as important dated from before living memory, a somewhat 'safer' period to recall, whose feuds, betrayals and persecutions were not such 'live' issues in the community as those of the late twentieth century. I collected very few tellings of events of the past two generations or so; these tended to refer to very localised matters.

Family History

It is obvious that blood relationships and blood-lines play a key role in Yezidi social organisation. From their parents Yezidis inherit not only a tribe and a caste, but also a well-defined set of relationships with specific families in other castes. These relationships between pîr, sheykh and murîd bring with them accepted religious and social practices and obligations.[8] As one would expect, accounts of family history serve this social order. Each of the sheykhly families claim descent from one of three holy figures: the Shemsanis from Sheykh Shems, the Adanis from Sheykh Ḥesen, and the Qatanis from the brothers of Sheykh Adi.[9] Members of each of these groups have specific tasks – some have unusual attributes, such as the ability of Sheykh Mend's descendants to handle snakes – and they must marry within their group; they are perceived publicly to have an especially close association with the venerated *khas* by their lineage, even if they are privately regarded with ambivalence. There are also tensions and rivalries between the groups. Members of the pîr caste fall into four main branches, each of which is also associated with a holy ancestor. As with the sheykhs, the lineages and their sub-clans sometimes have special attributes and some of the clans have complex rules on intermarriage. The claim of the sheykh and pîr classes to their religious authority, and thus to their social privilege, rests on their lineage.

Although the Yezidis do not keep oral public 'king-lists' in the way that some societies do, they do keep genealogies. Some families now write these down in 'family trees' rather like the *silsilas* of the Sufi orders (one very detailed example was shown to me by a murîd family in Shari'e),[10] but most remain oral. Most of my informants could recite their ancestors' names up to, say, three or five generations back, though they often claimed to know ten or so, and where memory failed, an absent relative was usually cited as 'knowing these things better.' Typical genealogies contained modern family history, where informants knew their own ancestry in detail as far back as three generations or so, and often, further back, especially if this could be traced to a well-known clan chief. This was usually secular, containing accounts of conflicts and alliances, births, deaths and marriages, with no obviously mythic or supernatural elements. Those living in collective villages knew the sites of their families' former villages, even where they were too young to remember these themselves; in many cases they knew of previous moves by their tribe. This 'secular' modern genealogy was combined with 'religious' genealogy, in that the relevant *khas* or companion of Sheykh Adi was also cited as the defining religious ancestor. Between the distant ancestors and their own parents and grandparents, detailed genealogies were often not known, and there were rarely if ever enough names in the list to extend as far back as Sheykh ʿAdi. This supported Henige's remark (1974: 27) on the subject of telescoped genealogies:

> Since the purpose of these genealogies is both to reflect and to justify current social patterns based on kinship considerations, it serves no purpose to preserve the memory of useless ancestors.

Some figures who had lived during the period between the distant ancestors and the most recent generations were well known, mainly because they were the subjects of widely-known songs and prose narratives. Informants were particularly likely to know about these and mention them if they were from the same tribe, or better still, if they were claimed as a direct ancestor; conversely, they knew less about them if they were from a different tribe or area.[11]

'History' and 'Legend'

Although it is relatively easy for an outsider to distinguish between 'secular' modern history and 'religious' ancient history, with their different chronological patterns, it seems very unlikely that the Yezidis would consider this a valid distinction. Many elderly Yezidis have a literal belief in both the supernatural and the religious myths. A typical example was Mr N., an illiterate murîd from Baʿdrê, who considered *jinns* to be a feature of everyday life, and also described 'the time of the prophets' (i.e. Abraham, Solomon, etc.) as a historical period. A middle-aged murîd from Sharіʿe, Mr P., when asked about Êzdî Mîrza, thought carefully and then said that he had lived 'before the second Qadisiyya' (a mythical event difficult for outsiders to date). The older Yezidis are, of course not devoid of a linear view of time; they are perfectly able to understand and apply linear chronology in their retelling of secular traditions of the more recent past (i.e. the past hundred and fifty years or so), and have a clear idea of how their community has interacted with non-Yezidis during this period. Yet they can also use 'sacred' chronology to link events widely separated in linear time. It is very unlikely that they would perceive any tension or inconsistency between 'sacred' and 'secular' chronology, or any difference between their ordering of recent or 'secular' history and of the ancient, 'legendary', past.

It is undeniable that much of the traditional material of the pre-Sheykh Adi period is unlikely to be considered factual by the literate younger generation, some of whom also expressed scepticism to me about the deeds of Sheykh Adi himself. Nevertheless, as described in Chapter Two, these people, who had attended State schools and in some cases university as well, still had greater faith in Yezidi discourses of modern history, including the oral traditions dealing with battles and love-stories of the past two centuries, than those of the State. Many Yezidis during the last generation have had pragmatic reasons for supporting the Iraqi government rather than the Kurdish nationalists, but it seems unlikely that a Yezidi child growing up amid the collectivisations, repressions and propaganda of late twentieth-century Iraq would reject the discourses of family and local community on modern history and heartily espouse the State discourses learned at school.

It is clear that what is 'legendary' for one person may be believed wholeheartedly by another. Although the oral traditions which will be considered in this book are considered by the Yezidis in general to be 'historical', that is, literally true, the 'legendary' material is also a relevant part of the discourse on the past. One need not believe that something actually happened for it to have some meaning, and the 'legendary' traditions will colour the view of history of those young Yezidis who do not literally believe in them, affecting their responses to and perceptions of other events.

GENRE

Definitions of genre in folklore and oral studies have very naturally varied with the theoretical perspectives of the scholars concerned.[12] For the purposes of this study, which considers a specific cultural context and is not a work of comparative folklore, such widespread classificatory terms as 'myth' and 'folk-tale' are of limited use in a theoretical framework without a full understanding of the relationship between these terms and the terms used within the community. If these terms are indeed universal phenomena, their definitions are open to some discussion; I shall use them only in the process of defining some of the Kurdish terms where their meaning is clear enough to be helpful, and will try to avoid using them as categories in their own right in analysis or discussion of the Yezidi material, where the Kurdish terms will be used. Many features of the performance and transmission of these genres are changing, but these changes reflect the situation within the specific cultural environment of the Yezidi community, and are not to be seen as universal processes or stages of development common to all societies.

In written literature, genre is often considered to be a matter of formal structure, of 'shape', as it were; Greek tragedy is drama in iambic trimeter with choral lyric, Virgilian epic is a narrative poem in hexameters. Naturally there is a close and complex relationship between this outward form and the content; the subject matter must be appropriate, and treated appropriately. Yet the question of oral genre is more challenging, especially in the context of a language such as Kurmanji which has not yet developed many of the better-known literary forms, and whose oral forms are little studied.

I have found few literary theorists who explicitly address the oral among the forms of human communication worthy of study. The work of M. M. Bakhtin is a welcome exception. He defines 'speech genres' as follows (1986: 60):

> each separate utterance is individual ... but each sphere in which language is used develops its own *relatively stable types* of these utterances. These we may call *speech genres*.

Provided one places a strong stress on the word 'relatively' in this definition, Bakhtin's view, as expounded in this essay, does full justice to the fluidity of spoken language forms, their ability to borrow from and allude to each other, to change and develop, whilst still retaining certain dominant associations in the minds of speakers and listeners. Moreover, his view of the dialogic aspect of discourse, of its existence in the mind of the hearer even when there is no reply to an utterance, is consistent with the issue of the performance and its allusions to past and future performances. Various folklorists have discussed the problem of genre; one may perhaps single out the discussion of Ben-Amos (1976: Introduction); definitions of genre as a 'form of discourse' makes clear the role of context, of the role and status of the genre within the community. In the following account of the major genres I encountered, I have tried to give as full a description as possible of the interplay between form, content, and performance – what Dundes has termed texture, text and context (Dundes 1964).

Even where spoken genres are relatively informal and have not been assigned names, performers and observers have clear, if sometimes unconscious, ideas about their conventions. Speech communities are sensitive to the differences between various oral forms of communication. They have different expectations from a poetry recital, a folk concert, and a stand-up comic routine. Members of audiences will also have a clear, though probably not unanimous, idea of how well a performance worked as an example of a particular form. The Yezidi community proved to be no exception and comments on performances were often forthcoming, though explanations of why certain performances were better than others were often more difficult to interpret.

In the Kurdish context, as in many others, emic (local) and etic (outsider) genres of oral tradition do not usually match. The difficulties of reconciling ethnic systems of defining oral tradition, where genre constitutes a mode of discourse, with the analytical categories constructed by outsiders for the purposes of classification, have long been discussed by scholars (e.g. Ben-Amos 1976: 215–37, Finnegan 1992: 144). In Kurdish folklore study, an additional complication for both outsiders and locals is the variety and inconsistency of terminologies and classificatory systems found in different areas, and different traditions of study. Even the most commonly found Kurdish generic terms are rarely understood without ambiguity throughout the entire Kurmanji-speaking area.

Classification purely by theme, in other words the grouping together of material about a certain individual, place or series of events which takes no account of genre, runs the risk of losing the meanings of individual performances. For example, *Derwêshê 'Evdî* is a popular story in the Yezidi community which will be discussed in detail in Chapters Four and Five; I have encountered a prose version, a narrative song, and several lyrical songs consisting only of dialogue between protagonists. Each of these forms in which the *Derwêshê 'Evdî* theme was presented concentrated on a different aspect of the story and was performed in different ways, on different occasions, for different effects. A strictly thematic approach would not take account of this multiplicity. Conversely, a purely phenomenological or functional approach would lose the connection between these forms of the tradition which are, after all, associated in the mind of the audience; often the performances may derive some of their power from the audience's knowledge of other parts of the story, heard in other types of performance, which are not included. A lyrical love song, for example, gains extra poignancy if the audience knows that the story ends tragically, even if the end of the story is not told.

Whilst some grasp of the forms of discourse and the way they are used is crucial to our understanding of the traditions as a social product, the material must also be studied thematically. This is not only necessary for the construction of a coherent account of Yezidi attitudes, but will also enable tellings of the same tradition which use different forms to be compared. Thus, whilst genre, i.e. the 'relatively stable' forms of discourse used, will be discussed, the examples quoted will be arranged thematically, by story. This chapter will make some general observations on the most distinctive of the relevant genres and their uses in the community; later chapters will concentrate on the larger themes of battle, love and lamentation. This arrangement admittedly has its shortcomings; of course many traditions do not fall conveniently into larger categories. The *Derwêshê 'Evdî* theme is both a love story and a story of martial heroism. Nevertheless this framework seems the most reasonable way of reconciling the considerations of form and theme.

Genres Observed in the Field

Although it would be desirable to consider all spoken genres for their contribution to Yezidi oral tradition, this cannot be possible until scholars have a good understanding of genre and register in Kurmanji, a point which is still some distance away – very few Kurmanji genres have been described in any detail. Nor have they been fitted into theoretical schemes, such as that of Abrahams, who posits a spectrum of genres broadly separating into 'primarily active involvement' (such as conversation) and 'involvement primarily through vicarious identification' (such as epic or legend) (1976: 197). Bakhtin's distinction between primary genres 'developed in unmediated speech communion' and secondary genres of 'developed and organised cultural communication' organises the genres differently (1986: 62); in the Yezidi context his distinction is relevant, contrasting 'everyday' and 'artistic' genres. Almost all the material to be discussed in the next three chapters is 'artistic'; it has an aesthetic value as well as imparting knowledge, and the skill of its composition and performance are important factors in its success; thus, to use Bakhtin's terminology, it falls into the 'secondary' genres. The lyric and narrative songs, the set-piece stories and the women's lament, all have Kurdish names and are seen as appropriate objects for discussion by informants. As far as Abrahams' system is concerned, the majority of the material is consciously performed to an audience, and would be positioned towards the 'vicarious' end of the spectrum; however, the women's lament considered in Chapter Six would be situated nearer the middle as it is, in many cases, a discourse of personal emotion referring to a performer's own experience, but at the same time using imagery of the 'vicarious' artistic genres and subject to audience evaluation; audience members may also spontaneously join the lament.

I will describe here the most important genres I encountered in the field, in terms of form and content, performance conventions and status. My account will inevitably be incomplete; I hope to cast some light on the relationship of these genres with each other by using contextual information based on the Yezidis' descriptions of their *folklor.* The term 'metafolklore' was first coined by Alan Dundes (1966) to describe folkloristic commentary about folklore genres, particularly jokes about jokes, proverbs about proverbs, etc.. It has been extended somewhat by Ben-Amos (1976: 226) to mean:

> . . . the conception a culture has of its own folkloric communication as it is represented in the distinction of forms, the attribution of names to them, and the sense of the social appropriateness of their application in various cultural situations.

I will make use of the metafolklore available from Kurdish folklorists and my Yezidi informants.

The terminology for the various forms of oral tradition which will be set out below is based on my own understanding of local terms and their applications, and varies in some cases from the observations of scholars discussing folklore in Kurdistan in general. Questioning members of the community about the terminology was of course not easy; the informants, though usually eager to be helpful, justifiably found abstract questions about terms which they considered self-evident to be baffling, or worse, irrelevant. However, questions about the uses of the different traditions within the community were well understood and received ready, and usually consistent, replies. I hope that the descriptions of these well-known 'artistic' genres will also serve as a basis for the study of the 'everyday' genres which are so difficult to discuss with informants as, unlike the artistic genres, they are often not even objectified to the extent of having formal names. Everyday conversation has clearly identifiable stylistic features in common with the artistic genres, though we know little as yet of how allusion is made, of the ways in which register is marked, and other less obvious aspects of meaning in Kurdish.

The variations in terminology associated with performance and performers throughout Kurdistan meant that a single song might be classified under different headings in different collections; in the field, informants were not always in agreement. However certain broad distinctions may be made. The definitions used in this work will follow local usage as far as possible, supplemented by evidence from fieldwork and secondary literature, much of which is not specific to the Yezidis, but which nevertheless yields some relevant data. Many of the terms used in Kurdish are also used in Arabic, Persian or Turkish, often with very different meanings. Before the description of the relevant major forms of discourse, some more general terms must be noted.

The term *qesse* was applied by the Yezidis of Northern Iraq to songs and stories in general;[13] this included many types of sung and spoken material. *Meqam* was sometimes used in the context of folklore; it is a very general term, originally Arabic, meaning nothing more specific than 'song'. The genres which were most often encountered in the field as vehicles for Yezidi oral tradition were: the sung 'folklore song', *strana folklorî*, the various forms of spoken prose narrative including the *çîrok*, and the women's lament, *şîn*. Much of the material which presents Yezidi history, and a large proportion of Yezidi social comment, is conveyed through these genres. Once the salient points of each genre have been noted, it will then be possible to discuss the status of the genres in the community.

Lyrical and Narrative Song

In conversation with Yezidis about secular oral traditions, the form of oral tradition most commonly cited as important and pleasing was the *stran*. Literally, this word merely means 'song'. J. Bedir Khan defines it as 'le genre exclusivement musical, correspondant à peu près au Lied allemand' (1932: 9). His discussion is of Kurdish folklore in general rather than of Yezidi tradition, and must be treated with some caution, but his parallel with the Lied is useful. Like the Kurdish term, the German term literally means 'song', but the term can have a more specific meaning; it often denotes a poetic song, often romantic in theme, where both words and melody are important, and artistry is demonstrated in both vocal and musical performance. These characteristics are shared by the term *stran* as it is often used in the Yezidi context, where it can denote a particular type of emotional song. Occasionally the more precise term *strana folklorî*, which may be translated 'traditional song' was used, particularly by literate informants who were conversant with current trends in the collection of Kurdish folklore. This was more precise, but most informants referred only to *stran*, whilst it was obvious from what they said that they meant *strana folklorî*, rather than contemporary or popular song. The *stran* collected during fieldwork mostly describe events which happened before living memory, but not all are old; some deal with recent events, using traditional form and performance conventions. In much of Turkish and Syrian Kurdistan these *stran* are known as *lawiq* or *lawik*.

The range of *stran* is broad; the Jelîl brothers' *Zargotina K'urda*, hereafter ZK (Jelîl 1978), the most wide-ranging and authoritative collection of Kurmanji oral traditions to date, which draws on predominantly Yezidi sources, has several sections of *stran*, namely *stran* of history (*tarîxî*), *stran* of love (*bengîtî*), *stran* for dancing (*govend*), and *stran* of lament (*şînî*). This was largely borne out by a Sheykhani singer, Mr A., who listed and demonstrated several kinds of *stran* for my benefit; war (*şer*), more or less corresponding to the 'historical' *tarîxî*;[14] love (*evîn*), meaning the same as *bengîtî*; grief (*ẍerîbî*), which does not correspond to the lament *şîn*. In ZK the *stranêd şînî* are the women's laments for the dead which will be described in more detail later. Mr A. demonstrated a different type of song, where a lost hero is lamented by the singer who usually sings 'in character'. Although the term *stranêd şînî* is well understood amongst the Northern Iraqi Yezidis, the women's laments are more often termed *dîrok*.[15] Mr A. added that political songs (*stranêd siyasî*) had recently become popular. He went on to demonstrate a dance song; the Jelîls term such songs *stranêd govenda*, but they are known among the Northern Iraqi Yezidis as *peste*, or *beste*; [16] *stran* proper denotes a more melancholy, less rhythmic song. Another *stranbêj*, the Sinjari Mr B., considered that dance songs are not the proper business of serious singers, but of mere *mitirb*, common musicians who rely on performance for their living. One might just as well expect a doctor to put on a nurse's uniform, he added. However, the performances I have attended, and the audio and video tapes I have heard, suggest that *stran* without *peste* is now unusual; the *peste* tend to follow the *stran*, often without any break in the music.

In ZK, the Jelîls observe that 'in former times every *agha* and *beg* would have one or two singers who would sing *stran* about his lord and his deeds.' (Jelîl 1978 I: 40). The collection of *stran* made in the field did, for the most part, prove to be about individuals, and events which were believed to be historical. Although they covered a variety of subjects, the *stran* were notable for their lack of supernatural elements, except in certain love songs where the strength of the imagery deviated somewhat from realism. Even these love songs were, with a few exceptions, held to be about real people who had existed.[17] The Yezidi folklorist Dr Khelîl Jindî Rashow (KJR) has underlined the importance of *stran* in Yezidi discourse by describing it as a vehicle for the emotions of the people, expressing their happiness and griefs.[18]

Stran, as songs with musical accompaniment, could be distinguished from what are often called in Kurmanji *beyt* or, sometimes, *destan*, which are heroic and usually long narrative songs, often with some prose sections, performed without musical accompaniment.[19] *Destan* more properly means 'legend' in the widest sense; *beyt* denotes the specific genre. However, within the Yezidi community, *beyt* denotes a religious poem, so to avoid confusion, I will avoid the use of the term *beyt* and wherever possible refer to *destan* or 'long narrative poems'. Although *stran* could be performed without a musical accompaniment, in my experience this was usually through lack of an instrument or ability to play; I came across no examples of singers having these resources and choosing to perform *stran* without musical accompaniment. Although I made some recordings during the fieldwork of some of the most famous Kurdish *destan* sung by Muslim singers in Dihok and Amadiya, the Yezidi *stranbêj* seemed to perform only *stran* proper. The Yezidis seemed to regard the *stran* as their own, despite the fact that not all *stranbêj* are Yezidi (there have been various well-known Muslim singers of *lawik* in Turkey and Syria) and many *stran* refer to the deeds of non-Yezidis. Performers of the long narrative poems are much rarer among the Iraqi Yezidis; I heard stories such as *Mem and Zîn* and *Dimdim* told in prose narrative form, but only found Muslims able to sing these in verse form. These have certainly been performed among the Yezidis in the past (ZK features many examples collected from Caucasian Yezidis) but are clearly in decline in the community, though not yet extinct. One Sheykhani sheykh mentioned that some Sinjaris still had expertise in singing 'the long songs'; he added that the qewwals (whose activities are normally vehicles for the religious traditions) knew them too, and in 1999 I heard of a Yezidi performer of these now resident in Europe. Blau (1975: 6–7) attests to the knowledge and performance of *'Ashik Gherîb* 'the exiled[20] troubadour', a tradition known all over the non-Arab Islamic world, by the Yezidi Qasim Ḥeso; his performance seemed to be *cantefable*, a form of narrative performance including spoken prose and sung verse narrative.[21] Informants did distinguish between these two genres; Mr Y., an elderly Sinjari *stranbêj*, referred to the well known narrative poem *Dimdim* not as *stran* but as a *şi'r* 'poem'. Some of the legends usually associated with *destan* were put into the form of *stran* by the *stranbêj*. I collected some short versions of *Mem and Zîn* whose musical accompaniment, melody and performance style were those of *stran*. Other legends, such as that of *Khej and Siyabend*, were couched in the form of love lyric, with the protagonists addressing each other. However, few of the *stran* I encountered took their subject-matter from legend or folktale, and supernatural elements were rather rare. A clear distinction emerged between the (mostly) lyrical *stran*, based for the most part on historical events, and the narrative *destan* poems, with their subject-matter taken from various areas of legend and history.

In terms of structure there were also important differences. Unlike the *destan*, the *stran* has clearly identifiable stanzas and regular refrains, separated by musical interludes. In both types of poetry line length can be very variable, making meaningful syllable-counts difficult, and rhyme can be consistent for many lines, or for just a few.[22] Although Nikitine says that Kurdish folk poetry 'ignore à vrai dire le rythme et ne connaît que la rime' (1956: 270), many of the Badinani *destan* poems are highly rhythmic, with strong stresses in the lines, whereas the performers of *stran* tend to deliver very long lines very fast, with some extended melismas towards the end of the (clearly marked) stanzas. The usual Kurdish terminology used by commentators is *rêz* (line) and *bend* (stanza). At the end of each line or sense-unit in the *stran*, there is a fall in pitch, and at the end of the stanza a further fall, often followed by words of emotion such as *wey lo*. The way in which this is done varies with performer and performance. The melodies of the *stran* also differ considerably from those of the unaccompanied *destan/beyt*. Each of the *destan/beyt* poems I recorded had its own distinctive tune; *Memê Alan*, the oral poem more often known as *Mem and Zîn*, for example, is easily distinguishable from *Dimdim*; the rhythmic patterns of these songs are often beaten out by the performer as he sings. Each of the slow *stran* has its own melody, but the rhythm is not so pronounced as in the *destan*; the *peste*, as one would expect from dance music, have rhythms which are more pronounced than slow *stran*, but less so than the *destan* poems.

Though tempting, it would be simplistic to classify *stran* as 'lyric' and *destan* as 'epic'. It is true that in ZK the Jelîl brothers classify the most popular *destan* poems as 'epic' as does one of the prominent Southern Kurdish folklorists, Izzaddin Mustafa Rasul (1979: 32). However, Chyet makes a convincing case for defining the *destan* poetry recounting the tradition of *Mem and Zîn* as a Kurdish equivalent of *halk hikayesi*, the Turkish 'folk romance', a long narrative that blends prose and poetry (1991

I: 64–101). The *stran* are generally lyrical, in that they express strong emotion; they contain many words and phrases such as *wey lo*, more or less equivalent in meaning to the English 'alas', often sung between verses,[23] and are usually allusive to some degree, rarely contextualising their action. However, they are not always devoid of narrative and contain many accounts of heroism.

Performers

As with the genres themselves, the terminology for performers is confused. The word most commonly used by the Yezidis of Northern Iraq for professional or semi-professional singer is *stranbêj*, literally 'song-singer' (*stran* – song, *bêj* <gotin – to say); scholars discussing Kurmanji in general more often use the term *dengbêj* (*deng* – voice). The most precise definition, by the Jelîl brothers, equates the two terms and defines them as 'a person who has a pleasant voice and who sings *stran* about people and events'. However, many people distinguish between the singer who plays an instrument and is more likely to perform *stran/lawik* and the singer who performs unaccompanied, usually singing *destan/beyt*. Thus the Jelîls make this distinction between the *dengbêj* and the *aşiq* ('troubadour', literally 'lover'); the former sings without musical accompaniment, and the latter accompanies himself on the *saz*, a stringed instrument (1978 II: 26). However, *aşiq* is the Turkish *aşık*, a term prevalent in Central Asia, Northern Iran and the Caucasus, and rarely if ever used in Iraqi Kurdistan, where *stranbêj* is preferred. For the *lawik* singers of Syria and Eastern Turkey, *mitirb* is often used for those who sing with accompaniment. In Sinjar, the preferred instrument is the *tembûr* or long-necked lute, though the short-necked *oudh* or mandolin and the *kemanche* or spike-fiddle are also used; this latter seems particularly popular amongst the *lawik*-singers of the Tur Abdin. For the unaccompanied singers of *destan*, *dengbêj* is the preferred term in Badinan. The Yezidi *stranbêj* of Northern Iraq are usually semi-professional singers. As mentioned above, a senior Sinjari singer, Mr B., drew a strong contrast between the *stranbêj* and the common musicians or *mitirb*, who earned all their money from music. A *stranbêj* may belong to any caste, but in practice most, including the most admired, are murîd.[24] The most skilful are well-known throughout the Yezidi community in Northern Iraq, and in wider Kurdish society. Their performances can attract large audiences, though not on the same scale as such popular modern Kurdish singers as Şivan Perwer, Nasser Razazi, or Ciwan Hajo. Cassettes and videos change hands amongst Yezidis, are sold in larger towns such as Dihok, and are heard and seen by Yezidis in the diaspora.

Performance of the Stran

Stran and their *peste* are most often associated with celebrations of various kinds, such as parties and festivals, both religious and secular. They are often played at wedding parties (*dawet*); I observed *peste* in performance at one Yezidi wedding in Ba'drê. At another, *def û zurne* (frame drum and shawm), with no vocals, were played to accompany the dancing, as at the village *ṭiwaf*. During a stay in Ba'drê with a member of the Mîr's family, a number of spontaneous performances took place; local Sheykhani singers would visit and perform for the host and the other guests in the courtyard after dinner. These performances were partly prompted by the presence of a Western researcher of *folklor* in the town, but were seen as not particularly unusual; in the past, performances had been very common during relaxed gatherings in *dîwanxane* or guest-halls, and any competent performer present would be likely to be asked to sing. *Stran*, with their emotional content and subsequent dancing, were considered better entertainment than spoken stories.

When a well-known performer is present, a recital is expected; the visit of a *stranbêj* to my hosts in Ba'drê attracted a small crowd of family and neighbours, eager to hear the songs. Performances of the most famous Sinjari *stranbêj* are often recorded by the Yezidis on video; one example I saw was a performance by the well-known singers Feqîr Khidir, Lezgîn Seydo, Kheyro Khelef and Khodêda Abu Azad at a secular New Year party attended by Feroq Beg, of the Mîr's family. Religious songs and secular *stran* were sung before the *peste* and dancing began. Another performance, in the guest-room of a large house in Sinjar, featured Feqîr Khidir, Qarpal Sinjarî and Pîr Micho, who sang slow *stran* in succession. There is a strong element of competition in this environment; after some time the voice of one of the singers began to falter, and this was remarked on. Singers may compete by singing one after another; the first one to falter, whether from losing his voice, or from forgetting the song, is the loser. Similar competitive performances were once also a regular feature of *destan* poetry in both the Yezidi and Muslim communities; Muslim villagers from Sûriye and Sirsenk, near Amadiya, remembered them well.

In spite of its lesser status, it seems that *peste* is becoming an essential part of many performances. Even Mr B., who was so scornful of it, acknowledged that those prepared to play it were invited to perform more often and made more money. In the Kurdish context in general, Yezidi and non-Yezidi, Kurmanji and Sorani, dancing is associated with happy emotion and considered inappropriate at times of mourning. Dancing is an essential and joyous part of a party or celebration, but the emotive *stran* are also very much enjoyed by the audience, for reasons which will be discussed later. However, dancing during the slow *stran* with their often tragic themes would be inappropriate and disrespectful. This combination of slow *stran* and *peste* strikes a balance between strong emotion and the exuberant activity of dance.

The performances I have seen and heard were mostly informal; singers could stand, but were usually seated. Most singers accompanied themselves. The degree of strumming during the singing of individual lines or sense-units, or between them, was variable. Stanzas were separated from each other by short musical interludes, with repeated, rhythmic chords at the end, which signalled the beginning of a new stanza. The instrument might be played between stanzas only in some of the slower songs such as 'Ferîq Pasha'; for *peste* the singer would accompany himself or be accompanied as he sang. There was a great deal of opportunity for virtuosity; the words were often delivered very quickly. Singers often lingered on the last syllables of the line, either on one note or with a melisma. They sometimes emphasised lines with a few emphatic chords at the end. Between these songs there would often be no break in the music; the development of a musical theme or a change in tempo would alert the audience to the fact that a new song was about to begin. Sometimes a singer would give a spoken, prose explanation of the next song, recounting the story and giving its provenance; these are often omitted on the cassettes, but were noticeable on video; the performances I attended were probably atypical in this respect as the singer aimed his explanations at me and my requirements. There seemed to be no rules that specific *peste* should follow specific *stran*; the selection of an appropriate *peste* was at the performer's discretion. Nor must each *stran* be followed by *peste*; sometimes several *stran* followed each other, with *peste* at the end.

Performances are generally mixed, with women sometimes sitting further from the singer. Audiences appreciate virtuosity, which is shown in specific devices; if a singer sang a particularly long line, or performed it especially quickly, or lingered for a long time on a melisma, there would be appreciative cries of *tew, tew* 'Bravo!'. While the music was being played between stanzas in slow songs, the audience would sustain a gentle sound, almost a hum, '*û*', on a single note, like a drone. As soon as the *peste* with its well-defined and swifter rhythm began, the audience would clap in time to the music, and begin to dance. In the performances I attended the men got up to dance first, but the women would then dance with them. Most Kurdish dances are mixed, with men and women linking arms and dancing in long lines. There are some exceptions, such as the local 'Sheykhani' dance, performed by groups of young men.

Prose Narrative Genres

There is much to be done in identifying and describing spoken narrative prose genres in Kurmanji, a language long overdue for sociolinguistic study. The role of formal structure, choice of vocabulary and style of delivery in the meaning of utterances is not well understood. Like the Afghan storytelling encountered by Margaret Mills (1991: 21), Kurdish storytelling performances, whether consciously addressing an audience or part of the dialogue of 'ordinary' conversation, juxtapose various genres and verbal textures. I encountered many types of prose narrative during fieldwork in various contexts, including personal histories and description of events witnessed, accounts of events which had happened to the local community over the last two centuries or so, performances of folktales, and anecdotes. Local terminology had no need to define and acknowledge all of these differences. For example, the history collected from an elderly Hawerî sheykh in Khanek, in which he outlined the recent movements of his tribe and described their way of life, was not distinguished in formal terms from ordinary conversation and would probably only be referred to as his *axiftin* 'conversation', or *gotin* 'speech'. Nevertheless, there is a perceived divide between fact and fiction, and there are also a few stylistic features which distinguish narrative in general.

The term *çîrok* means 'story' and is used throughout Kurdistan. Its meaning seems to be very broad. J. Bedir Khan refers to *çiroqbêj*, who tell stories and legends, as opposed to *dengbêj*, who sing them (1932: 9). *Çîrok* thus includes prose versions of the great Kurdish legends which are performed in poetic form in the *beyt*. However, ZK includes, under the title of *çîrok*, various fables about animals and anecdotes about stock figures, such as *neçîrvan û rûvî* 'the hunter and the fox', and *axa û x̂ulam* 'the squire and the servant' (Jelîl 1978 II: 531); they are grouped together with *mijûlî* (lit. 'chat'). They are not grouped with prose stories about *Silêman pêxember* 'Solomon the prophet', *Iskender Zûqorne* 'Two-horned Alexander', and *Behlûl*, the 'Wise Fool'.

It seems that, in the Yezidi community and in wider Kurmanji-speaking society, *çîrok* can be as broad as the English 'story'. In general, *çîrok* is something made up, as distinct from historical (*tarîxî*) material. Thus, folktales are *çîrok* but legends may not be considered so, if they are believed to be true. Mr E., an elderly murîd in Ba'drê, told the story of Mem and Zîn in prose form, borrowing many phrases from the poem, and called it a *çîrok*; another told a legend of Solomon the prophet, but did not call it a *çîrok* because he believed it to be true. Historical traditions were not usually called *çîrok*, nor labelled with any other special term; they were just mentioned by name, for example, 'I will tell you *Êzdî Mîrza*'. Only one young man referred to *Êzdî Mîrza* and *Derwêshê 'Evdî* as *çîrok*, and this may reflect the fact that to an educated adult such histories seemed very remote anyway. It must be emphasised that this divide between fact and fiction is not always rigorously observed in ordinary conversation. *Çîrok* can sometimes mean an anecdote of a true event, as the English 'story' can be used in such contexts as 'Have you heard the story of how I met such-and-such a person?' However, there is enough differentiation between the two in the Yezidis' usage to justify making a distinction.

An obvious feature distinguishing *çîrok* from historical account is the introductory formula. There are certain stock phrases which introduce fictitious material in various Middle Eastern languages; these function as a sort of waiver, absolving the speaker from any responsibility if an untruth is told. The most commonly known in Kurmanji is *hebû tunebû*, literally 'there was and there was not', which is a shortened form of a formula which can vary slightly, but usually says something along the lines of 'there was and there was not, but nothing exists without God.' Any audience hearing this knows that it cannot rely on the veracity of what comes next. Many tales in the published collections have other introductory words, beginning with *dibêjin* 'they say', which also shifts responsibility for historicity away from the speaker, or *wextekê/çaxekê* 'once', which assigns the action to a vague period. Defining the time where something happened obviously sets the tone for the status of the action. Similarly, the *Mem and Zîn çîrok* I heard from an elderly murîd in Ba'drê began, '*rojekî bêjin ji rojêd Xwedê bû, bajarê Xorzemînê bajarekî gelek mezin bû* …' 'they say that once upon a time the city of Khorzemîn was a very great city …' and the subsequent description of the city is a direct imitation of the opening of a well-known telling of *Memê Alan*. Another story, as told by Mr N., an elderly murîd, began only '*bi zimanê Silêman pêxember*…', 'in the time of the prophet Solomon …', a time of ancient history for him, as he professed belief in the prophets, but probably a legendary time for younger educated Yezidis who might hear him tell it. The narratives of modern history as told to me had no such introductory formulae; they all began with a broad introductory statement such as 'Derwêshê 'Evdî was a Yezidi'.

There are various stylistic features shared by *çîrok* and factual narratives. One is the way in which dialogue was expressed. This was nearly always done by the means of direct rather than indirect speech, where even inconsequential remarks were sometimes included, providing a slight pause in the action; this gave the impression of simplicity but was not simply imitating real conversation; the rhythm pattern it created was distinctive and tended to be repeated with each conversation of the protagonists. To take a typical example, in Blau's Sinjari version of *'Ashik Gherîb*, (1975: 158) when a character speaks to a woman, the storyteller says, '*Gotê, 'Metê!' Go, 'Belê.' Go, 'Metê, çima hûn* …' 'He said, "Auntie!", she said, "Yes", he said, "Auntie, why do you …", and the story continues. The rhythm patterns of such repetitions become clearer when they are heard. One of many examples from my own collection, told by Mr H. in Shari'e, has a young man begin a conversation with his father (rise and fall in pitch is indicated by accents): '*Gotê, "Bábo!", gotê "à", gotê "Bábo, ez…"*', 'he said, "Father!", he said "yes", he said, "Father, I … "' and the story continues. The first syllables of *gotê* and *babo* are stressed; the pitch of the voice rises on *gotê babo* and falls on *gotê 'a'*. This is more than an opportunity for thought on the part of the storyteller; it also has aesthetic functions. The combination of pitch and rhythm is quite distinctive, and interrupts the general patterns of pitch and rhythm in the telling, where most sentences are considerably longer. This small device, varying according to the protagonists, occurs on numerous occasions in historical narrative and non-historical *çîrok*, and occurs in conversation where a raconteur is describing an incident. It may be delivered slowly or quickly, but it is a device and not merely an unconscious reproduction of everyday speech.

Another small, but characteristic feature of both historical and fictional narrative in Kurmanji, is the use of combinations of two, or sometimes even three verbs together. It usually seems to be done for the purposes of emphasis; in KJR's transcription of an account of the career of Dawûdê Dawûd by his son, the government are said to have *rabûn leşker şandin*, literally 'they arose, sent soldiers [against Dawûd]' or perhaps 'they upped and sent soldiers'; there is little difference in sense from merely saying *leşker şandin* 'they sent soldiers'. This device was also used in conversation by raconteurs in Badinan; one particularly frequent example, used in the context of refugees leaving Kurdistan, was *reviya çû*, 'lit. he ran away [and] went', but more accurately translated 'he was off!', spoken with a stress on the *çû*, and often accompanied by a dismissive arm gesture. The context of meaning in which this construction was used, and the accompanying pitch of the voice and hand gestures, indicated that this usage of two or more verbs in a short clause was meant to convey precipitate action.

There is no restriction on members of any specific Yezidi caste learning and performing secular narratives, and learning to tell prose narrative presumably takes less specialised training than learning to sing *stran*. It would be a reasonable assumption that a large section of the community would know both historical prose narratives and *çîrok* proper, but it was an unwelcome surprise to discover that in fact very few people did. Of the small number of full narratives I did manage to collect in Badinan from both Yezidi and Muslim communities, all were performed by middle-aged or elderly storytellers. In every collective village or town visited, informants consistently said 'Old people know these things'. This was not, apparently, an instance of the situation described in the Jordanian Bedouin context by Shryock, where only certain members of the community had the status of 'authoritative source' of historical tradition, and where this rarely included younger people (1997:151–2); in the Yezidi context, the 'authoritative sources', though elderly, like their Bedouin counterparts, were often rather low-status individuals. It really did seem to be the case that most younger people were more ignorant of such traditions – they were sometimes able to give a bald summary of stories, especially those which corresponded to well-known *stran*, but did not know them well enough to 'tell' them, and it seemed unlikely that they would know a great deal more by the time they were older themselves. No special word for a teller of stories was used;

instead, informants would say, 'So-and-so knows stories'. Mr H. had once been able to sing his tales as *stran*, but his singing voice had now failed; it was clear that he had not been asked to tell them for some time.

A Sinjari informant who had lived in Ba'drê for almost twenty years remembered that the traditional time for the telling of *çîrok* and *serpêhatî* (adventures) was during winter nights in the *dîwanxanê* (guest-room) of a prosperous person. *Stran* were also sung, and sometimes the various performances, by different performers, would go on till morning. In the collectives of Khanek and Shari'e, and the town of Ba'drê, informants consistently spoke of such gatherings in the past tense. Some said (as noted above) that nowadays people preferred to watch television; others said that in the present unfortunate times it was inappropriate to tell *qesse* 'songs and stories', implying that they were associated with enjoyment. Festivals and parties seemed to be exceptions to this and in Shari'e informants said that they were now the usual occasions for the performance of *çîrok*, rather like the *stran*. All of the informants asked to tell a story, whether historical or folktale, claimed to have forgotten some or all of the stories they once knew, though some remembered the names of stories they had once known well. This response cannot simply be attributed to modesty; most informants, even women, were quite willing to be recorded, and gave what they knew, but mentioned other stories they had once known which they could not remember.

Life histories and narratives of personal recollections also seemed to be told relatively rarely. Elderly individuals of high status in the community, for example the sheykhs, were not surprised to be asked about their past experiences. However, they were outnumbered by less influential octogenarians and nonagenarians, mostly murîds, who were as taken aback as the women when I asked them for an interview. One resident of the Khanek collective said he could remember massacres before and during the First World War, but he did not often have the opportunity to recount his reminiscences.

It was noticeable that there was no longer any traditional regular occasion for the performance of set-piece narratives; all the performances of both 'historical' and fictional narrative which I attended were prompted by my requests, and clearly affected by my presence. For all performances, both performer and audience sat comfortably, and the performer might take tea or a cigarette during the narrative. Tempo and tone varied according to the material, of course, but also according to the style of the performer. A performer with a larger and more attentive audience responded to this, with more expansive illustrative gestures and more eye-contact with the audience. As prose narrative does not necessarily have a fixed wording, there was a great deal of opportunity for virtuosity. My recordings were made in villages and audience members knew the tellers personally; they had no hesitation in contributing where they thought it necessary. During one telling of *Mem and Zîn* in Ba'drê the audience reminded the performer, Mr E., not to forget the episode where three fairy princesses decide to transport Zîn to Mem's bedroom. This had clearly become part of the 'received version' of the story, as performed on Iraqi radio, and a version which did not feature it would not be tolerated. It was noticeable that fewer people gathered to hear stories than *stran*; at the performances I attended less than ten came to listen to stories, whereas for the *stran*, audiences were usually more than twenty even for *ad hoc* village performances.

Women's Lament

This is a very distinctive form of discourse, performed by a specific group (women only) at certain prescribed times. It exists throughout Kurdish society in both Kurmanji- and Sorani-speaking areas. According to Dr Shukriya Rasool of the University of Salahaddin, an acknowledged authority on the subject, laments for the dead are always sung by women, but melodic form, idiom and gesture vary from tribe to tribe, as does terminology; the Yezidi form is common to all Yezidi tribes. Yezidi informants confirmed this. Even the Arabic-speaking Yezidis of the villages of Ba'shîqe and Beḥzanê have the same type of Kurdish lament as other Yezidis. Mrs R., a well-known semi-professional singer of laments (a murîd), who was brought up in the Arabic-speaking area but had moved to Ba'drê, made the interesting comment that although Arabic was their everyday language, Kurdish was *reḥemtir*, 'more merciful', and better suited to laments. Sheykhanis living in Germany also confirmed that the semi-professional laments from Georgia published by the Jelîl brothers were of the same type as those performed in Sheykhan.

In Badinan women's lament is known as *şîn*, which means 'mourning' in general, or *stranêd şînê* 'songs of mourning.' This latter term is also used among the Yezidis, who also use *dîrok* or *dîlok* to denote the lament.[25] *Şîn* is a more general term; it can mean the whole set of arrangements and rituals associated with mourning; it can also mean the gathering of women who sit down together and cry; as Mrs R. expressed it, 'I sing the *dîrok*, and they [the audience, the family of the deceased, who listen and cry] do *şîn*.' The phrase *şîn û şapor*, used by Kurdish folklorists, means the practice of singing the song whilst striking oneself and tearing one's hair, upon the death of a close relative. I did not hear the latter term among the Yezidi community, but the practice is one of the features which distinguishes Yezidi lament from that of some other Kurds, and I observed it in the commemoration of the dead at a graveyard during the Yezidi New Year festival; there were differences between this and the *şîn* I saw performed in a house later the same day. According to Mrs R., Muslim Kurds did not strike themselves, but merely sat together and cried. This is inaccurate and may reflect a general Yezidi lack of familiarity with the finer points of Muslim customs. Arabs tore their clothes, she added, but not Muslim Kurds. Yezidi laments, on the other hand, were *bi lêdanê*, 'with blows'; Yezidi women struck their chests and eyes and, for the deaths of younger men in particular, cut their braids off.[26] All the laments I heard were commemorative, for those who had died some time ago; the occasion did not arise to attend and observe the mourning, or *taziye*, following a death in the Yezidi community.

Performance

The correct context is crucial for performance of this genre. Laments must be performed, as a duty, during times of mourning; conversely they are not associated with happy times and should only be performed within the appropriate context of a period of mourning or a festival of commemoration. Informants could not simply perform to order; one must wait either for a *taziye* after a death or for a socially sanctioned occasion for commemoration of the dead.[27] For instance, during my interview of Mrs R., a man surreptitiously asked her to sing a lament for me. Her response was *ne, heram e*, 'no, it is forbidden'. I did not hear this exchange at the time, but it was clearly audible on the recording. It was an occasion of commemoration which provided me with an opportunity for observation and collection of lament. These restrictions were not confined to my own experience as a foreign researcher; the Jelîl brothers had to request permission from community leaders to collect laments from a famous singer, and their recordings were made during the commemoration of a particular individual.[28] They also had to retire from the performance themselves, leaving their recording equipment, as it was an occasion for women. For the lamentations I observed at the Yezidi New Year, the participants were often accompanied to the graveyard by adult male relatives, but the men within earshot stood back from the lamentation and made their non-involvement clear. The only active participatory males were qewwals who played sacred music. I also attended a lament performed by a widow in a house, with other women, unmarried girls, children and babies present; only the women took part. I have not observed unmarried girls singing the songs of lamentation among either the Yezidis or the Barzani women of Qosh Tepe; however, they do attend.

There is an important distinction between laments by women for family members and laments for the dead by known performers who travel around their area to perform for the bereaved. The form of the song is similar but the content will of course be different. A well-known performer might not know the deceased at all; nevertheless she will make her song appropriate to the deceased's age and sex, and will always concentrate on his or her good points. The *dîrok* of relatives, of course, is more personal. Most women living in villages or collective villages could perform *stranêd şînî* (songs of lamentation) for family members, but relatively few women were skilled enough to be well known for it. These were usually older semi-professionals; it is not clear whether this was a formally established rule or simply a matter of convenience; the number of taboos surrounding death in the Yezidi community would make it very difficult for a young bride or a woman in her childbearing years to perform *şîn* frequently. Two women in particular were consistently mentioned as being famous throughout the Yezidi community in Badinan; I spoke to one of them, Mrs R., about her work. ZK records the laments of one woman, Ḥisreta Ḥeso, whose fame extended from Tbilisi to the Georgian border (Jelîl 1978 I: 36). Only a Yezidi woman could perform the *dîrok* for a deceased Yezidi, but her caste was not important, in contrast with some of the more specifically religious rites of death, such as washing the corpse, which require the presence of pîr and sheykh (Kreyenbroek 1995: 160). A well-known performer might travel some distance for a *taziye*; personal acquaintance with the deceased was not an issue as long as she knew the family.

The women's lament is performed by unaccompanied voices. In this respect it differs strongly from the *stran* discussed earlier. However, in terms of melody and structure there are similarities. Sense-units or 'lines' may be of variable length, with a fall in pitch on the final syllable; several of these may be grouped together with two or three falls in pitch on the final syllables of the 'stanza'. Between stanzas the performer or others present may sob or beat their breasts rhythmically. The length of the lament is at the discretion of the performer, since it is an extemporised genre; within a traditional structure it is composed as it is performed. It is clear that stock elements are used by semi-professionals at least, though informants were unanimous that no two songs were identical. The use of stock elements, and of appropriate imagery, will be discussed with reference to specific laments in Chapter Six.

The lament is not a straightforward occasion where one clearly distinguished individual or group performs to a well-defined audience, but a performance of participants. It is true that not all the women present at the laments I observed made an audible contribution of song, speech or weeping, but all were apparently free to do so, though the verbal contributions tended to be dominated by a few. As participants rather than audience members, the women present at the laments were emotionally involved in the performance of the genre. The performances aroused strong emotion in participants, including those who did not make verbal contributions.

GENRE AND GENDER

In the oral traditions of many societies there are links between genre and gender. Certain forms may be performed only by men, or only by women. Within the Yezidi context, I encountered no genres as such which were only available to men, though it is likely that such genres existed and were not considered appropriate to describe to a female researcher. It is probable that epithalamia, as performed by the bridegroom's male friends and supporters, are different from women's songs. Lescot attests to 'mischievous' songs sung before Kurdish weddings in general by the groom and his companions, and to Yezidi women's songs sung by the friends of a bride when she goes to the stream for the first time after her marriage. ('Tawusparêz' 1943: 764–8). Ribald songs are also probably gender-specific; a few of those performed by males have been collected, for example Makas 1926: 95, a song addressing the female genitals, apparently sung by young boys to embarrass and annoy girls. Ribald songs performed by women are rumoured to exist, but polite conversation precludes their discussion and they are not featured in the folklore collections. Among the polite and generally high-status genres which were the object of my investigations, the most obvious examples of women's song I encountered were laments for the dead and work songs, which were sung to accompany women's tasks in the village. Of these genres, only laments have been considered in this work; not enough examples of the low-status women's work songs are currently available for study, either from my fieldwork or from previous collections.[29]

It seems that, in the wider Kurdish society, there is no *a priori* reason why a woman cannot be a *stranbêj* or *dengbêj*; women are not specifically barred from singing or composing heroic or historical songs. There are some indications of women's role in composition in the secondary literature, but no studies have specifically focused on the issue. Bois alludes to the pre-eminence of women in composition of love and war-songs in an article whose primary focus is written literature (Bois 1955: 32). Jaba notes that the wife and daughters of one dead hero composed many laments in his honour, which are still sung 'to this day' (1860: 56). This seems to imply that these laments are not *şîn*, which would be composed extempore for a female audience, with no attempt at verbatim repetition later on; rather they are 'heroic' laments of the type performed by *stranbêj*, like the lament sung by 'Edûlê for Derwêshê 'Evdî in the version sung by Israel Ohanyan (see Part II). The Kurdish novelist Mehmet Uzun, who has spent time in Syria and met several noted *dengbêj* there, remarks that women play their part as much as men, that they listen, perform and compose, and that the number of famous Kurdish female *dengbêj* is 'not small'(1992: 32, 37).

In the Yezidi context it was extremely difficult to collect specific data on gender and performance during the fieldwork. The problem of finding translators contributed to this, as did certain social factors within the Yezidi community. Various Yezidis told me about Ḥezo, a Sinjari woman who had been taught the songs of the great *stranbêj* Biroyê Sherqî. It seems that *stranbêj* in general were much more common among Sinjari than Sheykhani Yezidis; no Iraqi Yezidi female singers of *stran* who were not from Sinjar were mentioned at all. Female singers tended to learn songs from members of their families; it would not be considered appropriate to send them out to learn from singers who were not relations. Modesty, or 'shame' (*şerm*), had prevented Ḥezo from making recordings, though she did sing in public; it is not clear whether she had a musical accompaniment or played an instrument herself while she sang.[30] The context in which a woman performed depended on the wishes of her family; a husband, for example, might forbid his wife to sing in public. This was consistent with interviews with Hawerî and Dina women in Khanek, none of whom claimed to be a *stranbêj* or to know the great heroic songs, but who did know some 'historical' songs and stories; examples cited included *Mîrza Mohammed* (a secular 'historical' tradition), and *Rustem Zal* (a well-known figure in Iranian folklore, cf. Jelîl 1978 II: 103). Nevertheless, these women said that *şerm*, or modesty, prevented them from performing in front of men. Some described gatherings of men and women where the men would tell *qesse*; women did not, though (according to female informants) some knew them better than the men. Others, especially Sinjaris, described segregated gatherings. When the men were out, the women would make their children listen while they told the stories. The few recordings of women singing which I made were done in a closed room with only women and children present. A child brought up in the village would hear a range of oral traditions from its mother and her friends; transmission of most of the *stran* may generally have been the province of specialist singers, but mothers certainly played a crucial role in passing on a variety of traditional stories and songs which may have included some of the *stran*.

The collections made by the scholars of the former Soviet republics include a small group of traditions sung by women which nevertheless furnish some concrete examples; in these communities *şerm* did not prevent the women from making recordings. ZK includes short autobiographical sketches of several Yezidi women. Most are the daughters of singers, and the notes say that they learned from their fathers. They perform a range of material; Gulîzera 'Etar, for example, is said to know 'many young girls' songs', whilst Kida Ûso, who learned from her father and passed the songs on to her son, performed a version of the well-known Kurdish *destan* called *Zembilfirosh*, 'The Basket Seller' (Jelîl 1978 II: 498).

In some parts of the Near and Middle East, fictional and legendary oral traditions, such as folktales, are considered the special province of women, who are expected to know fewer 'historical' traditions. Although the women who spoke to me about their knowledge were in general more reticent than men and less confident of their abilities, and cited more examples of 'fictional' rather than 'historical' traditions among their repertoire, there could have been various social reasons for this. As it was simply not possible to focus on the knowledge of women as opposed to that of men (for reasons outlined in Chapter One), it remains far from clear whether this was in fact the case. There certainly were some women who knew 'historical' traditions well, though most of these were from knowledgeable families and learned their traditions from relations. In terms of secular Yezidi oral traditions, there was no indication that any of the major genres were in theory closed to women to learn and perform. It seems that only variable circumstances, such as the attitudes of an individual's family or community, imposed restraints on them. Of course, some genres were exclusively available to women.

COMPOSITION AND TRANSMISSION

Since past studies of oral traditions have been mainly text-based and did little to describe genre and context, it is difficult to study the genres from a diachronic perspective. However, many members of the community can still remember traditional fora for performance of oral traditions, and there are dominant accounts of their composition which must be taken seriously. The community's perceptions of the origins and transmissions of the traditions are of course closely linked to their current status; not only do these perceptions contribute to a better understanding of the present role of the genres but also give indications of the genres' likely future.

The processes of composition and change are easier to evaluate in the case of the *stran* and *destan* poems than in the case of the prose narratives, due to the relative abundance of examples of *stran* in the field and in the published collections. In the case of *şîn* there have not been enough data collected in the past to study the genre diachronically, although the similarity of Jelîl's Yezidi material from the Caucasus, acknowledged by Sheykhani Yezidis, indicates considerable stability of both form and imagery, because the Caucasian community has been divided from the Iraqi community for so long.

Stran

The Yezidis of Badinan have a very clear perception of the origins of the 'traditional songs'. In this case it is legitimate to use the term 'origins' as the songs are believed to have been composed by individuals (some of whose names have been preserved by posterity), and to have remained unchanged, without innovations by performers, over many centuries. This will be examined more closely with reference to the *stran* of *Ferîq Pasha* and *Dawûdê Dawûd* in the next chapter. Most informants believe that the traditions currently performed in Sinjar were composed by one *stranbêj*, Biroyê Sherqî, a Yezidi, who was court poet at the *dîwan* of Ibrahim Pasha Milli, and who came from the Millî stronghold of Wêranshehir (Viranşehır in Turkey) to Sinjar after the fall of Sultan Abdulhamid. However, singers themselves acknowledged that whilst he was clearly a particularly influential *stranbêj*, he could not possibly have composed all the traditions relating to a variety of periods, not to mention those dating from the twentieth century. All the variants of *Ferîq Pasha* collected (see next chapter) have enough in common to posit a common origin. The two versions of *Dawûdê Dawûd*, one collected during the fieldwork in Badinan, the other collected by Jelîlê Jelîl in Syria (1985: 156), are clearly forms of the same song. It is quite possible, over time, for a composition by one *stranbêj* to spread over some distance and become part of the repertoire of several singers. However, the lyrics of *Derwêshê 'Evdî* which will be examined in Chapter Five were collected by the Jelîl brothers in the former Soviet Union; they seem to have more than one origin and also differ from the Sinjarî *stran*.

The *stranbêj* of Sinjar have not merely preserved a group of songs by one singer. Quite clearly, new songs have been composed. *Dawûdê Dawûd* is an obvious example; his rebellions took place during the 1920s and 30s. The *stran Şerê Mala Şeşo*, 'The battle of the house of Shesho', is about a vendetta between two Sinjari families; the fighting recounted took place during the 1970s. Contemporary *stranbêj* also compose *stran* about love; a recent love-song by the renowned Kheyro Khelef became very popular in Sheykhan, with many recordings made of it. Mehmed Uzun says, of *dengbêj* in the wider Kurdish context, that a singer must know his craft well and bring his own talents to it before he is good enough to make *gotin* (lit. 'speech') and *stran* about new events (1992: 34). This seems also to apply to the Yezidi *stranbêj*; many can perform, but only the best can gain popular approval for their compositions, which will then be passed on.

Biroyê Sherqî taught the singers Kiçê, Pîr Giro, Sheykhmûs, Ḥezo and Qasim Meyro, who in turn taught Lezgîn Seydo, Sheykh Derwêsh, Khelef Elias (and thus Kheyro Kelef), Pîr Micho and Feqîr Khidir. This implies the existence of some sort of apprenticeship or school. Mehmed Uzun, who places great emphasis on the levels of technical skill acquired by trained singers, refers to those singers eminent enough to compose as having a 'school'. This may have been relatively informal; Uzun's own novel based on the life of a well-known Kurdish *dengbêj* (1991) describes groups of apprentices lodging with the singer and travelling with him from the winter to the summer pastures. All the well-known *stranbêj* who featured in discussion and on my recordings were, according to informants, pupils of one singer or another, probably at a relatively early age in most cases. One young man who said he had learned some of the *stran* from repeated listening to a master's performances, rather than from being personally accepted as a pupil by the master, did not claim a large repertoire, nor did he call himself a *stranbêj*. It seems that anyone with serious ambitions to be a *stranbêj* would have to be publicly accepted as a pupil by a competent teacher. Many of the Sinjari singers, and of those cited in ZK, learned from their fathers or some singer in their own area. The local view that innovation did not take place in the *stran* did make some allowance for differences in performance and virtuosity between different singers. Informants would make such observations as 'So-and-so sings a good *Derwêshê 'Evdî*'. A singer's training and the identity of his master was also a factor in his reputation. Recently, more methods of learning have become open to would-be singers; if unable to be taught directly by a master, they need no longer wait for performances to learn from him by imitation, but can watch videos or listen to cassettes. These indirect methods were apparently becoming more common in the Kurdish autonomous zone with the prevalent interest in *folklor*, but in 1992 no-one who had learned in such a way would be accepted as a truly authentic *stranbêj*.

Prose Narrative

In the case of the generally known *çîrok*, modern resources such as recordings and broadcasts have contributed to the transmission of dominant versions, and the most well-known *çîrok*, such as *Mem and Zîn*, seem to have become 'fossilised' into a generally known version; substantial innovations or omissions are noted by the audience. As for historical prose narrative, there is little direct evidence, but it would be reasonable to assume that the same conditions pertain as for the *stran*, namely that once a particular version has gained currency within the community, major innovations are discouraged. It would appear that, for the most part, prose narrative dealing with historical events is now most often performed as an accompaniment to and explanation of the *stran*; the evidence of the informants in the field seems to indicate that prose narratives are rarely performed for their own sake, except where there is a special interest, such as family history or a politically significant theme.

It is not clear how far *çîrok* are formally taught. Those historical narrative traditions which explain and correspond to the lyrical *stran* are taught and passed on along with the *stran*. It is also unclear how easy it is under present circumstances for personal recollections of the elderly to become oral tradition, i.e. a historical account passed on through the generations, unless these are preserved by a *stran* with its accompanying explanation. Various informants described being taught about the events of history, especially family history, by grandparents or great-uncles, who often reminisced about the important events of their youth; they said that knowledge of these had now declined since the death of these relations. It is true that one would expect people to say knowledge had declined even where it had not, in the same way that people would always say life was better in the old villages even when it had been harder, but the upheavals in Kurdish community life and the decline in the fora for public performance of these traditions would seem to support popular opinion here. Prose accounts of community history now seem to be part of the private domain, rarely given even in the context of the extended family, and young people are claiming a lack of knowledge which, far from being a result of modesty and a reluctance to claim inappropriate expertise, seems to be a source of pain to some. It seems highly unlikely that immediate family history is no longer being transmitted, but on a wider tribal and community level, knowledge among young people of those traditions which are preserved neither in writing nor in a reasonably durable genre such as *stran* is in decline.

Women's Lament

Although, according to Mrs R., every village has one or two women who know how to perform reasonably, the distances travelled by the well-known performers of *şîn* are an indication of their pre-eminence and the value placed on their skills. Women in environments such as Khanek learn to practise these rituals of commemoration by participating in them. It is not clear whether a woman becomes pre-eminent by becoming a pupil of a well-known performer, or whether her fame spreads further afield from her performances within her family group. Mrs R. said that young women were not seeking to learn the skill nowadays.

RELATIVE STATUS AND FUTURE PROSPECTS

All of the traditional forms of Kurdish 'folkloric' discourse are under threat from the decline in arenas for performance and competition from new forms, such as the modern political Kurdish song. However, some have better prospects for survival than others. The traditional *stran* enjoy a position of prestige, and are especially closely associated with the Yezidi community. The recent awakening of interest in folklore and the availability of *stran* collected elsewhere increases the interest of younger Yezidis in the form. *Stran* are still performed frequently, and their association with large gatherings such as weddings and parties assures a wide audience. However, there are good reasons for supposing that many members of the audience find them very difficult to understand. The Sinjari dialect is not always well understood by Sheykhanis; unfamiliar vocabulary and the style of delivery, which alternates between great speed and lingering on single syllables, conspire against the comprehensibility of the song's words. This was amply demonstrated when first a native Kurdish speaker of Dihok, and then a young Sheykhani Yezidi, found great difficulty in deciphering some passages from my collection for transliteration and translation. Even the *stranbêj* Mr B., who at first declared that all the songs were well-known to the audience, acknowledged when pressed that they might be difficult for young Sheykhanis to understand in their entirety. It seems that the lyrical nature of the songs is what ensures their popularity, and that those among the audience who cannot understand every word literally have a somewhat impressionistic, emotional understanding of the songs. The quality of the voice of the singer and his virtuosity are factors in this; deep emotions can be conveyed by performance technique and musical expression as well as by the words. The dancing of the *peste* is also extremely popular. It was noticed above that the *stranbêj* often prefix the musical performance with a prose narrative account of the story; this is, incidentally, by no means peculiar to Kurdish songs – for instance, the Jordanian Bedouin also give explanatory stories as a 'foundation' to poems on historical subjects (Shryock 1997: 201). Similarly, the sacred Yezidi *qewls* are also usually explained by a religious *çîrok*. As the number of occasions where historical prose narrative is performed declines, this may become the primary opportunity of hearing such narrative for most of the audience.

The *çîrok* and historical prose narratives, although associated with the same performance environment as *stran*, would be seen as a poor second at parties and weddings, where dancing is considered essential. Local gatherings seemed by 1992 to be dominated more often by contemporary political discussion and by television than by traditional songs and stories. Young people seemed less interested in historical prose narratives than in the *stran*; the only performers found were elderly. *Çîrok* well-known throughout Kurdistan were becoming standardised by broadcast and recording. The move to collect folklore seemed to be more associated with verse than prose forms; prestigious forms were still being collected and the collection of oral history from people of low status had not yet begun. Prose narrative, both historical and fictional, seemed to be in decline.

Although one might expect the *şîn*, as a woman's genre with relatively low status, to be in decline, this does not seem to be the case. Local folklorists, with the exception of a single specialist, show little interest in it. However, amongst the Yezidis, performing *şîn* is still seen as a necessity. Few young women were interested in specialising in this, but as of 1992 there was no shortage of skilled individuals.

The traditional songs, both lyrical and narrative, and the prose narratives which will be considered in the next three chapters, are both history and literature for the Yezidis. The lyrical *stran* are composed and performed with certain aesthetics in mind; they concentrate on certain moments, personalities and situations from the past and on their emotional impact. The prose narratives, on the other hand, are more obviously designed for the transmission of information; they also have their own aesthetics and stylistic devices, their own agendas and conventions. The women's lament is an emotional discourse, often intensely personal; this will be explored further in Chapter Six. All these forms of discourse, and the subject matter associated with them, are well known amongst the older members of the Yezidi community in Badinan. Many of them expressed a passionate attachment to these embodiments of their history. Amongst the younger Yezidis, there was less detailed knowledge of the events of the past, but the traditions still had a resonance. Even for those with no belief in their religion, the 'legendary' traditions, such as those surrounding Sheykh Adi, coloured their world-view because they were so closely associated with the attitudes and practices of the communities in which they had grown up; such traditions could be embraced or rejected, but could never be neutral to them. The secular traditions of the last two centuries or so were in many ways less challenging and more readily believable for those educated in State schools. These traditions were not part of the Iraqi mainstream; they were largely ignored by literate historical studies, and closely associated with the identity of the Yezidi communities of the area. Moreover, the secular traditions were also very flexible; those dealing with events in Ottoman Turkey, with their wider Kurdish cultural reality, could easily be incorporated into Kurdish nationalist thinking, whereas the many traditions emphasising Yezidi distinctiveness could be used by other parties to distinguish them from other Kurds.[31] Partial and localised as they are, both the 'traditional' and the younger Yezidis see these artistic tellings of secular events as their own distinctive history.

CHAPTER FOUR

Battles, Heroes and Villains: Portrayals of Conflict

INTRODUCTION

It is easy for outsiders to overestimate the frequency with which traditional Yezidi society has resorted to violence to resolve both internal and external conflicts. Roger Lescot's memorable image of the tribesmen of Teref and 'Eldîna in Sinjar, who passed the time on summer nights by exchanging insults and gunfire from the comfort of their own homes, sticks in the European mind (1938: 180). It is all too easy to forget that not only Kurdish tribal structures but also Yezidi religious hierarchies provide for the resolution of many local disputes without violence, by negotiation and the mediation of senior figures. Moreover, with the increase in power of the state during the twentieth century, greater recourse was had to Iraqi law rather than local systems. Nevertheless, blood-feud and honour killings remain widespread in Kurdistan, and, as the history of the Iraqi Kurdish movement shows, armed resistance is still a common response to outside threat.

Since conflict is such an important part of Yezidi life, it is no surprise to discover that it is also an important theme in Yezidi oral tradition. Many of the lyrical *stran* describe battles great and small; narrative poetry recounts the exploits of martial heroes. The great events and personalities of past conflicts are recalled in conversation. Each genre has its own conventions and stock elements, and the process of discerning an historical individual amid the stock elements of the tradition can sometimes be a challenge for the outsider; the Yezidis, of course, with their multi-layered understanding of the messages conveyed by the various genres, would rarely need to engage in such an exercise. Such oral traditions may retain considerable power and influence, at least in sections of the community. One of the very few people still alive today who played a part in the events of the traditional *stran* is Qasim Shesho, who was involved in a blood-feud of the 1970s, the subject of the Sinjari stran *Şerê Mala Şeşo*, 'The Battle of the House of Shesho'. He expresses a distinct ambivalence at being immortalised in the *stran*; he considers the song to be dangerous, and that it is quite possible that young men might hear it and be inflamed by it into perpetuating the conflict, perhaps causing more deaths.

In my analysis of the portrayal of conflict in Yezidi oral tradition, I will pay particular attention to the conventions by which battles are described, the description of heroes, and the depiction of villains, especially the rather nebulous figure of 'the government'. Given the complexity of the interplay of the various genres used, I have opted to consider specific performances of a small number of individual traditions in some detail, rather than make very broad and possibly unjustifiable comparisons across a great breadth of traditions. I will present the traditions, where possible, alongside some of the relevant written records, in the hope of providing some insight into what the Yezidis see fit to include and omit; it will also illustrate the effect of the choice of genre on the traditions. The *stran* in particular, more frequently performed among the Iraqi Yezidis than narrative poetry, can be seen in many ways as 'texts', but their performances differ considerably, and the focus on specific traditions will enable the poetics and artistry of individual performances to be described, and a picture built up of the impressions conveyed by the different genres in which the traditions are transmitted. The three traditions which will be considered in detail are: *Ferîq Pasha*, whose campaigns are still a byword for religious persecution, *Dawûdê Dawûd*, the most famous Yezidi rebel against government forces, and *Derwêsh* or *Derwîshê 'Evdî*, the pre-eminent Yezidi martial hero. The first two of these will illustrate how *stran* in particular (as opposed to prose narrative) present conflict, and the third will show various ways in which *stran* differs from narrative poetry and prose accounts. Both the Ferîq and Derwêsh were nineteenth-century figures, but Dawûd is still part of living memory, described to me by various elderly people. These three traditions all recount events in which Yezidis participated and where their Yezidism was an issue; they are amongst the best-remembered episodes in Yezidi history, famous enough to be well known to many other Kurds. They are among the 'defining memories' of the Yezidi historical discourse.

Ferîq Pasha, the 'Lord Lieutenant'

'The calamity that now looms largest in the communal memory is the "Year of the General", 1892, when 'Umar Wahbī Pasha descended on their villages with fire and sword, giving them the choice between adoption of Islam or death . . .' Such was the impression of C.J. Edmonds, as recorded in his diaries between 1930 and 1945 (1967: 60), and the persecution by the Ferîq is still well known today.

In 1892, Lieutenant-General 'Umar Wehbī Pasha was sent to the Mosul *vilayet* from Istanbul to reclaim outstanding taxes. Apparently he had a special brief to convert as many Yezidis as possible to Islam with the eventual aim of instituting companies of (ex-)Yezidi 'Hamidiyeh' irregular cavalry. The Yezidis' traditional aversion to military service, which had motivated the 1872 petition requesting exemption on religious grounds, had long been a source of irritation to the Ottoman administration. 'Umar Wehbī Pasha forced conversion to Islam on a number of Yezidi dignitaries, including the Mîr, and when other Yezidis protested, sent punitive expeditions to Yezidi communities. Soldiers set up camp in villages and proceeded to harass the population. When fighting broke out, the Sheykhani Yezidis in particular, who were farmers, were unable to defend themselves. Villagers were massacred, the shrine at Lalêsh was pillaged and turned over to Muslim control.[1] Those Yezidis who resisted conversion to Islam, including the Mîr's brother, were tortured. With the effective fall of Sheykhan as a centre of Yezidism, the religious centre shifted to Sinjar, which offered sanctuary to Sheykhani refugees. It became a centre for anti-Muslim feeling and for visionaries such as Kochek Mîrza who predicted the imminent collapse of Islam and triumph of Yezidism. The military expeditions sent there by the Ferîq failed, and only served to strengthen the growing influence of tribes such as the Feqîran, led by Hemo Shêro, at the expense of entrenched tribes such as the Mêrkan who were felt to be suspect as they included Muslims in their number. Intervention by the British Foreign Office, combined, according to some sources, with the advice of Ibrahim Pasha Milli, whose confederation included Yezidi tribes, persuaded the Sultan to recall 'Umar Wehbī Pasha in early 1893 (Guest 1993: 131–2; 134–42; Fuccaro 1999: 34–5).

During the first engagement in Sinjar in the summer of 1892, the police colonel in charge of the government force reported ten Yezidis killed and thirty-five wounded, with two soldiers killed and four wounded. One hundred and twenty prisoners were taken to Mosul. During another engagement in November of the same year, the government forces were defeated, led into an ambush by tribesmen who had promised cooperation in exchange for the safety of their villages. An expedition led by 'Umar Wehbī Pasha himself also failed; he then agreed to let the Sinjari Yezidis keep their religion as long as they paid their taxes. After the Pasha was dismissed from his post, the Sinjari Yezidis could not pay their taxes as they did not have access to much of their livestock; Kochek Mîrza's predictions also made the community restive. After another battle in 1893, government forces and the Yezidi Sifûq Agha negotiated an uneasy peace.

The Ferîq Pasha *Stran*

Most, if not all, of my informants knew of Ferîq Pasha, but none of those I interviewed felt their knowledge to be detailed enough to warrant its recording as a narrative. However, the tradition was clearly flourishing in *stran* form, as it featured on several of the cassettes I acquired. Four of these performances were of sufficient recording quality (just) to be fully transcribed and compared; these were sung by five *stranbêj*. Unfortunately I was unable to obtain positive identification of three of these singers. The first was mistakenly identified by the supplier of the tapes, a Muslim from Sinjar, as Qarpal, a well-known Sinjari singer. However, comparison with Qarpal's other recordings, particularly with a video in the collection of a knowledgeable friend, made it clear that this voice was not that of Qarpal. I am still not in a position to suggest a more positive identity, and will use 'Qarpal' for want of a better alternative. The second was included in a recording labelled 'Jerdo and Kheyro'; there were two voices, one singing the first stanzas and the other, an older man, singing the last. Neither was the voice of the famous singer Kheyro Khelef, which is distinctive. The name 'Jerdo' or 'Rat', unknown to my informants, is likely to be a pseudonym; such names are sometimes used; Kheyro is not an uncommon name. The third performance in my collection is sung, confusingly enough, by the more famous Kheyro, Kheyro Khelef; the fourth is by Lezgîn Seydo. The fifth recording, by Pîr Micho, only included part of the song. Later I was shown another performance by Pîr Micho, on video, recorded in Europe, in the collection of Pîr Khidir Silêman. I was unable to transcribe this, though I did note down some interesting passages. Texts and translations of these are in Part II.

These *Ferîq Pasha*s are clearly performances of the same song. They all have many phrases and sometimes whole lines in common; in fact there are remarkably few phrases or lines in any one which are not in any of the others. Occasionally different vocabulary is used to express similar sentiments. There are various major common elements.

The terms of discourse of emotion within the song are very similar in all performances. All (except that of 'Jerdo and Kheyro' where the first few lines are not recorded) begin with a striking image of emotional anguish; the world, or the heart, of the speaker, is 'like the hoop of a sieve'. Sometimes this is an introductory remark by the singer as 'narrator'; sometimes it is put into the mouth of one of the women in the song. In Kurdish it is relatively common to express emotional pain by saying that the heart feels narrow or constricted, or that it is burning. It is quite typical of Kurdish folk poetry to combine such a usage with an object or scene from everyday life, in this case the sieve, to create an arresting image. Alongside the personal anguish goes the curse on the enemy; all the performances contain the wish that God will not allow the house of Ferîq Pasha to endure. There is also anxiety in the song, expressed by the women watching the battle, because they cannot hear the sound of a particular man's gun.

All the performances featured the same protagonists, except that of Pîr Micho, who had his own reasons for making changes (see below). The heroic fighters mentioned in all the performances are called Osê Mejdî (elder brother of Pîr Kemal, grandfather of the present Baba Chawûsh);

Miḥemê 'Evdo (father of Saleh); Sifûqê Meto (father of Berjes), not the Sifûq Agha of the Musqoran known as Sifûq Pasha, who was 'Chief of the Mountain', but a member of the influential Meḥmûdî clan of the Simoqan tribe;[2] Dawûdê 'Isa (father of the famous Dawûdê Dawûd of the Mêrkan tribe); 'Elî Agha, whose gun was not heard during the battle, was a chief of the 'Elî Jermkan (Lescot 1938: 176). There are also two women, 'Big' and 'Little' Gulê – differentiated by their age – who observe and comment; in some performances, a woman called Zerîfka Osê also plays a part. The locations and tribes mentioned are similarly consistent, such as the 'shady tree' and the Sinjari peak of Chilmêra. The village of Girê 'Ereba belonged to the Ûsivan, a clan of the Mala Khalitî tribe, which, along with the Mêrkan, Mûsqoran, Bekiran and Habbabat tribes, formed a group called the Jenewîyan (Lescot 1938: 257).[3] These protagonists only represent a small group of the Sinjari Yezidi tribes, and other tribes who did not fight alongside them are strongly criticised, especially the Khwerkan.

The contents of the exhortatory speech made to the fighters before the battle are also very similar in the different performances. Their Yezidi identity is clearly stated, either by references to Yezidi heritage, or to the help of the holy being Sultan Êzdî (Kreyenbroek 1995: 94). The men are urged to fight bravely and, usually, not to take their eyes off the Ferîq's army. The speaker hopes that they will drive the army to various distant places, or that the army's casualties will be so numerous that it will take some time to collect them. The battle is described in an impressionistic way; its sounds are mentioned in all the performances, and one performance mentions the sight of falling shells. All the performances say the battle lasted for three days. This is clearly a stock element, raising the obvious question of how far all these parts of the song are characteristic of Kurdish lyric in general and how far they are peculiar to *Ferîq Pasha*.

The constituents listed above, developed to various degrees, in differing orders and with varying amounts of repetition, make up the entire content of the performances (with the exception of a section of Kheyro's performance, where he suddenly mentions some new characters who may well come from another song). One cannot seriously avoid the conclusion that these are performances of one original composition. It is unlikely to be a composition of Biroyê Sherqî, who must have arrived in Sinjar some twenty years or more after this battle took place – it is so impressionistic that whoever composed it must have had ready access to the protagonists and witnesses very soon after the event. Mr B., a senior *stranbêj*, even suggested to me that it may have been composed by one of the women who watched the events unfold. In the absence of evidence, however, further speculation on the *Ur-Ferîq Pasha stran* is unlikely to be revealing, so I will turn instead to types of variation on the common theme used by the *stranbêj* and the ways in which they use the material to enhance their performances.

In many instances phrases, lines and groups of lines within the songs are identical. The line *Xodê o ava neke mala Ferîq Pasha*, 'O God, do not leave the house of Ferîq Pasha standing', for example, is used many times with little or no variation. It is also common, however, for small variations in these common elements to be inserted by different singers. 'Qarpal' uses the following words in stanzas 2, 4, 6, 7 and 8:

Şad û nişûdêd Osê Mecdî kekê Kemêl, gelek hene ax	The famous ones, the heroes, of Osê Mejdî, Kemal's elder brother, there are many, oh,
Sê denga dibêje Miḥemê 'Evdo bavê Salayê Sifûqê Meto bavê Berces,	He calls three times, to Mihemê Evdo, Saleh's father, Sifûqê Meto, Berjes' father,

('Qarpal' 2: 2–3, 4: 2–3, 6: 6, 7: 5–7, 8: 6–7).

He does not vary this except in stanza 7 when he makes the first of these lines longer, not lowering the pitch until he has sung *sê denga dibêje*, and beginning the next line with a higher note on *Miḥemê 'Evdo*.

Şad û neşûdêd Osê Mecdî, kekê Kemêl, gelek hene, sê denga dibêje	The famous ones, the heroes, of Osê Mejdî, Kemal's elder brother, there are many, he calls three times, to
Miḥemê 'Evdo bavê Saleh ax Ewî Sifûqê Meto bavê Berces . . .	Mihemê 'Evdo, father of Saleh, [To] that Sifûqê Meto, Berjes' father . . .

(7: 5–7).

Nevertheless he keeps to the same words. Other singers treat these lines differently. Lezgîn Seydo varies the word order; in stanza 1: 5 he has *gelek hene* 'there are many' at the end of the line, in stanza 2: 2 at the beginning; using it at the beginning signals that this particular section is about to be repeated. 'Jerdo and Kheyro' and Kheyro Khelef use epithets describing the protagonists, such as *Miḥemê 'Evdo siwarê Bozê*, 'Miḥemê 'Evdo, rider of Bozê' ('Jerdo and Kheyro' 6: 6; Kheyro Khelef 1: 7, 4: 5). Kheyro Khelef and Lezgîn occasionally lengthen these lines with emphatic words and phrases such as *wellê* 'by God' and *Xodê zane*, 'God knows', as in:

Ewê gelek hene şad û nişûdêd, *Xodê zane*, Osê Mecdî kekê Kemêl,	They are many, *God knows*, the famous ones, the heroes, of Osê Mejdî, Kemal's elder brother,
Mane sê denga gazî dike Sifûqê Meto bavê Berces, *wellah* Miḥemê 'Evdo bavê Saleh, Dawûdê 'Isa bavê Dêwêd,	He calls out three times, to Sifûqê Meto, Berjes' father, *oh God*, Miḥemê 'Evdo, Saleh's father, and Dawûdê 'Isa, Dawûd's father,

(Lezgîn 8: 3–4).

Thus although these lines are common to all versions, they are not always performed in the same way; such variations can be observed in other lines and groups of lines which are common to all the songs. The small additions often do not change the meaning greatly, but can give differences in emphasis or emotional tone.

In Kurdish verbal art in general, both prose and verse, one noticeable feature is the use of two (usually) alliterative nouns with similar meanings, linked by the word 'and'. Like the common use of two verbs next to each other, this device appears to give more vividness, and thus more force, to a narrative; it is also frequently used in conversation. The *stranbêj* tend to use the same examples of these, most obviously '*Erz û 'eyêl*'; which I have translated 'kith and kin'.[4] ('Qarpal' 2: 6; 'Kheyro' 6: 8; Kheyro Khelef 2: 5; Lezgîn 2: 7, 9, 11: 2; Pîr Micho 1: 6); *şad û neşûd* 'famous ones, heroes', is very common in these songs ('Qarpal' 2: 2, 4: 2, 6: 6, 7: 5; 8: 6; 'Jerdo' 3: 1; 5: 2; Kheyro Khelef 1: 4, 2: 2, 4: 5, 5: 7, 6: 4; Lezgîn 1: 5, 7, 2: 2, 5: 3, 8: 3, 9: 4, 10: 9).

Sometimes the different singers use different vocabulary, although they clearly have the same idea in their minds. An instance of this occurs in the expression of the wish that Ferîq Pasha's army will not be able to claim its dead for some time. 'Jerdo and Kheyro' and Kheyro Khelef wish that the *qoç û 'ereba*, 'coaches and carts', of the government will not collect their dead for a year and three months:

Belê bi Xodê, li çemê Bekira qoç û 'erebanê ḥukumetê xelas nekin cenaz û leşa.	Yes, by God, and the coaches and carts of the government will not have finished with bodies and corpses. ('Kheyro' 7: 10).

and:

Bi Xodê koç û erebanê ḥukumetê li çemê Bekira xelas nekin meytan û laşa.'	By God, may those coaches and carts of the Government at the river Bekiran not finish with their bodies, their corpses. (Kheyro Khelef 5: 10–11).

This idea is expressed slightly differently by 'Qarpal':

... serî sê rojî tamam, dewleta ḥukumeta Ferîq Paşa ax, Ce bavo bi tirimbêla xelas nake laşêd kuştîyan û birîndaran.	... when three days have passed, Ferîq Pasha's government, oh, For certain, they won't have finished collecting the bodies of their killed and wounded in their cars. ('Qarpal' 8: 8–9).

Lezgîn (11: 6) also uses the word *tirimbêl*, which is the same word as 'automobile'. Since we may safely assume that the *stran* of Ferîq Pasha was composed not long after the events of 1892–3, *tirimbêl* is clearly an anachronism supplied by a later singer, or singers. The word *'erebe* is still understood in many areas; in Diyarbakir it is used for 'car'.[5]

Another example is in the first speech of the female observer, usually Little Gulê. 'Qarpal' has:

Lê lê xwehîngê vê sibê tu karê xwe bike,	Oh, sister, this morning you do your work,
Emê çinê serbanê Çelmêra ganê min bi gorî diyarî sûke,	We will go to the peak of Chilmêra, my life, just by the town,
	(3: 4–5).

whereas Pîr Micho, for instance, has:

Lê xwehingê rabim biçime serê çiyayê Şingalê,	Oh, sister, let me up and go to the top of Mount Sinjar,
Serbanê Çilmêra pêşberî sûkê,	The peak of Chilmêra, looking out over the town,
	(2: 3–4).

Both clearly have the idea in their minds, that the women are going up to find a vantage point to look out over the town, but express it in different ways. They are expressing the same concept, part of the train of thought of the original composition, but using different vocabulary.

Given that there is an 'original' composition, how far is it justifiable to speak of 'mistakes' or 'misunderstandings' on the part of performers? There is certainly a feeling among audience members that certain singers give a more accurate telling of the song than others. Tiny differences in phrases used at parallel points are easy to see. For instance, 'Qarpal's' seventh stanza begins as follows:

Ezîdo, kavlê bavê Reşo bişewite bi geneka,	Oh Yezidi, let the ruins of Resho's father burn up, green bushes and all,
	(7: 1)

whereas Pîr Micho, in a parallel line, has:

Kavlê bavê Ḥemo gelek e,	The ruins of Ḥemo's father are many,
	(3: 1).

He seems to have replaced *genek* with the more common word *gelek*. However, such similar alternatives, which also make reasonable sense, might well reflect earlier 'mishearings' or perhaps, different interpretations of the wording of the original. However it is not fair to consider them as 'incorrect' either. Certainly the audience does not seem to consider them as such. The fact that each works well within its own context shows that the tradition retains its life as it develops.

Nevertheless there are some points where change is perceived as 'incorrect' by audiences. The most obvious such area is the list of names of protagonists, the part of the song which most clearly does not consist of stock elements and which distinguishes that song from all others. A case in point is Pîr Micho's performance on video, where the name of the well-known leader Ḥemo Shêro, father of Seydo, is inserted among the heroes, and Dawûdê Dawûd is mentioned instead of his father Dawûdê 'Isa. When challenged on these changes by Pîr Khidir Silêman and others afterwards, Pîr Micho conceded that the inclusion of Dawûdê Dawûd had been a slip of the tongue, that is, a mistake in performance, but said that he had included Ḥemo as a sop to Seydo's son who was in the audience. Later on he hardened his position, saying that Ḥemo had played a valiant part in that engagement, fighting bravely over the body of Kemal (the brother of Osê Mejdî) but that he had not been included in the song for reasons of Sinjari internal politics and rivalries. He, Pîr Micho, was only including him to reflect the truth. Such an addition was clearly considered to be taking a great liberty with the tradition, requiring justification. The *stran* are after all a form of Yezidi history.[6]

So what are we to make of the Yezidis' repeated assertions that the songs do not change? It is clear that Pîr Micho had to explain himself to his audience when he made perceptible alterations to a sensitive area. Among the older Yezidis, there are clearly many Sinjaris and Sheykhanis who can detect such changes. Some of those whom I met were able to recite part of the song, but only a few lines at a time. It is obvious on consideration of performances by different singers that there are not only differences in vocabulary but also in the arrangement of material. However, these differences were not fully acknowledged by informants when they recited sections; they certainly did not say 'This is *Ferîq Pasha* as So-and-so sings it.' If I were to counter with 'So-and-so sings it differently' they would either not accept this, or hint in more or less diplomatic terms that So-and-so was wrong. It seems that the knowledgeable members of the audience have a strong idea of what should and should not be included in this *stran*, but that their concept of it as an oral 'text' does not consider word-for-word uniformity to be crucial. In general, innovation, or introduction of new material into the song, is frowned upon, especially in certain core areas; these include the melody, the key protagonists, and (probably) the key locations. There also seem to be certain key images, such as the sieve, which are strongly associated with that particular *stran*. For the less knowledgeable members of the audiences, particularly the younger Sheykhanis, the songs are more difficult to understand, especially for those performers with a particularly fast delivery. These audience members would not be able to distinguish anything less than major differences clearly and indeed would probably not be very concerned about smaller innovations; for them, the power of the song lies in its expression of emotion and performance technique, and in general phrasing.

Artistry in Performance

It is easy to see that although each performance contains more or less the same elements, there is considerable variety in their arrangement, in the emphasis placed on each, and that each singer is using the elements to craft his own performance. The longest performance is by Lezgîn, but Kheyro Khelef's version has more individual elements which are repeated less often. The stanzas are of varying length even within individual versions. The scope of the musical accompaniment also varies considerably.

Stanzas are clearly marked by musical interludes or pauses between them and may be introduced by different devices.[7] The most common of these is to begin with words expressing strong emotion, such as *lê dayê*, literally 'o mother', or *lê lê*, 'oh, alas' or even *Ezdî o* 'O Yezidi' ('Qarpal' 6: 1, 7: 1; 'Jerdo' 2: 1, 4: 1, 'Kheyro' 7: 1); such expressions of emotion are common in Kurdish lyric. Although many do have literal meanings and are not 'nonsense syllables', they are not always interpreted by their audience in terms of these literal meanings, but add emotional colour. A very common device is to begin a new stanza with the last words of the previous one, as with 'Qarpal's' first two stanzas:

Dilê minî teng e Mîna bû tara bêjingê Xwedê ava neke mala Ferîq Paşa li beyana sibê Ewê mal û malbata şînê ba Sifûqê Meto bavê Berces milkê Feqîra wella Rebenê bi dara zivingê û.	My heart is tight, Like the hoop of a sieve Oh God, do not let the house of Ferîq Pasha be standing at dawn tomorrow, That is a house and home of mourning for Sifûqê Meto, Berjes' father, property of the Feqîran, oh God, Wretched ones by the shady tree. (1: 1–6).
Bi dara zivingê Şad û nişûdêd Osê Mecdîn kekê Kemêl gelek hene ax	By the shady tree The famous ones, the heroes, of Osê Mejdî, Kemal's elder brother, there are many, oh,
Sê denga dibêje Miḥemê 'Evdo bavê Salayê Sifûqê Meto bavê Berces , 'Gelî bav û bira, yê mêrî çêbin, lep hilînin, Bi izna Sultan Êzdî û emê vî ro vê nizamê bişkênînîn û Ce bi xwedê ji îro paşve şer kefte ser derê Kur Bimbarek, ser 'erz û 'eyêl, Ser mîratê darê tifingê'.	He calls three times, to Mihemê Evdo, father of Saleh, Sifûqê Meto, Berjes' father, 'Dear fathers and brothers, do the deeds of men, raise your hands, If Sultan Êzdî permits, we will this day break this system, and As God's my witness, from today onwards war has come upon Kur Bimbarek, on our kith and kin, On the cursed wood of [our] rifles'. (2: 1–7).

This repetition is usually associated with shorter, rather than longer, instrumental breaks between the stanzas. The device of repetition gives a clear opening to the stanza; where there are words of emotion, these set the mood.

'Qarpal's' first seven stanzas are relatively short (less than eight lines long) but thereafter they lengthen to about ten lines; 'Jerdo' begins with shorter stanzas, 'Kheyro' has longer ones. Lezgîn's stanzas are generally longer than eight lines; Kheyro Khelef's are irregular, with the majority longer than eight lines, but no discernible pattern or progression in stanza length. Pîr Micho has a little under or over ten lines. The amount of instrumental accompaniment also varies; 'Qarpal' generally has no musical accompaniment while he sings and very short gaps between stanzas with only a repeated chord. Only when he has finished *Ferîq Pasha* and is moving on to the next song does his musical accompaniment have melody rather than mere repetition of a chord. 'Jerdo' has slow, quiet repeated chords while he sings and melodies between stanzas; these melodic interludes lengthen when his stanzas lengthen. Kheyro Khelef and Lezgîn do not generally play as they sing but do play between stanzas.

The stanzas seem to be arranged with some care. Each singer introduces his song differently but clearly. 'Qarpal''s first stanza consists of introductory remarks about how tragic events are, a curse on the Ferîq, introduction of Sifûqê Meto, and ends with the specific of the *dara zivingê* 'shady tree'. Kheyro Khelef prefers to begin with the action of the army's sudden attack. Lezgîn has the girl calling out. All include the motif of the world being like the circle of a sieve. The repeated lines may be used to considerable effect in the structure of stanzas. 'Qarpal's' second stanza introduces the leaders and outlines their opposition to the Ferîq, adding that war has come into the Yezidis' midst. After stanza 3, which concerns Little Gulê, he returns to the leaders in stanza 4, repeating much of what he said previously, and adding the wish to drive Ferîq Pasha to Kirkuk. The core lines about the famous heroes (as quoted above) are repeated in the middle of stanzas 6, 7, and 8, with different flourishes at the end:

Şad û neşûdêd Osê Mecdîn kekê Kemêl gelek hene, sê denga dibêje Miḥemê 'Evdo bavê Saleh Sifûqê Meto bavê Berces,	The famous ones, the heroes, of Osê Mejdî, Kemal's elder brother, there are many, he calls three times, Mihemê Evdo, father of Saleh, Sifûqê Meto, Berjes' father,
'Gelî bav û bira, mêrî çêbin, lep hilînin,	'Dear fathers and brothers, do the deeds of men, raise your hands,
Bi izna sultan Êzdî, emê îro vê nizamê bişkênînîn,	If Sultan Êzdî permits, we will this day break this force,
Emê berê nizama Ferîq Paşa bidîn mîratê Diyarbakir.	We will drive away this force of Ferîq Pasha to cursed Diyarbakir.'

(6: 6–9).

Şad û neşûdêd Osê Mecdî, kekê Kemêl, gelek hene, sê denga dibêje	The famous ones, the heroes, of Osê Mejdî, Kemal's elder brother, there are many, he calls three times,
Miḥemê 'Evdo bavê Saleh ax Ewî Sifûqê Meto bavê Berces, 'Gelî bav û bira, yê mêrî çêbin, lep hilînin, Bi izna Siltan Êzdî û emê îro vê nizamê bişkênînin û Ce bi Xwedê ji nîro û paşve ev namûs, namûsa Xodê ye, namûsa wî Mîrza, mala koçeka o.'	To Mihemê Evdo, Saleh's father, oh, [To] that Sifûqê Meto, Berjes' father, 'Dear fathers and brothers, do the deeds of men, raise your hands, If Sultan Êzdî permits, we will this day break this force, As God's my witness, from today onwards this honour, this is God's honour, the honour of that Mîrza, of the kochek clan.' (7: 5–10).
Şad û neşûdêd Osê Mecdî, kekê Kemêl gelek hene, sê denga dibêje Miḥemê 'Evdo bavê Saleh ax	The famous ones, the heroes, of Osê Mejdî, Kemal's elder brother, there are many, he calls three times, to Mihemê Evdo, father of Saleh, oh,
Sifûqê Meto bavê Berces, 'Gelî bav û birayê mêrî çêbin, lep hilînin,	Sifûqê Meto, Berjes' father, 'Dear fathers and brothers, do the deeds of men, raise your hands,
Bi izna Siltan Êzdî, serî sê rojî tamam, dewleta ḥukumeta Ferîq Paşa ax, Ce bavo bi tirimbêla xelas nake laşêd kuştîyan û birîndaran.'	If Sultan Êzdî permits, when three days have passed, Ferîq Pasha's government, oh, For certain, they won't have finished collecting the bodies of their killed and wounded in their cars.' (8: 6–9).

The section ending each stanza makes a different point; firstly, the wish to drive Ferîq Pasha to Diyarbakir, (like Kirkuk, a distant place, but in a different direction), then the honour for the Yezidis, and finally, the wish that the government will not be able to collect their dead for three days. Several of 'Qarpal's' stanzas have an obvious parallel structure, with the repetition of the core lines leading the audience on to the varying motifs at the end of the stanza. The structure of 'Jerdo and Kheyro's' performance is very similar. Kheyro Khelef's song is slightly different. He introduces the leaders in his first stanza, and makes them describe their need to protect themselves in the second. The third concerns the girl who comments on the battle and is anxious about one of the fighters. Stanzas 4–6 contain much more description of the site and action of the battle than 'Qarpal' and 'Jerdo and Kheyro', but also include the core lines about the leaders with an expansion of their speeches, building up to the final lines of these stanzas, which are a description of the bloodshed, a wish that the government will not be able to collect its dead for a year and three months, and a wish to drive Ferîq Pasha's army to Kirkuk. Lezgîn's performance also includes repetition of these core lines in different stanzas, but like Kheyro Khelef, he includes a wealth of other details and the result is a more complex product. One of the most noticeable aspects of Lezgîn's structural arrangement is the role played by 'Little' Gulê, who speaks to 'Big' Gulê, and is mentioned far more often than in the other versions. Lezgîn mentions her by name in stanzas 1, 4, 7 and 10; 'Qarpal' only in stanza 3; 'Jerdo' has Gulê in stanza 2, and possibly in 8 with Zerîfka Osê; Kheyro Khelef has Zerîfka Osê addressing a woman called Gulê,[8] in stanza 3. Pîr Micho mentions Gulê only in stanza 2.

After stanza 6 Kheyro Khelef's performance moves into another song, with very similar melody and vocabulary, without warning. He suddenly introduces characters not mentioned elsewhere, and none of the familiar characters are mentioned again. The pause between the end of stanza 6, which states a clear wish to drive Ferîq Pasha's army off towards Kirkuk, and the beginning of stanza 7 which brings in the new characters, is no longer than pauses between other stanzas; the tune does not change, though there are more of the emotional *lê dayê*s than usual at the beginning of this stanza. The audience does not appear to react particularly strongly. One wonders whether Kheyro Khelef felt that this second theme was particularly appropriate for following *Ferîq Pasha*, or whether he felt the performance needed a few more tragic stanzas, and this was well-remembered and convenient. Whichever is true, this example shows the degree of freedom with which songs may progress from one to another during a performance.

Kheyro Khelef's performance of his *Ferîq Pasha* stanzas is a good example of how the *stranbêj* uses his skill to fashion traditional elements into a performance. He may fairly be described as the most flamboyant of the singers; he is certainly one of the most famous and admired of the Sinjari *stranbêj*. His performance here is enthusiastically received by its audience, and some of the devices he uses are worth noting as they are typical of the genre. In this performance, he does not generally play while he sings; when his substantial melodic interludes between stanzas finish, all attention is thus on his singing.

He moves into *Ferîq Pasha* from another stran, *'Ebdelleh Beg*. Although the music does not stop, he signals to the audience that a new song is coming by changing the melody. His first stanza sets the mood with an introduction of *lê dayê*, sung slowly:

Lê lê dayê	Alas, alas, mother,
Lê dayê ax	Alas, mother, oh,
Lê belê Xodê zane vê sibê 'esker bi ser me dihatin, dinya li me teng bû weke tara bêjingê,	Yes, God knows, this morning soldiers came upon us, our world became narrow as the hoop of a sieve,

Lê lê Xodê zane gelek hene şade û nişûdê Osê Mecdî kekê Kemal,	Oh, God knows, there are many, the famous ones, the heroes, of Osê Mejdî, Kemal's elder brother,
Ewî Dawûdê 'Isa babê Dewê, Ewe Mihemedê Osê xodê zanibe Sifûqê Meto babê Berces, Ewî Mihemê 'Evdo siwarê Bozê babê Saleh, Belê wellah sê denga gazî dike segmanê Êzîdiya, sêwir û tekbîrêd giran dane ra- Serî geliyê Kirsê bin dara zivingê.	That Dawûdê 'Isa, Dawûd's father, That Mihemedê Osê, God knows, Sifûqê Meto, Berjes' father, 'Miḥemê 'Evdo, rider of Bozê, Saleh's father, Yes, by God, he calls three times to the Yezidi marksmen, he stirs them up with great thoughts, Above the Kirsê valley under the shady tree.

He puts the initial information of the attack and the comment (that the world is as narrow as a sieve) into one long line, sung very quickly, after which he repeats a chord several times before beginning the next line. He then moves on to the heroes' names, but instead of putting them all into two or even one line, they are spread out over four, lingering on the last syllables of those names that are at the end of the line. He only spends so long over the names in this introductory stanza, not in later stanzas. As he finishes their names, he provides a 'false climax', as it were, to the stanza by lowering the pitch as if he were finishing the stanza; however, he lets the discerning among the audience know that this is not really the end by refraining from playing during the last word. (When a stanza is really at an end, Kheyro begins to strum during the last word or so). He then finishes setting the scene by saying that Miḥemê 'Evdo cried out three times, but not going into details of what he said, and by locating him at a specific geographical point – the shady tree near a particular valley.

'Ah!', 'Oh!' say the audience appreciatively as he performs a melodic interlude, at the end of which he signals the beginning of the new stanza with rhythmic repeated chords, and recalls them to the song by repeating the last words of the previous stanza:

Belê bira li bin dara zivingê Gelek hene şade û nişûdêd Miḥemê 'Evdo bavê Saleh,	Yes brothers, under the shady tree, There are many, the famous ones, the heroes of Miḥemê 'Evdo, Saleh's father,
Sê denga gazî dike, 'Segmane Êzîdiya bikin bilezînin, berê xwe ji kozik û çepera megêrînin,	He calls three times, 'Yezidi marksmen, act now, be busy, don't turn your gaze from their trenches and dugouts,
Ew çavê xwe ji nizamê Ferîq Paşa ẍalibe girane mane metirsînin,	Don't let your eyes be frightened of Ferîq Pasha's overwhelming forces,

'Erz û 'eyal gûlî sorê xwe vê sibê ji destê nizamê bifikînin,	Liberate your kith and kin, your red-braids this morning from the hand of [his] force,
Ce bi Xodê destê me ji gulî sorê me qut be	As God's my witness, let our hands be separated from our red-braids,
Destê me da nema ẍêrî tifingê.	In our hands there is nothing left but the gun.'

He gives his audience the leader's speech they have been waiting for, stressing the fact that the Yezidis are defending what is dearest to them.

Stanzas 3 and 4 focus on Zerîfka Osê, her anxieties and what she has seen of the battle. However, more detail of the battle itself, as viewed from above, is given in stanza 5. Its beginning parallels stanza 4, which began:

Lê dayê	Alas, mother,
Lê dayê diyarî min û kûrana Bekira bişewite wa bi bera,	Oh, let my region and the Bekiran valley burn, stones and all,
	(4: 1–2).

Stanza 5 begins in a very similar way, and its first two lines are greeted by *Tew, tew!* 'Bravo!' from the audience:

Lê dayê, lê dayê,	Alas, mother,
Diyarî min û kûrana Bekira bişewite wa bi kaşa	Let my region and Bekiran valley burn up, hills and all,
Xwedê danî ser çemê Zoqayê li gundê me Girê 'Ereba, sê bêlûkêd giranê ji 'eskerê Ferîq Paşa,	By God, they attacked by the river Zoqa, at our village, Girê 'Ereba, three full companies of Ferîq Pasha's army,
Ew minê dêna xo dayê, bi destê pêyayêd Şingariya kitekitê reşoka mîratêd Hadî Paşa,	I was looking at it, in the hands of the Sinjari foot-soldiers, the musket-fire of Hadî Pasha's cursed ones,
Di destê pêyayêd 'eskerê Ferîq Paşa mîratêd topa, Xodê zane dîsa dubarî van reşaşa	In the hands of Ferîq Pasha's infantry, the cursed cannon, God knows, again the repeating machine-guns,
Ew minê dênê xwe dayê, binê 'eskerê meşiya li aliya ẍerbî ṛa gehişte birka 'Êlî Paşa	I was looking at it, below the soldiers, below the army was marching, on the western side 'Elî Pasha's regiment arrived,
Belê li aliya şerqê ṛa kete çemê Reşe, gelek hene şad û nişûde xortêd Ûsiva xortêd Mêrka û Bekira,	Yes, to the east, where the river Resha is, they are many, there are many, the famous, the heroes, Ûsivan lads, Mêrkan and Bekiran lads,
Ew dibêjê,'Gelî bav û bira mêrî çêbin, lep hilînin enişka bi kozika meteresa bikutînin,	He said, 'Dear fathers and brothers, do the deeds of men, raise your hands, elbows to the trenches, strike their positions,

Ew çeqmaqê tifinga rakin îşeka tê bixînin.	Raise the bolts of your rifles, load them with cartridges.
Bela ji pê 'eskerê Ferîq Paşa venagerîn mala saleke sê heyva,	May this army of Ferîq Pasha not return home for a year and three months,
Bi Xodê koç û erebanê ḥukumetê li çemê Bekira xelas nekin meytan û laşa.'	By God, may those coaches and carts of the Government at the river Bekiran not finish with their bodies, their corpses.'

This description of the battle, gives more details of its location, action and participants than before. The lines are quite long and all performed at great speed, with usually only one breath per line. It seems that the ability to sing long lines is prestigious, and is part of that same ability to sing for a long time without forgetting or losing one's voice which is so esteemed by the Yezidis; certainly a succession of several long lines forming a substantial stanza seems to please audiences. Kheyro and the others often lengthen lines by adding such emphatic words as *mane*, *weleh* and *lê belê* or even *mi dî* 'I saw'; some of these long lines receive appreciative shouts of *tew*.

Comparison of these performances of *Ferîq Pasha* shows that although the ingredients and much of the phraseology of the *stran* are fixed, the *stranbêj* has the freedom to structure the material as he sees fit for the purposes of his performance. However, perceptible innovation is frowned upon.

Dawûdê Dawûd

Dawûdê Dawûd was a chief of the Mêrkan, or Mihirkan, of Mount Sinjar in the first half of the twentieth century. Described by Edmonds as 'the stormy petrel of Sinjar', (1967: 62) he is well known throughout the Yezidi, Muslim and Christian communities of Badinan for his resistance to the government.[9]

The key feature of Dawûd's political activity was his opposition to the British appointment of Ḥemo Shêro as paramount 'Chief of the Mountain' at the end of the Great War, a title he held until his death in his nineties in 1933. The Yezidis called him 'the Pasha of the mountain'; he received a salary of 600 rupees from the government (Lescot 1938: 184). In terms of State systems of authority, his significance was limited, and he had no official position in the local Iraqi administration (Fuccaro 1999: 92); however, among the Yezidis, according to Empson (1928: 95), the position of 'Chief of the Mountain' was second only to that of the Mîr in temporal terms. There seems to have been some difference between Yezidi perceptions of authority and those of the government. For years Ḥemo had taken a resolutely anti-Turkish stance; as we have seen, oral tradition (sometimes) assigns him an honourable role in the conflict with the forces of 'Umar Wehbī Pasha, and a number of Christians remained under his protection during the War and afterwards.

Dawûd's objections to Ḥemo were not merely personal; Ḥemo and his tribe, the Feqîran, which had only come to prominence in the time of his father, were regarded with suspicion by many of the longer-established Sinjari tribes. Dawûd was a traditional leader of aristocratic tribal background; he described Ḥemo as a 'beggar' who had first relied on the commoners and then on the British and Iraqis (Edmonds 1967: 63). Empson (*loc. cit.*) notes that one of the main sources of conflict with Ḥemo Shêro was the contrast between Dawûd's religious conservatism and Ḥemo's lack of orthodoxy. Dawûd was aligned during the last years of Ottoman rule and later in the 1920s with a number of tribes of a broadly 'pro-Muslim' complexion, which contained Muslims as well as Yezidis, and also included certain anti-Christian figures such as 'Eto and Meto of the Habbabat. Although in earlier years he might have been in a position to receive government support, it seems unlikely that by the end of the War Dawûd himself was pro-Turkish, given that he and Ḥemo led the tribesmen to shelter in the caves of Sinjar from an Ottoman attack in 1918 (Guest 1993: 180). He was apparently hostile to all external government forces, and became more so with the passing of time, and his alliance was not so much 'pro-Muslim' as 'anti-Ḥemo' (Fuccaro 1999: 96). Although Ḥemo retained his office to the end of his life, in his old age much of his administrative work was carried out by his son Khodêda, who, according to Lescot (1938: 184), had not inherited his prestige, though he was recognised by the Iraqi government (on whom he relied for his authority) as Ḥemo's successor. Dawûd continued to challenge Ḥemo whenever possible. For example, when in his eighties, Ḥemo abducted the fifteen-year-old daughter of a Feqîran chief and refused to pay compensation to her father, Muradê Serhan. British attempts to intervene did not succeed, and when Dawûd took the side of the father, open war almost broke out and was narrowly averted (Lescot 1938: 184). Edmonds (1967: 61) remarks that by this time Ḥemo had become 'a despotic old dotard'.

Dawûdê Dawûd rebelled openly against the government twice. The first rebellion, over the period 1924–5, centred on Dawûd's opposition to Ḥemo's status; the amount of support given to Dawûd from other tribes on the Mountain shows the strength of anti-Ḥemo feeling there. Many tribes were fragmented, with some sections following Ḥemo and others following Dawûd. Fuccaro's account rightly counsels against any interpretation of these events as a popular uprising against national government, because it was so localised (1999: 101); nevertheless, Dawûd himself was implacably opposed to the government, even offering in 1924 to make common cause with Ḥemo in an anti-government alliance. He became a symbol of resistance locally and both Yezidi and wider Kurdish discourses now give him a much broader significance in the history of the Kurdish struggle.

After various initial skirmishes, the decisive event remembered in Yezidi accounts of the time is the bombing by the RAF of the villages of Zêrwan and Mêrkan where Dawûd was based. This took place over several days, whilst Dawûd's allies, Sheykh Khelef of the Haskan and Sheykh Khidir of the Qîran, fought against Ḥemo's forces elsewhere. Although *The Times* of 21 April 1925 blandly mentions planes escorting armoured cars sent to 'overawe' Dawûd it is clear that this, one of the earlier instances of the British policy of using air power to subdue troublesome colonial populations, was much more heavy and hostile than was publicly admitted, even allowing for some exaggeration in contemporary Yezidi accounts of hundreds dead and wounded. One of the planes was brought down by Sinjari rifle-fire.

Dawûd's second rebellion, in late 1935, was over the sensitive issue of military service. Under the British mandate, which ended in 1932, there had been no compulsory military service; attempts from 1924 onwards to form an all-Yezidi squadron within the Iraq Levies, initially intended to bring the tribes closer to the British, had foundered in the late 1920s due to Yezidi non-cooperation (Browne 1932: 33; Fuccaro 1999: 111–2). However, in 1934 the newly independent Iraqi government passed the National Defence Law, which initiated compulsory service. This law seems also to have met with mixed reactions outside the Yezidi community. *L'Asie française* (août-sept 1935: 241) reported that despite the justification of the law by the minister of defence, Ja'far Pasha al-'Askeri, on the grounds that it would give Iraq greater security, many Iraqis were unhappy with it and considerable numbers of young men born between 1914 and 1917 were attempting to leave the country and having their passports withheld. Within the Yezidi community the law must have caused consternation, but when Dawûd's refusal to register the Mêrkan for service became an open revolt, none of the other Sinjari chiefs followed him; indeed Sinjari villages loyal to the government were used as a base by the government forces in their armed response (Lescot 1938: 192–3). Although Longrigg (1953: 242) describes the battle itself as 'bloodless', the Yezidi oral tradition differs; it is clear that government forces won a decisive victory. Dawûd took refuge in Syria with the Arab chieftain Daḥḥam al-Hadi, who, like Dawûd, was feuding with the Shammar Sheykh 'Ajīl. According to Lescot (1938: 187) Daḥḥam attempted unsuccessfully to convert Dawûd to Islam. Dawûd was soon arrested and interned.

According to several accounts, government reprisals were brutal, no doubt because the rebellion was construed as evidence of the perceived threat posed to the Iraqi state by the non-Muslim minorities, a feeling which had also led to massacres of Christians in 1933. Those responsible received severe sentences and certain Christians whose role in Dawûd's rebellion was unclear, but who were known to have been associated with earlier activity on behalf of non-Muslims, were executed. Mêrkan villages were burned. However, many of those imprisoned were released within the next year through the intervention of C. J. Edmonds with Rashid 'Ali, Minister of the Interior, and, after the coup of October 1936, with the new Prime Minister Ḥikmat Sulayman (Lescot 1938: 193; Edmonds 1967: 63–4; Fuccaro 1999: 165).

Whether present, or absent as fugitive or prisoner, Dawûd's influence was felt on Mount Sinjar. After his flight to Syria in 1935, many of his supporters tried to join him (Longrigg 1953: 242). When Edmonds visited Sinjar for the last time in 1945, he was petitioned for Dawûd's release by Sheykh Beḥrî, guardian of one of the shrines of Sherefedîn (1967: 69).

Dawûdê Dawûd: The Oral Traditions

Dawûd is part of living memory, commemorated in various forms of oral tradition. Here I will consider the *stran* called *Dawûdê Dawûd* and an account of his life given by his son 'Emer to Khelîl Jindî Rashow in 1977 (Silêman and Jindî 1979: 185ff). The two *Dawûdê Dawûd stran* performances given here are from different sources. One is from my own collection of pre-recorded material, and the other was recorded by Jelîlê Jelîl in Syria (Jelîl 1985: 156). I have used Jindî's account of Dawûd mainly because I was unable to secure any kind of detailed description of the man or of his career in my own interviews. Most Sheykhanis claimed they did not know the story in enough detail to tell it to me. I did have a brief meeting with a Sinjari who remembered him well, but I was unable to arrange to come again to Ba'drê, where he lived, at a time when he was there. He described Dawûd as 'a small red man, always in prison or waging war'; despite Dawûd's ordinary appearance, he considered him to be an extraordinary man, and admired him enormously.

Khelîl Jindî Rashow wrote in the introduction to his interview with Dawûd's son (and has since confirmed to me) that it comes from the mouth of 'Emerê Dawûd. It can be seen that some nominal and verbal forms are slightly 'normalised' towards those of the Sheykhani dialect of Silêman and Jindî rather than the Sinjari of 'Emerê Dawûd. Thus the transcription has third person singular verbal forms such as *biçit* 'he goes', the subjunctive *bistînit* '(may) he take'; in the Sinjari dialect, these ought to be *biçe*, *bistîne*. The common verb 'to fall' is given as *keftin*; in Sinjari we would expect *ketin*. (Blau 1975: 61–2, 65). However, the transcription convincingly follows the rhythms and patterns of spoken anecdote. Direct speech is directly introduced, and the person of the verb is not changed, as in *'Emerê Dawûd digot tête bîra min* ... "Emerê Dawûd said, I recall ...' and *belê 'Emerê Dawûd dibêjit babê min* ... 'But, 'Emerê Dawûd says, my father ...'. Later in the account, explanations of Sinjari names are put into the form of footnotes, presumably to avoid detracting from the flow of the narrative.[10] Strong opinions, no doubt 'Emer's own, are expressed.

The two relevant *stran* performances which I have included in Part II are both known as *Dawûdê Dawûd*. One is by the Syrian *stranbêj* Silo Koro and the other by 'Pîr Qewwal', the pseudonym of a relation of Pîr Giro and Pîr Micho. I will not discuss their performance techniques in any detail; one is taken from a published work (Jelîl 1985) which does not include an account of the performance, and the recording I have in my own collection uses techniques to enhance the performance which are typical of the Sinjari *stranbêj*, and which I have outlined in my description of the *Ferîq Pasha* traditions. At this stage I will make some brief observations on the differences between the two, and on the arrangement of material, and will include a few quotations to give a flavour of the song.

Both versions are variants of the same song, though Silo's is longer and seems more complete. Each begins with painful emotions and with an arresting image, of plucking the head off the partridge and lily, both beautiful things in the imagery of Kurdish folklore; this is expressed by a woman called Shêrîn, who is mourning the loss of her son Memo. She calls for help, which does not come. Silo's performance adds a comment about the treachery of other Sinjaris; his first stanza is as follows:

Lê dayê, lê dayê, lê dayê,	Alas, oh mother, alas, alas,
Şêrînê digo, 'Memo, lawo, pêjna Memê min nayê,	Shêrîn said, 'Memo, my lad, the figure of my Memo doesn't come to me,
Bira serê kewê sorî sosinî jêkin,	Let them pluck off the head of the partridge, red as an iris,
Bigeṛênin li devê dayrê qehwocaẍê bi Beẍdayê ,	Let them bring it as far as the office of the head of barracks in Baghdad.
Bira navê kuştina Memo bela bibe li dinyayê,	Let the news of the killing of Memo become a disaster in the world.
Reşoyê Qulo xêrê nebîne şeṛ jê nayê,	May Resho Qulo not see good fortune, there is no fighting from him,
Ḥisênê Berces kiçûk û mezinê çiyayê Şengalê anîne ṛayê,	Ḥuseyn Berjes made the great and the small of Mount Sinjar change their opinion,
Ezê çi bikim, berê xortê cana dane sefera Kerbelayê,	What shall I do? He sent our handsome lads off to Kerbela,
Berê Dawûdê Dawûd, bavê Hadî, keke 'Eyşanê, ketiye sefera ser Ḥilayê.'	Dawûdê Dawûd, Hadi's father, 'Eyshan's elder brother, made the journey to Hillah.'

The personalities mentioned are consistent, though there seems to be a little garbling.

Like the *Ferîq Pasha* stran, the fighters are addressed and encouraged to fight well. Both performances phrase this in a similar way:

Dawûdê Dêwûd bi sê denga gazî dike 'Ûdêmê Ḥezo Ḥesoke Hemzî Silemanê Mehmûd,bavê me, mêrî çêbikin bixebitin,	Dawûdê Dawûd calls out three times to Ûdêmê Ḥezo, Ḥesokê Hemzî, Silêmanê Meḥmûd, 'Oh you fathers of ours, do the work of men, keep struggling,
Vê sibê hûnê dest hilînin . . . mêra bikujin xwîna narincî ber 'erdê weşînin, Destê xwe li qebdê xencera bişidînin, Çavê xwe ji bêlûkê 'eskera, nizama Înglîzî bişkînin,	This morning you will raise your hand, . . . kill men, make the orange blood pour forth on the earth, Squeeze the handle of your daggers in your hands, [Don't take] your eye from the companies of soldiers, break the English force,
Bira vê sibêkê dîsayê, Em dest bi kiçik û mezinê Êzdiyê çiyayê Şingalê bikin, . . . textê 'emrê Gezî bergehê wê Beẍdayê. . .'	This morning again let it happen, We will begin with the great and small of the Yezidis of Mount Sinjar, . . . the throne in the time of Ghazi . . . the view of Baghdad. . .' ('Pîr Qewwal' 3: 6–12).

In their description of the battle, both mention the arrival of the army of Sheykh 'Isa Effendi, though Silo adds other details: Memo shot down a warplane, Silêmanê Meḥmûd stabbed a man holding a rifle, the sound of weapons 'stirred up the world' and 'set the world on fire'. Both site the action near the the peak of Chilmêra and the wood in the Bekiran valley; both allude to the barracks of Baghdad and Kerbela and Hillah, in the South of Iraq, where some of Dawûd's fighters were exiled and imprisoned.

As with the *Ferîq Pasha stran*, each performer arranges the material in his own way. Silo has two long stanzas together (5 and 6) but in general alternates long stanzas with short repeated refrains (2, 4, 7) calling for help which does not come and saying that Sinjar is treacherous. Stanza 4 is as follows:

De nayê, de nayê, Şêrînê digo, 'Ezê hawar dikim, hawar nayê, Hawar heye, lê hindad ji me ra nayê, Ez çi bikim, qublit û şemalê çîyayê Şengalê ṭemam xayînin,	Oh, it doesn't come, it doesn't come, Shêrîn said 'I am calling for help, help doesn't come, There is help, but real help doesn't come to me. What shall I do? The South and the North of Mount Sinjar are full of treachery.
Kesek di hawar û hindada Dawûdê Dawûd bavê Hadî kekê Eyşanê li min nayê.	No-one comes to me with real help for Dawûdê Dawûd, Hadi's father, Eyshan's elder brother.

'Pîr Qewwal' has a similar short stanza, also used as a refrain (1, 2, 4). Silo focuses more strongly on Shêrîn and Memo; both *stranbêj* open with Sherîn's anxieties about him, but Silo comes back to him in stanzas 3, 5 and 6. Stanza 5, given below, includes his reply to her, telling her about his exploits in the battle. The pathos of the lost son addressing his mother in this stanza is obvious:

Lê, lê, lê dayê, lê, lê, lê dayê, Şêrînê digo, 'Memo lawo, şeṛeke qewimî li dara geliyê Bekira, li gaza Çilemêri, li navsera çiyayê Şengalê, Ji xema dilê min û te ṛa li wî banî,	Alas, alas mother, alas mother, Shêrîn said, 'Memo, my lad, a battle happened at the wood in Bekiran valley, in the district of Chilmêra, in the middle of Mount Sinjar, To the pain of your heart and mine in this high place,
Me qaleke giran danîbû li navsera çiyayê Şengalê li wî banî, Mi dî 'eskerê Şêx 'Isa Efendî, baş qumandarê dewletê Ḥusêîn Foucê Paşa bi 'emrê melik Ẍazî, li kozik û çeperê Memo, bi hewa kete banî,	We made a great noise in the middle of Mount Sinjar, in this high place, We saw the soldiers of Sheykh 'Isa Effendi, the commander-in-chief of the country of Huseyn Fewzî Pasha by command of king Ghazi, at Memo's trenches and dugouts, they flew overhead.'
Giṛegiṛa midiṛi'a, dengê reşaş û bêlafiṛa dinya tev hilanî,	The firing of Mausers, the noise of automatic rifles and aircraft stirred up the world,
Şêrînê digo, 'Memo lawo, pêjna Memê min nayê,	Shêrîn said, 'Memo, young man, the figure of my Memo doesn't come to me,
Ez nizanim Memê mi kanî.' Memê digo, 'Yadê, ezî vame, Li pêşiya bêlûk 'eskerê Şerîfo ṛawestame, Wexta mi dest davîte desgîra tivingê, derpa 'ewil mi lêdabû, şifêrê bêlafira bi çengekî, Mi nehîşt ew teyara ḥerbî bi xêr û silamet bi hewa keve banî.'	I don't know where my Memo is.' Memo said, 'Oh mother, I'm here, I have stopped in front of the company of Sherifo's soldiers When I put my hand to the grip of my gun, my first shot hit the pilot of the plane in the arm. I didn't allow that warplane to fly over in peace.'

Silo stresses Shêrîn's role; she makes the exhortatory speech, (3: 5–10); as noted above, 'Pîr Qewwal' has Dawûd himself address the fighters (3: 6–10). Until the point at which 'Pîr Qewwal' breaks off, both *stranbêj* cover much the same ground. It is clear that the same body of material is being varied in performance as with the *Ferîq Pasha* songs, though there is a lesser degree of variation, as one would expect from a more recently composed song.

Derwêshê ʿEvdî

The geographical extent of this tradition over Iraq, Georgia and Armenia is one indication of its appeal. Its hero, Derwêsh, is not only a martial hero but also loves 'Edûlê, the daughter of his paramount chieftain, Zor Temer Pasha. He is a Yezidi and his beloved is a Muslim, and their love ends tragically. This love is the focus of most tellings of the tradition in Northern Iraq, and I will examine this further in the next chapter. However, narrative poems have also been composed which emphasise his exploits in battle. Admittedly, these are now rarely performed among the Yezidis of Northern Iraq; I did not manage to collect any, but since my return from the field I have been reliably informed of some performances given by Northern Iraqi Yezidi singers. The examples I will present here were collected by the Jelîls in the former Soviet Union; they may well not be quite the same as those being performed among Iraqi Yezidis, but they present Derwêsh as a Kurdish martial hero in terms highly consistent with other Kurdish epics such as *Dimdim*. This type of hero is quite common across wide areas of Kurdistan, and these performances are worth considering because the terms in which their hero is presented would be very familiar to the older Yezidis at least.

The Yezidis believe that Derwêsh, 'Edûlê and Zor Temer Pasha are all historical individuals; given the amount and nature of the information still preserved about them, there is no good reason to doubt this. According to Jelîl's ZK, Zor Temer Pasha, 'Edûlê's father, was the father of Ibrahim Pasha Milli, which would place him in the mid-late nineteenth century. I have been unable to date the events of the story more precisely. According to ZK (Jelîl 1978, II: 475), the story retained its significance in the time of Silêman Beg, the son of Ibrahim Pasha, who did not want it to be told because it showed his family as responsible for Derwêsh's death. Derwêsh, according to Jelîl, belonged to the Pashê section of the Milli confederation; the Yezidis of this group were settled mostly round the Viranşehir area in Turkey after the end of the Ottoman empire, with some villages in Syria (1985: 312).

Detailed accounts of the performances included in ZK are not available, so this discussion will by necessity consider them as texts. There are two substantial narrative poems, by Israel Ohanyan and 'Egitê Têjir. These also contain some lyrical sections. The other *Derwêshê 'Evdî* songs collected by Jelîl are predominantly lyrical with short narrative sections, some of which are exactly the same as parts of the narrative poems. There is clearly a close relationship between the narrative and lyrical traditions in the Caucasus. In all of Jelîl's versions, the name Derwêsh has metathesised to 'Dewrêsh'.

The performance by Israel Ohanyan, an Armenian singer, is an 'epic' style narrative poem. The singer, clearly a virtuoso from his many contributions to the Jelîls' collection, had learned his songs among the

Reshkotan, a Kurdish tribe in the Diyarbakir area, unlike other performers who had lived all their lives in the Caucasus. Hence it is hardly surprising that the contents of this poem are rather different from the others. This performance may be summarised briefly thus:

A prose introduction (spoken) describes 'Evdî's prowess in fighting for Zor Temer Pasha, the friendship between the two men, and the love between Derwêsh, 'Evdî's son, and 'Edûlê. The Gêsan, an Arab tribe, gather at their *dîwanxane* 'guest-hall', and send a message to Zor Temer Pasha of the Milan that they will attack and massacre his tribe. This message is received at Zor Temer Pasha's *dîwanxane*, where everyone is terrified; 'Edûlê suggests asking Derwêsh for help. She writes to Derwêsh[11] explaining the situation. When he receives the message Derwêsh reads it to his father 'Evdî and his brother Se'dûn, and tells them that Zor Temer Pasha and 'Edûlê have offered 'Edûlê's hand to whoever will fight. Derwêsh asks his father to let him take Se'dûn, 'Elî and Bozan, and fight. 'Evdî weeps and tries to dissuade him by telling him that Zor Temer Pasha is dishonourable, but Derwêsh cannot stop thinking of 'Edûlê. Derwêsh goes to the *dîwankhane* of Zor Temer Pasha, claims 'Edûlê by accepting a cup of coffee from her, and leaves. Derwêsh and his companions ride away, and both Derwêsh's father and 'Elî and Bozan's mother beg 'Edûlê to intercede. 'Edûlê goes after Derwêsh and pleads with him, but he rejects her pleas. Derwêsh and 'Edûlê kiss. Derwêsh urges his comrades on, and they leave.

The comrades stop by a stream, and Derwêsh goes ahead to reconnoitre. He finds an encampment, and meets some young girls, who are afraid of him. He accompanies them to a tent where he meets an old man, a former comrade of 'Evdî, who tells him where the Gêsan are, and tries to dissuade him from fighting one thousand Gêsan warriors in a quarrel that is not his, but belongs to Zor Temer Pasha. Derwêsh is not persuaded and returns to his friends. The comrades ride together until they see the Gêsan warriors and attack them. In the first attack two hundred Gêsan, and 'Elî (the champion of Zor Temer Pasha) and Silêman are killed. In the second attack four hundred Gêsan and Se'dûn are killed. Yusif the scribe records Derwêsh's valour. Derwêsh kills another three hundred; the other, 'Elî, the Yezidi, and Bozan are killed. Derwêsh kills another fifty, but his horse trips and he falls, and is killed by the remaining fifty warriors and the two Gêsan leaders. Yusif the scribe returns to Zor Temer Pasha with the news. 'Edûlê hears the news and weeps, and makes a lyrical lament for Derwêsh. Then she stabs herself.

One characteristic feature of oral narrative which is immediately obvious in this performance is the repetition of entire sections, such as the contents of the threatening letter from the Gêsan. Equally obvious are the instances where the singer 'nods', such as Derwêsh's saying to his father that 'Edûlê's hand has been offered to whoever will fight, when no previous mention has been made of this.[12] However, these are insignificant in comparison with the clear structure and skilful characterisation of this telling. It is a highly developed narrative containing many elements which do not occur elsewhere, and each of the characters speaks plausibly and appropriately. The following section, stanza 9, illustrates the calibre of the performance, its detail and its focus on the crucial moment when Derwêsh claims 'Edûlê and thus seals his own fate:

Bi Dewrêş ṛa siwar bû 'Elî û Bozan, Se'dûnê birane,	Elî and Bozan, and Se'dûn his brother rode with Derwêsh,
Ev herçar derketin, berê xo dane dîwana Zor Temer Paşayê Milane.	All four rode out and made for the guest-hall of Zor Temer Pasha of the Milan.
Giregir fêriz û pelewanê Kîka û Mila di dîwana Zor Temer Paşa da li hev civiyane.	The big, the brave and the champions of the Kîkan and Milan were gathered in the guest-hall of Zor Temer Pasha.
Dibê, Dewrêş nêzîk bû devê derê dîwana wane,	They say, Derwêsh drew near to the door of their guest-hall,
Hidman çev bi miḥîna ket, bû ḥîşîna Hidmane,	Hidman's eye fell on a mare, there was a loud neigh from Hidman,
Alê dîwanê se kirin ḥîşîna Hidmane,	The people in the guest-hall heard the neighing of Hidman,
Gotin, 'Ev Dewrêşê 'Evdî hate dîwana girane'.	They said, 'This is Derwêshê 'Evdî who has come to the great guest-hall.'
Dewrêş û 'Elî û Bozan û Se'dûnê bira peya bûn ji hespane,	Derwêsh and 'Elî and Bozan and Se'dûn his brother got down from their horses,
Kişiyane dîwana girane,	Drew near to the great guest-hall,
Tev ji ber Dewrêş ṛa ṛabûn û sekinîn ji piyane.	Everyone got up from respect for Derwêsh and stayed on their feet.
Dewrêş ṛûnişt li ser doşeka ḥerba girane,	Derwêsh sat down on the cushion of great battles,
Li tenişta wî ṛûnişt 'Elî û Bozan û Se'dûnê birane.	By his side sat 'Elî and Bozan and Se'dûn his brother.
'Edûlê se kir, ko Dewrêş hate dîwana girane,	'Edûlê saw that Derwêsh had come into the great hall,
Fîncana qawê danî ser destane,	She took a cup of coffee in her hand,
Anî geṛand li nava fêriz û pelewanê Kîkan û Milane,	She carried it around among the brave and the champions of the Kîkan and Milan,
Çû sekinî li ber Dewrêş, vî fêriz û pelewanê hane,	She came up to Derwêsh, this brave man, this champion, and stopped,
Dewrêş ṛabû piya, fîncana qawê hilanî ser destane,	Derwêsh rose to his feet, took up the cup of coffee in his hands,
Qawe danî ser dev û lêvane,	Held the cup to his mouth, his lips,

Di nava odêda devê xo xiste ḥinarê rûyê ‘Edûlê û ṛamûsane.	In the middle of the room, he put his mouth to ‘Edûlê’s cheek, lovely as a pomegranate, and kissed her.

The poem contains a series of encounters with others who try to dissuade Derwêsh from entering into an impossible battle. ‘Evdî tries to undermine Derwêsh’s loyalty to Zor Temer Pasha (7: 5–15), ‘Edûlê, at Derwêsh’s parents’ instigation, says that Derwêsh’s family is without a master if he leaves with his brother (11: 2–4), and the old Gêsan man tells Derwêsh that Zor Temer Pasha’s quarrel is not his (15: 36–9). These points in the narrative will be examined more closely later in the chapter.

The other *Derwêshê ‘Evdî* narrative presented by Jelîl is performed by ‘Egîtê Têjir of the Ḥesenî tribe, who were among the earliest Yezidi immigrants from Turkey into Russian Armenia in the early 19th century (Guest 1993: 193). A ‘Mîr’ (not identified further) calls for Derwêsh. When he arrives, the Mîr asks him how many men a man can face in the heat of war. Derwêsh replies that a man would be brave to fight. The Mîr has him bound. ‘Edûlê sees him and scolds the Mîr, who has Derwêsh released and proposes going hunting the next day. A servant comes to fetch Derwêsh, and he saddles his horse. They go to the ‘Egyptian garden’, and the Mîr asks Derwêsh for meat from a young gazelle; eating gazelle is taboo for Yezidis (Kreyenbroek 1995: 149). Derwêsh criticises the request, but complies. The Mîr falls asleep. Derwêsh keeps watch and sees seventeen hundred warriors of Ḥisênê Jerdê; he wakes the Mîr, who asks Derwêsh to take him away. Derwêsh says he will fight. He attacks the Jerdan (obviously, with no hope of survival); women watching wonder at his valour. ‘Edûlê says that but for the shame it would cause to her family, she would have cried out that she belonged to Derwêsh and not to them.

This is also a developed narrative, though it is noticeable that the enemy is different and that the Zor Temer Pasha figure is simply called ‘Mîr’ (an ‘emir’ rather than the Yezidi Mîr of Sheykhan); ‘Edûlê is named, and it is clear that she is from the Kîkan, a group within the confederation of the Milan. Many of the interactions between Derwêsh and the Mîr are reminiscent of other stories of Kurdish oral literature, such as those tellings of *Dimdim* which trace a complex relationship between the hero and the Persian Shah. The first four stanzas are enough to demonstrate that this is rather different from the telling of Israel Ohanyan; there is far less detail. Indeed, at times, the story moves rather abruptly:

Mîro go, ‘Kuro, cot qewaz, ṛabin pêye,	Mîr said ‘Boy, you two bodyguards, get to your feet,
Gazî Dewrêşê ‘Evdî kin, bira bê yalê dîwanxanêye!’	Call Derwêshê ‘Evdî, let him come to the side of the guest-hall!’
Wexta Dewrêş hate yalê dîwanêye,	When Derwêsh came to the side of the guest-hall,

Mîr go, 'Dewrêşo lawo, min ṛa bêje rastiyêye,
Çika ṛojê oẍirmê giran, ṛeqe ṛeqe darê darṛima, firxînê me'negiya, nalînê şêr û 'erfûta, ḥawe ḥawê lawê kurmanca, mêr beranberî çend mêra dertêye?'

Mîr said, 'Derwêsh lad, tell me the truth,
On the day of heavy destiny, with the crashing of wood on wood, the waggons and horses, the wailing of lionhearts and heroes, the shouting of young Kurmancî lads, how many men can a man face?

Dewrêş go, 'Serê mîrê xwe kim, bi ṛastiyêye,
Ṛojê oẍirmê giran, wexta ṛeqe ṛeqe darê darṛîma, firxînê me'negiya, nalînê şêr û 'erfûta, ḥawe ḥawê lawê kurmanca, çiqas merî çê be ancax mêr beranberî mêr dertêye'.'

Derwêsh said, 'I swear on the head of my king, truly,
On the day of heavy destiny, with the crashing of wood on wood, the waggons and horses, the wailing of lionhearts and heroes, the shouting of young Kurmancî lads, how brave a man would be if he were to come out to face another man.'

Mîr got, 'Kuṛo, cot qewaz, ṛabin pêye!
Nigê Dewrêş bavne qeydêye!
Stiyê wî bikine lelêye!
Sivê van çaxa ezê berê Dewrêş bidime ḥevsêye!'

Mîr said, 'Boy, you two bodyguards, get to your feet!
Bind the foot of Derwêshê 'Evdî with fetters!
Put his neck in the stocks!
In the morning I will put him into prison!'

A knowledge of key facts is required to understand this telling fully – even Derwêsh's death is not actually mentioned. There are various lyrical passages, and in general it is more '*stran*-like' than Israel Ohanyan's telling. Although both of these narrative tellings are structured and told according to the conventions of oral literature, it is fair to say that Israel Ohanyan's gives the impression of being 'closer' to the historical events, with a higher proportion of specific detail among the stock elements.

BATTLES

It is clear that descriptions of battle vary considerably according to genre. A cursory glance at the *stran* of *Ferîq Pasha* and *Dawûdê Dawûd* shows that this genre has many stock elements – an individual calling out to others at the beginning, an exhortatory speech, a curse on the enemy. The narrative poems give a fuller account, but there are still stock elements – the improbably large numbers of enemy slain, the unlucky chance leading to the hero's death. It is the prose accounts which are most comprehensible to the outsider seeking 'historical information'.

The reader wonders why, in these so-called *stran* of battle, so little attention seems to be devoted to the action of the battle itself; what description there is looks suspiciously like a collection of stock elements. In the *stran* of *Ferîq Pasha*, the position of known individuals and groups within the battle is described in most detail by Kheyro Khelef and even he does not give a narrative account of the actions of all these persons and groups. The 'three days' duration of the battle with Ferîq Pasha's army is clearly a stylistically appropriate, rather than historically accurate, length of time, particularly since it is also hoped in 'Qarpal's' version that the government troops will not be able to collect their dead for three days. For a full picture of the action of the battle, contextual details of the action must be supplied by a knowledgeable individual, usually the *stranbêj*, who introduces his songs with a prose narrative.

It is the names of the protagonists rather than the features of the battle which stand out as distinctive in each of these *stran*. Great attention is paid to the identities of those involved, with names given in full each time and not abbreviated in subsequent repetitions. Each man's own name and his father's name are given, or sometimes the name of a son or brother. The reaction to Pîr Micho's addition of a name in *Ferîq Pasha* shows that inclusion in *stran* is a major mechanism in the preservation for posterity of the role of certain individuals in historical events.[13] Each song repeats its names several times, an effective strategy for reducing the likelihood of their being garbled. Details of place are similarly carefully enunciated and repeated. In *Ferîq Pasha*, for instance, Girê 'Ereba is a Sinjari village, as are Zêrwan, Ûsivan and Bekiran (Lescot 1938: 251–61). The latter two are also the names of tribes. The 'shady tree' is clearly a local landmark, though I have been unable to discover its exact location. Chilmêra, literally 'forty men', is the peak of Sinjar, where a Yezidi shrine is located. It is a common feature of much rural and localised social memory that past events are very closely linked to local geographical features – in some ways, one can say, the landscape is a 'map' of the history.[14] However, this is a Sinjari map, and its details must be obscure to many Sheykhanis. Moreover, in *Dawûdê Dawûd*, the allusion to Kerbela and Hillah is not explained; the audience must know that many of Dawûd's supporters were imprisoned or exiled there. Within the battle itself, there are few distinctive incidents. A striking exception to this is in Silo's *Dawûdê Dawûd*, where Memo, responding to Shêrîn's calls, refers to shooting down a warplane (5: 9–12). This must surely be the British plane which was brought down by rifle-fire when overflying Dawûd's territory in 1925. However, the references to King Ghazi imply that it is Dawûd's second campaign, since he succeeded on the death of Fayṣal in 1933, and the song is associated with the second campaign by contemporary Yezidis.

Thus it is clear that the purpose of the *stran* of battle is not to impart knowledge of the circumstances and course of the battle, or even its context. What, then, does it give its audience? The answer, of course, lies in the songs' subjectivity; they describe the emotional effect of the battle on one, or more, observers. Most of the songs are in direct speech, sung in character, describing what individuals saw, heard and felt. We have seen that Kheyro Khelef emphasises this very strongly in his description of the battle:

Ew minê dênê xwe dayê, binê 'eskerê meşiya li aliya ẍerbî ṛa gehişte birka 'Êlî Paşa	I was looking at it, below the soldiers, below the army was marching, on the western side 'Elî Pasha's regiment arrived,
Belê li aliya şerqê ṛa kete çemê Reşe, gelek hene şad û nişûde xortêd Ûsiva xortêd Mêrka û Bekira, Ew dibêjê,'Gelî bav û bira mêrî çêbin, lep hilînin enişka bi kozika meteresa bikutînin,	Yes, to the east, where the river Resha is, they are many, there are many, the famous, the heroes, Ûsivan lads, Mêrkan and Bekiran lads, He said, 'Dear fathers and brothers, do the deeds of men, raise your hands, elbows to the trenches, strike their positions,
Ew çeqmaqê tifinga rakin fîşeka tê bixînin. Bela ji pê 'eskerê Ferîq Paşa venagerîn mala saleke sê heyva,	Raise those bolts of your rifles, load them with cartridges. May this army of Ferîq Pasha not return home for a year and three months,
Bi Xodê koç û erebanê ḥukumetê li çemê Bekira xelas nekin meytan û laşa.'	By God, may those coaches and carts of the Government at the river Bekiran not finish with their bodies, their corpses.'

(5: 6–11)

Like the other *stranbêj*, Kheyro's descriptions of the battles are often couched in visual terms:

Sê bêlûkêd 'eskerê Ferîq Paşa di ẍalib di giranin Xodê danî gundê me ser çemê Zoqê li Girê 'Ereba,	Three companies of Ferîq Pasha's army, overwhelmingly powerful, by God, hit our village, on the river Zoqa, at Girê 'Ereba,
Lê belê Xodê zane berê topa dabûne Bekira ser malê me de, gûlê topa dirijin weki mûman û çîra ...	Yes, God knows, their shells had a direct hit on Bekira, on our houses, the shells and bullets cascade down like candles and lamps ...

(4: 3–4).

There is also much emphasis, in all the performances, on the proximity of the battle to the Yezidis' own homes and special places. The sounds of the battle also figure prominently in the singers' descriptions:

Mi dî li bayana sibê, bû gumînê topa, bû lekelekê xopanê van reşeşa,	I saw in the dawn of the morning there was the whining of shells, the ruinous firing of automatic rifles,
Li destê segmanê malêd êzdiya dabû reqîne xopanê kitekita bêşetaşa...	In the hands of the marksmen from the Yezidi houses, the lethal firing, the crack-crack of machine-guns...

(Lezgîn 10: 7–8).

This focus on the impressions of individual narrators gives immediacy – the narrators are not impersonal, but closely associated with the fighters, and speaking directly to the audience. It is worth examining these narrators and their comments more closely.

Some of these narrators are named, but there are also certain references to unnamed first-person observers who are more difficult to place. For example, a singer may say *mi dî*, 'I saw', without having introduced the speaker earlier in the stanza. The stanzas are often quite self-contained, and one cannot assume that the same character who was speaking at the end of one stanza is still speaking at the beginning of the next. One might plausibly account for these unidentified 'narrators' by suggesting that the song has lost its coherence slightly over the years, and that in the 'original' song the identity of the speaker at this point would have been clearer. However, this would be to miss the point – at the point of performance, clear indication of who is speaking is not a priority for the *stranbêj*.[15] Narrators are usually introduced when they call out, usually with *sê denga*, literally 'three cries', to another character or group of people. In many *stran*, including these two, such observing narrators are women. These named women are said to be historical individuals; checking women's names from Kurdish oral tradition in written sources is even more difficult than searching for men's names, but in the case of *Ferîq Pasha* and *Dawûdê Dawûd* at least, informants such as Qasim Shesho and Mr B. knew their descendants personally. Such female characters occur elsewhere in my collection, and also in *stran* collected and published elsewhere, such as *Bavê Behcet* 'Behjet's father', which has a character called Nefiya (Jigerxwîn 1988: 186, 189), or *Bavê Fexrîya*, 'Fekhrîya's father', which has Meyrê (Jelîl 1978, I: 315). Given the care with which the names of characters are preserved, they also are likely to be historical figures.

In *Ferîq Pasha* the women who 'narrate', or perhaps, 'comment', in the various performances are Little Gulê and Zerîfka Osê. There are two points at which they narrate. The first is at or near the beginning of the song; one woman calls out to another, proposing to go up to the peak of Chilmêra to see the battle. Both 'Qarpal' and 'Jerdo' have Little Gulê doing this. 'Jerdo's' second stanza runs thus:

Ezîdo	Oh Yezidi,
Gula kiçik bi sê denga dibêje Gula mezin,	Little Gulê calls out three times to Big Gulê,
'Lê lê xwehîngê vê sibê tu karê xwe bike û emê çînê serbanê Çelmêra ganê li gorî diyarî sûkê,	'Oh, sister, this morning you do your work and we will go up to the height of Chilmêra, my life, just near the town,
Xwedê o ava neke mala Ferîq Paşa	Oh God, do not let the house of Ferîq Pasha stand,
Tarî kûbara sibê xêvet û çadirê xwe danîne li	In the darkness and rain of the morning they pitched their tents,
Mîratêd wê gêdûkê.'	At that cursed pass.'

Pîr Micho has this in his second stanza; Kheyro Khelef does not include it, and Lezgîn changes it considerably; in his version, Little Gulê calls to the other woman at the beginning:

Belê e ye	Alas, yes,
Gula kiçik sê denga gazî dike li beṛiyê Gula mezin,	Little Gulê calls out three times in the wilderness to Big Gulê,
De lê lê xwehînge sibê dinya li me bû xopana dara bêjingê,	'Oh sister, in the morning my whole world was destroyed like the wood of a sieve,
Ew sibeyê dinya li me bû xopana dara bêjingê ...	This morning my whole world is destroyed, like the wood of a sieve ... (1: 1–4).

He leaves the wish to go to Chilmêra until stanza 4. The other motif has a woman calling out during the battle, trying to make herself heard, and expressing anxiety about Miḥemê 'Elî Agha, as in 'Kheyro's' stanza 8:

Xwedê vê carê	Oh God, at this time,
Zerîvka Osê bang dike	Zerîfka Osê is shouting,
'Lê lê Gulê xwehîngê, wezê bang dikim, dengê min dernayê,	'Oh, Gulê, sister, I am shouting, my voice does not carry,
Ezê bang dikim, dengê mi dernayê, dengê top û tifingê 'eskerê Ferîq Paşa agirê Xodê berda bûye dinyayê,	I am shouting, my voice does not carry, the noise of the shells and guns of Ferîq Pasha's soldiers, the fire, by God, the world is lost,
Mendikaniya xayîne çûyê ḥedayetê, çûye xaletê, çûye rayê,	The Mendikan are treacherous, they went over to Islam, they changed their allegiance,
Evê bi sê rojî dew û dûwe gêdûke x̌erbî dengê tifinga Miḥemê 'Elî Ax̌a bavê Milḥim tucar û bi cara nayê,	For three days at the Western end of the pass the sound of the rifle of Miḥemê 'Elî Agha, Milḥem's father has not come, not once,

Bi xodê ji qadîm ziman	By God, since ancient days the
Xwerkaniya xayîne roja,	Xwerkan have been treacherous, on the day
Mirinê tucara hîndadeke me li ba nayê.'	Of death, no help is coming to us.'

Kheyro Khelef's stanza 3 contains similar points, though the fighter is called simply 'Elî Agha. Both 'Kheyro' and Kheyro Khelef have Zerîfka doing this. 'Qarpal' and Lezgîn include this element of anxiety about Mihemê 'Elî Agha ('Qarpal' 5: 2; Lezgîn 3: 7; 6: 7, 13: 2–3), but not in specific, close association with a girl's name; Lezgîn has more detailed description of the battle in stanzas introduced by Little Gulê's call (stanzas 4, 7, 10); he does not mention Zerîfka. Pîr Micho's song, which is only partial, does not include this element.

The *Dawûdê Dawûd stran* has only one female character, Shêrîn, the mother of Memo, who plays a very clear and prominent role, especially in Silo's version. Silo overtly puts most of the song into the mouth of Shêrîn, and her role is much more obvious in his performance than in that of 'Pîr Qewwal'. Her anxiety about Memo is mentioned right at the beginning of Silo's song, after the introductory *lê dayê*. In every refrain Silo has Shêrîn saying 'I call for help, help does not come . . .'; 'Pîr Qewwal' has the same refrain without specifically saying that the words are spoken by Shêrîn. The motif of calling for help (which does not come) is quite common in Kurdish traditional song generally, and was memorably used by the Kurdish popular singer Şivan Perwer in his song *Hawar*, about the bombing of Halabja. In *Ferîq Pasha*, Kheyro Khelef has Zerîfka Osê say that she is calling for help, but it does not come (3: 3); 'Qarpal' does not attribute it, saying simply that help does not come. In Silo's performance of *Dawûdê Dawûd*, Shêrîn makes the exhortatory speech to the fighters (3: 5–8); in 'Pîr Qewwal's', Dawûd himself does this (3: 6–10). Silo's stanzas 5 and 6, which describe the battle, are put into the mouth of Shêrîn, with a response by Memo; this antiphonal structure, whereby characters answer each other, is also common in the *stran* and further examples will be considered in Chapter Five.

It is quite striking that all these expressions of emotions of grief and anxiety in these *stran* are associated explicitly with women, or not attributed at all. If one were to take a diachronic approach to the song, one could suggest that the 'unattributed' expressions of emotion were once associated with the female characters who express them in the other performances and that they have become 'detached' from them over time. What is important, however, is that they are never spoken by a male character, nor is there any evidence that they ever were. Emotions of vulnerability, such as grief, fear and anxiety, are associated with women rather than men in these *stran*. Women are witnesses of the action, and descriptions of events are ascribed to them. These *stran* do not seem to be atypical; women certainly describe events and their emotional impact in other *stran*. That is not to say that men never express such emotions in other *stran* – *'Eysha Balê*, which will be considered more fully in Chapter Six, articulates a man's grief at the death of his beloved, and the *Bîsharê Cheto* collected by Jigerkhwîn (1988: 181) where, as in Israel Ohanyan's narrative poem of *Derwêshê 'Evdî*, the hero's father expresses grief and fear for his son and attempts to persuade him not to fight. Nevertheless, in the *stran* of battle, female characters are more closely associated with emotions of vulnerability than male, and in these particular examples, much of the conflict is portrayed through their eyes, in terms of those negative emotions.[16] This is true even of the Ferîq Pasha *stran*, which commemorates a skirmish which the Yezidis won.

In Israel Ohanyan's masterly performance of *Derwêshê 'Evdî*, description of the battle itself is rather short (stanzas 17–19) but it is the focus of the narrative. All the previous episodes in the story lead to the battle, Derwêsh's death, and 'Edûlê's response. Patterns are set up – of armed response to an outside threat, first by 'Evdî, Derwêsh's father, and then by Derwêsh himself, and, most importantly, of repeated attempts to deter Derwêsh from fighting, made in turn by the most important figures in his life – his father, 'Edûlê (representing 'Evdî and the mother of his companions 'Elî and Bozan), and then a benign outsider, 'Evdî's former comrade-in-arms. The outsider warns him of the odds against him, and when the battle begins, the enormous numbers involved dominate the account of the fighting. The battle consists of a number of smaller sections enumerating the (obviously highly improbable) number of enemies killed and naming those of Derwêsh's supporters who die, picked off one by one; each of these subsections is introduced by the same description of the sounds of battle, reminiscent of the sensory immediacy of the descriptions of battle in the *stran*:

Bû çingîna şûra, bû terqînê mertala, bû ḥişînê hespa û li hev dabû,	There was the clashing of swords, the ringing of shields, the neighing of horses and they came together,
Mêr têne kuştin bi seda û xûn ṛijiya bû,	Men were killed in their hundreds and blood flowed,
Ji neyara dusid hate kuştin, ji Zor Temer Paşa kuştî 'Elî û Silêman bû.	Of the enemy, two hundred were killed, of Zor Temer Pasha's men 'Elî and Suleyman were killed.
Şeṛ sekinî, bîna xwe berda bû,	The battle stopped, the fighters had lost their breath,
Ṛabûne ser xwe, dîsa li hev dabû,	They retreated, and again rushed together,

Bû çingînê şûra, bû ḥîşînê hespa, bû terqînê mertala, dê dev ji ewledê xwe berda bû,	There was the clashing of swords, the neighing of horses, the ringing of shields, mothers lost their children,
Hingî ko şeṛ giran bû.	The battle was so great at that time.
Ji ḥeyşsid siwarî hate kuştin çarsid, çarsid mabû.	Of eight hundred warriors, four hundred had been killed, four hundred remained.
Bi van siwara ṛa hate kuştin Se'dûnê bira bû.	With these warriors Se'dûn, Derwêsh's brother was killed.
Dewrêş û 'Elî û Bozan mabû,	Derwêsh and 'Elî and Bozan remained,
Ûsiv, başkatibê wan, sekinî bû li dera habû,	Yusif, their chief scribe, had stopped and was at that place,
Ûsiv dinhêre, mêraniya Dewrêş çawa bû,	Yusif could see how valiant Derwêsh was,
Dinivîsîne, û li ber çevê wi xuya bû,	He wrote, and before his eyes it was clear,
Careke dinê şeṛ giran bû,	One more time the battle was heavy,
Dewrêş û 'Elî û Bozan ketine nava van her çarsid siwarê habû.	Derwêsh and 'Elî and Bozan fell upon those four hundred warriors.

(17: 12–26).

It is important that the enemy only gains the opportunity to fall on Derwêsh and kill him by an unfortunate accident:

Divê, serê Dewrêşê 'Evdî, lawkê êzdî, hêja kete şeṛ û deqê girane,	They say, Derwêshê 'Evdî, the Yezidi lad, again rushed into battle and into the heaviest fighting,
Lingê Hidman kete qulê cird û mişkane,	Hidman's leg fell into a rat or mouse hole,
Lingê Hidman şkestin ji herdû çokane,	Hidman's legs broke at both knees,
Dewrêş qulibî, kete ser piştane,	Derwêsh toppled, fell on his back,
Ḥafirê Gêsî û 'Ecîl Birahîm, şêxê wane,	Ḥafir Gêsî and 'Ajîl Birahîm, their sheykh,
Û vî pêncî siwarê han ajotine ser laşê Dewrêşê 'Evdî, siwarê Hidmane,	and these fifty warriors of theirs fell upon the body of Dewrêşê 'Evdî, rider of Hidman,
Ji hespa peya bûn, wî dane ber şûrane.	They leaped down from their horses and put him to the sword.

(19: 10–16).

'Egîtê Têjir's performance does not have the pattern of encounters leading inexorably to the battle, though his answer to the Mîr's question about courage prefigures the fighting; here the conflict arises suddenly when

Derwêsh and the Mîr encounter hostile forces in the open. The Mîr does give him the choice of retreat, but Derwêsh chooses to fight, once again against insuperable odds. When the battle does happen, the women and girls of the town of Birê come to look (13: 8–10); like their sisters in the *stran*, they observe and comment.

MARTIAL HEROES

'Manliness', *mêrxasî* or *mêranî* in Kurdish tribal culture has been succinctly defined by van Bruinessen (2000: 15) as a combination of generosity and courage. The presentation of Derwêshê 'Evdî's manliness in the Caucasian narrative poems, particularly that of Israel Ohanyan, has much in common with that of other Kurdish martial heroes, such as Prince Goldenhand, the hero of *Dimdim*, and even, to a certain extent, Memê Alan. In both these narratives, Derwêsh rushes into a battle against insuperable odds, and it is worth examining his motivation.

In the first of the narratives, this question is aired during the course of several unsuccessful attempts to dissuade him from fighting. Obviously Israel Ohanyan cannot change the end of the story which all his audience knows, but he does make Derwêsh's actions consistent. There are several coherent forces pushing Derwêsh to his fatal confrontation. There are three key encounters which make his motivation clear. The first is his conversation with his father after he receives 'Edûlê's letter telling him about the threat from the Gêsan. This is recounted in stanzas 6 and 7:

Dibê, 'Bavo, dilê min liyane, liyane,	He said, 'Father, my heart is longing, longing,
Tu bide min 'Elî û Bozane,	You give me 'Elî and Bozan,
Tu bide min Se'dûnê birane,	You give me my brother Se'dûn,
Ezim, ko heṛim fîncanê hilînim ji ser destê 'Edûla qîza Zor Temer Paşayê Milane,	I'll do it, I will go and take the cup from the hand of 'Edûlê, daughter of Zor Temer Pasha of the Milan,
Ezim, diqelînim ḥezar û ḥevsid siwarê Gêsane,	I will roast one thousand five hundred Gêsa warriors,
Ezim, konê Zor Temer Paşa xilas bikim ji devê şûrane.	I will deliver the camp of Zor Temer Pasha from the (mouth of the) swords.
Bavo, Zor Temer Paşa emekdare,	Father, Zor Temer Pasha is righteous,
Emekê wî li ber çevê min xûyane.'	His righteousness is clear to my eyes.'
Dibê, 'Evdî giriya û stêr ji çevê bavê wî bariyane,	They say, 'Evdî wept and tears trickled down from the father's eye,
Go, 'Weyî weyî li min û vî bextî hane,	He said, 'Alas, alas for me and that honour of theirs,

Lawo, sebir bike, sebir ji ba Xudane,
Ezê du xebera ji kuṛê xwe ṛa bêjim, bala xwe bide vê xebera hane.'
Go, 'Lawo, 'emrê min hijde salî bû, ez şivanê mala Zor Temer Paşayê Milame,

Lad, be patient, patience belongs to God,
I will say two words to my son, pay attention to these words.'

He said, 'Lad, when I was eighteen years old, I was the shepherd to the family of Zor Temer Pasha of the Milan,

Carekê dîsa li ser serê wî ṛabû fermaneke girane,
Kîka, Mila ji ber Gêsa ṛeviyane,

Another time again there was a death sentence passed on him,
The Kîkan and Milan fled from the Gêsan,

Ez ṛabûm siwar bûm li miḥîna Zor Temer Paşa Milane,
Mi şûr girêda, mertal avîte zendane,
Ez dageṛiyame nava neyarane.
Dibe çingînê şûra, terqînê mertalane,'
Go, 'Lawo, min sed ji wan kuştin û tev ji ber bavê te ṛeviyane,
Min konê Zor Temer Paşa xilas kir ji destê neyarane,
Paşî Zor Temer Paşa çi got? Go, "Evdê êzdiye, li çiyayê Şengalê dibe dizê kerane.'

I got up and rode the mare of Zor Temer Pasha of the Milan,
I strapped on my sword, tossed aside my shield from my forearms,
I fell upon the enemy.
There was the clashing of swords, the ringing of shields,'
He said, 'Lad, I killed a hundred of them and they all fled from your father,
I delivered the camp of Zor Temer Pasha from the hand of the enemy,
Afterwards what did Zor Temer Pasha say? He said, "Evdî is a Yezidi, on Sinjar mountain he is a donkey-thief'.

Tu ji ya bavê xo bikî, Zor Temer Paşa bêbexte, emekḥerame.'

You take it from your father, Zor Temer Pasha is treacherous and dishonourable'.

Dewrêş dibê: 'Bavo, dilê min liyane, liyane,
Sûretê 'Edûla Zor Temer Paşa li ber çevê min xûyane,
Ez bextê teda, tu dilê min neşkênî ji boy vî şeṛê hane,
Tu bide min 'Elî û Bozane,
Tu bide min Se'dûnê birane,
Emê siwar bibin li hespane,
Heṛine dîwana Zor Temer Paşa Milane,
Emê binheṛin ṛay, şêwr û tekbîra wane.'

Derwêsh said, 'Father, my heart is longing, longing,
The image of 'Edûlê, child of Zor Temer Pasha, appears before my eyes,
I throw myself on your mercy, do not break my heart over this battle,
You give me 'Elî and Bozan,
You give me Se'dûn my brother,
We will ride on our horses,
Go to the guest-hall of Zor Temer Pasha of the Milan,
We will find out their views, their counsels and their thoughts.'

This has something in common with his conversation with the old Gêsan man, 'Evdî's former comrade-in-arms:

Kal go, 'Xorto, tu ne Dewrêşê 'Evdiyî? Tu ji mi ṛa bêje bi ṛastiye,	The old man said, 'Lad, are you not Derwêshê 'Evdî? You tell me truly,
Tu derewa dikî, tu ne li deva digeṛî,	You are lying, you are not looking for camels,
Tucar mi te nedîtiye,	Never have I seen you,
Tu gelekî bi xezebî, te cilê hesin xwe kiriye,	You are full of anger, you have clad yourself in clothes of iron,
Te tasa hesin ser serê xwe daniye,	You have put an iron helmet on your head,
Û te şûr û mertalê xwe girêdaye,	And girded yourself with sword and shield,
Ji apê xweṛa bêje, binhêṛe, îşê te çiye?'	Come, tell your uncle, what are you here for?'
Dewrêş go, 'Apo, ezê ji teṛa bêjim bi ṛastiye,	Derwêsh said, 'Uncle, I will tell you truly,
Di nava me û Gêsa da neyartiye,	Between us and the Gêsan is hatred,
Ez hatime, ko komê bibînim, koma wan li kuê derêye.'	I have come to see their camp, to see where their tents are'.
Go, 'Lawo, tu xortekî gelekî ḥeyî,	He said, 'Lad, you are a vengeful young man,
Min û bavê te, me bi ḥev ṛa hevaltî kiriye,	I and your father, we became comrades together,
Bila min bike, tu mekeve vî şeṛiye,	Take my advice, do not involve yourself in this war,
Em Misilmanin û tu Êzdiye,	We are Muslims and you are Yezidi,
Û heq û ḥesabê te li ṛiḥê te çiye?	And what use is your justice, your old scores, to your soul?
Ji me geṛe, di nava me û mala Zor Temer Paşa da neyartiye.'	Turn away from us, the hatred is between us and the house of Zor Temer Pasha'.
Dewrêş go: 'Apo, erê, biṛa ez Êzdîme,	Derwêsh said, 'Uncle, yes, indeed I am Yezidi,
Bes ez eşîra Zor Temer Paşayê milîme!	But I am of the tribe of Zor Temer Pasha of the Milan!
Min nan û avê wî zeḥf xariye.'	I have eaten and drunk with him so many times.'
Evî kalî gote Dewrês, go, 'Lawo, înca ezê te ṛa bêjim bi ṛastiye,	This old man spoke to Derwêsh and said, 'Lad, this time I will tell you truly,

Ḥezar siwar tevî Ḥafirê Gêsî, 'Ecîl Birahîm li girê Leylanê, li gola Xatûniyê sekiniye,	One thousand warriors with Hafir Gêsî and 'Ajîl Birahîm are camped on the hill of Leylan, at the lake of Khatûnî,
Lawo, ez ketime bextê te Xudê da, tu xo bernedî vî agiriye.'	Lad, I am falling on your mercy, by God, do not lose yourself in this fire'.
Dewrêş go, 'Apo, bi Xudê, ez hatime ji bona vî agiriye.'	Derwêsh said, 'Uncle, by God, I have come for this fire.'

(15: 24–46).

Derwêsh is clearly in the patronage of Zor Temer Pasha, and owes allegiance to him, despite the attempts of 'Evdî and the old Gêsan warrior to undermine this. Both try to play on Derwêsh's Yezidi identity; 'Evdî says that Zor Temer Pasha slandered their family, and the old man says that Muslim rivalries should not be relevant to Derwêsh. The young man counters these differently; to his father he gives 'Edûlê as the reason for fighting, and on initial receipt of the letter he mentions her before the justice of Zor Temer Pasha's cause. To the old man, he declares his tribal loyalty to Zor Temer Pasha, and his bond to him is expressed in terms of eating his food and drink. Beside his bond to Zor Temer Pasha, Derwêsh is also driven by his awareness of his own honour. When 'Edulê herself pleads with him, he uses it to justify his actions:

Dewrêş go, "Edûlê, bese ji van te'n û niçane,	Dewrêş said, "Edûlê, enough of this reproach and hissing,
Ez nadim 'Elî û Se'dûnê birane,	I won't give 'Elî and Se'dûn my brother,
Ê gelek kûçikê wa Kîka û Mila hene,	There are many dogs among those Kîkan and Milan,
Wê kenê xwe mi bikin û wê bidin hilobiyane.'	They will smile at me and give me their contempt.'

(11: 5–8).

Death is an honourable course, he says in his brief exhortatory speech to his friends:

Dewrêş gazî kir, 'Gelî birano, gelî hevalno,	Derwêsh called, 'My brothers, my comrades,
Ji berêda kuştin ṛiya mêrane,	Killing has long since been the way of men.
Meriv têye kuştin, namûsa xo nade destê neyarane,	When a person is killed he gives none of his honour to his enemies,
Dilqewî bin, bi emrê Xudane.'	Be stout-hearted, by God's will.'

(13: 3–6).

Derwêsh does not go unwillingly into the fighting, pushed by a tribal code of honour, but enters into it with passion. The old Gêsan man describes him as *bi xezeb*, ‘full of rage’ (15: 27), and when he fights he is like various avenging angels – Gabriel, and Ezra’îl, the angel of death, and again *melkemot*, the angel of death (18: 2; 19: 4). His *mêranî* is recorded by the scribe. Egîtê Têjir’s description of his fighting is consistent with this; he falls screaming on the enemy, and the young women comment on this:

Qîz û bûkê şeherê Bîrê ṛadivin temaşê, Divê, ‘Hela lêbinêṛin, tê bêjî, melkemotê mêrê kulêye’.	The daughters and brides of the town of Bîrê came up to look, They said, ‘Look at this, you would say it is the angel of death, the sorrow of men,
Qîzek dibê, ‘Bira xwedê bide siḥetê, mêrekî tenê peşmûdê kir aqas siyarê cerdêye’.	One girl said, ‘May God preserve us, one man alone has had such an effect on so many horsemen of the Jerdan.’ (13: 8–10).

In this part of the poem he is characterised as *Dewrêşê dîn*, ‘mad Derwêsh’ (13: 1) and he refers to himself in this way (12: 1). Since Derwêsh is elsewhere perfectly sane, it is probable that this refers to the frenzy denoted by the English word ‘berserk’, which has been described by observers of battles in many cultures.

In the *stran* of battle, as we have seen, observers often articulate negative feelings about the battle. However, they do admire courage, as in these lines from *Ferîq Pasha*:

Belê bi xodê aferim bona mêrêd weke Miḥemê ‘Evdo bavê Saleh, li ‘esra êvarê Tara şîrê zirav siwarî dihajotine li nav çadiran.	Yes by God, I congratulate men like Miḥemê ‘Evdo, Saleh’s father, in the evening twilight, With his thin sword alone the brave horseman was attacking them among their tents. (6: 10–11).

The ‘observers’ of the battles in the *stran* occasionally refer to the feelings of the fighters; Pîr Micho, for instance, says:

Dengê tifingêd Ferîq Paşa li xortêd Êzîdîya bûye şekir …	The sound of Ferîq Pasha’s guns was sugar-sweet to the young Yezidis … (4: 2)

However, the fighters’ intentions and feelings are most clearly articulated in the exhortatory speeches. These are clearly a common feature of *stran* of battle; my own collection includes various examples which have them, such as *Temer Pasha* sung by Ḥisên Omerî, and Nikitine’s selection also includes them (1947–50, 1956: 259–68). Many of the sentiments expressed, and some of the words and phrases, are the same in both *Ferîq Pasha* and *Dawûdê Dawûd*. Typical exhortations include *dest hilînin*, 'raise your hands', *destê xwe çeqmaqê mîratê beşetaşa bipelînin* 'feel the trigger of your cursed weapons with your hands' and *destê xwe li qebdê xencerê bişîdînin* 'squeeze the handle of your daggers with your hands'. Their basic pattern is an encouragement to the fighters to be brave, to rely on their weapons, and (sometimes) to protect their Yezidi homes and families; they end with a statement of their ultimate aim – to drive the enemy far away, or to kill huge numbers of them. Perhaps the most striking aspect of these speeches, to the outsider, is the emphasis on being brave, on facing up to the enemy, as in Kheyro Khelef's stanza 2:

Belê bira li bin dara zivingê Gelek hene şade û nişûdêd Mihemê 'Evdo bavê Saleh,	Yes, brothers under the shady tree, There are many, the famous ones, the heroes of Mihemê 'Evdo, Saleh's father,
Sê denga gazî dike, 'Segmane Êzîdiya bikin bilezînin, berê xwe ji kozik û çepera megêrînin,	He calls three times, 'Yezidi marksmen, act now, be busy, don't turn your gaze from their trenches and dugouts,
Ew çavê xwe ji nizamê Ferîq Paşa ẍalibe girane mane metirsînin, 'Erz û 'eyal gûlî sorê xwe vê sibê ji destê nizamê bifikînin,	Don't let your eyes be frightened of Ferîq Pasha's overwhelming forces, Liberate your kith and kin, your red-braids this morning from the hand of [his] force,
Ce bi Xodê destê me ji gulî sorê me qut be Destê me da nema ẍêrî tifingê.	As God's my witness, let our hands be separated from our red-braids, In our hands there is nothing left but the gun.'

'Do not take your eyes off the enemy' also means 'do not turn your back', 'do not run away'. The protection of the Yezidis' wives and families is an important motivator (e.g. 'Kheyro' 6: 8–9). This is not unique to these *stran*. One of Nikitine's examples has '... don't run away from the battlefield. There is such a thing as flight, but it is for old women' (1956: 260). Such a recurrent emphasis on facing the enemy bravely suggests a strong conception that courage is not the same as fearlessness, that fear is natural in the face of the enemy. The Yezidis may expect that every man will do his duty, and the heroes do fight bravely, but the *stran* acknowledge the difficulty of overcoming fear in battle.

Despite the stereotypical ways in which heroism is expressed in the *stran*, there is a strong awareness that the ideals of *mêranî* 'bravery' are not always easy to live up to. Another dimension of the presentation of the women who watch and comment on the battle is their ability to comment unfavourably on the performance of individual men. The women of the *stran* have no compunction in cursing those they think have behaved badly, whether it be the Mendikan or Khwerkan, or Reshoyê Qulo. This reflects a real issue in Yezidi, and Kurdish, life; in the discussion of love songs and stories in the next chapter I will discuss the issue of *namûs*, of 'shame' and modesty for women and their need to retain a blameless reputation, but it is also true that men also have concerns with their own reputations and the way others see them. Yezidi women, especially in Sinjar, may be excluded from various public decision-making processes, but in private life they have opinions and express them. Ideals of masculine behaviour are undoubtedly problematic for Yezidi men; no man wants to be put to shame in front of women.

Unlike Derwêsh and the defenders of Sinjar against the Ferîq, Dawûdê Dawûd is still part of living memory, and an iconic figure in Kurdish discourses of resistance. It is perhaps not a surprise, given the subjective, impressionistic nature of the *stran*, that Dawûd plays rather a small part in the song that bears his name;[17] Dawûd's rebellion is the context for a woman's grief for her son. It is 'Emerê Dawûd's account which tells us much more about the man – as his son would wish him to be remembered, at any rate. 'Emer would have known that Silêman and Jindî's book would have an impact among the Yezidis: it would be the first book of its kind, and would probably reach some non-Yezidis as well. Thus he was knowingly constructing a highly influential account of his father's life. If there is any justice at all in Lescot's reference to the 'chaos of shifting friendships and transitory hatreds of which the history of Sinjar is composed' (1938: 180), then one can be pretty sure of the existence of opposing discourses on Dawûd in the Yezidi community, which 'Emer would be trying to discredit or contradict. There would also have been constraints on him and Khelîlê Jindî to produce a statement which would be acceptable in the Iraqi political climate of 1977.

Dawûd is clearly a hero. He is presented as honourable and honest throughout, but caught up in corrupt politics and Government machinations:

Hoya serekî ew bû serokêd Êzdîya – bi teḥrîka îngilîz – bûne dû tay (beş). Hindek nokerêd îngilîz bûn û bi ḥukmê wan dirazî bûn, mîna Se'îd Begê, mîrê Êzdîyayê wî demî ḥukumeta îngilîz eve kir heta ku ev serokina êk li êkî bidet û hemû pêkve lawaz bin û ew bişêt bête ser ḥazirîyê. 'Emerê Dawûd digot, 'Têtê bîra min mûçexorêd ferensî li Sûrîya dihatin û pare dînan û	While he was one of the leaders, the leadership of the Yezidis, at the instigation of the English, split into two factions. Some were servants of the English and were contented with their rule, like Se'îd Beg, the Yezidi Mîr at that time; the English government did this so that this would set leaders one against another and everyone would be weakened together, and it would be able to

didane serokêd hindek êla, û bextê wan pê dikiṛî û razî kirin ku ‘erdê Singarê pêxine ser xaka Sûriya.’ Belê ‘Emer dibêjit, ‘Babê min qayil nebû pare ji wan hilgirt û daxwazîya wan qebul ket. Got, “Şingar parçeke ji ‘erdê Îraqê.” Ango welat peristina xo diyar kir. Her hosa bi ḥukmê îngîlîz razî nedibû.’

dominate. ‘Emerê Dawûd said, ‘I recall that French agents came from Syria and offered money and gave it to the heads of various tribes, and bought their loyalty and made them agree that the territory of Sinjar be annexed to the land of Syria.’ Well, ‘Emerê Dawûd says, ‘my father was not willing to take money from them and agree to their wish. He said, ‘Sinjar is part of the country of Iraq.’ So he made his patriotism clear. But he remained unhappy with English rule.’

‘Van egera êk û dû girtin û ḥêcet bo Înglîz çêbû pajone ser Dawûdê Dawûd. Ṛabû Şêx ‘Icîl şêxê êla Şemeriya teḥrîk kirin ku biçit ‘erdê Ezdîyêd Şingarê jê bistînit. Dawûd ev serşoriye qebûl nekir û bersingê wan girt…’

‘These conditions set one person against another and made it necessary for the English to attack Dawûde Dawûd. Up came Sheykh ‘Ajîl, sheykh of the Shammar tribe, whom they incited to go to the Yezidi territory in Sinjar and take it from them. Dawûde Dawûd did not agree to this plan and confronted them …’

Dawûd refused to accept French bribes. His first battle arose from his resistance to an attempt by an Arab chief to take Yezidi property. Later, his final conviction was the result of entrapment by his enemies:

‘Miṣerefê Mûsil Se‘dî al-Qizaz şande pê Dawûdê Dawûd û Şêx Xelef û bextê xo dayê çu lê neket. Wî demî jî Esma‘îl Ḥeqî Resûl qaîmeqamê Şingarê bû … . .’

‘The prefect of Mosul, Sa‘di al-Qizaz, sent a message to Dawûde Dawûd and Sheykh Khelef and gave his word nothing would happen to them. At that time Asma‘īl Haqī Rasul was Qaimaqam of Sinjar …’

‘Demê dadgeha Dawûdê Dawûd û Şêx Xelef hatine danan, çu li ser Şêx Xelef derneêxistin û berdan. Belê xefik û torêd qayîm di rêka Dawûdî da vedabûn, ku berê wî dane bendîxanêya Mûsil …’

‘When the case against Dawûde Dawûd and Sheykh Khelef came to court, no charges were brought out against Sheykh Khelef and he was left alone. But they had set strong traps and snares for Dawûd, so that they could send him to Mosul prison …’

‘Emer’s description of Dawûd’s character emphasises his strong principles, his adherence to the Yezidi religion, his protection of other Yezidis, and his avoidance of impurity to such an extent that he would not tolerate impure speech or behaviour. ‘Emer illustrates his point with an anecdote of

Dawûd's anger with a man who had sworn at a Yezidi. 'Emer clearly wants to portray his father as a model Yezidi:

Di ser vê hemûkê ṛa Dawûdê Dawûd miroveki xodan xîret û bext bû. Serşoṛî û nexoşî, çucara, qebûl nekir. Her hosa piyawekî dîndar û ṛêya ola xo bû. Digotin peyva derew di devî ṛa dernedikeft û nedivîya guh lêbit. Axiftina gotiba jî diviya dû ta nebit û bête cî.	Besides all this, Dawûdê Dawûd was a man of passion and honour. He never agreed to vice and wickedness. In every way he was a religious man, following his faith. They say he never let a wicked lying word pass his lips and would not permit himself to hear one. If he had said something, it had to be done immediately, without his repeating it.

It is likely that Dawûd's political opponents and their descendants continued to question Dawûd's credentials as a good Yezidi, given his alliances with local tribal Muslims, his opposition to Ḥemo Shêro and an ambivalence, alluded to by 'Emer, towards Mîr Se'îd Beg,[18] and that 'Emer is trying to counter this. What is interesting is that here he constructs Yezidi virtue almost entirely in terms of purity; Dawûd refrains from dishonesty and polluting behaviour. 'Emer does not focus particularly on Dawûd's undoubted courage.

VILLAINS

One of the most obvious features of the Ferîq Pasha *stran* is how little it says about its eponymous villain. It is really about the impact on Sinjari Yezidis of an attack by his troops, and the Ferîq himself remains a shadowy figure, a cipher for the real enemy, which is the government. There are other enemies in the *stran* and the narrative poems, but tribal enemies are often not fully characterised. In Ferîq Pasha the Mendikan are said to be 'treacherous' but this is clearly a transient and political response to their refusing to fight. Similarly, in *Dawûdê Dawûd*, Reshoyê Qulo (leader of the Mala Khalitî village of 'Eldîna) is cursed for reasons not made clear, but is not characterised further. These people may be glorified in other *stran* for other actions. It is 'the government' which is consistently negatively characterised in Kurdish oral tradition of the late Ottoman and Mandatory period, despite the fact that many prominent Kurds aligned themselves with the government and held official posts. The terms in which government is presented reflect the most common situations in which Kurds encountered it. Even in the twentieth century, government-provided facilities, such as education and healthcare, were much more scarce in Kurdish areas of both Turkey and Iraq than in more urban areas; the government's role in remote areas was authoritarian, and apt to be perceived as repressive. Even by 1925, Sinjari Yezidis still tended to perceive the State government as 'an extraneous power which induced fears of taxation and conscription' (Fuccaro 1999: 100). Most dramatically, the Yezidi oral tradition well remembers those *ferman*, or official decrees, sanctioning violence against them. The term came to be applied to any campaign of violence by government, or government-backed forces; Yezidis I met used it to describe the campaigns of Ferîq Pasha, who appears to have had an official brief to convert as many Yezidis as possible, but 'Emerê Dawûd also uses it of the British attack on Dawûd's villages in 1925.

The oral tradition commemorates in poetic form many small skirmishes with the army, and encounters with petty officials. The treatment of these representatives varies considerably; sometimes they are distinguished from the government which commands them, as in the lyric poem *Bisharê Cheto* collected by Nikitine, about Kurdish leaders in the Muş area of Turkey (1956: 267).

> I am Bishar, blond Bishar. I can no longer live with the Turkish government, with its tricks and prevarications. Let it be understood for my soul and body: I will not fire on the rank and file. They are only the children of the State. I will fire on the *Kaimakam* (district governor), the *binbaşı* (colonel), the *yüzbaşı* (captain), the *mülazım* (lieutenant) ... Jemîl calls out to Bishar: '... Keep hold of your Martini rifle, don't move the Mauser from your shoulder, do not fire on the rank-and-file, they are the children of the State. Look at all the ones whose sword hangs by their side, whose belt is sewn with gold and silver, throw those ones down ...

In other traditions government servants are not strongly differentiated from the government itself; in such cases they, and through them the government, are portrayed as objects of ridicule. One performance I saw on video, by the *stranbêj* Kheyro Khelef, included a *stran* called *Resho û Chawîsh*, 'Resho and the Sergeant'. In a spoken preface to the song, Kheyro Khelef said that it was based on an incident which happened near Sinjar in the early years of the twentieth century. In the song itself, a Yezidi called Resho was going innocently about his business when a sergeant stopped him for no good reason, beat him and locked him up. A message was sent to his tribe, and a Yezidi called Silêman arrived to rescue him, carrying a club. They then had a dispute about religion during which the sergeant insulted the Yezidi faith. The song concerns the revenge taken on the sergeant by Silêman and the rescued Resho. The Yezidi audience in the video relished the sound beating and the insults given to the sergeant; they laughed when Silêman threw him into cow dung until he was 'dappled', and were delighted when Resho then threw him into some water. In the song, everyone cheered Resho when he came home. It is easy to see how such an incident could become an anecdote and then a *stran*. One element in its enduring appeal is the way that an agent of oppression gets his just deserts.

'Emerê Dawûd's account of his father's life portrays one great enemy, the British government. Ḥemo Shêro, whose relationship with Dawûd dominated the latter's political career, is conspicuous by his absence, and his appointment as paramount chief of the Mountain is only alluded to by the reference to the leadership, at the instigation of the British, splitting into two factions. Details of other Sinjari political figures of the time are not given either, apart from the passing references to the Qaimaqam of Sinjar and to the guarantees supplied by the prefect Osê Sa'di al-Qizaz. There is no comment on Sheykh Khelef, who was rewarded by the government for deserting Dawûd's cause. This reluctance to blame other members of the Yezidi and Sinjari community in print is probably a result of the same eagerness to present a united front and minimise community differences which I noticed during my fieldwork. It is hardly surprising that 'Emer's account of events differs from that of British sources; Dawûd's refusal to attend a meeting, which, according to the *Times* of 21 April 1925, was the reason for the action taken against him, is portrayed by 'Emer as a mere pretext, and set in the context of the Mandatory authorities' plan of using Sheykh 'Ajîl to provoke Dawûd. The *Times* also downplays the implications of using air power against a largely civilian population unfamiliar with aircraft.[19] 'Emer describes the subsequent fighting and retribution as a *ferman* 'for the Yezidi people', again glossing over the divisions amongst the Yezidis of Sinjar.

However, the focus on the British seems to reflect the anti-British post-colonial discourse which was still apparent in Badinan in the early 1990s. Not only does 'Emer stress the brutality of the Mandatory forces, but in his account of Dawûd's second rebellion, the Government, which forced conscription on the Yezidis, attacked Dawûd and gave brutal punishments, is said to be English. However, the mandate had finished in 1932. It seems that, in common with many of my Badinani informants, 'Emer believed that the British continued to control everything from behind the scenes; it is clear from written sources, however, that their influence was confined to certain areas only and that matters relating to non-Muslim minorities were a particularly sensitive area in which the Iraqi government perceived British imperialism at work and wished to show strength in countering this (Fuccaro 1999: 133).[20] For instance, as a British national, I was often asked by Christians in Badinan why 'the British' perpetrated a massacre of Christians in Simêl in 1936. In spite of the role of the British in preparing the climate in which this took place, the massacre itself was an action of the Iraqi army; in fact one of the aims of its authors was to humiliate the British (Elliot 1996: 11). Such representations of British interference must also have been acceptable in the climate of 1970s Iraq, given that 'Emer's interview was allowed to be published in this form.

Non-Governmental figures of authority

Central State governments are most negatively portrayed in Yezidi discourses, but there are also lesser villains. 'Emerê Dawûd, for instance, speaks dismissively of them:

'Belê çu cara baweriya mirovî li çîna koneperest û derebeg û dagirkera neêt. Ne şeref heye, ne bext û bawerî jî heye. Ser û binê wan ẍedire! Xodan ziman û peyvêd hilûne. Dîn û îmana wan pareye!!'

'But when people trust the class of old-fashioned people and feudal lords and occupiers it never comes to anything. There is neither honour, not fortune nor trust. From head to toe they are treachery! Their tongues and their words are smooth. Money is their faith and their religion!'

One wonders how far this is a nod in the direction of Ba'ath anti-feudalist ideas of social order, rather than a contrast with Dawûd; Dawûd himself was a prime example of an old-fashioned feudal lord, with his pride in his ancestry, his concern to maintain the autonomy of the tribes, and his contempt for the newly powerful Ḥemo Shêro.

It is worth examining the presentation of some of these figures of authority in the narrative poetry. Vilchevsky's proposition that Kurdish folklore reflects the interests of the ruling classes (Nikitine 1956: 258) is justifiable up to a point, since it is demonstrable that many important people did hire the services of poets to present them and their interests in a good light. However, as Margaret Mills has shown in the Afghan context, skilled performers are quite capable of making subtle critiques of their patrons (Mills 1991: *passim*). Moreover, a great many oral traditions are performed outside the *dîwanxane* of great men, and there is a strong populist bias in Kurdish folklore, which can provide an outlet for criticism of high-ranking people. This is easily seen in those anecdotes where high-status figures such as senior clerics and aghas are ridiculed for their hypocrisy, and common sense often wins the day over learning. It also finds its way into the accounts of the heroic deeds of history, and can be seen in the tellings of *Derwêshê 'Evdî* collected in the Caucasus.

In Israel Ohanyan's telling, Zor Temer Pasha is not shown as being especially heroic in martial terms – he has others to do his fighting for him – but he is not lacking in honour. He treats 'Evdî fairly and it is not at all clear that 'Evdî's assertion that Zor Temer Pasha slandered him is to be believed. Egitê Têjir's telling, however, depicts the 'Mîr' in a very ambivalent way, with many negative features. The initial, riddling exchange is rather curious and deserves further consideration:

Mîr go, 'Dewrêşo lawo, min ṛa bêje rastiyêye,

Mîr said, 'Derwêsh lad, tell me the truth,

Çika ṛojê oẍirmê giran, ṛeqe ṛeqe darê darṛima, firxînê me'negiya, nalînê şêr û 'erfûta, ḥawe ḥawê lawê kurmanca, mêr beranberî çend mêra dertêye?'	On the day of heavy destiny, with the crashing of wood on wood, the waggons and horses, the wailing of lionhearts and heroes, the shouting of young Kurmanji lads, how many men can a man face? (2: 2–3).

Derwêsh replies:

Ṛojê oẍirmê giran, wexta ṛeqe ṛeqe darê darṛîma, firxînê me'negiya, nalînê şêr û 'erfûta, ḥawe ḥawê lawê kurmanca, çiqas merî çê be ancax mêr beranberî mêr derêye'.'	On the day of heavy destiny, with the crashing of wood on wood, the waggons and horses, the wailing of lionhearts and heroes, the shouting of young Kurmanji lads, how brave a man would be if he were to come out to face another man.' (3: 2).

The Mîr is displeased; stanza 4 says:

Mîr got, 'Kuṛo, cot qewaz, ṛabin pêye!	Mîr said, 'Boy, you two bodyguards, get to your feet!
Nigê Dewrêş bavne qeydêye!	Bind the foot of Derwêshê 'Evdî with fetters!
Stiyê wî bikine lelêye!	Put his neck in the stocks!
Sivê van çaxa ezê berê Dewrêş bidime ḥevsêye!'	In the morning I will put him into prison!'

It is clear that by his questioning the Mîr is testing Derwêsh; he seems to be requesting a commitment from Derwêsh to fight unquestioningly for him and is angered by Derwêsh's failure to state unequivocal loyalty immediately. He is quick to exert his power over him by having him bound. After releasing him at 'Edûlê's request, he rather capriciously shows him favour, takes him hunting, and demands choice gazelle meat, taboo amongst Iraqi Yezidis at least and probably also for a Caucasian Yezidi audience. Certainly his motives are not so clearly depicted as those of Zor Temer Pasha in Israel Ohanyan's telling, and one is tempted to wonder whether a more fully explained original storyline, known to the audience, lies behind the whole of Derwêsh's interaction with him. Elsewhere in Kurdish oral tradition, kings and high-ranking lords can be presented with some ambivalence when they interact with heroes. Variants of the Kurdish epic *Dimdim* trace a complex relationship between the hero and his King, which begins with testing, moves towards trust and ultimately ends in confrontation (Jelîl 1960: 120–133). It is noticeable that the Mîr himself is not particularly courageous. He panics when he sees the enemy warriors, and has to be reassured by Derwêsh (stanzas 11 and 12).

CONCLUSION

The various genres clearly have different conventions for describing violent conflict. The poetry, especially the lyrical *stran*, has very impressionistic descriptions of battle, told from the viewpoint of individuals. There are also strong gender roles, with emotions of vulnerability articulated by women, and declarations of strength and the joy of battle associated (in general) with men.[21] The motif of the exhortatory speech can clearly be associated with both men and women, as *Dawûdê Dawûd* shows; the speeches are similar in both performances, but Silo has Shêrîn deliver it (3: 5–11) and 'Pîr Qewwal' has Dawûd (3: 6–10). Nikitine refers to the 'culte du Combat' (1956: 268) among the Kurds which is expressed in lyrical songs, but the feelings articulated in the *stran* on the subject are more complex and reflect the community's ambivalence on the subject. In *stran*, observers are often women who present war as a calamity for the community. Young men themselves are drawn to it and indeed prove their honour by it. In these martial lyrics and also the narratives, battle is the test of a man, but it is also a fearful thing. The *Ferîq Pasha* and *Dawûdê Dawûd stran* both present their articulations of male virtue and pleasure in battle within the context of lamentation articulated by women; the lamentation and anxiety far outweigh the pleasure. This is a somewhat surprising vision of battle from a society which, by all accounts, places a high value on machismo, but the (admittedly few) published sources show that it is not confined to these Sinjari songs. Even in Nikitine's selection of lyrics (1956: 259–68), there are many references to the destruction wrought by conflict. This predominantly negative portrayal of battle is clearly not true for all Kurmanji lyrical songs, but there is a significant group of *stran* with this characteristic. It is possible, though by no means certain, that within the Yezidi historical discourse, where past persecution is an important theme, those traditions which survive are likely to depict responses to external threats, and that such presentations of battle play a greater role than in the wider Kurdish discourse.

The portrayal of warriors in Yezidi oral tradition, in common with wider Kurmanji tradition, places a high value on military prowess and manly courage. Derwêsh is drawn to his mortal combat not only by his interpretation of his code of honour – those who attempt to dissuade him keep reminding him that battle is not the only possible option – but also by passion for the fight, and, of course, for 'Edûlê. However, despite the lure of battle for young men, the *stran* do not ignore the fact that it can be a terrifying experience for the fighters themselves, as well as a disaster for the community, and that courage can require a great deal of effort. Although courage is a keynote of manliness, there are other types of Yezidi heroism. The undoubted courage of Dawûdê Dawûd is not dwelt on by his son 'Emer, who chooses instead to present him as a pure and virtuous Yezidi, betrayed by a corrupt system. In his comments and those of non-Yezidi writers, we can discern a struggle in Yezidi discourses between supporters of Dawûd and Ḥemo Shêro over which of them was the better Yezidi, Dawûd, the old-fashioned Yezidi tribal leader of established family, or Ḥemo, the son of a newly successful religious family. 'Emer, like my own informants, is careful not to make the details of such conflicts public to outsiders.

Resistance to central governments in particular, whether successful or not, continues to be valued among Yezidis and more widely in the Kurdish community, in the climate of self-determination prevailing at the beginning of the twenty-first century. It seems likely that in the future, Mulla Mustafa Barzani, who had some great military successes but ultimately failed in his rebellions, will be remembered as a greater hero than his son Mes'ûd. However, Mes'ûd, who has made many compromises, including cooperating with Saddam's forces against his Kurdish political rival, has won far greater political success than his father, especially in terms of relations with international groups and foreign powers. Similarly, the small scale of Dawûd's rebellions, his failure to win over the whole of Sinjar and his ultimate lack of success do not affect his heroic status. He never constituted a threat to the survival of any government, but his great achievement is to have defied the central authorities. Dawûd is much better known now in Badinan, inside and outside the Yezidi community, than is his rival Ḥemo Shêro, whose status he so envied. However, the overt respect currently given to headstrong heroes such as Dawûd belies the pragmatism of the Yezidi community, whose political adaptability has enabled them to survive the past turbulent century. They are inspirational figureheads rather than role-models.

Of course, the warrior is not the only type of hero in Yezidi oral tradition. Derwêshê 'Evdî is also portrayed as a lover, or as a good Yezidi in the context of the relationship with 'Edûlê. These aspects are more strongly stressed in genres other than the narrative poems discussed so far, and will be considered in the next chapter.

CHAPTER FIVE

Representations of Romantic Love

INTRODUCTION

Love is a dominant theme in Kurdish oral literature; its very popularity raises the question of why society finds it so appealing. The stories and songs are not only entertaining, but also speak to their audience at a profound level. They address areas of conflict between accepted social behaviour and personal will, and thus illuminate some of the tensions between individual and community. This chapter will focus mostly on the *stran* of love, still held in great affection among the Yezidis; these are not merely an enunciation of social preoccupations, but also a varied and complex form of verbal art. Thus there are specific images and sentiments associated with love in the *stran* which are strongly resonant when used in other contexts. This chapter will consider the sentiments articulated in Yezidi oral tradition, and begin to explore the imagery used. There is, of course, much in common between the love songs and stories performed within the Yezidi community and those told in Kurdistan generally; indeed, many songs and stories are common to both. However, the choice of subject-matter and the way in which it is told in the Yezidi community tend to reflect the special concerns of that community more closely.

The Kurds share their interest in love stories with many of their Middle Eastern neighbours; the tensions in these other societies, and their expression in verbal art, have been convincingly analysed in various works (e.g. Abu Lughod 1988, Grima 1992). There are numerous social points in common with Kurdish communities, including the Yezidis, and many common themes, such as that of the 'star-crossed' lovers. However, Kurdish love songs and stories are distinctive in that they are usually explicitly grounded in a Kurdish context. Those featuring historical individuals – a majority in the Yezidi oral tradition – contain many details of Kurdish village life. Some songs are rather sexually explicit by comparison with 'polite' literature from the Iranophone region. Despite this apparent 'realism', however, there is an undoubted element of fantasy in some of the 'tellings' of these love stories, especially in the *stran*, and particularly in relation to the representation of women.

The theme of love shows itself in many genres, especially poetic ones; of the *stran* in my collection, the vast majority are songs of love. Since most of my tapes were recorded at parties and copied for retailing to the public, this predominance of love songs may be taken as a fair indication of audience preferences. Many of the long narrative poems performed by Kurdish Muslim *dengbêj* on cassette, radio and television, (and still, occasionally, in the villages), were love stories, such as *Mem and Zîn* and *Khej and Siyabend*. Love was also one of the dominant themes in the songs of commercial artists whose music was played in both public and private spaces in Badinan; not only Kurdish singers, but also the popular *arabesk* singers of Turkey, and popular Arab singers, are admired. Although many of the Kurdish love songs played and broadcast in Badinan were modern rather than traditional, they still use similar vocabulary and images to the *stran* of the Yezidis, and commercial singers such as Şivan Perwer have recorded older love songs with modern instrumentation. The Kurdish commercial descendant of the traditional 'folkloric' love song is easily recognisable, and its allusion to Kurdish village life is part of its appeal.

It should be said at the outset that all the material which will be considered in this chapter concerns heterosexual love. I have not encountered any examples, either during fieldwork or in the published collections of material, which describe love between men or between women in terms similar to those used for love between the sexes.[1] However, within the realm of heterosexual love a wide variety of situations are described; both lovers may be unmarried, or one or both may be married to another. The love may be requited or not; lovers may be old or young.

Like the last chapter, this will consider a small number of oral traditions in detail – songs and stories about the love of Derwêshê 'Evdî and 'Edûlê, and Besê (or Besna). Derwêsh, as we have seen, is well remembered among the Yezidis; Besa Khelîl, to use her full name, is less famous, but her story is fairly typical of the lyrical *stran*. She was a young woman, believed to be a historical individual, who was married against her will to a much older man.

LOVE AND MARRIAGE IN KURDISTAN

This complex subject, which could warrant a book in itself, forms part of various anthropological studies of Kurdish communities (e.g. Hansen 1961: 115–38, Yalçin-Heckmann 1991: 211–55). I shall confine myself here to a few observations which can be said to be generally true in Iraqi Kurdistan, and which apply to both Muslim and Yezidi communities.

Marriage is the norm in Kurdistan. In Iraqi Kurdistan in recent years, with more of the population receiving state education, the age at which people marry has risen. Many of those who now have grown-up children were married by their late teens; often girls were married in their early teens. It is now common for those in higher education to wait until they have finished their studies before they are married. Those men who became *pêşmerge* in the resistance movement in the years before 1991 spent most of their time in the mountains, and many married later than their peers in the villages and towns; those who did marry during their careers as *pêşmerge* often spent very little time with their wives and children. With the rise in later marriages has come a trend towards monogamy, which though compulsory for Christians and Jews, was not so for Muslim men, who could have up to four wives, nor for Yezidis, who could have as many wives as they could afford. Overall, marriages in rural areas take place earlier, especially for girls, and are more likely to be polygamous. However, it must be emphasised that these are general trends, with many variations.

Marriages in Kurdistan are alliances between families and are usually arranged. Parents may identify a partner for their child while he or she is still an infant. Elaborate negotiations are carried out by representatives of families before betrothal and marriage take place ('Tawûsparêz' 1943). Patrilateral parallel-cousin marriage, which is widespread throughout the Middle East, is common, but not overwhelmingly so, in both Yezidi and Muslim communities; there are many Kurdish proverbs both supportive and critical of it (cf. Abu-Lughod 1986: 56–8). A bride almost always goes to live with her husband's family – her relationship with her mother-in-law is again the subject of proverbs. For a period of time at least, her primary loyalties and affections are assumed to lie with her birth family, rather than her married family; this tension is rather dramatically illustrated by the case of the Yezidi Princess Wansa, who shot and wounded her husband, the Mîr Se'îd Beg, because he had agreed to have her brother killed (Guest 1993: 190).

The degree of choice exercised by a prospective bride, or indeed, a groom, varies according to the attitudes of his or her family. A well-educated, middle-class (and rather beautiful) friend of mine, a very desirable potential bride, received several proposals during 1992. She was allowed to refuse them all, and was not at all eager to be married; nevertheless she felt that, for the good name of her family, she must one day accept an offer.[2] Another woman from an educated family had been promised to a distant relation when she was still a child, and had married him, but had not had a happy relationship with her husband's family. Her parents greatly regretted their decision to follow their obligation to the other family by giving her to them. However, the elderly Sheykh K. whom I met in Khanek considered it right and proper to marry his daughters off according to his wishes, and even joked that daughters were preferable to sons because of the large amounts of bride-price received by the father.

There is no doubt that, as more young men and women receive secondary and higher education and move into the professional classes, their freedom of movement will give them a greater chance of meeting partners not previously known to their families. However, even in the village environment, the sexes have never been totally segregated. Men and women meet at festivals and family celebrations, especially at weddings, and dance together in large groups. They thus have the opportunity of seeing each other, and of exchanging limited conversation. The community would not sanction men and women meeting alone, but according to accounts of Kurdish village life, such meetings do take place secretly. Even informants whose own marriages were arranged for them and who claimed never to have been in love themselves knew people who had fallen in love when they were young; some of these had married each other.

It is the control of marriage by the family rather than by the protagonists which produces that conflict between the wishes of the individual on the one hand, and the behaviour approved by society on the other, that permeates so many Kurdish love songs and stories. Few love stories (apart from those in folktales) end in a happy marriage, and love songs often have a strong element of sadness because something is keeping the lovers apart. Many of the *stran* collected during the fieldwork described situations where lovers were unable to marry for various reasons, and, as will be discussed later, these songs draw much of their emotional power from this essentially tragic conflict between society and the individual. It is extremely difficult to assess how often in Kurdish society those already in love with one person are forced to marry another, and how often those already married fall in love with someone forbidden to them, when the evidence is anecdotal. Modesty might prevent an individual from openly acknowledging feelings considered unacceptable in the community; the ever-present rumours of liaisons and affairs are likely to be fuelled by personal and family enmities. This is a particularly difficult area for an outsider to fathom. Lindisfarne (1990: 1–2) gives a vivid description of how researchers living for a considerable time in a community (in her case the Durrani of Afghanistan) can be unaware of liaisons taking place close by. What can be said with confidence is that love and marriage are regarded as separate, and their coincidence as unusual and fortunate for the lovers, perhaps less desirable for the family. Some informants said that love had grown after marriage.

There is one way open to lovers who wish to marry each other against the wishes of their families, and that is *revandin* (cf. Yalçin-Heckmann 1991: 247–53). This term translates as 'abduction', as it is the causative form of the verb *revîn*, 'to run away'. However, its use in Kurdish is often more akin to the English 'elopement'. The distinction between elopement and abduction may be very unclear. If the woman is willing, then her choice of partner is made very public; this is unacceptable to her family, who should be seen to control her sexuality, and they are likely to present it as an abduction.[3] Whichever is the case, the woman must marry the man who takes her away. The usual pattern of events, as described by Badinani informants, is that after running away, the couple stay under the protection of an influential person, locally or at a distance, depending on the degree of insult felt by the woman's family, and the consequent danger to the lovers' safety. Usually, if the suitor is felt by the woman's family to be from an appropriate social group, a decent interval will be allowed to elapse and then overtures would be made to the father of the woman under the mediation of the influential protector. A cash settlement may often be made in lieu of bride-price and the married couple can return to the area. This is the most preferable option, as relations between families can then normalise, the woman can continue to visit her family, and her father will not have lost face. *Revandin*, though not considered the ideal way of making a marriage, is certainly considered acceptable if the criteria given above are fulfilled, and it is fair to say that it is a social institution in itself. Complications arise, however, if there are differences in status, or worse, religious faith, between the parties. Marriage between members of different communities in Badinan is not approved of; in some cases, the woman's family may not welcome the marriage but feel powerless to resist a settlement. For instance, during my stay a young Christian girl eloped with a local Muslim man who already had one wife. They stayed with a local agha pending the initiation of negotiations. The case caused a great deal of anger in the Christian community, who felt that as a minority they risked reprisals if they refused to accept a settlement. By my return home, the case was nearing resolution, but the woman, whilst not suffering complete ostracism, would effectively lose her membership of the Christian community.

Love and Marriage in the Yezidi Community

What has been said above about society in Badinan also applies to the Yezidi community, often to a greater degree. The constraints surrounding the choice of marriage partner are even greater for Yezidis than for Muslims; not only are some rural fathers, like Sheykh K., ready to marry off their daughters very young, but the caste system and the ban on exogamy also result in a smaller selection of appropriate marriage partners and an even greater reduction in the individual's freedom to choose. Lineage is of course an important factor in the Yezidis' perception of religious power and authority, and appropriate marriage is the mechanism by which lineage is perpetuated. Numerous Yezidis, rural and urban, said to me that endogamy was the only way to maintain the 'purity' of the Yezidis as a whole, and of the castes and sub-castes within the Yezidi community.[4] The Yezidi preoccupation with order and purity sees exogamy as polluting. A marriage with an outsider is not only repugnant to Yezidis in religious terms but also a challenge to the genealogical purity at the foundations of the community's power structures.[5] Marriage with a Yezidi of an inappropriate caste would constitute a similar challenge, and mean that neither member would have a proper place in Yezidi society. It was noted in Chapter Two that the Yezidis of Northern Iraq are undoubtedly more conservative on the subject of marriage than some Yezidi communities. Both the Yezidis of Germany, most of whom originally came from Turkey, and those of the former Soviet Union, have had to grapple with the issue of exogamy, a prospect which appals the Yezidis of Northern Iraq; indeed several well-known religious figures, including Feqîr Hejî, Baba Chawûsh, and the Baba Sheykh, participated in a video aimed at the Yezidis in Germany, during which they urged them to preserve the purity of the Yezidis and not to marry outside the community.[6] I saw this revulsion against exogamy clearly expressed during a conversation with a high-ranking lady from the Mîr's family, when I injudiciously referred to the ostracised Princess Wansa. Her response was that one ought not to speak about her, not because she shot her husband, the Yezidi Mîr Se'îd Beg, but because she later married a Muslim.

The institution of *revandin*, followed by a reasonably amicable settlement, seems to be relatively common in Yezidi society, especially in Sinjar. Fawziya Rahman, a Sinjari Muslim, recalls her father harbouring several eloping Yezidi couples at his house in Sinjar in the 1960s. Given that those who marry outside caste or outside the community can only choose ostracism (or death, if the aggrieved families find them) it follows that those who elope and make a settlement must be from the same caste and from appropriate social groups, otherwise a settlement would not be possible. The high incidence of *revandin* would seem to argue either that Yezidi couples are more assertive than lovers in other groups, or that Yezidi families are often unsympathetic to the wishes of their children, and try to force them into unwanted marriages quite frequently – a plausible scenario, given that Yezidi fathers receive a bride-price for their daughters and may keep it, whereas among Muslims dowry is, in theory, a resource for the bride and bride-price is returnable on divorce. It is certainly the case that the Yezidis, proportionately, have a smaller educated middle class than other groups, and that the modern trends towards monogamy and marrying later are less advanced. Sheykhani Yezidis often cited Sinjar as particularly 'backward' (their term) in these respects; how far this is true when Sinjaris are compared with rural Sheykhanis is unclear.

As with the Muslim community, the honour of a Yezidi family is strongly associated with the status and behaviour of its women. As the community is so close-knit, rumours spread very easily and women have to be particularly careful of their reputations. Conversely, men have to be circumspect in the way they speak to or about women of other families to avoid antagonising fathers, brothers and husbands. The Sinjaris are considered by other Yezidis to be particularly sensitive on this issue. Even the singing of a *stran* may cause offence if it is a love song addressed to an identifiable woman; as Kheyro Khelef, a Sinjari himself, attested in the introduction to one of his songs, which I saw on video, a singer must take great care not to reveal too much in a love song, as Sinjaris are quick to anger. There seems to be something of a grey area here; according to Pîr Khidir Silêman, who cited several examples, the identity of the women to whom the songs of contemporary *stranbêj* are addressed is often generally known, but her family do not always take offence. Much depends on how blatantly the *stranbêj* alludes to the woman's true identity, and of course on the attitude of her relations. However, Kheyro was not overstating the case; the popular *stranbêj* Qarpal Sinjari is said to have composed songs about a particular woman for years. He continued to sing about her even after her marriage to another man, whereupon the angry husband killed him.

The subject of romantic love is obviously closely linked to relationships of gender and power. If male prestige is closely associated with the status and behaviour of women, this gives women a certain power over men. As Pitt-Rivers says (1977: 80):

> Feminine power is not overt, but, due to their participation in the familial honour (as the repositories of its moral and sacred aspects) women hold in their hands the power not merely to put pressure on their menfolk but actually to 'ruin' them.

Yezidi society is consistent with other Middle Eastern groups in the importance it ascribes to *namûs*, the measure of women's modesty and men's honour. In a fascinating discussion of love and sexual behaviour in the Middle East in general, and more specifically among the Durrani in Afghanistan, Lindisfarne considers sexual liaison as a subversive tactic carried out by women and argues that Durrani women whose menfolk are weak are more likely to have adulterous liaisons, whereas women from politically and economically strong families are more likely to suffer from problems such as *jinn* possession (1990: 14–16). My inability to spend long periods living in Yezidi villages prevented any insight into the incidence of extra-marital affairs there, though I did hear of several among non-Yezidis in Dihok, but this complex relationship between gender and power, both overt and covert, certainly does exist in Yezidi society. The oral traditions do hint at such 'subversive' tactics on the part of women; these will be considered later in the chapter.

LOVE STORIES AND SONGS IN THE YEZIDI COMMUNITY

It was very easy to find *stran* of love among the Yezidi folklore. The songs tended to be almost entirely lyrical with few narrative sections; as in the historical *stran* described in the previous chapter, the singer would speak 'in character' as one, or sometimes both, of the lovers. Antiphonal songs, with alternate sections spoken by each of the lovers, are common among both the Yezidi *stran* and Kurdish love songs generally. Sometimes different singers, or different groups, will sing the parts of the two characters; in Şivan's recording of *Gelavêj*, for instance, he and his wife Gulistan take the roles. However, in the Yezidi *stran* tradition it is normal for one singer to sing the entire song. An example of this is the version of Besê which will be discussed later in the chapter. The obvious consequence of this lack of narrative is that, to appreciate the song fully, the audience must have some knowledge of the story in its entirety. The songs tend to be highly allusive, often referring to tragic events. For example, the *stran* of *Khej and Siyabend* in my collection, recorded in 1978 by Pîr Micho, enunciates the quarrel of the lovers who had eloped to Mount Sipan in Turkey. Siyabend praises the beauty of the girl Khej (or Khejê), and wishes for more time with her; she says she has caused her family to pursue them. He suggests she goes back to her family. The story is so well-known that the audience will be aware that after the quarrel, Siyabend rushed away and fell to his death from a precipice, and that Khejê jumped because she could not bear to live without him. Knowing the story's tragic end adds extra pathos for the audience and is necessary for full understanding of the song. As general knowledge of traditional stories declines, it is of course incumbent on the *stranbêj* to contextualise songs of love, like the other *stran*, for the audience by explaining their background.

It is worth mentioning briefly some of the most common terms associated with love in Badinan. The most commonly used verb for 'like' or 'love' is *hez kirin*. Nouns with similar ambiguity include *dost* and *heval*, which often mean 'friend' or 'comrade' but, when used in a relationship between a man and a woman, are often interpreted as 'boyfriend' or 'girlfriend'.[7] The word *yar* unambiguously means 'lover', as do *dildar* and *evîndar*. Romantic love itself is usually called *evîn*, or sometimes, as in Israel Ohanyan's narrative, simply *dil* 'heart' – he says that there was *dil* between Derwêsh and 'Edûlê. *Dil ketin* and *dil dan* both mean 'fall in love'. There are many euphemisms for sexual intercourse; one commonly used word is *ramûsan* 'kiss', which like the French *baiser*, also means 'sex'. *Maç* also means 'kiss' but has fewer sexual overtones – one gives *maç* to all sorts of friends and relations.

The areas of concern already identified, namely the conflict between love and duty and the problems of intermarriage between communities, are clearly reflected in the body of *stran* collected during the fieldwork. *Revandin* is a common element of many songs. As we have seen, it features not only in such 'legendary' stories as *Khej and Siyabend*, whose historicity is not uniformly accepted by the Yezidis, but also in the 'historical' songs (the great majority of those performed by *stranbêj*) whose protagonists are accepted as historical individuals. For instance, a song showing the politics of elopement in more detail is *Matrano* 'O Bishop', also called *'Elî and Meryem*. These two lovers are both Muslims, and Meryem is the daughter of the Walî of Van. Since he is so powerful, they know they cannot expect protection from other Muslims in the area, so they take refuge with the Christian bishop, or Matran. Faced with an army sent by the Walî, the bishop refuses to surrender the lovers, and is eventually killed.

Tragedy is not always the dominant theme of Yezidi representations of love; there is a lighter side. Often this is shown in the upbeat *peste* which are often mixed with the *stran* in performances. *Kênê*, as sung by Lezgîn Seydo, is a good example of this. He tells her, *Bi şevê tu doşeka min î, bi rojê tu liḥêfa min î ...* 'By night you are my mattress, by day you are my quilt', adding how much he loves her, and that he hopes he can be alone with her, finishing his stanza with 'Oh Kênê, give me a kiss!' The word used is *ramûsan* which, as we have seen, is ambiguous. There are many such songs, performed with good humour and a rather self-conscious naughtiness. There are also songs which use stock tragic elements with irony; Kheyro Khelef plays on the common motif of the wandering lover in his performance of *Sodalê*, when he describes looking for his beloved girl in various places in Turkey, Iraq and Iran, and gives a description of what the girls were like, in terms of looks and willingness, in each place.

Some songs combine intentional humour with pathos and sadness, such as the group called *Kherabo!* 'Bad boy!' where a girl reproaches her beloved. The scenario of these songs is quite variable; a common situation is that of a girl who reviles a young man for marrying another instead of her. The lovers are often unnamed. According to the Kurdish poet and folklorist Jigerkhwîn, in these songs the girl may call the young man *Nebaşo*, 'wicked one', *Neqenco*, 'horrible one' and *Pîso*, 'filthy one' (1988: 127). One performance of this, from the Mardin area, was published in the Kurdish periodical *Hawar* by Roger Lescot ('Tawûsparêz' 1942). It is an interesting song, and I have included it in Part II, though, strictly speaking, it cannot be safely assumed to be a 'Yezidi' oral tradition; it came from the Omeriyan, a tribe with Yezidi and Muslim sections. The girl gives contradictory statements about her feelings; for instance the final stanza says:

Xerabo, wile, tu Xerabo,	Bad boy, my God, you're bad,
Malê te pir e, ji canê te ṛe edabo!	Your wealth is great, may it torment you!
Tu bi şêxkî diwanzde elmî bo,	If you were a sheykh learned in twelve sciences,
Sed werdê te di bêrîka mi de bo	And if I had one hundred of your charms in my pocket
Qenyatiya dilê mi bi te nabo!	My heart would not be more satisfied with you!

(14: 1–5).

There is also conscious irony; having called him 'bad boy' herself, she calls down numerous colourful curses, including infertility and failure of crops, on anyone else who says to him 'you are bad.' Amid the descriptions of the pain of love, expressed by both girl and boy in the song, is some humour; the girl venomously describes the boy's new bride as the worst kind of broken-down old nag, whilst she herself is a thoroughbred. A convincing variety of emotions felt by the girl, including anger, love and sorrow, are expressed in quick succession; the complexity of this portrayal rings true in psychological terms. The song is not 'sophisticated' in the ordinary sense; it is not court poetry, nor is it urbane. It describes a situation between peasants which is probably relatively common, almost everyday; however, it also contains complexity of characterisation, clarity of presentation, and irony.

Like the songs about other historical events, many of the songs performed among the Yezidis are about people from other areas and communities; *Matrano*, which presumably originated in the Van area of Turkey, is just one example of a story which must at one time have been circulating over a larger area. The fact that love songs are about real people puts Kheyro's remarks about how easily a *stranbêj* can give offence by his songs into perspective. It would hardly be convincing to compose a song and claim it was about a fantasy woman if the customary practice is to base songs on the lives of real individuals. The perception of the love songs as historical also raises the question of how lovers are commemorated, and what criteria their story must fulfil to be considered worthy of song. The historical record as given by the *stran* makes little mention of couples who fell in love and then married each other, or of couples who had no strong attachments elsewhere before their marriage and grew to love each other over time, but one can hardly assume that because this genre has ignored them they did not exist. I heard of several such couples, all within the context of personal or immediate family history. The *stran* give a fascinating insight into Yezidi preoccupations, but one cannot be beguiled by their apparent 'realism'; their 'artistic agenda' means that there are whole areas of experience and discourse which they ignore.

Derwêshê ʿEvdî and ʿEdûlê

Let us return to the love between the Yezidi warrior and the chief's daughter. This is an extremely popular aspect of the story; of the six performances printed by Jelîl (1978 I: 279–98), four are love lyrics. I will consider only two of these, mainly because they all contain much the same material, rearranged in different ways according to the wishes of the performer, like the *Ferîq Pasha* performances discussed in the previous chapter. A full discussion of all five would require greater performance detail than that furnished by Jelîl. After the *stran* I will also consider a very brief prose summary, given to me in English by Pîr Khidir Silêman, which exemplifies a modern Iraqi Yezidi perspective on the story.

The performance collected by Jelîl (1978 I: 292–4) from Meḥmûdê 'Elîyê Temo, a Yezidi sheykh, is put into the mouth of the girl who loves Derwêsh, though she is not named. She begins by saying that other people do not care for him, but she does; she compares him to a flawless pomegranate. She then describes an incident in her father's tent where she served coffee to Derwêsh and in her agitation she spilt a little on his cloak. She took a gold piece which belonged to her father from inside her clothes, and went to a shop. She bought seven cakes of soap, wore them away, and dried up the waters of the river Pa, but could not get the cloak clean. She then says that spring has come; members of her family are dying or being arrested, but when she meets the eye of Derwêsh all seems well. The next verse changes abruptly; the Mîr orders Derwêsh to be brought to him, and asks how many men a man can face in the heat of battle. Derwêsh replies that a true man comes out to face men; the Mîr has him put in chains. Derwêsh says he is worth three hundred and sixty-six fighting men; the Mîr asks for meat from a young gazelle, but Derwêsh replies that what the Mîr really wants is for Derwêsh to fight for him, that the Mîr is his fate. The girl finishes by saying that she will love no-one after Derwêsh.

'Egîtê Têjir's lyrical song does not name the girl either (Jelîl 1978 I: 294–5). She describes the pastures of the Kîkan and Milan, and all the famous people there, but says it is destitute without Derwêsh. She then describes how she went to the crowded guest-room, and spilt coffee on Derwêsh's cloak. Taking a gold piece from her headdress, she asked a man to get her seven cakes of soap from town. She weeps; the soap is worn away, her hands swollen, the river – the Mûrad this time – dried up, but the stain has not washed out. Then she adds that it is spring; members of her family are dying, but when she meets the eye of Derwêsh, all is well.

Although I have described these songs as 'lyrical' it is obvious that they contain narrative sections, particularly that of Meḥmûdê 'Elîyê Temo, which incorporates many details of the riddling exchange between the Mîr and Derwêsh, and the Mîr's abrupt demands, which were discussed in Chapter Four. Similarly, the finely-crafted narrative of Israel Ohanyan contains a substantial lyrical section at the end, where 'Edulê offers riches to anyone who can bring her news of Derwêsh, describes an encounter where he was angry with her, and says she would not exchange him for a number of famous and rich people. She then describes in graphic physical terms the effect on her of losing him, and says she will deck his horse out beautifully, so that people will know how beloved he was – an allusion to Caucasian funerary custom. Narrative and lyric can be closely intertwined in Kurdish oral tradition. Nevertheless these two love songs purport to be 'Edulê's words; their narrative sections are framed within her own expressions of her feelings and their primary focus is her emotional state; they are predominantly, if not entirely, lyrical.

One of the major narrative episodes in the Caucasian songs is the exchange with the king, leading to the binding of Derwêsh. Meḥmûdê 'Elîyê Temo's song moves quite abruptly from 'Edûlê's remarks about her love for Derwêsh to the riddles, and then moves again; the seventh and final stanza is as follows:

Dewrêş go, 'Mîr, ezê wî kim îlahiye,	Derwêsh said, 'Mîr, I will do what God orders,
Ezê gava ṛavim pêye, ezê te temem kim sêsid û şest û şêş mêrê di ṛimêye.'	When I get to my feet, I will be equal to three hundred and sixty-six men for you with my spear.'
Mîr go, 'Dewrêşo, dilê min dibêye kivava kara karxezalêye.'	Mîr said, 'Derwêsh, my heart wishes for a kebab of the meat of a young gazelle,'
Dewrêş go, 'Mîro, dilê min dibêye, Dilê te ne kivava kara karxezalêye,	Derwêsh said, 'Mîr, my heart is longing, Your heart does not wish for a kebab of the meat of a young gazelle,
Tu dixwazî min bişînî pêşiya ḥezar ḥevsid mêrê 'eskerê 'Emerê Unise, min hatî xezêye.'	You want to send me to face one thousand seven hundred fighting men of 'Emerê Ûnise, you have come to me as my fate.'
Wey delal, ezê pey Dewrêşê 'Evdî, lewandê şevê, lawkê êzdî ṛa, kesekî ṛa navêjim, "tu delalî."'	Alas my love, after Derwêshê 'Evdî, the reckless one of the night, the Yezidi lad, I will say to no-one "you are beloved".

The hunting motif is directly linked with Derwêsh's final battle. 'Egîtê Têjir does not use these exchanges between the king and Derwêsh in his lyric – they are major constituents of his narrative, which was discussed in Chapter Four.

The 'coffee-spilling' episode is interesting; it differs substantially from Derwêsh's symbolic taking of the coffee-cup from 'Edûlê in Israel Ohanyan's narrative, which made public his claim to her, but it seems more than coincidence that narrative and lyrical songs should have important elements so strongly associated with the passing of coffee-cups between Derwêsh and 'Edûlê. Though lovers are often described as 'guests' in Kurdish love lyric, coffee-cups are not a particularly common stock element. The spilling of the coffee is presented as calamitous, more than a social embarrassment for 'Edûlê. Meḥmûdê 'Elîyê Temo emphasises the lengths she went to to remove the stain:

Divê, navê kapêk pol pere cem min tinebû,	At this time I had no money about me,
Minê destê xwe bire nava sîng û berê xwe, zêrekî diha dîtibû xercê şeherê bavê minî ḥevt sala bû,	I put my hand on my breast inside my clothes, I saw a piece of gold there – my father's going-to-town money for seven years,
Minê hildabû, ezê çûme dikanê van 'etara,	I took it out, I went to the shop of those grocers,

Minê go, dikançiyo, ha, dikançiyo, minê niqitka qawê ṛijandiye ser ‘eba Dewrêşê ‘Evdî,	I said, shopkeeper, shopkeeper, I spilt a drop of coffee on the cloak of Derwêshê ‘Evdî,
Minê hildabû ḥevt qalib sabûne, teşt û sîtile, ezê çûme ber çemê Payê vê mîrayê,	I took seven cakes of soap, a bowl and a cauldron, I went to the Pa, that river of kings,
Çemê Payê mîrayê ava çil çar kaniya bû.	The river Pa, of kings had the waters of forty four streams.
Ava çîl çar kaniya mi çikiya bû,	The waters of forty-four streams dried up for me,
Tilî pêçiyê min maşiya bû,	My fingers were swollen,
Ḥevt qalib sabûna min ḥeliya bû,	I wore away seven cakes of soap,
Teşt û sîtilê min qul bibû,	My bowl and cauldron had holes in them,
Hela hê niqitka qawê ser ‘eba Dewrêşê ‘Evdî neçûbû.	But still the drop of coffee on the cloak of Derwêshê ‘Evdî had not gone.
Wey delal, wey delal, wey delal, wey delal, wey delal,	Alas beloved, alas,
Ezê pey Dewrêşê ‘Evdî, lawkê Êzdiya ṛa, navê mêra naynime ser xwe.	After Derwêshê ‘Evdî I will not link the name of any men with my own.

This incident emphasises the effect of Derwêsh on ‘Edûlê’s composure, but the unsuccessful washing of the cloak is also important. Another performance, by an Armenian, Sarkis Bozoyan, collected by Jelîl (1978 I: 278–81) but not included in Part II, makes it clear that the stain has an importance beyond the literal:

5. Kubara sibê ṛabûm, min qolî zêṛê serê xwe qetand, çûme li Ḥemayê, li Ḥekayê, li Şamê, li Bexdayê, derê dikanê wan beqala, min da ḥevt qalib ṛeqîya sabûnê hildam pêda-pêda meşîyam, çûme ser ava Xamûrê, minê ‘ebayê Besrayê Dewrêşê şêx ‘Evdî, ḥûtê binîya beṛîya jêrîn, sîyarê Senemê, xudanê zeng û zêṛîn, şûştîye, ḥevt qalib sabûnê destê mida mefîyaye, ava Xamûrê, bextê min poṛkuṛê, ser mida miçiqiye, ‘eba Besra Dewrêşê şêx ‘Evdî temîz nebû ji vê qiṛêcê, ko li derdê ‘eba Besra ma dilê mi jî.	In the early morning I rose, I took a gold piece from my headdress, I went to Ḥema, to Ḥeka, to Damascus, to Baghdad, the places where those grocers had their shops, I got seven cakes of hard soap, I took them, step by step I walked, I went to the waters of the Khabûr, I washed the cloak from Baṣra which belonged to Derwêsh Sheykh ‘Evdî, the giant in the furthest desert, rider of Senem, lord of riches and gold; seven cakes of soap wore away in my hand, the Khabûr, and fortune dried up for me, the curly-haired one, Derwêsh Sheykh ‘Evdî’s cloak from Basra was not clean of this stain, and the mark on the cloak stayed in my heart too.

The indelibility of her feelings for Derwêsh are paralleled by the mark on the cloak. It is also conceivable that the audience of this lyric would be familiar with those narratives, such as Ohanyan's, where the taking of the cup constitutes a claim to the girl; if this is in their minds, then the spilling of the coffee may well be a bad omen. However, this is speculation; the lyrics do not mention that the cup is offered as a challenge, and that he who accepts it will win 'Edûlê. It is always problematic to speculate on the contextual knowledge of an audience without fieldwork amongst that audience. A direct link between the 'claim' motif of the narrative and the 'stain' motif of the lyrics is difficult to argue, not only because of the differences between them, but also because Israel Ohanyan learned his songs in the Diyarbakir area where he grew up, whereas the singers of the lyrics, with the exception of Sarkis Bozoyan (the only other non-Yezidi), had lived all their lives in Soviet Armenia. Yet it does seem that an episode concerning a cup of coffee is associated, albeit vaguely, with the story of an encounter between Derwêsh and 'Edûlê. Each strand of the oral tradition interprets it differently; for Ohanyan, it is one of those fleeting and poignant moments in the story where they publicly affirm their love (the moment where Derwêsh leans down from his horse to kiss 'Edûlê is another); for Meḥmûdê 'Elîyê Temo and 'Egîtê Têjir it is a symbolic and somehow disastrous moment.

Like the *stran* of battle, the love lyrics combine certain motifs and episodes distinctive to the story being told with many stock elements. Sometimes a specific phrase or verse associated with a certain oral tradition is discernible, which may be used and developed differently. Such an example in *Derwêshê 'Evdî* is *ez ne Kîkî me, ez ne Millî me . . .*, 'I am not Kîkî, I am not Millî . . .,' where 'Edûlê denies her paternal tribal identity and claims association with Derwêsh instead. 'Egîtê Têjir's narrative has this as a climax at the end of 'Edûlê's lament, followed by *ez berdilka Dewrêşê 'Evdî, lawkê êzdîme*, 'I am the lover of Derwêshê 'Evdî, the Yezidi lad.' However, she says it is a statement she would have made if it had not shamed her family. The sentiment is also used in Sinjari *stran*; in my own collection, after the initial *Delal, delal*, Pîr Giro introduces his performance of *Derwêshê 'Evdî* with it.

It is noticeable that none of the examples collected in the Caucasus, neither the lyrics nor the narratives, emphasises that the love between Derwêsh and 'Edûlê is forbidden; they concentrate on the tragedy of his death and 'Edûlê's loss. It is interesting to compare the presentation of these with a Badinani Yezidi telling, as recounted to me in English by Pîr Khidir Silêman:

> Derwêshê 'Evdî was a Yezidi, and he and his father 'Evdî, as Sinjaris, belonged to the Milli confederacy of Kurdish tribes. The daughter of the Milli chieftain, Zor Temer Pasha, whose name was 'Edlê or

> ‘Edûlê, loved Derwêsh and he loved her. Derwêsh fought heroically for the Milli tribes against the Arab Shammar tribe. As he was Yezidi and she was a Muslim it was forbidden for them to marry. Derwêsh approached the Yezidi authorities for permission to marry ‘Edûlê, as she was willing to become a Yezidi. The Yezidi Mîr referred it to the highest religious authority, the Baba Sheykh, who refused on the grounds of lack of precedent. Derwêsh then asked a group of qewwals in his village. They also said ‘No’, but when ‘Edûlê put on a lovely dress, and Derwêsh asked ‘Would you marry such a girl?’ the qewwals replied ‘Yes, even if she was Jewish.’ Derwêsh declared ‘I have been lying with her for many nights, but I have kept a dagger lying between us, and I have not touched her, because I am waiting for permission.’ The qewwals were moved by his virtue, but the Baba Sheykh remained adamant. Derwêsh then determined to go beyond human authority and find out the will of Melek Tawus, the Peacock Angel, and the most powerful divine being below God himself. When he next went into battle, his horse fell under him. His brother offered him his own, but Derwêsh refused, saying that it was the will of Melek Tawus that he should fight on foot and not return to marry ‘Edûlê. He was killed, and ‘Edûlê took poison.

It is worth pointing out that Pîr Khidir gave the account in response to my asking him about ‘the story of Derwêshê ‘Evdî’; it did not arise from a discussion of mixed marriage, hence the emphasis on prohibition and permission is all his own. Certainly he was trying to give all the most important elements so that a foreigner could understand the major elements of the story. He has used some common folkloric elements; the motif of displaying a girl to religious figures who express admiration for her beauty is found in some *stran*, and in many tellings of *Memê Alan*, for instance, the two lovers sleep chastely alongside each other with a dagger placed between them. What is particularly striking about Pîr Khidir’s telling, however, is the way in which his Derwêsh is shown to be a virtuous Yezidi. His loyalty is never compromised; he fights heroically for his overlord, and seeks permission from the Yezidi authorities to make the marriage he wants. He refrains from sexual intercourse with his beloved because his religious authorities have not given permission. Finally he submits to the divine will of the Peacock Angel, who disposes of the world as he sees fit (Kreyenbroek 1995: 74, 76; Guest 1993: 208). The will of Melek Tawus shows itself in the form of fate. Derwêsh respects the hierarchical and ordered nature of Yezidi society, with its permissions and taboos; he does not jeopardise his membership of the community by eloping with ‘Edûlê, but takes his case to a higher court, as it were, each time he is refused.

The love between members of different faiths is identified almost immediately as the issue of most importance in Pîr Khidir’s telling. It is true that the performances from Soviet Armenia belong to different genres, but the forbidden nature of the love between Derwêsh and 'Edûlê is not a great concern for them; the tragedy lies elsewhere.[8] Jelîl even notes that 'Edûlê is the fiancée (*dergîstî*) of Derwêsh without further comment (1978 II: 476). Given that the Yezidis of Northern Iraq are more conservative on the subject of marriage than their co-religionists elsewhere, it is not surprising that this prose telling reflects this. In this telling, it is the forbidden nature of the love which is the driving force behind the story; even Derwêsh's death is linked, via the will of Melek Tawus, with this love.

Besa Khelîl

Songs based on this story have been attested in various areas; under the pseudonym 'Herekol Azizan', Jeladet Bedir Khan published a performance called *Besna* (1933), which was collected from the well-known singer from Turkey, Ehmed Ferman Kîkî (EFK); it will be referred to as the EFK *Besna*. Bedir Khan also refers to a variant form of it recorded by 'Isa Derwêsh from Zakho. Among the Badinani Yezidis she is called Besê; her full name is Besa Khelîl. The song I will consider here (referred to below as the Sheykhani *Besê*) was collected and transcribed in Sheykhan during the 1970s by Khelîl Jindî Rashow; unfortunately it lacks performance details. Most of the song consists of Besê's own words, with a few stanzas from her lover; she has been married off to a much older man, Ibrahim Temo, who is repulsive to her. According to Bedir Khan, the historical Besna, who was from the Omerîyan tribe, did elope with her lover after some years and went to another area; this part of the story seems to be less well known among the Yezidis. Although she was probably a Muslim, Besê's story, still performed in Sheykhan in the 1970s, retained its significance in the Yezidi community.

Besê describes herself as especially fine and beautiful in various ways, and expresses her bitterness (that all this has been wasted). She longs to divorce herself from her husband, and wishes her lover would marry her. She stresses her own beauty, and curses her parents for marrying her to her mean husband. She then reiterates this, adding that her husband has three wives, and is old and impotent. Her lover answers, urging her to elope. She describes her lover's beautiful appearance and her willingness to give herself to him. He then gives a description of her beauty and refers to his own distress at her marriage. She describes herself again in erotic terms, and he again extols her beauty. The EFK *Besna*, on the other hand, is a different song about the same people, though it contains various points in common with the Sheykhani song; some of these are stock elements very common in Kurdish love songs. It consists entirely of Besna's words; there is no dialogue with her lover, who is never very clearly defined. It also contains various references to the locality of Mardin. Ehmed Ferman Kîkî, was, of course, one of the Kîkan; Yezidis would claim a connection with the traditions of the Kîkan and Milan via Biroyê Sherqî, the Yezidi who was court poet to the last of the great Milan chieftains.

The imagery and style of Besa Khelîl are rather forceful but also typical of Kurdish love lyric in many ways; hence they are best considered in comparison with the imagery and style of the *Derwêsh* songs in particular, and with other Sheykhani and Sinjari songs in general.

THE IMAGERY AND STYLE OF KURDISH LOVE LYRIC

In Kurdish love poetry, there is a whole range of sentiments and images associated with the erotic, each of which has its own overtones and is instantly recognisable to its audience.

As one would expect, lovers extol each others' desirability; girls also praise their own. Both the Sheykhani Besê and the *Hawar* Besna begin by praising their own loveliness. The first stanza of the Sheykhani Besê is as follows:

Lê lê dayê,	O mother,
Min kiḥêla serê ṭewlayê,	I am the thoroughbred filly, the best in the stable,
Min x̆ezala serê şewlayê,	I am the gazelle, the best in the grasslands,
Min tifinga bergirê dev gundayê,	I am the gun defending the village, (1: 1–4).

The girl in Lescot's *Kherabo* also describes herself as a thoroughbred, in contrast with her lover's new wife:

Çewa te dev ji mi, kihêla serê tewla berda, tuê li bergîla şix̆ulê Rismiliya û Qibaliya dihesilî.	How did you give me up, the best thoroughbred mare in the stable, for that nag of Rishmili and Qibali stock?
Mi ji te ṛe ne go, 'Di meha biharê, bergîla li şwîna kihêla metewilî!'	Didn't I say to you 'In spring, you must not harness old nags instead of thoroughbreds!' (11: 3–4).

Besê's reference to the gun as something precious is a reflection of the value placed on firearms.

Besê is also *x̆ezala serê şewlayê* 'the best gazelle in the countryside' (1: 3) and 'like a gazelle' (4: 6). Many images from nature, each with its own overtones, are used in descriptions of physical attributes. Gazelles, associated with grace and beauty, are particularly resonant – beautiful women in love lyric are often compared to them, and they also feature in the more 'legendary' types of oral tradition; for instance, the story of *Khej and Siyabend* turns on the sighting of a gazelle, and in 'Egîtê Têjir's narrative poem of *Derwêshê 'Evdî*, the Mîr specifically demands gazelle meat, the eating of which is taboo for Yezidis, when he has been testing Derwêsh's loyalty (9: 3). These rather curious exchanges between these two characters seem to come from older folkloric tradition rather than from any nineteenth-century tribal battle.

As well as animals, lovers may also be compared with birds. EFK's Besna compares herself to a wild duck; the boy in Lescot's *Kherabo* compares the girl to wild birds (8: 5), and the girl calls him *bazê dilê min*, literally 'the hawk of my heart' or 'my hawk' (3: 7; 8: 5). Though it does not feature in *Besa Khelîl*, the nightingale is a bird closely associated with love in written Middle Eastern genres, and this is also true of the Yezidi *stran*. In Pîr Giro's performance of *Sodalê* in my collection, it is mentioned; Khidir Feqîr also has a song called *Bilbilo*, 'O nightingale.' ZK also includes a song called 'The Nightingale visited the rose' (Jelîl 1978 I: 395). These creatures are all portrayed positively. Others are less pleasant; when Besê's lover is agonising about the vileness of her husband, he talks of the owl (8: 3). The EFK Besna compares her husband to an owl, and in Lescot's *Kherabo* it is mentioned along with the jackal and the corpses in the cemetery as one of the unpleasant things which felt sympathy for the lovers (4: 6). Besê also compares her husband Ibrahim Temo to a (gelded) ox, not only unattractive but also impotent (5: 14).

Though not a strong feature of the Sheykhani *Besa Khelîl*, plants are also a common image in Kurdish love lyric. The erotic associations of the pomegranate are clear in the *Derwêshê 'Evdî* lyrics. Meḥmûdê 'Elîyê Temo's lyric compares Derwêsh to a perfect, flawless, and seedless pomegranate, an impossible perfection, as an indication of his worth to her:

Wey delal, wey delal, wey delal, wey delal, wey delal,	Alas, alas my love,
Ber dilê 'evdalî xwedê da, tiyo netişteko,	You who are nothing to the heart of any servant of God,
Ber dilê min 'evdala xwedê da, hinarî deşta Bêlacûkê, xurê kalan û pîran bêḥeb û bêdendiko ...,	But to me, a servant of God, you are a pomegranate of the plain of Bêlajuk, food of the grandfathers and grandmothers, flawless with no seeds ...,
	(1: 1–3)

In Israel Ohanyan's narrative, 'Edûlê's mouth and cheeks are compared to pomegranates (12: 3, 21). *Lawkê Simoqî*, as sung by Ehmed Ferman Kikî and printed in *Hawar* ('Stranvan' 1933), has an almost identical image of going to an orchard of pomegranates. Flowers such as roses, *gul*, are often used for the description of female loveliness. Less obviously, the *riḥan* or wild basil, not ordinarily considered a particularly beautiful plant, has very strong erotic overtones in the *stran*, probably because of its fragrance, and lovers are often compared to it. Khidir Feqîr's *Esmerê*, in my collection, refers to the girl as *gul û riḥan* 'rose and basil'. Lovers may also be compared to trees; from my own collection, in *Gulê*, Khidir Feqîr compares the girl to a fig tree and another singer performing *Esmerê* compares his beloved to a mulberry.

Lovers are often depicted as being tall and slender. The opening of stanza 4 of the Sheykhani *Besê* is typical of the way she describes herself:

De lê lê dayê,	De lê lê dayê
Ew Besê bang dike dibêje,	Besê is calling, she says:
Lê le Ḥitê Nurê, sibhane Ellah xelk ji min ṛedibêje bi şêranî, Besê xoka Nurê,	Oh, Ḥitê, Nurê, by God, people say to me 'You are very lovely, Besê, Nurê's sister,
De xodê zane nav û navkêla min qendîle,	God knows my waist is slim as a candle,
Taxê sîng û berê min nebûne çiṛa şîre,	My breasts are like a drop of milk,
Ew şah û biskê min kara ẍezala nebûne têla tembûrê,	With my hair, my fringe, I am like a young gazelle, like the neck of a lute, (4: 1–6).

She is slim as a candle (3: 4, 4: 4, 5: 4); the term is also used in the EFK *Besna*. She is also slender 'like the neck of a lute' (4: 5) and, by implication, like a poppy in the fields (9: 1). In Lescot's *Kherabo*, the girl frequently refers to her beloved's *bejna zirav*, or 'slim figure' (4: 6; 10: 2). In some songs, this can lead to startling comparisons – my collection contains a song called *'Edûlê and 'Emer Agha*, performed either by Lezgîn Seydo or Silêman Khershênî, where the girl is said to be 'as tall as a minaret in Diyarbakir'. Hair and eyes are often described, either literally, as in Besê's lover's references to her dark eyes (6: 2) or by comparison with something else, such as Besna's description of her eyes 'like [those of] lambs', which occurs in the EFK *Besna*.

The *Besa Khelîl* tradition featured here is quite typical of Kurdish love lyric in the attention paid to the girl's breasts. In both Kurmanji and Sorani love songs a woman's breasts are a particular focus of eroticism; indeed they seem to be the primary focus. There are two terms, or sets of terms used; one, *sîng* or *sîng û ber*, literally 'chest' or 'chest and front' denotes the pair of breasts as a single entity, as it were, in much the same way that the single word 'cleavage' can have the meaning, in British usage, of a pair of breasts partly exposed by a low-cut dress. The phrase *taxê* (or *taximê*) *sîng û ber* means the line or shape of the breasts. There is also the word *memik* which means the individual breast itself, often compared to fruit, for instance. In *Besa Khelîl* the girl mentions her breasts during her description of her beauty in stanza 3, stanzas 1 and 2 being devoted to her bitterness at the waste of her quality, and her hatred for her husband. Her breasts, she says (*sîng û ber*), are like the snow on the top of Mount Alagöz, in the

Caucasus (3: 5). Apart from emphasising their whiteness, this image makes a direct connection with another powerful area of imagery, namely the mountains, which in Kurdish discourse are a defining feature of Kurdistan, a harsh environment in which to live, but a refuge in times of danger. Their beauty, and that of the plants and animals which live in them, is a commonplace in Kurdish folklore, which often recalls features of the semi-nomadic Kurdish life which had all but finished by the end of the twentieth century. The patterns of this life were highly seasonal; the freezing winters were spent in the valleys or on the plains, but for many members of the semi-nomadic tribes, the summer was spent in the *zozan* or summer pastures, which remained green and cool much longer than the plains. These are idealised in Kurdish folklore, and indeed in much contemporary discourse; before the Gulf War, the mountains of Badinan were a popular summer retreat for Iraqis from the big cities. For the semi-nomadic Kurds, not only was the time in the *zozan* a season of relative plenty, but the long days and mild weather of summer provided far greater opportunities for lovers to meet secretly.[9] This is also the case, of course, for lovers in the villages, but the *zozan* are particularly strongly associated with freedom and beauty, and have a special link with the erotic. The connection with the *zozan* is made explicitly later in the poem (7: 6), when Besê says her *sîng û ber* are like the *zozan* of Sherefedîn. The *zozan* are pastures, and the idea of a woman's breasts as nourishment for her lover is quite common. In Israel Ohanyan's long narrative, 'Edûlê, again recalling the *zozan*, describes her chest as *mêrg û çîman*, 'pasture and meadow', for Derwêsh (23: 7). This idea, as well as that of colour, also underlies Besê's repeated description of her breasts as 'like a drop of milk' (4: 4, 5: 5) There is quite clearly a tension between this and the biological function of breasts in providing nourishment for babies and young children.

The individual breasts, the *memik,* are often compared literally to fruits of various sorts – again the idea of food, along with the obvious consideration of shape. In some Sorani songs they are compared to melons, or lemons.[10] The EFK Besna likens her breasts to apples, first of Malatya – interestingly, these are said to be 'both bitter and sweet'- and then of Zînar in Mardin. Pert nipples are clearly extremely desirable, as is obvious in the most overtly erotic part of the Sheykhani *Besa Khelîl*, stanza 9:

Belê Besê bang dike, dibêjê,	Yes, Besê is calling, she says, 'I am
'Qurban, bejna min zirave, kûlilka nava bendêre,	your sacrifice, my figure is slim, a poppy in the fields,
Ew kirasekî di ber bejna min kara ẍezala daye,	This dress is covering a figure like a young gazelle,
Erê xode dizane medrumê gewre,	Yes, God knows, a grey dress,
Serê memika têre dabû dere,	You can just see the points of my nipples,

Erê herçî xortê nuhatî di ber bejna Besê de razê,	Yes, whichever young man sleeps next to Besê's body,
Di dilê xo de, li vê dinyayê nahêlî, ne tu kûle, ne tu kesere,	In his heart, he will forget all pain, all sorrow in this world',
De eman wayê, torîn wayê.	Pity me, beautiful one.

It is her breasts, tantalisingly visible through her dress, which are described to make the point that her body is irresistible. The girl in Lescot's *Kherabo* also describes her nipples:

Serê memikê mi, rebena Xwedê, mînayî tiriyê Çêlikê Eliyê Remo, di çax û benga xwe de dekemilî.	My nipples, poor one of God that I am, are like the grapes of Chêlikê 'Eliyê Remo, when they are mature on the vine.
Serê memikê mi, rebena Xwedê, mîna Qesrê Pirota, serê Miḥela Meşkîna avakirî.	My nipples, poor one of God that I am, are like Pirota Castle, which dominates the district of Meshkîna.
	(2: 4–5).

They are not only likened to grapes, but also – presumably to emphasise their pertness – to a castle. Kherabo's lover also gives the idea of breasts as nourishment a rather gruesome twist:

Tu rabe, ji mi ṛe gwîzaneke berbera bîne!	Get up, bring me a barber's razor!
Ezê serê memikê xwe biçipilînim, ji kala ṛe bikim taştê, ji xorta ṛe bikim firavînê.	I will cut my nipple off, I will make it into breakfast for the old men, lunch for the young men,
Bazê dilê min rojika rojiya se meha digire, bila êvarê pê fitara xwe bişkênîne.	My hawk has been fasting for three months longer than Ramadan, let him break his fast and feast in the evening.
	(3: 5–7).

Her threat to get rid of this major source of her attraction emphasises her desperation.

The Sheykhani *Besê* makes various comparisons linking the breasts with complex ideas, such as that of the *zozan* and of nourishment; where these links are made, a wealth of associations are invoked. Her breasts seem to be the key erotic attribute, used to symbolise her sexual desirability. She wishes that the young man of her choice would 'buy her breasts' (3: 8), i.e. marry her. An unappealing picture of Ibrahim Temo, her husband, is built up over the song; we discover he is miserly (stanza 4), he has three wives and he is impotent (stanza 5). The fact that he has full (though unwelcome) sexual access to Besê is shown by *li ber sîng û berê Besê razayê* 'he slept on Besê's breast'. This point, and her addition that he is like an old ox, is a climactic point in her description of him, and of her statement of her unhappiness; the song then features for the first time the words of her lover, who is anxious about the effect of all this unhappiness on her.

Female desirability in Kurdish love lyric is not only a matter of nature, but also of artifice. Attributes of a woman which are often described are her clothes, jewellery and make-up. The wearing of finery and care for one's appearance is associated with desirability and happiness, and conversely a lack of care is associated with unhappiness. In her grief, the 'Edûlê of Israel Ohanyan's long narrative will throw away her jewellery and cut her hair, and make them into ornaments for Derwêsh's horse, (26: 2–4), a reference to the Caucasian *kotel* ceremony which will be described in the next chapter. In Kheyro Khelef's performance of *Halîma*, in my own collection, the girl is so unhappy that she has not worn any kohl on her eyes for three days; more such examples occur in the laments which will be discussed in the next chapter.

Descriptions of desirable men are, in general, far less explicit than those of women. Besê names her lover and expresses her wish to marry him, but says little about his appearance, apart from a reference to his white clothes (for Yezidis, associated with religious purity and hence with festivals) and his dagger (7: 2). Similarly, although 'Edûlê is greatly affected by seeing Derwêsh and spills the coffee, and later aligns herself with him rather than her own family, she says little about his appearance. There are a few conventions for describing male appearance. A man's moustache is often a focus of female interest; like the ideal girl, the ideal boy is tall and slim, though it is clear that heroes like Derwêsh are strong and powerful as well. We might also hear of other qualities, such as being 'sweet' – Sarkîs Bozoyan's *Derwêshê 'Evdî* has 'Edûlê refer to Derwêsh's mouth as 'sugar'; the folklorist Jigerkhwîn has a *Kherabo* very similar to that of Lescot, where the girl calls her lover 'you who are sweeter than buckets full of sugar' (1988: 125). Pîr Giro's *Derwêshê 'Evdî* in my own collection has the same image. However, we rarely hear what they look like, still less what their bodies are like. There is no doubt that the girls express strong feelings of desire for the young men, but these are usually couched in other terms. The girl may speak of the effect the young man has on her; she may also say what she would like to do for him. She might abandon her usual work to make clothes or some other present, as does Kheyro Khelef's *Sêvê* in my collection, who offers to make her lover a *şal û şepik* or traditional Kurdish costume. She may also invite him to come to her, with the implication that a sexual encounter is offered.

Although there is humour in many of the songs, the concept of love as a painful experience is extremely pervasive. This is hardly surprising in view of the fact that it is the difficult situations which are seen as fit subjects for love lyric. The Sheykhani Besê finishes each of the first seven stanzas with:

... lê lê, li min poşmane dayê.	... oh, mother, I am bitter.

The term *poşman* often means 'remorseful', but is perhaps better translated as 'bitter' given that she is not personally responsible for the situation. She blames Ibrahim Temo and her parents rather than her lover, who fears that she might die of distress:

Eve çend roje tu ji ḥisabê mêrê xirab tu dihonîji, tu dikey bimirî,	For days now you have been fretting because of your vile husband, it will be the death of you,

(6: 3)

Although the detail and length of description of her husband's repulsiveness implies very strongly that she would have been unhappy with him anyway, her love for her own young man has exacerbated the situation and made her position intolerable.

Lescot's *Kherabo* is slightly different from *Besê* in that the reproach is focused strongly on the lover. The girl fondly recalls meetings which involved *gilîk*, 'complaints' and *gazin*, 'reproaches':

Ez û Xerabê bi tenê şevê nîvê şeva li zikaka biniya mala li hev runiştin.	Alone with my bad boy at midnight, I used to sit in the street, below the houses.
Me gilîkê xwe pev kirin û gazindê xwe dihiştin,	We exchanged our complaints and let our reproaches go,
Kundê şkêra, wawîke ber devê çema, li halê min û bejna zirav diponiştin,	The owl on the heap of stones, the jackal by the river, nodded their heads sadly, full of pity for me and my slim one,
Mirîkê gorê di mezela, ê go îsal hezar û pênc sed sal mirî bûn, kefenê xwe li cemcûmê serê xwe gerandin, li ser qebrê xwe rûniştin,	The dead in the graves, who have been dead fifteen hundred years, wound their shrouds around their skulls and sat on their tombs,
Li halê min û bejna zirav diponiştin.	Nodded their heads sadly, full of pity for me and my slim one.
Ez bi te ṛe dost bûm, tu bi mi ṛe dijmin bûyî.	I was a friend to you, you were an enemy to me.
Tu li paş xanîka li min dikelistî, te derbek bi tifingê berda mi, ez dikuştim.	You were spying behind my house, you fired your gun at me, you killed me.[11]
Şevê nîvê şeva, te bi destê tola jina xwe girt, û ez li ber dîwara dihiştim.	At dead of night, taking your cursed wife by the hand, you left me alone.

(4: 4–11).

The fact that even the unpleasant creatures felt sorry for them makes it clear that they were not merely bickering with each other, but also complaining about their sad lot. The subject of sorrow is taken up later in the song:

Kul û kederê te gelek in, şak berdane ser vî dilî.	The griefs and sorrows you have caused are many, they tear at my heart.
Kul û kederê ji bîra nakim, heya axê mezelan, kêlê di kevirî.	I won't forget the grief and sorrow, until [I am in] the dust of the grave, under the tombstone.
Kul û kederê te pir bûne, tucar dernakevin ji vî dilî ...	Your grief and sorrows were great, they will never leave this heart ... (11: 7–9).

Even before the calamity of his marriage took place, the two young lovers were pitiable, as the image of the dead in the graveyard shows.

A lover is often presented as unhappy, either because his or her love is unrequited or because he or she cannot be with the beloved. The sadness of love may be expressed by either the man or the woman. A number of Sinjari stran are entitled *Leylê and Mejnûn*; the name *Mejnûn*, of course, implies not only unhappiness but madness; this is not necessarily a part of the tale in the Kurdish *stran* of that name, but there is in Kurdish love lyric in general a very common association of love with sickness. It is not always clear whether love itself is seen as a sickness, or merely the cause of sickness. In Israel Ohanyan's long narrative, 'Edûlê expresses the effect of her love for Derwêsh in painful physical terms:

Mi go, lo, lo, lo, delê , te goştê min ḥeland, teyê hestiyê min ṛizand, bala xwe bidê tilî pêçiyê minî zerî zeytûnî, bînana mom û şima diḥelin, bi enîşka milê miva bû bizmêre.'	I said, alas, my dear, you have dissolved my flesh, you have withered me to the bone, look, my fingers and toes, olive-yellow, are dissolving like wax or candles, nails pierce my elbow and shoulder.' (25: 5)

This type of imagery is used in other *stran* in my collection. In Kheyro Khelef's performance of the well-known Yezidi love story, *Resho and Khansê*, Khansê says that Resho is mortally ill. Like the heroine of *Kherabo*, she is full of grief, and ascribes his sickness to their being fetched home when they tried to elope. In *Ziravê*, sung by Sheykh Mûs, and *Pitê*, sung by Khidir Feqîr, a young man who is sick says that a visit from his beloved will be the best cure for him.

However, the pleasure and comfort of love is by no means neglected in lyrical song; 'Edulê says, in 'Egîtê Têjir's lyric:

Ḥevt birê min, wekî heṛine ber kuştinê,	Even if seven of my brothers are about to be killed,
Kalebavê min ber şûştinê,	My grandfather is about to be washed,
Pîrediya min ber mirinê,	My grandmother is about to die,

Wexta çevê min çevê Dewrêşê Evdî, ḥûtê binê beṛiyê, qeremanî Sindî, dikeve, min tirê, ḥemû saẍin li ṛûbara dinê.	When my eye falls on the eye of Derwêshê 'Evdî, giant of the desert, hero of Sindî, to me it seems that all is well in spite of the world.

(6: 3–6).

This sentiment also occurs in the performance of Meḥmûdê 'Elîyê Temo (3: 3–6). In Lescot's *Kherabo* too, the young man asks for a kiss, saying that he will never regret it, and that it is worth extra punishment after death:

Wexta Ezraîl dakeve, rûhê mi distîne,	When 'Ezra'îl comes down and takes my soul,
Wê gavê, bila diwanzde mîkweta zêdî heqê mi li mi xîne,	Then, let him give me twelve hammer blows more than I deserve,
Bila heqê ramîsanê keleşgewra mi ji mi hilîne.	To make me pay for the kiss of my lovely girl!

(11: 16–18).

He says he is prepared to pay an especially high price after death for the kiss. The paradox of pain and pleasure, love and anger, permeates Lescot's *Kherabo*.

In close association with the concept of the lover as unhappy is the motif of the (usually male) lover wandering, either because he is looking for the beloved, or trying to forget her. Kheyro Khelef's *Sodalê* has been mentioned earlier in the chapter, and describes the lover visiting many places throughout what might be termed 'Greater Kurdistan' and beyond. Place-names may be used because they are exotic, or locally significant, but it is hard to understand the reasons for their selection without knowing the significance of each place-name in the area which produced each form of the tradition. Some examples are obvious; in Sarkîs Bozoyan's performance of *Derwêshê 'Evdî*, 'Edûlê went to Damascus and Baghdad, among other places, to find soap to clean Derwêsh's cloak – the intention is clearly to indicate the lengths she went to, and thus to give an index of her devotion to him.

Since men have greater freedom of movement it is usually the young man who travels and the woman who stays behind, eager for news of him. In Israel Ohanyan's narrative, 'Edûlê's extravagant offers to those who bring news reflect her status:

Heçî kesê, ko ciwaba Dewrêşê 'Evdî, siwarê Hidman, lawkê êzîdî, delalê malê, xêmê binê beṛiyê, ji nava ḥezar û pênsid siwarê Gêsa ji miṛa bîne,	Whoever brings me news of Dewrêşê 'Evdî, rider of Hidman, the Yezidi lad, beloved of our home, whose tent is in the desert, from among the one thousand five hundred warriors of the Gêsan,

Ezê bidimê çar aşê bavê min li ber ava Misêrbînê,

Hege bi herçar aşa qayîl nebe, ezê bidimê de ḥeb caniyê bavê min hene, kiḥêlin, 'eslîne, ezê bidim bi ṛiḥînê,
Çar qesr û qonaxê bavê min hene, ezê bidimê li bajarê Misêrbînê,
Eger herçar qesr û qonaxa qayîl nebe, ezê di ser da bidimê ḥezar û pênsid zêṛê osmanlî ji xizînê.'

I will give him four of my father's mills on the banks of the water of Nusaybin,

And if he is not satisfied with all four mills, I will give him ten of my father's colts, thoroughbreds, of pure stock, I will give them as insurance,
My father has four fortresses and mansions in Nusaybin town, I will give them,
If he is not satisfied with all four fortresses and mansions, I will give him in addition one thousand five hundred Osmanli gold pieces from the treasury.'

(22: 8–12).

and later:

'Edûlê gazî dike, 'Gelî Kîkano, gelî Milano, ḥeçî kesê ciwabekî xêrê ji alê delalê malê, Dewrêşê 'Evdî, lawkê êzîdî ji xêmê binê beṛiyê, ji nava ḥezar û pênsid siwarê Gêsa ji miṛa bîne, ezê bidimê malê diniyayê, ḥezar û pênsid zêṛê di altûze . . .,

'Edûlê called, 'People of the Kîkan, people of the Milan, whoever brings good news from the dear one of my house, Derwêshê 'Evdî, the Yezidi lad, from the tent in the desert, from among a thousand five hundred Gêsan warriors, I will give him worldly goods, one thousand five hundred pieces of pure gold . . .,

(24: 4)

Of course, the news would have to be good, though 'Edûlê knows very well that good news would be impossible. Similar sentiments are expressed in my own collection of *stran*. In Pîr Giro's performance of *'Edulê and Genj Khelîl*, the girl asks passers by for news of her lover.

Just as the mention of faraway or famous places can be used to illustrate points, so also well-known individuals, from history and myth, are used. In Israel Ohanyan's performance, 'Edulê says:

Mi go, 'Lo, lo, lo, delêl, ez te nadim bi Ḥemmê,
bi Kinê, bi herdu fêriz û pêlewana, ko li xêmê binê beṛiyê ji kuştinê, ji malê alemê nabin têre,

Ez te nadim bi kuṛê Birahîm Paşa ji mala zengo zêṛe,

I said, 'Oh, my dear, I wouldn't give you up for Ḥemmê,
for Kinê, for those two brave men and champions, that even in the tent in the desert are not sated from killing, from the wealth of the world.

I wouldn't give you up for the son of Brahim Pasha whose house is golden with wealth,

Ez te nadim bi kuṛê Bedirxan Begê, mîrê Bota ji maleke del û têre.'	I wouldn't give you up for the son of Bedirkhan Beg, the Emir of Botan, from a house brave and full [of riches].' (24: 11–14).
'Lo, lo, lo, lo, lo, delêl, Ez te nadim bi sultanê dînê Êzîdxanê, Ku li çiyayê Şengalê îsal ḥezar û pênsid salê wan qediyayê, quruşekî wan negihîştiye destê dewletê, neketiye kassa xundkêre ...'	'Alas, alas, my beloved, I would not give you up for the son of the Sultan of the Yezidis, Who on Mount Sinjar this year one thousand five hundred years have passed, but not a penny of theirs has reached the hand of the Ottoman Sultan, nor fallen into the coffers of the Shah ...' (25: 1–3).

Her remark on the reputation of the Sinjaris is interesting, given that the immediate provenance of this performance is non-Yezidi. Such usages of exempla are also quite common in the *stran*, which means that it is difficult to understand fully any one tradition without knowing others.

The rejection of famous people in favour of the beloved has much in common with a motif present in *Derwêshê 'Evdî*, where the lover who is speaking draws a contrast between the attitude of ordinary people to the beloved and her or his own strong feelings. Meḥmûdê 'Elîyê Temo's lyric begins with such a point; he contrasts the attitudes of other people who do not value Derwêsh with 'Edûlê's attitude; she says that to her he is a flawless pomegranate (1: 2–3).

The *dîwanxane* scene is important in all the performances of *Derwêshê 'Evdî* in ZK. It belongs to Zor Temer Pasha and is a reflection of his wealth and status. It is also a public space, with many people meeting there, and is thus an appropriate setting for the public declaration of the feelings of the lovers. In Israel Ohanyan's performance, as we have seen, Derwêsh makes his feelings plain by claiming her; in the other lyrics, she betrays her own emotion by spilling coffee. In Pîr Micho's *stran* of *Derwêshê 'Evdî* in my own collection, and also in Sarkîs Bozoyan's lyric collected by Jelîl, she imagines bringing him water (usually offered to guests on arrival) when he comes to her father's tent. Scenes where young women offer food or drink, and where lovers are described as 'guests', occur elsewhere in the *stran* and their symbolism is obvious. Such scenes are a plausible part of life; one of the best chances a young woman in a traditional village household might have for a good look at a man would be if he were a guest in her father's house. There are a few other settings for encounters between lovers which are common in the *stran*; a *Kherabo* in my collection, performed by Ḥesen Sinjarî, has the lovers' first encounter taking place by the stream. Two older

Yezidi women I interviewed in Khanek described how the stream had been a frequent meeting place for women, who washed clothes and fetched water from there, and sometimes lovers met there too, as girls could easily claim a legitimate excuse for being there. *'Elî Pismamo*, 'Oh, cousin 'Elî', performed by Lezgîn Seydo, says that there were too many people by the stream. Some songs, such as *Pitê* sung by Khidir Feqîr, and *Nezanê*, sung by Kheyro Khelef, have the lovers meeting at weddings and feasts. In Pîr Giro's *'Edûlê û Genc Xelîl*, 'Edûlê and Handsome Khelîl', the girl sees her beloved from the roof; traditional Kurdish village houses have flat roofs, which families use as a common space and sleeping area in the summer. Where locations are given for encounters between lovers – as *Besa Khelîl* shows, some songs do not describe them at all – they are usually everyday rural settings.

CONCLUSIONS: FANTASY, REALITY AND THE PORTRAYAL OF WOMEN

We have seen that lyrical love songs are very popular amongst the Yezidis, and that many are based on real individuals and situations of the past. They can articulate particular areas of preoccupation, such as exogamy. Most of the songs performed by the Yezidi *stranbêj* of Northern Iraq are not about kings and queens in palaces, but are firmly rooted in the everyday lives of villagers, or of the semi-nomadic tribes. Moreover, the love which is articulated is not courtly love, though it is constrained by the rules of *namûs* prevailing in Kurdish society. One of the disadvantages of discussing a small number of traditions is the difficulty of showing the wide range of scenarios in these songs; lovers may be married or unmarried, monogamous or polygamous, older or younger, rich or poor, and their somewhat untidy private lives make them more believable. Both women and men speak in the songs, articulating a complex and credible range of emotions, many of them conflicting. The characters are certainly not abstractions of virtue.

The songs are believed to be about individuals who lived in the past, and accordingly they are set in a world where tribes are semi-nomadic, pitching their summer camps in the mountains. People live in tents; 'Edûlê, a chieftain's daughter, wears a traditional headdress adorned with gold Osmanli lira. When Derwêsh dies, she wants to adorn his horse for a traditional ceremony. All these details, if not totally obsolete, are certainly no longer a part of everyday life in Kurdistan, where most people now live in urban communities. Even the Yezidis, most of whom have remained rural for longer than their neighbours, now live for the most part in urban collectives rather than villages; they still cultivate crops and pasture their animals, but their social life is changing. Yet these details have been preserved in songs and stories still performed by Sinjari *stranbêj* at the close of the twentieth century.

What is the relationship between these songs and 'real' Yezidi life and feelings about love? It must be complex; on the one hand, the truth and relevance of the songs are much prized, whilst on the other, the very fact that there are many loving relationships in Yezidi society, such as those within marriage, which are not normally deemed appropriate for lyrical song, makes it clear that the songs can only cover part of the general discourse about heterosexual love. As a well-defined form of oral literature, these songs have an aesthetic suited to the telling of particular kinds of truth, but not necessarily to a 'realistic' representation of love in Yezidi society.

The interplay of fantasy and reality within Kurdish love songs and stories raises obvious questions about gender roles. The previous chapter discussed women's considerable role in the *stran* of battle. However, in the *stran* of love, their role is greater; a large amount of attention is devoted to the description of women and their feelings. These women certainly do not hesitate to speak their mind. 'Edûlê's statement 'I am not Kiki or Milli' effectively rejects her family and associates her with Derwêsh, a social inferior and a Yezidi to boot. Bêsê cries out to her husband, 'Hey, Ibrahim! I stick my fingers in your eyes!' (2: 2). Kherabo's lover wishes death and destruction on him (5: 1–4; 6: 1–4), and describes his wife in derisory terms (11: 3–5; 13: 5). As we have seen, these women sometimes draw a contrast between their own attitudes and values and those of ordinary society (Egitê Têjir I, 14: 4–5; Meḥmûdê 'Elîyê Temo 1: 2–3).

Yezidi and other Kurdish women are indeed often strong and assertive on their own ground, but the clearly defined roles of the sexes in Yezidi society limit the range of their activities. The cherished examples of female power, such as the redoubtable Mayan Khatun, who shaped Yezidi politics for two generations (Guest 1993: 176–92), remain exceptions to the rule. It is undoubtedly simplistic to speak of the power of women versus that of men in Yezidi society. There are certainly female hierarchies – older matriarchs like Mayan can enjoy considerable influence, more so than some younger men, whereas the position of a new bride such as Besê is very junior. Moreover, Kurdish women, especially older ones, play a vital role in the upholding of customs regarding *namûs* – they are often quick to criticise behaviour they consider inappropriate. They have even been known to carry out honour killings of younger women who have been violated or who have had liaisons with men.[12] Women who overstep the bounds of propriety are relatively common fantasy figures in Kurdish folklore; several heroic tales feature hitherto unconquered warriors who wrestle with the hero, and, as the hero is about to win, are unmasked and revealed as women (e.g. Bedir Khan 1938: *passim*; MacKenzie 1990 II: 23). I saw evidence of this continued interest during my own fieldwork in the popularity of portraits of women dressed in *pêshmerge* costume. However, practising female warriors in real life are relatively few, particularly in Iraqi Kurdistan. The PKK (Kurdish Workers' Party) in Turkey, the KDPI (Kurdish Democratic Party – Iran) and Komela in Iran recruited much greater numbers of female *pêshmerge* than the Kurdish parties in Iraq. Indeed there are persistent rumours that one of the the most well-known Iraqi female *pêshmerge*, a Christian woman called Margaret George, was murdered by Iraqi Kurdish men offended by her lack of modesty (cf. Rohat 1995: 92–93). As far as the *stran* of love are concerned, fantasy elements such as female warriors are almost unknown.

Besê says *Ezê xo . . . . bi sê telaqa xo telaq kim* 'I will divorce myself . . . by saying "I divorce you" three times' (2: 8). Of course, this is an option only open to men, but Besê is wishing that she had this right.[13] In 'Elî Lezgîn's *Kherabo*, in my own collection, a woman says that if she ruled Dihok and Sinjar, women would be allowed to divorce cruel husbands. The case of the woman is often put very effectively in the *stran*, and genuine female grievances are aired. This is in striking contrast with the poetry of some other Iranian peoples; for instance, Grima (1992: 148, 154), draws attention to the idealised woman's voice in Pashto poetry composed and performed by men. In the example she quotes, the female protagonist, Meymuney, gives in passively to her fate – her husband has to kill her to salvage his own honour, though she is blameless. Unlike Meymuney, the women of Kurdish love lyric challenge the status quo with some vigour.

How far are these songs speaking with authentic women's voices? Various Kurdish informants, almost all men, have said that these are real women speaking. Indeed, some have claimed that certain songs were 'probably' composed by women, but there are various factors which arouse scepticism. The first is obvious – none of the songs I have collected is performed by a woman, and there is no firm evidence that they were composed by women. No female composer's name has been preserved in association with the songs I have encountered. It is unfortunate that we do not have examples of such love songs; it would be interesting to compare and contrast these with those composed and performed by men.

The feature of the songs which seems to point most convincingly to a male-dominated aesthetic is the description of women's bodies, which is far more detailed than the physical description of men. This feature is much more noticeable in the Iraqi material than in the Caucasian songs. Moreover, the particular interest in breasts, a very curvaceous and womanly body part, seems to preclude any reading of this material as dealing in a veiled way with homosexuality. In my own experience, married Yezidi women at least are quite capable of noticing and commenting on men's bodies, and of speculating on their likely sexual performance. Yet the women of the *stran* are very vague about men's bodies – they prefer to express desire in terms of the responses of their own bodies. They make their availability very clear to audiences in terms which cannot normally be articulated in public – their statements look very much like the fantasies of men. There is also the theme of 'irresistibility' – Besê says:

Erê herçî xortê nuhatî di ber bejna Besê de razê,	Yes, whichever young man sleeps next to Besê's body,
Di dilê xo de, li vê dinyayê nahêlî, ne tu kûle, ne tu kesere,	In his heart, he will forget all pain, all sorrow in this world,

(9: 5–6)

Pîr Khidir's pared-down narrative of the Derwêshê 'Evdî story featured 'Edûlê wearing an especially fine dress and stunning the qewwals with her beauty. This theme occurs elsewhere in the *stran* and is fully consistent with the attitude that a woman is responsible for the approaches made to her by a man, since the man cannot help himself – an attitude which many Yezidi women also subscribe to, but which is dictated by male concerns about power and control.

An audience can certainly empathise with the believable characters of the *stran* of love, and their contextual knowledge, still considerable in the older generation, will enhance their enjoyment, as they will know how the story ends even if the *stranbêj* does not say so, and will understand the various references to other people and places. Love is clearly presented in these songs as an excuse for unseemly behaviour. However, despite the transgressions by many of the lovers of the rules of *namûs*, the songs are not a clear-cut manifesto for action. It is clear that although most conservative Yezidis, men and women, will be moved by the enumerations of the woes of, say, Besa Khelîl, they would certainly not feel such sympathy if their own daughters ran away from their husbands with another man, as she did after several years of marriage. Yalçin-Heckmann notes that in a Muslim Kurdish community in Turkey, 'love' is often cited as the reason for elopement, or the making of otherwise unusual marriages. Where elopement happens, the family of the woman is shamed, though people who are less close to the couple may feel more sympathy for the couple; thus the community has a complex and varying attitude towards the issue (1991: 248). It is possible that this is also the case in Yezidi communities, with the added dimensions of caste and the ban on exogamy affecting their attitudes. Whether this is true or not, the statement of the lovers' point of view in the *stran*, though powerful, is clearly only part of a complex discourse on love and its relationship with *namûs*. The love songs and stories, especially the *stran*, seem to answer an emotional need in the community, by giving expression to these insoluble tensions between the wishes of the individual and those of society in a controlled way.

Thus it would not be correct to see the themes of love as a form of subversion which somehow operates against the rules of Yezidi society. Despite their articulation of women's concerns, the *stran* are not particularly liberating for less powerful women. The potentially subversive messages of past challenges to the social order, such as elopement and adultery, are contained by the placing of the issue in a socially appropriate place, namely the performance of verbal art. These stories and songs of love are neither pure fantasy nor reality, but a complex mixture of both. Their appeal lies partly in their evocation of an idealised (though often tragic) rural world, and partly in the presentation of situations which are realistic enough to arouse sympathetic emotion, and strike a chord with the personal experiences of members of the audience. The way in which emotions are evoked in audiences will be discussed in the next chapter, which will consider not only those *stran* which specifically address the death of a lover, family member or heroic figure, but also the types of lamentation performed by women after a death in the community.

CHAPTER SIX

Death, Loss and Lamentation in Yezidi Verbal Art

INTRODUCTION

After the suppression of the Kurdish uprising in 1991, a very large percentage of the population of the towns of Badinan fled to the mountainous Turkish and Iranian borders. Almost every family I met in 1992 had lost someone, usually a grandparent or a child, on the arduous journey, or in the squalid conditions of the temporary camps. Before this, many had lost young sons or brothers in the Iran-Iraq War and the Gulf War; there had also been a number of deaths and disappearances in custody, and deaths in conflict between *pêşmerge* and government forces. Few families had been left totally unscathed by the history of the previous decade. Even by 1992, when a substantial part of Iraqi Kurdistan was under Kurdish control, conditions were certainly not perceived as normal. The decline in prosperity brought about by two wars had been felt by everyone. For many people, the strong emotions brought on by recent bereavements were combined with intense anxiety about the future.

At such a time, a collector of *folklor* could hardly be unaware of discourses of loss and lamentation, especially the women's laments, which are low in status and are not usually made prominent to outsiders. This chapter will consider the treatment of the theme of death and grief in Yezidi poetry; after touching on the *stran* of grief, it will discuss women's lament, a genre in which very few examples have been collected. I will give a description of the poetry on the subject and an outline of the terms and images used therein, with some account of its significance for the community and for participating individuals. Anthropologists and others are justified in saying that that simply isolating a group of nouns from the language of the people under study, and using them as metaphors for social institutions and processes without any indication of their syntactic context runs the risk of misrepresenting the realities (e.g. Rosenberg 1990). I will try to avoid this error by giving as many examples as possible of syntactic use and social context.[1] However, where previous studies are so limited and extensive data is not available, I hope that simple description of performance and discussion of commonly mentioned concepts and their significance can be useful and informative as a first step, particularly for the women's lament.

Various academic disciplines have been applied to the study of emotion. Emotions are no longer considered to be objective realities, similar in all cultures; the dangers of projecting one's own perception of the significance of emotions, and their place in the individual and in society, onto other peoples, who may conceptualise emotion very differently, have been acknowledged. Recent studies have argued that, to use Grima's words, 'emotion is culturally constructed rather than universal' (1992: 6),[2] and discussions have moved towards a discourse-centred approach (cf. Lutz and Abu-Lughod 1990: 1–19). The terms of the discourse of those emotions expressed in the *stran* of grief and women's laments are well worth exploring in detail. However, any full analysis of a discourse of emotion requires close relationships within the community to uncover the important elements, compare them and observe their use in the social context. An account of a group of emotions, in this case those associated with loss, would be extremely complex under normal conditions. A full understanding of the idioms of emotion among the Yezidis would necessitate living within a community for a long period and gaining a great deal of trust at the best of times; in a time of crisis this becomes all the more difficult and my fieldwork conditions simply did not permit it. In honesty, I should add that it would also have necessitated a great deal of intrusion on the grief of others; this may not necessarily have been perceived as intrusive, but, no doubt because of my own cultural background, it made me extremely uncomfortable.

KURDISH LAMENTS

Kurdish laments, in the broad sense of material performed in mourning for a death, are wide-ranging and little studied. The most extensive study made so far was published by Margaret Rudenko, who had carried out her fieldwork in the former Soviet Union, where the Kurdish community is mostly Yezidi (Rudenko 1982); other relevant work is in progress.[3] However, it must be noted that the focus of her work is 'ceremonial' poetry which is performed at funerals, and none of the lamentation I observed among the Yezidis in Badinan took place within the context of a funeral. It is hardly surprising, therefore, that the data collected in Badinan is not uniformly consistent with Rudenko's observations. Rudenko herself fights shy of proposing a complex system of classification of Kurdish poetry of lamentation on the grounds that the field has been so little studied (Rudenko 1982: 16).

Before discussing forms of song associated with death it is worth noting briefly some of the most common terms used in Kurdish in association with death. The literal term for 'death' is *mirin*, a verbal noun, which has the past participle *mirî*, 'dead'. This blunt term was often used among the Yezidis, and indeed in Badinan generally, when talking about a dead person; members of the bereaved family were referred to as *xodanê mirî*, literally 'proprietor' or 'owner of the deceased'. However, when talking to the bereaved, or when writing, several euphemisms were used. The most common, used by the son of Dawûdê Dawûd in the formal context of his interview with Khelîlê Jindî Rashow, was *emrê Xodê kirin*, 'to fulfil God's command'. An alternative was *çûn*, literally 'to go', with its slightly longer form *çûn rehmetê*, 'to go to [God's] mercy'. *Bar kirin*, the verb used amongst nomadic groups for packing up and moving on, is also used in oral literature, though less often in ordinary conversation. When talking of someone who had died in fighting, the most common term used was *şehîd bûn*, 'to be martyred'. *Şehîd*, the (originally Arabic) word for 'witness', usually means 'martyr' in the Kurdish context, and is used by both Iraqi and Turkish Kurdish guerrilla movements to refer to those of their members who have died fighting. It has overtones of martyrdom for a cause, but in Iraq was applied to *pêşmerge* fighters who had died in accidents as well as in clashes with the Iraqi government, or with other Kurdish groups.

When a person dies in Kurdistan, it is considered a social duty to call on the bereaved family to pay one's respects; failure to do this is noticed and criticised.[4] Such visits may continue long after the funeral, especially when a family of high status loses a member, and others do not want to be seen to have neglected their duty towards them. Men give condolences; women mourn separately alongside female members of the bereaved family. This occasion of *taziye*, or 'condolence', is one of the occasions where women's lament is performed. The lament performed by women is only one of the forms of Kurdish poetry associated with death. Tragic *stran*, as we have seen, often deal with the death of a hero; according to Rudenko, many of these have their origin in songs composed for funerals and performed there by well-known singers; this is quite likely, though I have not so far found any examples where this could be proved. Singers may also perform such ceremonial songs in public after the death of a famous person. An example of such a song, performed by a Syrian Kurdish male singer after the death of Mulla Mustafa Barzani, was kindly given to me by Fawziya Rahman; he had died in the USA and was initially buried in Iran, but such commemorative occasions were held in various parts of Kurdistan. According to Rudenko, men's ceremonial laments concentrate on heroic and epic elements, such as valour and battle, whereas those of women are more emotional and lyrical (1982: 13). A Caucasian custom which was once a forum for eulogies among Yezidis is the *kotel* ceremony, performed exclusively by and for men, when the horse of the deceased, laden with his effects, was driven around before his house. According to Rudenko, this ceremony was by the early 1980s practised only in remote areas in the former Soviet Union, but *kotel* songs were sung publicly and often thought to be simply heroic songs (1982: 14). The folklorist Hejiyê Jindî stresses the link between a warrior and his horse (1962: 19):

> In Kurdish epic song, the horse and the hero of the song ... fall together and together become one. Often the death of the hero and the horse are bound together. When the hero dies, his horse also, for the dignity and respect of the hero, is bound to the gates of the house of death. Thus the *dengbêj* sing songs of strength and heroism, about the hero and also about his horse.

This is fully consistent with the part played by Derwêshê 'Evdî's horse Hidman in Israel Ohanyan's long narrative poem; indeed, towards the end 'Edûlê says:

Ezê ṛabim, xilxalê lingê xwe bişkênim, ji Hidman ṛa bikime cotekî nêle,	I will get up, I will break the anklet on my leg, I will make for Hidman a new harness,
Ezê xizêma pozê xwe derxim, jê ṛa bikim hûr bizmêre,	I will pull the jewel from my nose, I will make from it fine nails,
Ezê keziyê xwe bibiṛim, ji Hidman ṛa bikim gulik û ṛîşî û du hevsêre,	I will cut my braid, I will make for Hidman a saddle-cloth and tassels and two bridles,
Ji îro peyda, wê berê te têkeve binê beṛiyê, nava ḥezar û pênsid siwarê Gêsa, xelqê bibêje, "Ev siwarê hanê çiqa bi ḥizne, çîqa bi delale û çi bi cemêle".'	From today onward, when you go to the desert, among one thousand five hundred Gêsa warriors, the people will say, "That warrior, how good he is, how beloved, how beautiful".' (26: 2–6).

Although I have referred to this lyrical poem at the end of Israel Ohanyan's narrative as an example of love poetry, it can in many ways be seen as a *stran* of grief. Shêrin's song about her lost Memo is also a kind of lament, though its setting is the rebellion of Dawûdê Dawûd. As will be shown later in the chapter, the imagery and motifs used in love poetry in particular are very closely linked to those used in lamentation. In the case of *stran*, the three categories of war, love and grief, which were suggested to me by the *stranbêj* Mr A., do not always have clearly defined boundaries between them.

Stran of Grief

The term *ẍerîbî* literally means 'strangeness'; if one is bereaved one is far from one's loved one. By implication, everyday things and people also become 'strange' to someone who is grieving. In the *stran*, the bereaved, rather like the lovers, do not care about ordinary concerns. The term *x̃erîb* is of course also common outside the *stran*; in the women's lament it is frequently applied to both deceased and bereaved. The English adjective 'estranged', although a literal translation, does not carry the registers of meaning of *x̃erîb*; in Kurdish society, where great importance is still attached to close family, community and place of origin, the pain of separation from one's own place is keenly felt. According to Rudenko (1982: 16) the term is used in songs sung at weddings about the bride's feelings on leaving her family and going to live among strangers. Kurds in Europe often describe themselves as *x̃erîb*, and members of their families in Kurdistan sometimes refer to them as *x̃erîbê min* or *x̃erîba min* 'my estranged' or 'my exiled one'.[5]

Chapter Four considered a *stran* sung from the point of view of a mother, Shêrîn, on the death of her grown-up son, Memo. There are various other *stran* of this type, but it is worth mentioning an example which is rather unusual in that it has religious significance. *Lavijê Pîrê* is a lament composed for a young man who has died, but it has a strong association with the valley of Lalêsh. Many Yezidis would define it, as Silêman and Jindî do, as a *dîrok* or woman's lament, but, like *stran*, it is now performed to mixed audiences by *stranbêj*, as well as by pilgrims to Lalêsh (1995: 182). A *çîrok* tells that Lavij's grieving mother met Sheykh Adi at Lalêsh. The saint showed her a vision of her son in Paradise, and asked whether she would really rather bring him back to earth, away from such happiness. She agreed that he should stay there.[6] *Lavijê Pîrê* is one of a small number of high-status oral traditions standing on the borderline between the sacred and the secular.

This study has so far considered oral traditions where emotions of grief and anxiety are predominantly articulated by women. However, there are *stran* where expressions of anguish are put into the mouth of a man. These are not the eulogies descibed above, but what Rudenko would call 'feminine' song, lyrical and emotional. An example of this is *'Eysha Balê*.

'Eysha Balê

This is the song of a man whose young wife has died. The *stran* was collected in Sheykhan in the 1970s by Dr Khelîl Jindî Rashow. The singer is probably the Sinjari Pîr Giro, but unfortunately the song is incomplete. The man begins by begging the girl to wake up; he describes his own frantic search for a cure for her sickness. Then he outlines how the world has been turned upside down; wild creatures are not in their proper places, and they have all heard the sad news. Even the weather has been against them; he describes the moment of her death. He returns to this in the next stanza. Then he wishes it had not happened, but remarks on the inevitability of death; a long list follows of famous people who could not cheat death, before he says that he does not want any other woman.

The lover begins the first stanza by addressing 'Eyshê directly, and makes her importance to him clear:

Yaman hevalê, yaman hevalê, yaman hevalê, rabe,	Oh help, my love, my love, wake up,
Yaman hevalê, hevaleke min li vê dinyayê . . .,	Oh help me, my love, the one I love most in this world . . .,
	(1: 1–2)

His desperation to help her is made clear later in the stanza:

Geriyam li eqlîma û li şehrestana	I searched the corners of the world, the cities,
Li doktor û hakîma	For doctors, for scholars,
Li dûbarî van dermana	Searching again for those remedies,
Yaman hevalê!	Oh help me, oh my love!
	(1: 9–12).

This recalls those *stran* of love where the lover wanders in search of the beloved. As will be seen later in this chapter, doctors play an important role in Yezidi poetry of lamentation. The lover also swears that after 'Eyshê he wants no woman:

Ezê sundxworî tobadarim piştî xelkekî xoyî delalî hoganî mîmbaşa keçkan û bûka	I have sworn an oath, a solemn vow, after my dear one, my precious love, commander of the cohorts of girls and brides,
Çucar û çucar li gerê govendê, li guhê dîlanê..	Never, never, in the circle of the dance, at the side of the dancing . . .
	(6: 20–21)

However, for most of the poem his strong feelings for her are shown not by direct descriptions of his emotions or his actions, but in other ways.

His initial description of 'Eyshê is fully consistent with the descriptions of the *stran* of love, though it lacks the overtly erotic elements:

Navê xelkekî minî delal 'Eyşanê	My dear one's name is 'Eysê,
Bejna zirave ji tayekî gulan û reş riḥane,	She is slim as a rose branch, as the dark basil,
Kesk dike li baẍa û li baẍestane,	Growing green in the garden, in the orchard,
Xelkekî minî delale	My dear, my beloved,
Nesaẍî bê hale,	She is grievously sick,
Mededî yamane.	She desperately needs help.
	(1: 3–8).

Again the imagery comes from nature; roses and wild basil, standard elements in love poetry, feature strongly. Gardens and cultivated greenery, in Kurdistan as elsewhere in the Middle East, are highly prized and are often the scene of encounters between lovers. His description of the moment before her death also focuses on those small details which are mentioned in so many *stran* of love – not only her lovely dark eyes, but also her ornaments, which make a gentle sound as she breathes her last.

Wextê herdû çavêd belek keftine ber firwarê,	When her two dark eyes began to close in death,
Min dîbû xişîna tok û mandel û zêr xizêma zêrî zere,	I saw, there was a gentle tinkling of her necklace, her gold nosering, yellow gold,
Min dî xelkekî minî delalî hogan herdû çavêd reş û belek ji mirinê ṛe wergîrane . . .,	I saw my dear one, my precious one, close both her lovely dark eyes in death. . .,

(3: 3–5)

The focus on the gold is very noticeable, not only in this image, which is repeated in stanza 4, but also in the mention of her *kimyonekî zêra*, a particularly fine and pure piece of gold (5: 3).[7] Not only are the women of Kurdish folklore particularly lovely and desirable in their finery, but the mention of gold, reiterated several times during the song, emphasises the fact that 'Eyshê was a bride, since gold is an important part of bride-wealth.

Stanza 2 of this song is particularly interesting for its representation of the folkloric world:

Herçi mirina xelkekî minî delal nebihîstî,	Who has not heard of the death of my beloved?
Şêr û heywana cî û mekan xo berdane,	The lions, the wild beasts have left their places, their homes,
Rojê li nîvro girtî meclis û dîwana,	The council-chambers and courts are closed at midday,
Mêr û melika selawat ji mirina 'Eyşê vedane,	Men and angels pay respects at 'Eyshê's death,
Ḥûriya li ezmanê heftê kef kutane,	The Houris of the seven heavens have been clapping their hands,
Quling li zozana dageriyana,	The cranes have come down from the *zozan*,
Xezalêd binê beṛiyê mendehoş bûne,	The gazelles in the desert are shocked,
Berê xo dane zozane,	They have left for the *zozan*,
Ew jî heywanêd Xodê bûn	They also were God's wild creatures
Hizna xelkekî minî delal kêşane	[Who] have shown their sadness for my dear one
Yaman hevalê!	Oh help, oh my love!

The principle behind this stanza is that the whole world has been turned upside down; busy places such as council-chambers and courts are deserted. Not only in this world but also beyond, creatures have heard of the tragedy. Desert and *zozan* animals – both cranes and gazelles are benign in Kurdish folklore – are changing places. The most important places in Kurdish folklore are mentioned here – the wild places where lions live, the desert or plain, the *zozan*, and human communities. There are also the heavens, where the Houris live; they, of course, are delighted to welcome 'Eyshê.

The inclusion of Houris and angels in this song, and the later mention of religious figures in Stanzas 5 and 6, should not obscure the essentially secular nature of this song. The mention of the caliph 'Ali after two heroes from oral tradition is particularly interesting; it is apparently not distasteful to the Yezidis despite their 'ultra-Sunni' reputation (Kreyenbroek 1995: 46):

Dinya dem û heywanêd xodê ne, herdem bi demê re, herdem bi wextê re,	This world and its centuries belong to God, every period, every time in its own time,
Dinya nemabû ji Aḥmedê lawê Tirkî re,	This world didn't last for Aḥmed the young Turk,
Dinya nemabû ji Boz Begê lawê pîre,	It didn't last for Boz Beg, the old woman's son,
Dinya nemabû ji 'Elî Şêr, şêrê Xodê re,	It didn't last for 'Elî Shêr, the lion of God,
Neh xelatî reb'l alemîn ji ezmana nazîlî 'erdê Xodê bûn,	The Lord of the Universe gave nine gifts to God's earth,
Sê jê hatibû jê re,	Three of them came to him,
Serê heft salî tamam şeṛ dikir bi kafirêd berî bedlê re,	For seven years he made war with the pagans in his time,
Yaman hevalê, yaman hevalê, yaman hevalê!	Oh help, help my love, my love!

(5: 4–11)

The list continues in the next stanza:

Dinya nemabu ji Noşê Rawan re,	This world didn't last for Anushîrwan,
Dinya nemabu ji Cimcimê Siltan re,	This world didn't last for Sultan Skull,
Dinya nemabu ji êkî wekî Hemze Pehlewan re	This world didn't last for someone like Hemze the Champion,
Dinya nemabu ji Rustemê Zalê re	This world didn't last for Rustem Zal,
Dinya nemabu ji 'Aşik Xerîb û Şa Sinemî ṛa	This world didn't last for 'Ashik Gherib and Shah Sinem,
Dinya nemabu ji Mem û Zînê re	This world didn't last for Mem and Zîn,

Dinya nemabu ji Siyabend û Xecê re,	This world didn't last for Siyabend and Khejê,
Dinya nemabu ji Mecnûn û Lêlê re,	This world didn't last for Mejnûn and Leylê
Dinya nemabu ji Silêman pêxember û Belqîz Xatûnê re,	This world didn't last for the prophet Solomon and the Queen of Sheba,
Kerem û êradêt barî te'ale hebûn vêre,	He had God's blessings and bounty here,
Kerem û êradêt ala te'ale ketine serî re,	God's blessings and bounty were bestowed on him,
Firiya, nava ezman û 'erdê re,	He flew between heaven and earth,
Min dî azmanê Xodê jêre kind bû	I saw God's heaven came down to him
'Erdê Xode jêre bilind bû ...,	God's earth rose up to him ...,

(6: 1–14).

However, it is clear from looking at the list as a whole that the 'religious' personalities are not playing any religious role in this song, but are merely there, along with other figures from the historical or 'legendary' past, to make a philosophical point. Solomon and the Queen of Sheba are listed, but they come alongside other proverbial lovers, 'Ashik Gherib, Shah Sinem, Mem and Zîn, Siyabend and Khejê, and Mejnûn and Leylê. The lovers come after the emperors, Anushirwan and Sultan Skull (a folkloric king who tried to cheat death), and the heroes, the Islamic Ḥemze Pehlewan and the Iranian Rustem Zal. Solomon himself is sometimes represented in Kurdish folklore, like Alexander and Shah 'Abbas, as a stereotypical monarch, and various stories have attached themselves to him. In this song, like 'Ali, he occurs not as a religious exemplum, positive or negative, but as an instance of someone who was given unusual gifts and privileges by God, but who still could not cheat death. Moreover, this *stran* does not deal with Yezidi beliefs about the afterlife and the possible fate of 'Eyshê. There are no devotional statements or entreaties to divine beings. In general, lamentation is a secular rather than a sacred phenomenon for the Yezidis, and, with a few notable exceptions such as *Lavijê Pîrê*, the *stranêd ẍerîbî* are personal statements of emotion grounded in a Yezidi view of the universe, rather than religious traditions.

WOMEN'S LAMENT

The women's lament I encountered amongst Yezidis in Northern Iraq can broadly be divided into two types, the semi-professional and the 'personal'. Each of these types will be described, and performance (where possible) and texts will be discussed. Major similarities and differences will be noted. Finally, an account will be given of the role played by the women's lament in the community and the purpose it serves for the participants themselves, as described by my informants.

Whether semi-professional or personal, the lament called *şîn*, described in Chapter Three, is generally agreed by Badinani Kurds to be a form of discourse exclusive to women. Rudenko describes women's funerary songs, which she calls *dilok* (1982: 13); these are about three or four lines long, usually with six or seven syllables to each line. However, some of the examples of *dilok* which Rudenko discusses are performed by males. In the Caucasus, men do perform *stran* or *kilamêd şînê*, 'songs of lamentation', usually in groups of three to five, with one as the main performer.[8] In Badinan, however, what was called *dîrok* or *dîlok*, which seems to encompass this form, was never ascribed to men by Yezidi informants. This is supported by the comments of outsiders. Bois (1966: 81–4) describes Yezidi mourning rituals, including visits made by women to the graveyard at the time of New Year, and refers only to women performing lamentation. In Badinan and Soran, the term *girîn* or *giriyan*, 'crying', is often applied to women's laments as a blanket term. The practice of weeping aloud seems to be one of the distinctive elements of the women's lament; among Yezidis, weeping is not considered inappropriate for men, but loud sobbing is usually considered unmanly. Murad (1993: 202) gives an example of a Yezidi man who wailed aloud during the mourning rituals; his extreme reaction to bereavement was seen as unusual but forgivable, given his close relationship to the deceased. Informants in Badinan were unanimous that lament was a women's genre, and I found no evidence there of any similar songs performed by men.

The paucity of collections so far made of Kurdish women's lament cannot simply be ascribed to problems of accessibility for male folklorists. Women's lament does not appear to enjoy the relatively high status of, say, the historical *stran*, in Kurdish society. Most of the men I questioned about women's lament asked why I was interested in such a 'miserable' genre; when within earshot of a lament, they kept away and appeared to find the lament distasteful and embarrassing. They showed sympathy towards the sufferings of the bereaved women, but the lament itself did not appear to trigger emotions in them in the same way as it did in the women.

In the *şîn*, the content is at the performer's discretion to a much greater extent than the *stran* or the long narrative poems. It consists of singing without musical accompaniment, though sometimes the participants will strike themselves rhythmically. It is composed extempore; even a well-known singer who does not know the deceased well, and who uses stock elements, will not perform the lament in the same way twice. Although one performer may sing the most, the others present are participants rather than audience; they may contribute to the song even if a semi-professional singer is leading it. The laments are extemporised song rather than 'texts' handed on from one individual to another; however, the genre, many of its images, and the rules governing its context, are traditional.

The distinction between semi-professional and 'personal' laments is valid not only because of the difference in standpoint between the semi-professional performer and the bereaved, but also because the (admittedly limited) samples available point to differences in form between the two. However, there are also important similarities between the two, which will also be examined, and at this early stage of Kurdish oral studies it is not worth separating the two into distinct forms of discourse, or genres. It is more accurate to say that they constitute two important elements of the varied form of discourse which is women's lament.

The material which will be considered here are consists of a number of the songs of Ḥizreta Ḥeso, a well-known performer amongst Yezidis in Georgia, as published in ZK, supplemented by the limited examples of wording and theme given by Mrs R., a semi-professional based in Sheykhan. These will be followed by an account of a performance of a lament initiated by a widow in Khanek and recorded during the 1992 fieldwork. This will be referred to as the 'Widow's Lament', though other women also made contributions to the performance. The former are examples of laments sung by semi-professionals for the relatives of others; the latter is sung by a bereaved woman for her own loved ones. Both groups are, of course, performed by Yezidis.

Semi-Professional Laments

It was noted in Chapter Three that the very limited samples of material given by Mrs R., a semi-professional singer in Ba'drê, resemble, in formal terms, the songs of another semi-professional, Ḥizreta Ḥeso, recorded in Jelîl 1978. Mrs R's examples were 2–4 lines long, with rhyming syllables at the end of each line; they also have some resemblance to the *dilok* of Rudenko. The occasion on which Ḥizreta Ḥeso performed, a ritual of mourning for 'Etarê Shero, was a *taziye* for women only, and presumably had much in common with those described by Mrs R. Since there is a strong consensus that Yezidi lament is reasonably uniform, and Ḥizret's songs constitute the only substantial evidence of Yezidi semi-professional women's lament currently available, they will be examined in the same context as the descriptions given by Mrs R. However, caution is necessary; Mrs R. only gave four examples, so it would be impossible to compare characteristics such as imagery with Jelîl's material. Since Mrs R. spoke rather than sang, and the examples in ZK give no indication of melody at all, the Badinani and Soviet material cannot be compared in terms of melody. Although it seems likely that the songs of Mrs R. and Ḥizret are of the same sub-genre, this cannot be proved for certain, and the two women provide two separate sets of evidence. Ḥizret's songs are not concrete evidence for the imagery used in Badinan, nor do Mrs R.'s comments on performance necessarily hold true in every detail for the Caucasus. Despite these caveats, the comments of various informants (particularly Mrs Hayat Rashow, a Sheykhani with some experience of women's lament) on the similarity of form and imagery between Ḥizret's songs and those performed among Sheykhani Yezidis, makes the Caucasian material worth considering here.

ZK gives 95 stanzas of lament sung by Ḥizret. They do not constitute a narrative, but a series of short pieces focusing on different scenarios and individuals. Each song is very short, but a full analysis of them all would be beyond the scope of this study, especially since the lack of performance detail would make it impossible to understand fully how they fit together. Since they are used in this book only as a sample of the use of language and imagery in Yezidi semi-professional lament, it will be adequate to take a selection of twenty as an illustration of the sentiments expressed and the devices used to express them.

As described in Chapter Three, the strict social rules governing the occasion of performance of lament made it impossible for me to make a recording of a semi-professional lament; all my evidence concerning performance comes from Mrs R.'s description. According to Mrs R., the initial period of mourning should last for seven days after a death; after this, *şîn* is continued on Wednesdays and Fridays until forty days have elapsed. When Mrs R. heard of a death she would take a car and go to the *taziye*; she travelled round the Yezidi villages throughout Sheykhan. In Georgia, Ḥizret was similarly well-known over a considerable area, and in Tbilisi bereaved families would always call her to sing a lament over the deceased (Jelîl 1978 II: 502–3). Mrs R. said that she would only sing if she knew the bereaved family, but personal acquaintance with the deceased was not necessary. She received some reward for her services, but it was not her sole, or even main, means of earning a living; she would sing for any Yezidi family regardless of whether they were rich or poor. When invited to perform, she would ask a few questions about the deceased, which would determine the substance of her lament. Although certain sentiments were dictated by the personality and circumstances of the deceased, every lament was different and improvised. She said that she sang according to her own inspiration '*dilê min dinivîsetin, devê min dibêjetin*', 'My heart writes, my mouth sings'. Mrs R.'s mother had known *şi'r* 'poems', and sung laments, but she was at pains to point out that her mother had not taught her formally; she had learned by observation when she was sitting at *taziye* and giving condolences, but not by formal training, '*kes min nîşan nekiriye*' 'nobody showed me'. Mrs R. was illiterate, Hizret 'semi-literate', though it is unclear exactly what Jelîl means by this (1978 II: 502). Although every village, according to Mrs R., had one or two women known for performing laments, not everyone had the skill in them, '*heye mirov zanit ... bêjit ... heye yani dil nezanit bêjetin*' 'there are people who know how to sing [laments] ... there are those, [whose] hearts don't know how to sing'. She portrayed her performance as a useful form of taking charge, saying that when people were sitting together after a death they did not know what to do, and if nobody performed they would not do anything except cry, and would become *'aciz* 'upset'.[9] After she had finished the bereaved family would continue with their own lamentation.

Mrs R. described the most important themes in her laments and their appropriate uses at some length, and it is her evidence which provides my account of key themes in semi-professional laments. For the discussion of imagery in semi-professional lament, however, I will examine the songs of Ḥizret which give a far broader range of evidence. According to Mrs R., what was said in a lament depended to a large extent on the identity of the deceased. There were several key facts about the deceased which she had to know before beginning a lament. One of the most important factors was gender; laments for men concentrated on their deeds, whereas those for women concentrated on their home and children; the number of children was important. Laments for the young differed from those for the elderly. She clearly wished to emphasise the special nature of laments for the young; all four of her examples given in Part II were explicitly for young people. She described her first example as being for children:

Ey yetîm sed ḥeyf û mixabin	Oh orphan, a hundred pities and regrets,
Ey yetîm li derî kolana bimînin	Oh orphan, let them remain at the street door,
Dane ṣoban û êvara	Morning and evening, they talked
Serî êhsînê wî li ber taq û dîwara	By the walls and the doorways about his good deeds,
Vê sibê çavêd wan nesekinin.	This morning, let their eyes not rest [from crying].

Her second example explicitly refers to young people:

Kuştiye çolê sed ḥeyf û mixabinê	He is killed in the wilderness, a hundred pities and regrets,
Xelkê cihêl çu li biyanêt avêtî bin	Young people went, to be cast away to a foreign place,
Lo lo birîndaro tu ji birînêd xo tu çawanî?	Oh wounded one, what state have your wounds left you in?

Her third and fourth examples were as follows:

Sed ḥeyf û mixabin xelqê nêzewicî li cîhê talî werin de ...	A hundred pities and regrets, that unmarried people come to the final place ...

and:

Xelqê dema xo nexwarî	A person who did not live out his time,
Xelqê kuçekokê dinya nedîtî	A little one who did not see the world

These directly echo words she used during the conversation, when she referred to the death of unmarried people, *xelqê nezewicî*, as particularly tragic; this is interesting in the light of Grima's observation that unmarried women and girls were excluded from the exchange of life stories among Paxtun women, on the grounds that they had not experienced anything worth telling (1992: 127). It is quite likely that for women in particular, marriage confers adult emotional status. Certainly, when discussing themes for laments over women, Mrs R. did not mention any aspects of girlhood, but cited only the married woman's house and children as appropriate subjects. She said that for those who died young, 'they say what a pity it is, he or she was young, hadn't married, hadn't seen the world'.[10] Even if a person was married and not particularly young, his or her relative youth would be mentioned. If a person had died under unusual circumstances, had been murdered, or killed in a car accident, Mrs R. would say so in her lament. Although the cause of death might be given, the issue of whether a person was murdered or died of natural causes did not necessarily influence what was said throughout the lament; similar sentiments would be expressed in both cases.

Laments for older people were much more straightforward in terms of theme, simply because longer lives provided more material. The person's age, children, family and customs (*adet*) could be described. Attention might also be paid to a person's moral worth (*qîmet*) and his good deeds (*başiya wî kirî*). Only good deeds and qualities were mentioned; everything beyond that, according to Mrs R., was God's business. She was at pains to point out that although death was ascribed to God's will '*em dibêjin xodê da xodê bir*', 'we say, "God gave and God took away"' the content of the lament was secular and not religious. The lament concentrated only on the life and virtues of the individual.[11]

Mrs R.'s comments covered a wide range of circumstances in which people die but she demonstrated only a tiny amount of material; Ḥizret's songs, on the other hand, give a much better indication of detail, but were performed on one occasion, in mourning for a specific individual, and must thus be assumed to constitute only a part of her repertoire.

Imagery and Emotion in the Semi-Professional Laments

Without performance details, one cannot evaluate how Ḥizret's songs work together to make a whole, but one can make general observations of how images work within individual songs. One of the most striking features of

Ḥizret's laments, for an outsider, is her use of images which are found elsewhere in Kurdish oral tradition, and which thus have enhanced meanings for her audience. These images can evoke a whole range of associations in very few words, and can give great poignancy to the poems, often without any direct reference to the death itself. Yezidi informants, notably Dr Khelîl and Mrs Hayat Rashow, have confirmed that this is also typical of Sheykhani semi-professional laments. To do justice to these short but highly evocative songs, I will for the most part quote them in full, numbered according to their listing in Part II. The first example begins with autumn nights, which have associations with melancholy and the genre of lyrical love song called *payizok*:[12]

1. Şevê payîzane dirêjin,	1. The nights of autumn are long,
Şarûr ṛûniştiye, bilbilê ḥalê dilê miṛa dibêjin,	The song-thrush has settled, the nightingale tells the condition of my heart,
Emê kerbê birînê birîndara, hinek keṛin, hinek gêjin.	We [feel] the pain of the wounded ones' injuries, some are deaf, some are dazed.

These associations are then reinforced by the reference to the nightingale, which can often give voice to emotion. As with the *stranêd xerîbî*, there is a clear link between the imagery of love lyric and that of these songs.

In Kurdish love songs, weddings feature strongly; they are usually represented as occasions of joy for families, and venues for encounters between lovers. This is played on in:

5. Emê heṛine mala birazavê,	5. We will go to the house of the best man,
Emê bêjin, 'Birazavê bira, ḥina xortê ṭûre nevêje avê,	We will say, 'Best man, brother, do not cast the lovely lad into the water yet,
Ḥeyfa min nayê girtina mêra, kuştina şêra, ḥeyfa min tê wê ḥeyfê, wekî jina wî ziviṛî mala bavê.'	I do not grieve at the capture of men, the killing of lionhearts, I grieve at this grief, that his wife has turned back to her father's house.'

and:

11. Me bariye berfa hûre,	11. A fine snow rained down on us,
Orṭa mala zeva û xezûrda bûye masûre,	Between the house of the bridegroom and father in law there was a difficulty,
Nizanim, xezûrê vî xortî çi jêṛa gotiye, zeva xeyîdiye, naçe mala xezûre.	I do not known what the father in law of this young man said to him, the bridegroom is offended, he is not going to the house of the father in law.

A happy occasion is anticipated but death prevents the young man from being married. Another example is also poignant:

15. Xerîbê min pak veṛêkin, Deste kincê zevatiyê lêkin, Ax û berê giran şakin.	15. Send off my exile clean and tidy, Put a bridegroom's outfit on him, Let the dust and heavy earth rejoice.

This does not describe the mechanics of a wedding taking place, but uses the vocabulary associated with it to describe the laying out and burial. For weddings and other celebrations, women would make themselves look as beautiful as possible, and in love songs they are often described in their wedding outfits. As in the love songs, there is a connection between a lack of care for the appearance and an unhappy emotional state:

3. Gulî ṛeşê, gulî alê, Ṛave neynikê bîne, serê xwe girêde, heṛe dewatê mala xalê,	3. Black braid, red braid, Get up, fetch a mirror and do your hair, go to a feast at your uncle's house,
Go, 'Feleka min min dixapîne, ṛoja çûyî îdî nayê.'	She said, 'My fate is cheating me, yesterday will not come again.'

One of the girls who are told to make themselves beautiful is being urged to be cheerful, but she refuses. Like many of Ḥizret's songs, this begins with a happy image and in the last line a melancholy note is introduced.

Many of the songs have strong associations between description of landscape and mood. Hizret uses the mention of specific locations to evoke mood in different ways:

4. Çemo, çemê Payê, Çem çikiyaye deng jê nayê,	4. Oh river, great river Pa, The river has dried up, it makes no sound,
Xazî xêra mala xwedêṛa, xortê ṭûre, dîsa mîna hêmanê berê, kêleka dayka xwe ṛûnişta, dîsa jêṛa bigota, 'Dayê,'	If only the joy of the house, by God, the lovely lad, would again do as he did before, [if only] he would sit by the side of his mother, and say again to her 'Mother',
Feleka min min dixapîne, mi ṛa nayê ṛayê.	My fate is cheating me, it does not go according to my wishes.

The metaphor compares the drying up of the river with the loss of a beloved son. Certain named places have their own associations:

20. Xemê gote Xeydê, Emê heṛin çiyayê Antanoskê, çiyangê seydê,	20. Sadness said to Anger, We will go to Antanosk mountain, a mountain of hunting,

Xortê ṭûre kire gazî, 'Ezê destê dê û bavê xwe nakevim, ḥeta ṛojek ṛoja şeva 'eydê.'	The lovely lad called out, 'I will not be in the hands of my mother and father until the eve of 'Eyd.'

No metaphor is needed here, as her audience will be aware that at the top of that particular hill is a Yezidi cemetery (Jelîl 1978 II: 481). More generally, description of weather is used to create or reinforce a mood; just as 'Eysha Balê's lover described how the a fog came down on them, so Ḥizret uses phrases such as *berfa hûr* 'fine snow' to evoke the emotional desolation of the bereaved.

Various terms are used for the state of both deceased and bereaved in the songs. The most important of these is *ẍerîb*. Its association with Kurdish songs about death is so strong that when, during my conversation with Mrs R., a man urged her to perform a lament, he used the words, 'Say *ẍerîbe*'; clearly this was felt to characterise the genre. The deceased, of course, are estranged, or exiled, from the living who cannot reach them (Rudenko 1982: 16):

12. Xerîbî ne ṭu kare, Forma ṛojê: bi ḥesavê, bi defterî, bi jimare, Wexta xerîbê xelqê xerîbiyê tên, xerîbê me xerîbiyêda dimînin mîna kulekeke pey keriyane.	12. There is no profit in exile, The rule of the day: by accounting, by copybooks, by numbers, When other people's exiles come back from exile, our exiles remain in exile like a lame sheep straggling behind the flocks.

and:

19. Dilê min dibêye, Şevê payîza dirêjin, diçin têye,	19. My heart is longing, The autumn nights are long, they go, they come,
Berê malxê mala, xortê ṭûre, daykê dergûşa, kewaniyê mala, dane welatê xerîbiyêye.	The head of the house, the lovely lads, the mothers of the babes, the mistresses of the houses, have gone to the land of exiles.

The latter example is ambiguous; the 'land of exile' may be death, but it may also be a more literal foreign country. The bereaved may also be described as *ẍerîb* in Kurdish women's laments; I made a recording of Barzani women in Qosh Tepe whose lament included '*em ẍerîb in*' stated repeatedly.

In Ḥizret's first song in this selection, the bereaved ones are referred to as both *gêj* 'dazed', and *keṛ* 'deaf'. Such usages imply that the bereavement has alienated the mourners from ordinary life, stopping them from behaving normally. Perhaps the most striking example of this occurs in:

2. Dayka dergûşê ji mala bavê berjêr bûye, Cotek karê xezala li wê dûye, Diya dergûşê çawa ji mal û mêra kûvî bûye.	2. The mother of the babe came down from the father's house, Two young gazelles behind her, The mother of the babe, how wild and distant from home, from men she has become.

The bereaved woman is said to have become *kûvî* 'wild', a term often used of animals, and is distanced from houses and people.

Besides the vocabulary of estrangement and separation, an image used here which is also used elsewhere in Kurdish poetry and song about death is the term *birîn*, 'wound'. This can refer not only to actual physical injury, but also to emotional or psychological damage suffered by the bereaved, and is one of a group of words which are similarly ambivalent, whose literal meanings of physical damage are used to express mental or emotional pain. Thus in 1 the living are described as *birîndar*, 'wounded', as well as dazed and deaf. This can also be seen in 17:

Me go, 'Birîndarin, nexaşin, ṭapa wan ṭinene . . .	We said, 'They are wounded, they are sick, they have no presence, (17: 3)

where the people are not only described as wounded but also sick.[13]

The physical organs which are most closely associated with the emotions in Kurdish are the heart and liver, and these songs contain references to them. The image of the heart being physically broken, similar to the English usage, occurs:

Emê çi bikin xwe vî dilê şkestî,	What shall we do with these broken hearts of ours? (18: 1)

and, more dramatically:

7. Kela girtiya serê çiya,	7. The fortress of the prisoners [is] at the top of the mountain,
Dûkî zirav lê kişiya, Minê bala xwe dayê xortê ṭûre pêşiya cendirma, ziravê dilê diya wî diqetiya.	A thin line of smoke rises from it, I looked for the lovely lad before the police-station, the frail heart of his mother snapped.

In another example, heart and liver are closely associated with each other and with love:

8. Sazbendo, sazî derda, Qasekî sazê xwe bîne xarda,	8. Saz player, teller of pains, Bring down your saz for a moment,

Têlê vî sazbendî şê û şêbiskê kewaniyanin, simêlê malxiya sosinîne, xazî xêra mala xudêṛa, dil-cegerê mi xeverda.	The strings of this saz player are like the chestnut-hair and braids of women, the moustache of the heads of families are like irises; if only the joy of the house, by God, my heart and liver, would speak.

The beloved man is described as 'my heart and liver'. He is set alongside other images associated with loveliness and attractiveness, the beautiful braids and fine moustaches.

Emotion is also described in more direct ways, as in *ḥeyfa min tê*, literally 'my grief comes' in number 5, quoted in full above. *Ḥeyf* itself can mean varying intensities of sadness, from a mild pity or regret to a strong grief. The common expression *ḥeyf e* 'it's a pity' can be used in a variety of situations, both trivial and serious. Number 22, as we have seen, begins:

22. Xemê gote Xeydê ...,	22. Sadness said to Anger ...,

The emotions of the mourners at the graveyard are externalised and personified – a rather 'literary' device. *Xeyid*, from an Arabic word meaning 'rage, passion, fury' carries a range of meanings centring round a concept which corresponds to the English 'offence'; here it means 'anger'.

Unlike many European environments, where politeness precludes the expression of anger among the recently bereaved, the Yezidis acknowledge such anger in their laments.

A sense of injustice may be expressed by the bereaved:

Go, 'Feleka min min dixapîne, ṛoja çûyî îdî nayê.'	She said, 'My fate is cheating me, yesterday will not come again.' (3: 3)

and:

Feleka min min dixapîne, miṛa nayê ṛayê.'	My fate is cheating me, it does not go according to my wishes. (4: 2–3).

Ḥizret describes and evokes emotion in a variety of ways, both directly and through imagery. The richness of the medium of Kurdish verbal art, with its wide range of meanings and associations corresponding to specific images, enables her to portray, and arouse, complex emotions in relatively few words. In this she appears to be very successful; according to Jelîl, she could move people to tears (1978 II: 502).

It seems to be a general feature that the full meaning of the song is brought out in the final line, and many of them set a general scene before moving to specifics. Thus in 1, the first two lines consist of rather melancholy references to the natural world, the autumn nights, the nightingale and the song-thrush, before the final line describes the condition of the people. A similar example is number 17:

17. Çiya gotê çiya,
Go, 'Ka xelqê li van ciya?'
Me go, 'Birîndarin, nexaşin, ṭapa wan ṭinene, meyê şandiye bilindciya, gelo kî êlêra dageriya?'

17. Mountain said to mountain,
'Where are the people in this place?'
We said, 'They are wounded, they are sick, they have no presence, we sent him out to the high places, but which clan did he come down with?'

The apparently impersonal mountains wonder about the state of the people, who describe their unhappiness in the final line. This is another expression of the strong connection between the people and the mountains which is felt throughout Kurdish folklore. Numbers 3, 5 and 17, quoted above, begin with seemingly happy wedding celebrations, which turn to sadness in the final line.

Even a cursory glance at this selection of semi-professional laments shows that certain characters recur in various songs. The *dayka dergûşê* 'mother of the babe' (literally 'of the cradle' (2 and 19) *xortê tûre*, 'lovely lad' (4, 6, 7, 9, 10, 19, 20) and the *zava*, 'bridegroom'(11, and indirectly, 5 and 15), are all mentioned several times and appear to be stock elements; the first two of these in particular look like formulaic phrases.[14] If this is so, then we may expect them to carry overtones of meaning beyond that of their literal translation, though more comparable texts are needed to evaluate this additional meaning. It is also notable that family members are often mentioned, especially close relations. The mother is the character most often referred to; 4 expresses a wish that a lost son would talk to his mother again, and 7 describes her reaction to his death. Fathers are not ignored; in 20, for example, the young man says that his mother and father will not be close to him again 'until the eve of 'Eyd' (it is unclear which 'eyd), but the emotions or wishes of fathers are not described in detail in these songs. The focus on the emotions of the bereaved mother is likely to be a common feature of Kurdish women's lament. In the Barzani lament collected at Qosh Tepe, great emphasis was placed on the *daika lava*, 'the mother of sons'. Ḥizret also mentions sisters:

14. Stêra sibê lêda,
Birê pişta xûşkê girêda,
Go, 'Îdî ez nayêm ṭixûbê weda,
Nizanim, şevekê mi bivînî di xewnêda.'

14. The morning star had set,
The brother fastened his sister's belt,
He said, 'Henceforth I shall not come to visit you,
I don't know, one night you may see me in a dream.'

The greater attention given to the emotional reactions of the female relations reflects the fact that this mourning is their special responsibility, not that of the men, who are not present.

It is worth noting that the deceased throughout these songs is male. This is, of course, in keeping with the fact that they were performed in mourning for one man. However, there are relatively few specifics in the songs. References are made to the physical attractiveness of the deceased; not only is he a *xortê tûre* 'lovely young man', but the colour of his moustache, one of the few male physical attributes commonly described in love songs, is also the focus of attention:

9. Simêleke sore bi sosinî,	9. A moustache is red as an iris,
Êleke giran ber derê mala bavê	A great clan has halted before the
xortê ṭûre disekinî,	house of the lovely lad's father,
Werin bala xwe bidine min vê	Come, give me your attention for
yekê, tê bêjî, simêla xortê ṭûre axê	this, you will say, the moustache of
goṛada ḥine kirî.	the lovely lad is hennaed with the earth of the grave.

In 15 his fine clothes are also mentioned. Yet it is never said that this *xortê tûre* actually *is* 'Etarê Shero, who was 73 when he died and clearly did not die before he was married, since some of the material in Jelîl 1978 was performed by his daughter Gulîzer. It is clear that a number of scenarios are described which are broadly applicable to the death of an adult male. Although Ḥizret takes on the persona of different individuals, speaking as the mother, sister, and possibly lover or bride (3: 3 seems to suggest this) of the deceased, none of these individuals is named; there is no indication that they are anything other than stock characters. This non-specific tone, along with a skilful use of language and image, is what one would expect in songs by a semi-professional who is lamenting a deceased person who is not a close relative.

'Personal' Laments

By 'personal' laments, I mean simply those sung by women for their deceased relations rather than by semi-professionals for the relations of others. It is not intended to imply that the laments of semi-professionals are 'impersonal', or insincere. Both performances which will be described were recorded during the Yezidi New Year festival (the first Wednesday in April; see Kreyenbroek 1995: 151), where the dead are lamented throughout the community. Women of all ages went to the cemetery at Khanek, gathered round family tombs on which they placed offerings, and lamented for various family members. They then ate a meal together at the cemetery, and qewwals processed round the cemetery playing sacred music. Later the same day, a widow sang a lament in her home. She was visited by other women who also participated.

Lamentation at the Graveyard

The styles of performance observed at the cemetery on the morning of the New Year festival and in the house in the afternoon were very different. The graveyard where lamentation took place was about a mile from the Yezidi collective village, though much nearer to the site of an older Yezidi village which had been destroyed. The women gathered there on the morning of the Yezidi New Year, but some women had visited the graveyard the previous day. At the cemetery, the women were in family groups, with the men who had driven them there standing at a discreet distance, chatting to each other or waiting by the cars. (The qewwals, all men of course, arrived much later, when most of the laments were almost over). Offerings such as food, money and cigarettes had been brought which were placed on graves; large pieces of cloth had been spread over some. Many of the graves also had rows of braids hanging from a line over them, along with small scraps of cloth.[15]

The women stood in groups round individual graves; these groups included women of all ages, from teenagers to the elderly. Most of the groups observed had brought along photographs of at least one deceased member of their family; these were often held aloft for all to see and then placed on the graves. Each of these groups followed its own lament without any reference to the surrounding groups; thus several laments could be heard simultaneously. Once a lament was established, it appeared that each woman became absorbed in her own mourning. Individuals would contribute stanzas of their own which varied widely in tune and wording, with some sung and some spoken. Often this was done while another woman was also lamenting.

To begin with, one woman would lead the lament whilst others wept. The stanzas were short. When one woman finished singing, another might begin, or, after a pause, the same woman might begin again. As this continued, several women might begin to sing at once; there seemed to be no fixed order in which women sang, and no fixed length to each woman's contribution. As the emotion built up, women would remove headscarves and loosen their hair; occasionally one individual would begin beating her breast and crying out 'Ah! Ah!' in regular rhythm; this would spread, with the sung laments declining, until most or all of the group members were beating their breasts and screaming, but was never sustained for longer than a few minutes in the groups I observed. Several families were observed carrying out the same process. When this broke up, lamenting in the form of singing would begin again. Some women also ululated. This became more frequent when the qewwals arrived, moving slowly around the graveyard playing the *def* or frame drum, and the *şebab* or flute. The group lamentations gradually broke up and large groups of women and children sat down together to eat a meal of meat and rice.

According to Pîr Khidir Silêman, it was a rare occurrence for an outsider to observe and record this commemoration of the dead at New Year. Although the women were aware that recordings were being made and consented to be photographed, a recording of sufficient quality to produce 'texts' of their laments would have involved an inappropriate degree of intrusion with recording equipment. The recordings made give a good impression of the sounds of the occasion, with all sorts of laments taking place simultaneously, but no one lament is heard clearly enough to allow transcription. Individual words and phrases, however, are clear.

By comparison with the lament recorded later in the day at the widow's home, the laments in the graveyard were much more fragmented and the women seemed much more agitated; what was particularly noticeable was that although the women were in family groups,[16] each individual made different contributions. In general, much of the vocabulary used was similar to that of the lament performed at home later in the day, with such words as *birîndar* 'wounded' and *x̌erîb* 'exiled, estranged' being common. Some songs emphasised grieving mothers with phrases such as *dilê daika* 'the mothers' hearts'; others referred to the deceased as 'brother' with repeated phrases such as *ay bira ay bira*, 'oh brother, oh brother'. The form of the songs was generally similar, with short stanzas of a few lines, and a fall in pitch at the end of the line. Some contributions were made loudly, with sobbing as part of the song; others were quieter; a few were simply spoken quietly. There were one or two examples whose musical forms differed strongly from the majority; one of these, which began *o delalê dilê min … lo lo lo …*, 'Beloved of my heart … oh,' had a melody and rhythm unlike the others and unlike historical *stran* – it sounded like a song the singer already knew rather than an improvisation.

My companion, Ms K., said that each woman was thinking of her own personal losses even when another person was being lamented. It was not clear how far each 'group lament', as it were, was for a specific individual or individuals, or for deceased loved ones in general. Certainly the individuals shown in the photographs were a focus for the group lament, but it is quite likely that each woman was thinking of others too. The idiosyncratic nature of contributions implies that they were products of personal feelings which varied according to the contributor.

The Widow's Lament

Later the same day at a house in Khanek I recorded a performance which bore a strong resemblance to Mrs R.'s description of *taziye*. Mrs J., a widow in her thirties, led the lamentation; I had been invited specifically to come and hear her sing. Although other women participated, it was felt that the occasion was her lament. During the performance, as I was told at the time, she lamented her husband, who was a *şehîd* 'martyr', her brother (or, possibly, brother-in-law), who had been a prisoner of war in Iran, and his wife, whom she refers to as 'sister', though she may have been a sister-in-law. This woman, according to my companion Ms K., was in prison. Other women also sang; the lament continued for about an hour. It contained a great deal of repetition and some very unclear references;[17] many of the words were unclear because of weeping, or other background noise; this became more of a problem as the lament progressed and more of the women wept. Since so much is unclear, I have not included this lament in Part II of this book; I shall not attempt to consider its broader structure, but will give a general description of the performance and its dynamics, and will quote samples of the lament, with a brief survey of its most important elements and images.

About ten women of various ages, and some children, were present. Initially Mrs J. led the lament; after about half an hour an older woman began to sing some stanzas. The two voices continued to alternate (not regularly, but spontaneously), while all the women in the room wept and some then sang. This lament lasted about an hour. There were pauses between stanzas, some longer than others. One might describe the atmosphere as relatively relaxed; it was certainly at no point comparable with the frenzies of the graveyard. There was very little interruption of one woman's song by another. Nevertheless, there was a good deal of expression of emotion. One woman sobbed between stanzas as Mrs J. sang; she herself sang at length later. Months later, a native speaker commenting on the recording described this woman as 'bitter'; certainly she was overcome at several points during her own song. As the performance continued, other women wept aloud; by the end, almost all were in tears, though one or two of the unmarried girls were not.

The women sat cross-legged, and occasionally hushed their children. Some of the older women, and Mrs J. herself, swayed back and forth rhythmically, and gently struck their knees in time to the lament. As the lament went on, more guests arrived and sat down; others got up quietly and left. Glasses of tea were served. The lament came to an abrupt end, precipitated by the recorder reaching the end of the cassette; this caused a diversion, though I tried to change it quietly. The singer finished her stanza and did not continue. The women then chatted, wiped each others' tears, and dispersed. Given the extempore nature of the genre and the way songs had arisen and ended at the graveyard, this was probably not a terribly unnatural way for the song to end; it seems quite usual that a singer simply finishes when she feels like it. Certainly, I observed a similar pattern among the Barzani women in the Qosh Tepe collective; a singer would stop and the women would chat. Occasionally one of the group would become upset and begin singing again, whereupon others would listen and sometimes join in.

Individual Contributions and Audience Reactions

Mrs J.'s song is clearly not a narrative, but an improvised lyrical form. In some ways, it seems less polished than the semi-professional laments, with their rhyme scheme, their neat balancing of images, and their concentration of meaning at strategic points such as the last line. However, it was not without structure; it was divided clearly into stanzas, which had pauses between them. Most of the stanzas centred on one issue or episode.

The lament had already begun when the recording started, and some words were inaudible due to the noise of setting up the equipment. The following summary gives an outline of the next part of Mrs J.'s lament, which concentrates mainly on one individual whom she addresses as *bira*, 'brother'. At first I assumed that this was her husband, since in Muslim laments it is possible for husbands to be addressed in this way.[18] However, Yezidis have since commented that this would be most unlikely in a Yezidi lament.

She described his death in terms of leaving for the *zozan*. She then mentioned going to Mosul to collect his body and expressed a wish to make him a fine coffin. Her loved one had been separated from her, she said; she mentioned her unfortunate sister and described her desolation. She then sang of the Iranian prisoners of war, her loved one's fatal wound, and how he looked in his coffin. Her loved one was unfairly killed; she called on doctors for help. She later dwelt on the fact that he died alone, with none of his own people by him. Then she described how she longed for him. She moved on to her brother who had been a prisoner for ten years, making her sister wretched. Again she called on a doctor, to help her sister, and to help her brother. She described various ways to heal her loved one's wound, from going to the *zozan* to making a pilgrimage to a shrine.

She then went on to say that she wished she had known what was happening to him when he fell into the hands of the infidels (the Iranians), and mentioned in more detail that he had been under the earth for some time. After this, other voices played a greater part. A second voice sang a stanza, and a third voice addressed a cousin, *pismamo*. The second woman sang again; indeed she dominated the second half of the lament. It is possible that she was Mrs J.'s mother (she was an older woman), as her lament at first concerned the miserable situation of Mrs J's 'sister' Nêrgiz. She mentioned her being taken to prison, and having her hands bound. Her children were without their father, *bêbab*, and without their mother's milk, *memikê şîrê*. This is a figure of speech; the children appear to be weaned, if her description of them as 'not big, not little' is to be believed. On festival days, she said, the children stayed at home instead of making visits and receiving sweets from neighbours and friends. By this time, several women were accompanying her by singing *ā* and *û* between stanzas; they continued to do this until the end of the lament. The third woman sang again, asking where the people had gone, and where the prisoners were, much as some of Ḥizret's songs had done. The second woman sang once more about Nêrgiz, referring to her as a 'gazelle pasturing in the wilderness' and her children as 'young gazelles'. This is again reminiscent of Ḥizret's song number 2, which talks of a woman with 'two young gazelles', surely her children, with her. The second woman then moved on from the plight of Nêrgiz to describe going to the mountains with small children and being under attack; her reference here to the *gelê Kurdistanê* 'the people of Kurdistan' makes it likely that she is referring to the Iraqi army's suppression of the Kurdish rebellion in 1991 and the subsequent mass flight to the mountains. She then described the death of a young male relative in Zakho hospital, where the staff were uncaring. This young man would never wear his bridegroom's clothes which were still in the wardrobe. Shortly after this, the lament ended.

It was noticeable that audible participation by other women present, expressed by weeping during or between stanzas, by their singing *ā* and *û* between stanzas, by their beating out the rhythm on their knees, and by their exclamations of grief and contribution of laments of their own, developed during this lament. Overall, the levels of these contributions were very low by comparison with the lamentation at the graveyard. Nevertheless they increased as this lament continued, and reached a maximum level during the account of the flight to the mountains. Even at this point, however, they were not so loud or so frequent as to interrupt the singing decisively.

The Imagery of the Widow's Lament

One of the most initially striking aspects of Mrs J.'s lament, which distinguishes it immediately from Ḥizret's songs, is the degree of specific detail. Individuals and places are named, though their identities and significance are not explained. As with many of the lyrical passages of the *stran*, the listener has to know the whole story to appreciate all the allusions. For instance, if Ms K. had not said that Mrs J. had a sister in prison, the references to Nêrgiz by Mrs J. and by the second singer would not have been at all clear.

Mrs J.'s lament deals primarily with her own griefs; it does not present a variety of mourners in different situations as do the laments of Ḥizret. There are considerable parallels between the way Mrs J. describes the condition of the deceased and the bereaved. There are examples of this in the following stanza:

Hey bira o bavê Faroqê min bira o	Oh brother, oh father of Faroq,
Bavê mêvanê me kula serê hemû kula o	Father of our guests, this is the grief of all griefs

Min go minê kuştî birîndarê berê sibê rakime ji piya	I said, I will go and take away the killed, the wounded one before morning
Wextê hûn çûne Mûsilê li berê sibê hûnê rakine ji piya	When you went to Mosul before morning, (I said) 'you take him away',
Min go xerîbo, welatê xeriba ketiyo	I said 'Oh exile, you who have come to a strange land,
Em rebene kuştî birîndara welatê xerîba ketine	We unfortunates, killed and wounded, have come to a land of exiles,
Wextê ço mi ser bavê mêvanê xwe sergirîm	Once I wept over the host of my guests,
Go, 'Hunê kuştî birîndarê li berê sibê carê rakinê ji piya.'	I said, 'You go and lift up the killed, the wounded one before morning.'

In line 5 she says that he has gone to a land of exiles, and then immediately says the same of the living. Similarly the terms *kuştî* 'killed' and *birîndar* 'wounded', are applied both to the deceased, for whom it is literally true, and, figuratively, to the living. This imagery is sustained for a considerable time:

Hey birao	Oh brother
Min go hakîmo çaxê tu were hêreo	Oh doctor, when you come, come here,
Hakîmo tu were hêreo	Doctor, you come here,
A tu ji daika mêva re dermanê xwe hûre hûre binhêre o	Oh, you look carefully at your medicine for the mother of the guests,
Dê bavê ḥemû kuştî birîndare	Mother and father are both killed and wounded,
Ew ji hemû xiyalê dile mi re dubarî birînêd van şêra o	Beyond all the dreams of my heart are the wounds of these lion-hearted ones, oh.

Her mention of 'mother and father' in line 5 of this stanza implies that the bereaved also need help for their hurt. Later she addresses the doctor again, asking him to come and examine the patient.

After this she gives some details of how she would help him herself:

Emê herin ziyaretê Memê Şivan rûnin ber serê kêlîkêd qebrî	We will go to the shrine of Mem Shivan, and sit at the head of the gravestone,
Heger miriyê me rabû ji xwe rabû û ne emê pê birinê birîndare ji kula dilê xwe re bikewîne.	If my dead one arose, rose of his own accord, we would cauterise the wound of the wounded with the grief of our hearts.

Among the Yezidis, the first resort for the treatment of many illnesses was (and sometimes still is) prayer, the services of a holy man, or the application of sacred earth from a shrine. Mem Shivan was the tutelary saint of a destroyed village whose inhabitants moved to the Khanek collective, where they rebuilt the shrine. Such scenarios are clearly imaginary, as the loved one is already in his grave before she tries to cure him and he appears to have been dead when she heard about his injury. Although her descriptions of his 'wound' may describe actual injuries, in general the imagery of wounds is a metaphor for his hurts and her own grief. Her statement of intention to tend and cure him demonstrate his value to her and her devotion to him. Similarly, we have seen that in the *stran* of love, women often volunteered to make or do something special for their beloved.

Not only does Mrs J. want to tend her wounded one; she says she will use a poultice of *ketan*, 'linen' or 'flax', a very fine and expensive fabric. Later in the lament, she wants to make him a shirt out of the same fabric:

Lê bila were ziyaretê Memê Şivan, emê kirasekî ji peyayê mala bavê xwe 'ezizî çêkin ji ketana, ji ketanekî nerme	But, come to the shrine of Memê Shivan, we will make a shirt for the darling of our father's house, from linen, from a soft linen,

She says she will make him a coffin of apple-wood and rose-wood:

Mi ço min gotê 'Erif û mata xwe,	I went, I said to 'Erif and my aunt,
'Rezîl û reben here Mûsilê	'Let the miserable, the wretched one, go to Mosul,
Û ezê herim ji xwe re Mûsilê bibînim,	And I will go and see Mosul for myself,
Ha û ezê tabûtê ji bavê mêvanê xo re çêkim aliyê ji darê sêvê û alî ji darê gûliyê	Yes, and I will make a coffin for the host of my guests, of apple-wood on one side and rose-wood on the other.'

Both woods are considered to be fine and desirable, and are expensive. She describes his physical appearance as if he were the hero of a love-song:

Wextê mi berê xwe dayê mi berê tabûtê rakir	When I looked, I opened the lid of the coffin,
Mi dî riḥa di hêştayê bi xewra xo de,	I saw the wild basil, he is still sleeping,

This is even more pronounced in the details of:

Ez qurbana serê tewêlê te me ...	I am wretched, longing for your hair ...
Destê se'eta me tilîyê gustilkê me	For your watch-hand, for your ring-finger,
Û bêjna mêranî me bêjnê bêjnê ziravê	And your manly figure, your figure, your lean figure ...

According to both Muslim and Yezidi informants, such heroic description is a commonplace of lament and does not necessarily imply that the deceased was particularly beautiful or heroic when alive. Nevertheless, it adds to the overall impression of his worth which Mrs J. creates in her lament, and fits in well with Mrs R.'s comment that one should only speak well of the dead in laments.

One element which is mentioned several times is the fact that the loved one was alone when he died. Mrs J. seems to find this particularly distressing:

Û hay delalê mala bavê mi wexte te keftî desta wa kafir û 'ecemê de	Oh beloved of my father's house, when you fell into the hands of those infidels and Persians,
Ê li welatê ẍerîba kes li ser te nebû ba te ...	Yes, in the land of exiles, nobody was with you, by you ...

In Kurdish society generally it is considered a terrible thing to die alone and *ẍerîb*, far from one's kin, but in Yezidi society there is an extra dimension; when one dies, one should have one's sheykh and pîr, and one's 'brother' or 'sister of the hereafter', at hand for religious reasons.

It seems clear that Mrs J. is using only concepts and images which are considered appropriate to the genre of lament; many of them can be seen in other laments. However, she is also creating an individual statement; she is elaborating on elements which are particularly appropriate to her situation, such as the concept of *birîndar* and of cure, and also on those which she finds particularly affecting and which will also arouse pathos in the audience. It seems that she uses stock elements of lament skilfully for her own purposes; she was introduced to me in Khanek as someone 'who can sing a good *dîrok*', and in Europe both Kurdish Muslims and Yezidis who have listened to the recording have commented on her skill.

CONCLUSIONS

Even the small range of material which could be surveyed here has shown that there is a great deal of common ground between the *stran* of grief and the two types of women's laments. Each draws its imagery from a large pool of evocative symbols and motifs. The deceased is represented as beautiful in the same ways as the heroes and heroines of love lyric. Of the women's laments, those of the semi-professional from the Caucasus are more uniform in structure, and contain a wide variety of stock elements with very few specifics. The 'personal' lament performed by a widow in Badinan contains many specific details, often repeated and developed at length.

The evidence provided by the account of Mrs R. and by the laments of Ḥizret and Mrs J. show that women's lament is a genre which is still flourishing, and which has purpose and value for those who perform and listen to it. According to Mrs R., *şîn* is not a religious but a social institution; her laments concentrated on the life of the deceased and did not include religious elements. The laments of both Ḥizret and Mrs J. are also secular; beyond the *welatê xerîba*, 'land of exiles', there is no mention of any afterlife, and certainly no mention of God beyond the type of exclamation common in conversation. This was also true of *'Eysha Balê*. Mrs R. was emphatic that, far from being a religious duty, *şîn* was actually sinful. Weeping, striking oneself and cutting off one's hair were repellent to God, but the strength of tradition was such that one could not refrain from *şîn* . *Ev adetê me, em nikarin nabêjin*, 'this is our custom, we cannot *not* say [*şîn*]', she said. Neglecting to perform *şîn* when someone had died was *bêqîmet*, 'unworthy'. If a family did not perform it, the reputation of both the deceased and the family would suffer; people would ask who the deceased had belonged to if his own people did not lament him. This would clearly be disastrous for the good name of a family; the importance of belonging to one's own people, and being acknowledged by them, is enormous among the Yezidis. A clear indicator of this importance is the fact that one of the most commonly used ways of expressing the misery and finality of death is to express it in terms of *xerîbî*, of estrangement or exile. This concept may perhaps be even more important for Yezidis, with their socio-religious preferences for living close to each other, than for other Kurds.

The women's lament is not only a social duty but also a meaningful experience for the participants. According to Mrs R., '*Her dilê xo dibêjite*', 'each speaks her own heart'. It is an occasion where women can express emotion relatively freely, and thus serves a cathartic purpose. This is also true among Muslim Kurds; some of the Barzani women of Qosh Tepe told me that lament had been helpful to them in their bereavement, though now, in 1992, they had had enough of it and wanted to resume normal life. According to Mrs Fawziya Rahman, *şîn* gives women the chance to 'let all the emotion out' and is ultimately helpful. Murad gives an example of a man who who wailed aloud at a Yezidi *taziye*; his wife said that he should be left to continue, as it would 'soothe his anguish' (1993: 202). Moreover, mourning is rightly depicted in songs of lamentation as a time when things are abnormal; in real life it is a time when people are far from everyday concerns, and customs and taboos are not as usual. Women abandon their customary restraint, uncover their hair and give vent to their emotions very loudly. It is perhaps not surprising that when deeply affected by grief, men are occasionally permitted to abandon masculine self-possession.

The women who are present are not always closely related to the deceased who is the subject of the initial lament, and who may be the focus of the *taziye*, but each woman thinks of her own losses and may contribute a lament of her own, about her own bereavement or loss. At a *taziye*, Murad was able to distinguish 'genuine' mourners from those who merely cried aloud once or twice (1993: 189), and then began to converse with other guests. My own experience, based on observation of laments which were not performed within the context of a *taziye*, is that after some time, even those not immediately concerned with the deceased were moved by the laments. However, it might be argued that, whereas all family, friends and neighbours, bereaved or not, would feel bound to visit for a *taziye* following a death, the women who would choose to attend the New Year commemoration would be those who had lost someone. Mrs R. said that at a *taziye* other women might be present who had lost relations in the war, and they would weep for their own losses. Thus Mrs J. concentrates on her brother and husband, but an older woman present at the performance focuses on Nêrgiz. However, despite the catharsis of the violent emotion of the *şîn*, I observed on various visits to Qosh Tepe that it can result in collapse and exhaustion, and that women often moved to calm down a person who had become too violently affected. Mrs R. may have had this type of 'management' of the bereaved in mind when she made her remark about the singer of the *şîn* controlling the occasion and helping the bereaved, who would only cry and become upset if left to themselves.

It is noticeable that laments, though performed in the context of death, are not concerned only with the deceased; Nêrgiz is not dead but in prison; her plight is still considered a fitting subject for inclusion in a lament. The Barzani women of Qosh Tepe did not refer to their lost men as dead, but as prisoners; they also lamented their current situation, especially their poverty and their distance from Barzan (Allison 1996). During Mrs J.'s lament, the part of the lament which provoked the most weeping among the other women present was the account of the flight from Iraqi forces to the mountains. This was an experience all had shared. Given that the lament is a vehicle for individual self-expression, its spontaneity, and the lack of fixed rules about starting and stopping laments, and about emotional responses to them, is hardly surprising. Emotional responses certainly vary; the range of contributions at the graveyard has been noted, and the Barzani laments at Qosh Tepe ranged from the hysterical, with violent weeping and collapse, to a gentle tone much more akin to Mrs J.'s lament. Murad interprets the strong emotion of Yezidi mourning rituals as a compensation for the sentiments the bereaved 'suppressed toward the deceased while he or she was alive' (1993: 203). However, the range of experience which is described in the laments, often only loosely associated with the deceased, would seem to suggest that it is not only the emotions felt towards the deceased, but a wider range of sorrows and frustrations that can be expressed in *şîn*.

It seems that there is a very real sense in which one might say that laments are not about the dead, but rather about the living. The dead are certainly extolled, but they also serve as a focus for the emotions and needs of the living; both semi-professional and personal laments describe the feelings of the bereaved. There is no doubt that the performance of lament triggers strong and swift emotional reactions in those present. Ms K. said in Khanek that hearing laments would make me cry. Jelîl notes that Ḥizret's laments provoked tears (1978 II: 502). Murad notes that the laments recited during the *taziye* stirred the passions of the listeners (1993: 191). However, the obvious presence of emotion does not mean that the sentiments of the laments should necessarily be taken at face value and equated with Western terms. Without knowing Mrs J. personally, we cannot know whether the heroic terms she uses to describe her husband reflect the way she perceived him when he was alive, or whether she is simply using an appropriate theme for lament. We do know that she has a reason for depicting him in this way, but the question of her motives in doing this goes far beyond a simplistic definition of 'sincerity' or 'insincerity'. She uses a range of culturally appropriate images to articulate her emotional state. It is possible that she feels a range of emotions, which we might term grief, misery, frustration, bitterness, or anger against her husband. She certainly uses some Kurdish nouns equivalent in meaning to these, but how far she would define her feelings in such terms is uncertain. One should not expect to find Western methods of location and description of emotions in Kurdistan. What can be said with confidence is that Mrs J. is using a known and accepted genre, and the imagery that goes with it, to make her individual emotional statement.

Although we can identify differences between the semi-professional and personal laments in terms of specificity and structural polish, these differences are not absolute. Not only do both types of lament draw on the same register of vocabulary and pool of imagery, but the Yezidi semi-professionals featured here do have an emotional involvement in the performance, and there is no evidence to indicate that in Yezidi society they are unusual in this. I have heard of examples of women who 'faked emotion' in their performances, from Dr Shukriya Rasool, but this was among Muslims in Soran. Mrs R. said that she began singing laments after the loss of her sister, whom she loved dearly; according to Jelîl, Ḥizret had lost various family members, and 'lightened the load on her heart with songs' (1978 II: 502). Mrs R. also said that the time her laments lasted depended on how upset she felt. Despite the fact that the semi-professional performers may not even know the deceased personally, it seems that they participate fully in the emotional event of the lament. The distinction between semi-professional and 'personal' laments blurs even further when we consider that the *taziye* is not a performance by an individual to an audience, but an event in which those present are participants, and may express their feelings with some spontaneity.

Women's lament, unlike the *stran* of grief, is not a particularly prestigious genre, but its social importance should ensure its survival. It is a vehicle which women choose for the expression of their emotions, and its performance is an occasion where women comfort themselves and each other. It is not a sophisticated genre; its images are drawn from the everyday life of the deceased and bereaved. Nevertheless, the skill and artistry of its performers can be easily seen by an outsider in the choice of image and the forms of expression used, and in the strong feelings it arouses in those who listen.

CHAPTER SEVEN

Conclusions

ORAL TRADITION AND IDENTITY

This study has considered the treatment of three important themes, war, love and death, in Yezidi oral tradition. Popular traditions must serve the community which uses them or they will perish, and the most widely circulated stories and songs predictably reflect the major contemporary concerns articulated by the Yezidis in other forms. The Yezidis' perception of their distinctive identity is reflected in their choice of specific songs and stories, in the broad themes they emphasise in their tellings, and, often, in the way they construct or reconstruct existing stories. The traditions which have been considered in this book, which for the most part are performed by and for Yezidis and which have Yezidis as their protagonists, reveal a preoccupation with Yezidi strength and separateness, at a time when the community feels vulnerable and fears assimilation or persecution.

It is clear that the type of Yezidi oral traditions featured in this book are part of Yezidi discourses of identity in Northern Iraq, but they are also grounded in the wider Kurdish oral tradition. Fuccaro has already dismantled 'the myth of splendid isolation' in her history of Yezidism under the British mandate (1999); the oral traditions recounting or alluding to the tribal past provide further proof, if any were needed, of Yezidi awareness of the close and complex relationships which have existed between Yezidis and non-Yezidis for centuries. The details of these songs and stories reveal links of tribal kinship, of *kerafet*, and of trade, between Yezidis and their neighbours which are often omitted in contemporary accounts of Yezidi separateness. The Yezidis of Northern Iraq share their overall folkloric 'map' with other Kurds of the area, with an emphasis on different local details. The mountains, the *zozan*, the wildlife of the *welat* or 'homeland' have similar associations for Yezidis as for other Kurds. These associations are extremely powerful and can evoke strong emotions.

In the light of this, the alienation of rural Yezidis in the face of official definitions of them as 'Arabs' becomes even clearer. Their world-view is very different from that of the Arab tribes with whom they come into contact, and certainly from that of urban Arabs. It is this essential Kurdishness of the Yezidis at the 'folkloric' level which made it necessary to devote Chapter 1 of this book to a discussion of the environment of Kurdistan and Kurdish oral tradition. Just as an understanding of the religious and cultural environment of Kurdistan is essential to comprehend the Yezidi religion, so an appreciation of the defining features of Kurdish oral tradition and the mechanisms by which it operates is crucial for any consideration of Yezidi oral traditions.

Within Yezidi discourses of identity in Northern Iraq, there are differences between Sheykhanis and Sinjaris. This raises obvious questions of how far one can discern a common identity. Whilst one could, in theory, divide and subdivide groups according to their expressions of their identity, one would eventually reach a *reductio ad absurdum* – each individual person defines her or his own identity uniquely. (There is an analogous problem in sociolinguistic research in finding an adequate definition of a 'speech community'.) Nevertheless, if one considers shared sentiments and idioms of their expression, there is clearly far more common ground in terms of identity between the Yezidis of Sheykhan and Sinjar than, say, between the Yezidis of Iraq and Turkey.

A similar problem of definition and scale arises when one considers oral traditions within 'Yezidi discourse'. A young Yezidi would learn traditional songs and stories from family, community, and at larger Yezidi gatherings. How far could one speak of 'canonicity', of a notional 'corpus' of oral traditions known to all, or even to most? In theory, there ought to be certain important traditions which an overwhelming majority of Yezidis know. They need not know such traditions in detail to regard them as part of their cultural property. The Yezidis' own religious poems, the *qewls*, are known in full to very few individuals, and relatively few people could give the titles of more than a few of them. Yet their existence is known by Yezidis in general. They are perceived as a discrete group; many people will have heard at least one of the more common ones, and most people know that they are holy texts. As distinctive and important Yezidi products, they 'belong' even to those Yezidis who do not know what they actually say.

During my fieldwork, I found that there was a considerable amount of consistency between informants on which themes of *stran* were particularly important. *Derwêshê 'Evdî*, *Ḥisênê 'Elkê* and *Êzdî Mîrza* were mentioned everywhere; *Ḥesen Hawerî* was mentioned wherever there were members of the Hawerî tribe, and *Dawûdê Dawûd* by Sinjaris. The prerecorded material collected features the same songs over and over again, performed by different *stranbêj*. The historical prose narratives cited as most important were on the same themes as the *stran*. Even those who were not able to tell these traditional stories in detail agreed on their importance. For most Yezidis, it seems that the secular traditions they know vary according to their village of origin, their tribe and their degree of education, but that there is a small core of traditions which everyone, or almost everyone knows. I have tried wherever possible to select the material for detailed discussion in this book from this small core.

It is inevitable that the varying historical discourses of different Yezidi families and communities must be in conflict with each other at some points. However, this did not become apparent from the interviews and material collected during the fieldwork. It is perhaps not surprising that Yezidis want to present a united front to an outsider, even to the extent of glossing over the bitter rivalry between Dawûdê Dawûd and Ḥemo Shêro. In published Yezidi discourse, Dawûd is represented as an enemy of imperialist government; his role as the leader of an anti-Ḥemo faction is omitted. The fact that I voiced an interest in *folklor* meant that I could safely be steered to the *stran*, most of which were composed before the end of the Ottoman empire, and therefore date from a period which, though bloodstained, is more 'safe' than the late twentieth century, with its unsettled scores and its barely forgiven *jash*. It seems to be acceptable for a *stranbêj* to sing in *Ferîq Pasha* that the Mendikan or the Khwerkan are treacherous, as everyone knows it predates living memory, though descendants of the protagonists, like Ḥemo's grandson, will still be pleased to hear their ancestors honoured. There are some details of *stran* which run counter to current Yezidi discourses, either by emphasising differences between Yezidis, like *Ferîq Pasha*, or in some other way, like *Silêmanê Mistê* which curses those who offend Islam; these are often preserved because of the degree of conservatism surrounding much of the phraseology of *stran*. Apparently such problematic sentiments can be somehow internalised and incorporated into general discourse, but this seems easier to do when the *stran* are of a certain age. The few more recent songs are more troublesome; Qasim Shesho still fears the impact of the song about his family's feud a generation after the events.

What I have found more surprising than the community's discretion about its own divisions is the lack of evidence of *stran* competing with each other. Those I have studied in my own collection are usually variants of the same song, or closely akin. I have wondered whether *stran* were ever composed, say, putting the case of the Mendikan or the Khwerkan, or arguing that Dawûd was totally wrong-headed and that the true heroes followed Ḥemo. This question remains unclear, but two points can be made. Firstly, there seems to be a rigorous 'natural selection' operating for *stran*; only the most valued compositions by the most acclaimed singers will survive, and secondly, the chain of singers, masters and pupils, is not very large; the current ageing generation was taught by a small number of singers, who were taught primarily by Biroyê Sherqî. It seems that this particular 'family tree' of singers and material is not only dominant, but has been the only one to survive – there must have been singers before Biro, but he seems to have dominated the scene after his arrival. It does not seem to be the usual practice for the current Sinjari *stranbêj* to perform very different variant forms of songs. If such counter-*Ferîq Pasha*s were ever composed, they do not seem to survive.

THEME AND GENRE

Oral tradition shows us clearly what is important to the Yezidis; certain martial and moral virtues are characterised as extremely valuable, the social danger of love is a matter of burning interest, and emotion is vented in discourses of loss. However, one must be wary of taking oral traditions at face value, and always be aware of genre and context. If folklore is 'a mirror of the heart of a people', it can sometimes distort. For example, it cannot be assumed that urban Yezidis want to live in villages just because oral tradition idealises village life, that they approve wholeheartedly of the behaviour of the romantic heroines they feel so strongly for on hearing *stran* of love, or that the prominent role of women in oral tradition reflects a correspondingly high status in society.

Almost all the material considered in this study has fallen within the genres of 'verbal art' – they are consciously performed, and a degree of performance skill and aesthetic value is expected by the audience. Even in the case of the women's 'personal' lament, a performance among participants, the women who attend take note of the skill of those who perform. Thus battles are described in stylised, impressionistic ways in the historical *stran*; they must be personalised and filled with emotional charge. The *stran* of love must describe dramatic or tragic situations, rather than amicable or happy marriages. The women's lament is a particularly interesting case. As a genre which uses improvisation and is not expected to repeat a previous composition, it would appear to be a form which allows free expression. Indeed the women who perform laments for their own deceased relations do seem to make their own individual statement. Yet there are strict rules governing what can be said; it is compulsory to speak well of the dead, and this is usually done by employing a variety of idioms which are also associated with love lyric. A widow who thoroughly disliked her husband may indeed grieve for his death, as it throws her own status into uncertainty, or she may even feel some relief, but whatever her feelings, she must perform a lament for him or have one performed, which must portray him as beautiful, virtuous and beloved. Thus we observe the paradox that the performer may say what she likes, as long as she says appropriate things. In such a case, it may be possible for an insider to notice small nuances in the performance giving an indication of a whole range of emotions lying behind the performance.

It is obvious that the choice of genre can enable a given traditional story to be used in a variety of ways; this has been perhaps best exemplified by the different presentations of the story of *Derwêshê 'Evdî*. The heroic narratives, or 'epic' tellings, focused on the hero's tragic death in battle; they explained how the battle came about, and included a lyrical section at the end describing the feelings of his lover on hearing of his death. The lyrical poems, which were in some ways similar to the fragmentary Sinjari *stran* on the theme, were put in the mouth of 'Edûlê and used a variety of common images associated with erotic love to depict the depth of her emotion and arouse strong feelings in the audience. The simple prose account given by Pîr Khidir Silêman depicted the tragedy of a hero in a situation made impossible by the conflict between his own wishes and the rules of his religion. By emphasising the impossibility of the two marrying as the underlying tragedy, this telling illustrated the conservatism of the Iraqi Yezidi community on exogamy. Of course, one cannot know whether the great majority of Iraqi Yezidis would have constructed the story in the same way as Pîr Khidir. However, it seems likely, from opinions voiced to me about exogamy, that many of them would view its focus as the impossibility of a Muslim girl and Yezidi man marrying.

The genre, or form of discourse in which a tradition is presented, affects the whole future of that tradition. Not only does it impose a pattern on it, but it also assigns it an appropriate performance environment which has important implications for the its survival as history. For instance, the story of a family feud such as *Şerê Mala Şeşo*, 'The Battle of the House of Shesho', may be commemorated in various ways. It is possible that an eye-witness might compose a *stran*. This is certainly a strong possibility in the opinion of the Yezidis, who seem to associate the vividness of the descriptions with immediacy of composition. The *stranbêj* Mr. B. said to me that Little Gulê, one of the eyewitnesses and narrators of the song, might have composed *Ferîq Pasha*. Though this is possible, it seems more probable to me that prose accounts, beginning with those of eye-witnesses or participants, will circulate and attract the attention of a composing singer. The degree to which prose narratives about, say, the Shesho feud, gain currency will depend on the interest of listeners; as we have seen, such tellings would have to compete for listeners' attention with other accounts and with material presented on television and radio. As time passes and the account grows more remote from listeners' immediate concerns, it will be more difficult to arouse interest. If one were to make a *stran* about such a feud, however, one could probably guarantee an enthusiastic audience, but one would then be subject to the stylistic limitations of *stran*; a *stran* of the lyrical type which predominates in Sinjar would need to be contextualised for wider audiences by a *stranbêj*.

A sung narrative, such as the long *Derwêshê 'Evdî* poems considered in Chapter 4, might initially seem the best option of all for ensuring longevity of a theme, since the story itself provides a mnemonic framework for the performer. However, within this framework the motifs used within the narrative may vary enormously, producing a rather different performance; this is obvious when Israel Ohanyan's performance is compared with that of 'Egitê Têjir. The conservatism of the *stran* is difficult to maintain for long narratives. Some examples of long Kurdish poetic narratives, such as *Dimdim*, have survived for centuries, in a rich variety of tellings. However, the survival of a long poetic narrative among the Yezidis of Northern Iraq seems less assured than that of *stran*. The great advantage currently enjoyed by the *stran* is that it does not depend on the declining *dîwan* and does not compete with television; it has an accepted place as part of the repertoire performed at parties, weddings and festivals. The commemoration of a localised event in a popular and widely circulated genre like *stran* can help ensure its survival as part of the wider discourse.

The Life of the *Stran*

This study may seem lacking in balance because it has spent more time discussing *stran* than any other form of Yezidi verbal art. This is simply because of the importance ascribed to these songs by the Yezidis themselves. A question about *qesse* or about 'old things' addressed to Yezidis would always receive a response which referred to the *stran* of the *stranbêj*. Informants were usually well aware that not all of the *stran* were about Yezidis, and that there were Muslim singers of this type of song; nevertheless it was always the first distinctive cultural product they mentioned. There was a clear perception that these *stran* were particularly closely associated with the Yezidi community. Even outside the community this link seems to be made; I once saw a Christian imitating various types of local songs and poetry – his 'Yezidi' example was a pretty fair imitation of the performance of a *stranbêj*. Yezidis were able to name both *stranbêj* and *stran* even when they were unable to recount the stories associated with those *stran*. The concept both of the *stran* as a group and of the storylines of the *stran* existed in people's minds. These concepts may not have been full or accurate, but they contributed to their attitudes towards their own identity, as the *stran* constituted something which they felt the Yezidi community had preserved while other communities had lost it.

For the Yezidis these *stran* seem to be totemic. Yet the events which inspire them are not necessarily the experiences of the community as a whole. Not only are some dealing with the deeds of far-away Muslims in nineteenth-century Turkey, but even among the defining Yezidi events, they appear to be minority discourses. They do not claim in any way to speak on behalf of Yezidis as a group. *Ferîq Pasha*, for instance, commemorates a distinctively Sinjari experience of that particular persecution. To my knowledge, there is no *stran* in common circulation about the slaughter of women and children in Sheykhan which was part of the same campaign. Furthermore, this *stran* is not even about the Ferîq himself, but about the response of a small group of Sinjari Yezidis to his *ferman* or persecution. Chapter 4 noted that the *nizam*, 'order' or 'system' of the Ferîq is never described in any detail; the government remains a vague entity.

Both Pîr Khidir Silêman, a Sheykhani with a high level of formal education, and Mr B., a fully-trained Sinjari singer well-versed in many kinds of traditional lore, referred to the *stran* as 'our history'. Their opinion is to be respected, but one should explore further what this means – what kind of history can it be that does not actually tell us what happened in the past? It is clear that the *stran* is not a form designed to convey information about history, but a lyrical genre which arouses emotion by describing the emotional impact of past events. These songs are personalised accounts of how individuals felt after seeing or hearing of historical events. Historical events are patterned to suit the song; description is stylised. Both of the *stran* discussed in Chapter 4 include similar elements, not only of vocabulary, but also of general theme; the loss of men in battle, the bravery of protagonists, the treachery of those who would not ally themselves with them, and the incomprehensibility and brutality of central government. It is the names of protagonists and locations of the action which are distinctive; these are given importance through repetition.

In my own attempts to make sense of the words of the *stran* I discovered that their language is often difficult even for native speakers to understand, and that this difficulty may be increased by the techniques of performance used by a singer. Not only are the politics of Sinjar, which are extremely complex and change constantly, a cause of some bewilderment to non-Sinjaris, but it is also difficult to understand local allusions. The audience, particularly its younger members, often seems to find the language used and the techniques of performance (such as singing at high speed) difficult to follow, and its appreciation of the *stran* is based on a combination of factors, including the voice of the performer, the music played, and certain striking motifs, rather than on literal comprehension of every word.

Stran are, of course, verbal art, or oral literature; the aesthetic dimension is crucial, far outweighing any informational content. After all, they consist mostly of stock elements. And yet one cannot ignore the authoritative voices which also define them as history. There is no doubt that they do have some annalistic function; it is clear that Pîr Micho took a great liberty in making an alteration to the list of protagonists in *Ferîq Pasha*. In previous times, when the contextual knowledge of audiences was greater, the allusions to emotive moments from the past would be very powerful, and reinforce individuals' feelings of belonging to the community, in much the same way as the performance of songs which were popular during the two World Wars are highly evocative for Europeans. They are not some kind of oral historical textbook but they invite reflection on the events of history, which audiences already know; they are articulations of social memory. By their understanding of the factual allusions of the *stran*, as well as of their complex, evocative imagery, audience members' identity as members of the group is reinforced.

However, the *stran* do more than this, because their emotional content arouses pathos and thought about an individual's own experiences. I spent some time during fieldwork and afterwards asking rather unsubtle questions along the lines of, 'If *stran* are so *xweş* 'pleasant', then why are they all about *kûl û keser* 'pain and sorrow'?'. With remarkable patience, Yezidi men and women of all ages would give very similar answers; that the sorrows of others, as exemplified in the *stran*, make a person think about their own sorrows, and that though this is painful, it also gives pleasure. In some cases there was an implication that some of the individual's own sorrows could not otherwise be articulated. In this way the experience of the individual is also linked with that of people in the past.

However, over the past generation or so, this situation has changed; the decline of the *dîwan*, and the rise of formal education among the Yezidis, has meant that much of the contextual knowledge of the events alluded to in *stran* has declined among younger members of audiences. This information may be supplied by the *stranbêj* in a spoken introduction, but the video and audio recordings of performances indicate that this is only done for certain songs, and that many songs follow on from the previous one without a break in the music. Even without such introductions, audiences can still understand some of the meanings of the *stran* – love songs, for example, are quite clear – and remain 'literate' in the most important meanings conveyed by folkloric imagery. Thus, even for those without detailed background knowledge, the emotional power of the *stran* is still kept, and there will still be the sense of participating in a Yezidi commemoration of past events.

The *stran* are still enjoyable, then, even to younger members of the contemporary audience. However, there may be factors other than young people's lack of contextual knowledge which conspire to make older *stran* difficult to understand. If one compares *Ferîq Pasha* with *Dawûdê Dawûd* as transcribed in this volume, one can see that the two performances of the latter are far closer to each other than the diverse performances of the former. Moreover, awareness of Dawûd in the Yezidi community (and in Badinan generally) is much greater than that of the Ferîq. During my fieldwork, informants from Sheykhan were able to give details such as his tribe, the fact that he had fought against the English, and approximate dates of when he had lived. This was not the case with the Ferîq, who could be recognised and dated to the end of the Ottoman empire by some older informants, but who was nothing more than a name vaguely associated with persecution for most of the young adults questioned. It cannot be denied that the *Dawûdê Dawûd* performances both have more consistent characterisation and clearer identification of the primary speaker, Shêrîn, than the *Ferîq Pasha* variants. The most obvious reason for this would appear to be the simple fact that *Dawûdê Dawûd* is far 'younger' than *Ferîq Pasha* and has passed through fewer transmissions and performances. It is clear that the *stranbêj* structure their performances of *stran* in different ways, to give them as much impact as possible. They may stretch out some sections, as Kheyro lingers over his listing of protagonists, compress others, or simply rearrange parts of the song. Their priorities are aesthetic; hence the various parts of the song become less and less clear. It is possible that after many performances and transmissions, the coherence of the song is lost completely. Such a process might explain why there are relatively few *stran* of this type about events earlier than the nineteenth century; if the characterisation of Ferîq Pasha is somewhat garbled after a century, a *stran* twice that age might lose its coherence altogether and cease to be performed.

It is easy to see a close relationship between the preservation of a historical event in oral tradition and its commemoration in *stran*. Where cause and effect lie is more difficult to discern – do the *stran*, by commemorating events, encourage the preservation of contextual knowledge, or does the contextual knowledge perpetuate the *stran* by enabling it to be understood? Perhaps the latter statement best describes the situation before the last generation or so – *stran* were only one of a number of traditional genres commemorating the events and world-view of the past. However, many of the mechanisms governing transmission and performance of other traditional genres have now all but broken down under the strain of social and political change, and for many young people, *stran* performed at weddings and parties may be the only traditional genre they hear regularly. In this case, the *stranbêj*'s explanation of the stories behind individual songs may be an important part of the audience's education in events of the past, and the most commonly performed *stran* may help to define which pre-twentieth century events are still remembered.

THE FUTURE

Many studies of oral tradition in modern societies reflect the gloomy predictions of the informants that 'folklore' of all sorts is in decline and about to disappear entirely. In some ways this is true of Kurdish oral tradition in general and Yezidi oral tradition in particular. Oral traditions are performed less often than formerly, and young people are less interested, for the most part, in listening to them.

Women's lament is protected by its necessity as a social duty; it is also part of cultural life for Kurdish Muslims, and for many non-Kurdish peoples in the Middle East and the Mediterranean area. It is hard to imagine lamentation becoming extinct unless the Yezidi community loses so many of its current characteristics that it becomes unrecognisable. However, it is conceivable that skilled practitioners will become less and less common, that it will be used less as a discourse of emotion for the singer (who may have the opportunity to express her emotions in other ways) and be the poorer as a result.

Other genres, whose performance is not enshrined in rigid social rules, are less privileged. Long narrative poems are already difficult to find amongst the Yezidis of Northern Iraq. Prose narratives about notable events and everyday life in the distant past are having to compete with other entertainments, especially television, for people's attention. Even the *stran*, valued as they are, are not immune to the threat of extinction. Young Yezidis might enjoy them at parties, but in their homes and cars they may be listening to Şivan Perwer, Ciwan Hajo, or any one of a number of other Kurdish, Turkish or Arab singers. Few, if any, young singers are currently training as apprentices with Sinjari *stranbêj*. I did not meet a single trainee, except for a young man teaching himself from Ordikhanê Jelîl's book of historical songs (Jelîl 1977). By 2025, it is hard to imagine that there will be a large number of singers of this particular 'school'.

However, all is not lost for traditional Kurdish verbal art. For the Kurds the heroic and often tragic world of life in the villages and nomad encampments of the past is very appealing. The concept of the beauty of the *zozan* or 'summer pastures' remains powerful for a Kurdistan where the overwhelming majority are sedentary. Before the mass exodus of 1991, many Iraqi Kurds had not been up into the mountains except on excursions for pleasure. However, rural life is felt to be the authentic Kurdish life, and its details, both of landscape and of lifestyle, have romantic associations; this goes for both Yezidis and Muslims. In 1992 it was clear that the reconstruction of the Kurdish villages destroyed by the Iraqi government was necessary for political, as much as economic, reasons; they had enormous symbolic value.

This rural idyll is emphasised everywhere in the Kurdish broadcast media; in the small but enthusiastic television channels operated by the parties in 1992, and later, in the satellite stations such as MED-TV and its later successors and competitors, images were portrayed of mountain landscapes, flowers and waterfalls, young men and women in traditional dress, and villages. Documentaries about *folklor* were quite common, and performances of traditional songs and dances, usually in traditional dress, were an everyday occurence. Modern poetry was also broadcast; like many contemporary Kurdish songs, it used numerous images from Kurdish folklore, as did many Kurdish political speeches. Such media were all busily engaged in nation-building, and did not hesitate to make use of a fund of imagery – the mountains, the *zozan*, the wild partridge, the *riḥan* or wild basil – which was well understood and which glorified the *welat* or homeland. There is newer imagery, of course, such as the Kurdish flag, or the blood of martyrs; these are used alongside the more traditional images. However, unless Kurdish national identity redefines itself completely in the near future (which seems unlikely), one can expect to see a continuation of the use of the imagery of the oral traditions. This will probably be in a simplified form, since most Kurds are urban and young Turkish Kurds in particular have often not been exposed to the same range of images and associations as their rural forbears.

Thus the imagery of the oral traditions at least will survive, for the Yezidis as for other Kurds. Some performances will be preserved, by repeated broadcast (in effect becoming a 'text'); other traditions will be incorporated into other types of performance, or other genres altogether. *Dimdim* has already become a novel and a play in Kurdish, but the illustrious work of Yaşar Kamal, among others, attests that villagers' relationship with the land and with each other provides a rich fund of inspiration and that Kurdish need not even be the language for such forms of creativity. The Iraqi Yezidis have begun to use literacy in less oblique ways, to record *stran*, prose accounts of events, and genealogies. However, Jasimê Jelîl, in the Caucasus, used oral tradition as an inspiration for his own creative work, and Yezidis from Iraq can no doubt be expected to follow suit. The Yezidi oral tradition will not die, but it will have a very different and probably much more 'textual' life in the future.

Part II

Kurdish Texts and Translations

Introduction

These texts are taken from various sources, with slightly differing transcription systems; for the sake of consistency, slight modifications have been made to the way some texts transcribe certain sounds. However, in those texts which I transcribed myself, I have tried to remain faithful to the performance by preserving the pronunciation of the speaker. Thus some slight inconsistencies may be detectable in words which are used many times, and at some points where the words do not seem to conform to 'standard' Kurdish grammar. All the translations, except that of the love song *Kherabo*, which is based on an existing French translation by Roger Lescot, are my own.

The *stran* I transcribed myself present many difficulties. The style of delivery is very rapid, and the recording quality is frequently poor. The singers may be idiosyncratic; Lezgîn, for instance, often pronounces the ends of words very indistinctly and also has a slight lisp. As I have described in Part I, it was simply not possible to sit down with the *stranbêj* and discuss the difficult words and phrases. Despite the invaluable help of native speakers, there still remain points where the wording is inaudible, or the correct interpretation is unclear. I have preserved inconsistencies in pronunciation, such as *Xwedê* and *Xodê* 'God', in an attempt to give a better impression of the performance. The grammar is also non-standard in some ways; for instance, word endings are sometimes changed to preserve the rhyme scheme at the ends of lines, a practice common in Kurdish oral literature. The gender of many nouns is also not always consistent with 'standard' forms of Kurmanji. The performance technique of the singers sometimes produces 'non-grammatical' forms – for example, words are occasionally lengthened at the end of lines, producing 'anomalous' verb endings such as *-ê-in*.

The account of the career of Dawûdê Dawûd, given by his son 'Emer, comes from Silêman and Jindî's ground-breaking book on Yezidism (1979). Kurmanji publications in Iraq, produced in the Arabic script, show considerable variation in transcription conventions. I have transcribed the section from the original edition, rather than the Latin-script edition (1995), which has some alterations consonant with European conventions of writing Kurmanji. My transcription has kept as closely as possible to the original edition, except where typographical errors are obvious, in an effort to imitate the original interview as closely as possible, given that some 'Sinjarisms' seem to have been 'Sheykhanised'. However, I have taken the liberty of adding some punctuation marks. Readers accustomed to systems of Kurmanji transcription used in Turkey and Europe will notice Badinani dialectal features, phonological and morphological and syntactic, which vary considerably from 'standard' (usually, Botan, Qamishli or Diyarbakir) Kurmanji.

The texts taken from the work of the Jelîl brothers come from two publications, *Zargotina K'urda* (1978) and *Folklora K'urdê Suriayê* (1985), the former in the Latin alphabet and the latter in Cyrillic. My transcription has differed from these in not distinguishing certain emphatic consonants; these are only differentiated from others in certain areas and are not part of the *Hawar* system. However I have kept some unusual spellings which might indicate differences in pronunciation, such as *çev* 'eye' where *çav* is more usual. In the examples from the Caucasus, distinctively Arabic sounds such as *'ain* and *ghain*, ṣ or ṭ in words borrowed from Arabic, are often either not pronounced, or pronounced as if they were Kurdish sounds. However, this is not true for all borrowings. I have followed Jelîl's lead on their notation. These texts are generally fairly clear, though there are some unusual pieces of vocabulary where the correct interpretation is debatable.

In the translation of this material, the perennial dilemma of rendering the original as closely as possible whilst trying to achieve some meaning in English was compounded by the unfamiliarity of the Kurdish genres. This was especially true of the emotional *stran.* Thus I have not reiterated every last 'alas', every *lê dayê*, in English; if I had, bathos would soon ensue. The common Kurdish device of using a pair of nouns with very similar meanings together is also not always natural in English; where possible, I have used English pairs with similar meanings. Thus *'erz û 'eyêl* is translated 'kith and kin'; the meaning is not identical but gives a similar effect. Tenses are used rather freely in some of the poetry; I have kept to more English norms, whist trying to be as faithful as possible to the Kurdish.

SECTION A

Stories and Songs of Battle

FERÎQ PASHA

Ferîq Pasha: "Qarpal"

1. Dilê minî teng e Mîna bû tara bêjingê Xwedê ava neke mala Ferîq Paşa li bayana sibê Ewê mal û malbata şînê ba Sifûqê Meto bavê Berces milkê Feqîra wella	1. My heart is tight, Like the hoop of a sieve, Oh God, don't let the house of Ferîq Pasha be standing at dawn tomorrow, That is a house and home of mourning for Sifûqê Meto, Berjes' father, property of the Feqîran, oh God,
Rebenê bi dara zivingê o.	Wretched ones by the shady tree.
2. Bi dara zivingê Şad û nişûdêd Osê Mecdî kekê Kemêl gelek hene ax	2. By the shady tree The famous ones, the heroes, of Osê Mejdî, Kemal's elder brother, there are many, oh,
Sê denga dibêje Miḥemê 'Evdo bavê Salayê Sifûqê Meto bavê Berces, 'Gelî bav û bira, yê mêrî çêbin, lep hilînin, Bi izna Siltan Êzdî û emê vî ro vê nizamê bişkênînin û Ce bi xwedê ji îro paşve şeṛ kefte ser derê Kur Bimbarek, ser 'erz û 'eyêl,	He calls three times, to Mihemê Evdo,[1] Saleh's father, Sifûqê Meto, Berjes' father, 'Dear fathers and brothers, do the deeds of men, raise your hands, If Sultan Êzdî permits,[2] we will this day break this system, and As God's my witness, from today onwards war has come upon Kur Bimbarek,[3] on our kith and kin,

1 The structure of this line makes it unclear who is calling whom (KJR); I have chosen to interpret it as Osê Mejdî, but it may be Miḥemê 'Evdo, who plays an important part in the fighting in some performances.

2 See Kreyenbroek 1995: 3, 79 for the identification of Sultan Êzîd or Êzî with Melek Tawus and Yazīd b. Mu'āwiya.

3 A place in Sinjar (KJR).

Ser mîratê darê tifingê.'

On the cursed[4] wood of [our] rifles.'

3. Ezîdo
Gula kiçik
Sê denga dibêje Gula mezin,
'Lê lê xwehîngê vê sibê tu karê xwe bike,
Emê çinê serbanê Çelmêra ganê min bi gorî diyarî sûke,
Xwedê o avaneke mala Ferîq Paşa ax
Li tarî kûbara sibê xîvet û çadirê xwe vegirtin li wî
Mîratê dûwê gêdûke.'

3. Oh Yezidi,
Little Gulê
Calls out three times to Big Gulê,
'Oh, sister, this morning you do your work,
We will go to the peak of Chilmêra, my life,[5] just by the town,
Oh God, do not let the house of Ferîq Pasha stand, ah,
In the dark of early morning they pitched their tents
At the cursed end of the pass.'

4. Ewî mîratê dûwê gêdûkê
Şad û neşûdêd Osê Mecdî kekê Kemêl gelek hene,
Sê denga dibêje Miḥemê 'Evdo bavê Saleh Sifûqê Meto bavê Berces,
'Gelî bav û bira, yê mêrî çêbin, lep hilînin,
Bi izna Siltan Êzdî û emê vî ro vê nizamê bişkênînîn û
Emê berê nizama Ferîq Paşa
Bidîn mîratê Kerkûkê.'

4. At that cursed end of the pass,
The famous ones, the heroes, of Osê Mejdî, Kemal's elder brother, there are many,
He calls three times, to Mihemê Evdo, Saleh's father, Sifûqê Meto, Berjes' father,
'Dear fathers and brothers, do the deeds of men, raise your hands,
If Sultan Êzdî permits, we will this day break this fighting force and
We will drive away Ferîq Pasha's force
To cursed Kirkuk.'

5. De hay nayê, hay nayê,
Dengê tifinga Milḥemê 'Elî Ax̌a li gêdûka x̌erbî nayê
Mendika çûne ḥedayatê Xwerkaniya xayîne
Pez û indada me li ba nayê.

5. Alas, alas, no help comes,
The sound of the gun of Milḥemê 'Elî Agha at the pass in the west doesn't come,
The Mendikan went over to Islam,[6] the Khwerkan are treacherous,
Our help, our aid, doesn't come to us.

6. Êzîdê o Êzîdo
Va Xwerka şeṛî nekir Êzîdo va Xwerka şeṛî nekir
Ev serî sê rojî tamam e,
Dengê topan û tifinga,
Wella mi gulî kir li ser serê Kûr Bimbarek, bûye şekir,

6. Oh Yezidi, Yezidi,
Those Khwerkan didn't fight, Yezidi, the Khwerkan didn't fight,
Three days have now passed,
There is the sound of bombs and guns,
By God, we heard it on top of Kûr Bimbarek, it was sugar-sweet,

4 This adjective is common throughout these lyrical songs; according to KJR, the places and objects have been polluted by the presence of Ferîq Pasha's troops and the necessity of fighting.

5 KJR: cf. as in Sor. *gyan*, Ps. *jan*. This would be an unusual usage in Kurm., especially between sisters, but I have found no preferable interpretation.

6 Thus KJR; *ḥedayat* literally means Islamic religious guidance.

Şad û neşûdêd Osê Mecdî kekê Kemêl gelek hene, sê denga dibêje Miḥemê 'Evdo bavê Saleh Sifûqê Meto bavê Berces,	The famous ones, the heroes, of Osê Mejdî, Kemal's elder brother, there are many, he calls three times, Mihemê Evdo, Saleh's father, Sifûqê Meto, Berjes' father,
'Gelî bav û bira, mêrî çêbin, lep hilînin,	'Dear fathers and brothers, do the deeds of men, raise your hands,
Bi izna Siltan Êzdî, emê îro vê nizamê bişkênînîn	If Sultan Êzdî permits, we will this day break this force,
Emê berê nizama Ferîq Paşa bidîn mîratê Diyarbakir.	We will drive away this force of Ferîq Pasha to cursed Diyarbakir.'
7. Ezîdo, kavlê bavê Reşo bişewite bi geneka,	7. Oh Yezidi, let the ruins of Resho's father burn up, green bushes and all,
Kavlê bavê Reşo bişewite bi geneka ax	Let the ruins of Resho's father burn, green bushes and all, oh,
Xwedê ava neke mala Ferîq Paşa	May God not let the house of Ferîq Paşa stand,
Tarî kûbara sibê xîvet û çadirê xwe danîne li mîratê girê dêrê yek bi yeka,	In the dark of early morning they pitched their tents one by one at the cursed hill of Dêrê,
Şad û neşûdêd Osê Mecdî, kekê Kemêl, gelek hene, sê denga dibêje	The famous ones, the heroes, of Osê Mejdî, Kemal's elder brother, there are many, he calls three times,
Miḥemê 'Evdo bavê Saleh ax	To Mihemê Evdo, Saleh's father, oh,
Ewî Sifûqê Meto bavê Berces,	[To] that Sifûqê Meto, Berjes' father,
'Gelî bav û bira, yê mêrî çêbin, lep hilînin,	'Dear fathers and brothers, do the deeds of men, raise your hands,
Bi izna Siltan Êzdî û emê îro vê nizamê bişkênînin û	If Sultan Êzdî permits, we will this day break this force,
Ce bi Xwedê ji nîro û paşve ev namûs, namûsa Xodê ye, namûsa wî Mîrza, mala koçeka o.'	As God's my witness, from today onwards this honour, this is God's honour, the honour of that Mîrza, of the kochek clan.'
8. Ezê bi diyarî bana Bekira ketim	8. I was going near the high place of Bekiran,
Bişewite ji dilê min û te ṛe wa bi kaşa ax	May it burn up, hills and all,[7] for my heart and yours, oh,
Ew xopanê Bekira bişewite wî bi kaşa	Let ruined Bekiran burn up, hills and all,
Li bayana sibê tête reqîna mîratêd tifinga,	At the dawn of the morning comes the firing of the cursed guns,
Li destê xortêd Êzdiya tête reqîne mîratê bêşetaşa,	In the hands of the young Yezidi men comes the firing of the cursed machine guns,
Şad û neşûdêd Osê Mecdî, kekê Kemêl, gelek hene, sê denga dibêje Miḥemê 'Evdo bavê Saleh ax	The famous ones, the heroes, of Osê Mejdî, Kemal's elder brother, there are many, he calls three times, to Miḥemê Evdo, Saleh's father, oh,

7 The word *kaşa* is difficult; as well as 'high ground' (KJR) or 'slope' (Izoli), it can mean 'tiles'.

Sifûqê Meto bavê Berces, 'Gelî bav û birayê mêrî çêbin, lep hilînin,

Sifûqê Meto, Berjes' father, 'Dear fathers and brothers, do the deeds of men, raise your hands,

Bi izna Siltan Êzdî, serî sê rojî tamam, dewleta ḥukumeta Ferîq Paşa ax,

If Sultan Êzdî permits, when three days have passed, Ferîq Pasha's government, oh,

Ce bavo bi tirimbêla xelas nake laşêd kuştiyan û birîndaran.

For certain, they won't have finished collecting the bodies of their killed and wounded in their cars'.

Ferîq Pasha: 'Jerdo and Kheyro'

'Jerdo'

[Recording begins after song has begun]

1. . . . gelek hene
Sê denga dibêje Miḥemê 'Evdo bavê Saleh Sifûqê Meto bavê Berces,
'Gelî bav û bira, mêrî çêbin, lep hilînin,

1. . . . there are many,
He calls three times, to Mihemê Evdo, Saleh's father, Sifûqê Meto, Berjes' father,
'Dear fathers and brothers, do the deeds of men, raise your hands,

Bi izna Siltan Êzdî emê evro vê nizamê bişkênînîn,
Ce bi Xwedê ji nîro paşve şeṛ kefte ser derê Kûr Bimbarê
Ser mîratê darê tifingê.'

If Sultan Êzdî permits, we will this day break this force,
As God's my witness, from today onwards war has come upon Kur Bimbarek,
On the cursed wood of our rifles.'

2. Ezîdo
Gula kiçik bi sê denga dibêje Gula mezin,
'Lê lê xwehîngê vê sibê tu karê xwe bike û emê çînê serbanê Çelmêra ganê li gorî diyarî sûkê,
Xwedê o ava neke mala Ferîq Paşa

2. Oh Yezidi,
Little Gulê calls out three times to Big Gulê,
'Oh, sister, this morning you do your work and we will go up to the height of Chilmêra, my life, just near the town,
Oh God, do not let the house of Ferîq Pasha stand,

Tarî kûbara sibê xêvet û çadirê xwe danîne li
Mîratêd wê gêdûkê.'

In the darkness and rain of the morning they pitched their tents,
At that cursed pass.'

3. Şad û neşûdêd Osê Mecdî kekê Kemêl gelek hene,

3. The famous ones, the heroes, of Osê Mejdî, Kemal's elder brother, there are many,

Sê denga dibêje Miḥemê 'Evdo bavê Saleh, Sifûqê Meto bavê Berces,
'Gelî bav û bira mêrî çêbin, lep hilînin,

He calls three times, to Mihemê Evdo, Saleh's father, Sifûqê Meto, Berjes' father,
'Dear fathers and brothers, do the deeds of men, raise your hands,

Bi izna Siltan Êzdî emê vê sibê vê nizamê bişkênînîn,

If Sultan Êzdî permits, this morning we will break this force,

Emê berê nizama Ferîq Paşa Bidîn miratê Kirkûkê.'

We will drive Ferîq Pasha's force away to cursed Kirkuk.'

4. Êzîdo, Êzîdo,
Kavlê bavê Reşo bişewite bi geneka
Kavlê bavê Reşo bişewite bi geneka ax
Xodê o ava neke mala Ferîq Paşa
Tarî kûbara sibê xîvet û çadirêd xwe danîne
Li mîratê girê Dêrê yek bi yeka.

4. Oh Yezidi,
Oh Yezidi, let the ruins of Resho's father burn, green bushes and all,
Let the ruins of Resho's father burn, green bushes and all, oh,
Oh God, do not let the house of Ferîq Pasha stand,
In the dark of early morning they have pitched their tents,
At the cursed hill of Dêrê, one by one.

5. Li wê mîratê girê Dêrê yek bi yeka
Şad û neşûdêd Osê Mecdî kekê Kemêl, gelek hene,
Sê denga dibêje Miḥemê 'Evdo bavê Saleh, Sifûqê Meto bavê Berces, 'Gelî bav û bira, mêrî çêbin, lep hilînin,
Bi izna Siltan Êzdî îro emê vê nizamê bişkênînin,
Ce bi xwedê ji îro paşve ev namûs namûsa Xodê ye namûsa Mîrza mala koçeka.'

5. One by one at that cursed hill of Dêrê,
The famous ones, the heroes, of Osê Mejdî, Kemal's elder brother, there are many,
He calls three times, to Mihemê Evdo, Saleh's father, Sifûqê Meto, Berjes' father, 'Dear fathers and brothers, do the deeds of men, raise your hands,
If Sultan Êzdî permits, today we will break this force,
As God's my witness, from today onwards this honour is the honour of God, the honour of Mîrza of the kochek clan.'

'Kheyro'

6. Lê dayê, lê dayê, lê dayê,
Diyarî min û kûrana Bekira bişewite wa bi bera,
Mi dî li vê bayana berê sibê, sê bêlûkê 'eskerê Ferîq Paşa danîne ser çeme Zoqa ye,
Li gundê me, li Girê 'Ereba,
Belê Xwedê zanibe berê topa dabûne Bekira, gulêd mîratêd topa ser malê me dirijin weke mûman û çira,
Mi dî Osê Mecdî, kekê Kemal, sê denga gazî dike Meḥmudê Osê, Dawûdê 'Isa babê Dawûd,
Ewî Sifûqê Meto bavê Berces, 'elimêd li Miḥemê 'Evdo bavê Saleh, siwarê Bozê, 'Gelî xortêd Şingaliya, bav û bira, lep hilînin,

6. Alas, oh mother,
Let my region and the valley of Bekiran burn up, stones and all,
I saw at that dawn before morning, three companies of Ferîq Pasha's soldiers camped at the River Zoqa,
At our village, at Girê 'Ereba,
Yes, God knows it, they dropped a direct hit on Bekiran, poured down on our houses like candles and lights,
I saw Osê Mejdî, Kemal's elder brother, he called three times to Meḥmudê Osê, Dawûdê 'Isa, Dawûd's father,
To that Sifûqê Meto, Berjes' father, the learned ones of Miḥemê 'Evdo, Saleh's father, rider of Bozê, 'Dear lads of Sinjar, fathers and brothers, raise your hands,

Berê xwe ji nizama Ferîq Paşa derînin, 'erz û eyalê şerîn metirsînin, Gulî sora ji destê nizama Ferîq Paşa vê sibê bifikînin,' Belê bi xodê aferim bona mêrêd weke Miḥemê 'Evdo bavê Saleh, li 'esra êvarê, Tara şîrê zirav siwarî dihajotine li nav çadiran.

7. Bêje Êzîdo, Êzîdo, Mane[9] ḥanekî me nema, gelî hogiran hevala dinêrim kûrana Bekira wa bi kaşa, Mi dî ji bayana berê sibê danîne ser çemê Zoqayê, gundê girê 'Ereba sê bêlûkêd girane ji 'eskerê Ferîq Paşa,

Nalîne kete mîratê reşaşa,

Li aliya x̱arbi ṛe pêşiya 'eskerê ... firqa 'Elî Paşa, Lê belê li aliyê şerqî ṛe pêşiya cêş ... kete çemê Reşa, Me dî Miḥemê 'Evdo, bavê Saleh, sê denga xortê Şingara kete kalî 'Gelî gûlî sora bav û bira mêrî çêbin, lep hilînin,

Enîşka bi kozika ... van meteresa,

Ca belê izna Xodê, Siltan Êzdî wezê bikim saleke sê heyv maye,

Belê bi Xodê, li çemê Bekira qoç û 'erebanê ḥukumetê xelas nekin cenaz û leşa.'

8. Xwedê vê carê Zerîvka Osê bang dike 'Lê lê Gulê xwehîngê, wezê bang dikim, dengê min dernayê,

Save yourselves from Ferîq Pasha's force, don't frighten our sweet kith and kin, Liberate your red-braids[8] from the hands of Ferîq Pasha's force this morning,' Yes by God, I congratulate men like Miḥemê 'Evdo, Saleh's father, in the evening twilight, With his thin sword alone the brave horseman was attacking them among their tents.

7. Say 'Yezidi, Yezidi', There was no real help for us any more, dear comrades, I see the valley of Bekiran, hills and all, I saw, since before dawn, at the river Zoqa, the village of Girê 'Ereba, three companies of Ferîq Pasha's army had encamped, The wailing of the the cursed automatic rifles, To the West, in front of the soldiers ... the battalion of 'Elî Pasha, But to the East, in front of the army ... lay the River Resha, I saw Miḥemê 'Evdo, Saleh's father, cry out to the Sinjari lads three times, 'Dear red-braids, fathers and brothers, do the deeds of men, raise your hands, Elbows in the trenches ... those [defensive] positions, For certain, if God and Sultan Êzdî permit, I'll see to it that when a year and three months have passed, Yes, by God, at the stream of Bekiran the coaches and carts of the government will not have finished with bodies and corpses.'

8. Oh God, at this time, Zerîfka Osê is shouting, 'Oh, Gulê, sister, I am shouting, my voice does not carry,

---

8 A reference to the traditional hairstyles of the Yezidis of Sinjar; the women had braids, like other rural Kurdish women. The men also wore their hair in many small but long braids. Red hair is presented as desirable in Yezidi lyrics.
9 This is an emphatic word, often used in Yezidi verbal art, which sometimes corresponds to 'indeed', 'certainly'; however, it is often more natural in English not to include it.

Ezê bang dikim, dengê mi dernayê,
dengê top û tifingê 'eskerê Ferîq Paşa
agirê Xodê berda bûye dinyayê,

I am shouting, my voice does not carry,
the noise of the shells and guns of Ferîq
Pasha's soldiers, the fire, by God, the
world is lost,

Mendikaniya xayîne çûyê ḥedayetê,
çûye xaletê, çûye rayê,

The Mendikan are treacherous, they went
over to Islam, they changed their allegiance,

Evê bi sê rojî dew û dûwe gêdûke x̌erbî
dengê tifinga Miḥemê 'Elî Ax̌a bavê
Milḥim tucar û bi cara nayê,

For three days at the Western end of the
pass the sound of the rifle of Miḥemê 'Elî
Agha, Milḥem's father has not come, not
once,

Bi xodê ji qadîm ziman Xwerkaniya
xayîne roja,
Mirinê tucara hîndadeke me li ba
nayê.'

By God, since ancient days the Xwerkan
have been treacherous, on the day
Of death, no help is coming to us.'

[The music changes with no pause, and the *stranbêj* begins *'Ebdelleh Beg*]

Ferîq Pasha: Kheyro Khelef

[The song (perhaps coincidentally) follows on directly from *'Ebdelleh Beg*]

1. Lê lê dayê
Lê dayê ax
Lê belê Xodê zane vê sibê 'esker bi ser
me dihatin, dinya li me teng bû weke
tara bêjingê,
Lê lê xodê zane gelek hene şade û
nişûdê Osê Mecdî kekê Kemal,

1. Alas, alas, mother,
Alas, mother, oh,
Yes, God knows, this morning soldiers
came upon us, our world became narrow
as the hoop of a sieve,
Oh, God knows, there are many, the
famous ones, the heroes, of Osê Mejdî,
Kemal's elder brother,

Ewî Dawûdê 'Isa babê Dewê,
Ewe Mihemedê Osê xodê zanibe
Sifûqê Meto babê Berces,
Ewî Mihemê 'Evdo siwarê Bozê babê
Saleh,
Belê wellah sê denga gazî dike segmanê
Êzîdiya, sêwir û tekbîrêd giran dane
ra-
Serî geliyê Kirsê bin dara zivingê.

That Dawûdê 'Isa, Dawûd's father,
That Mihemedê Osê, God knows, Sifûqê
Meto, Berjes' father,
That Miḥemê 'Evdo, rider of Bozê, Saleh's
father,
Yes, by God, he calls three times to the
Yezidi marksmen, he stirs them up with
great thoughts,
Above the Kirsê valley under the shady
tree.

2. Belê bira li bin dara zivingê
Gelek hene şad û nişûdêd Miḥemê
'Evdo bavê Saleh,
Sê denga gazî dike, 'Segmane Êzîdiya
bikin bilezînin, berê xwe ji kozik û
çepera megêrînin,
Ew çavê xwe ji nizamê Ferîq Paşa
x̌alibe girane mane metirsînin,

2. Yes, brothers under the shady tree,
There are many, the famous ones, the
heroes of Miḥemê 'Evdo, Saleh's father,
He calls three times, 'Yezidi marksmen,
act now, be busy, don't turn your gaze
from their trenches and dugouts,
Don't let your eyes be frightened of Ferîq
Pasha's overwhelming forces,

'Erz û 'eyal gûlî sorê xwe vê sibê ji destê nizamê bifikînin,	Liberate your kith and kin, your red-braids this morning from the hand of [his] force,
Ce bi Xodê destê me ji gulî sorê me qut be	As God's my witness, let our hands be separated from our red-braids,[10]
Destê me da nema ẍêrî tifingê.	In our hands there is nothing left but the gun.'
3. Lê lê hay nayê,	3. Alas, no help comes,
Zerîfka Ûsê bang dike, 'Lê lê Gulê xwehîngê dengê mi dernayê,	Zerîfka Osê calls 'Oh, Gulê, sister, my voice does not carry,
Berê ezê hawar dikim hawar nayê, dengê top û tifingê 'eskerê Ferîq Paşa û agirê Xwedê berda bûye dunyayê,	Before I was calling for help, help does not come, the noise of the bombs and guns of the soldiers of Ferîq Pasha and the fire of God, the world has been lost,
Bêjî Mandokan xayînin çobûne bi xaletê, çûne rayê,	You say the Mendikan are treacherous, they have gone astray, they have changed their allegiance,
Ew dengê tifingê 'Elî Aẍa bavê Milḥem ji gêdûka Barê nayê,	That sound of the gun of 'Elî Agha, Milḥem's father, does not come from the pass of Barê,
Bi Xwedê, Xwerkaniya xayîne ji qadim û zeman,	By God, the Khwerkan have been treacherous since ancient times,
Pez û hîndada dînê xwe nayê.	Help does not come to us from our own religion.'
4. Lê dayê	4. Alas, mother,
Lê dayê diyarî min û kûrana Bekira bişewite wa bi bera,	Oh, let my region and the Bekiran valley burn, stones and all,
Sê bêlûkêd 'eskerê Ferîq Paşa di ẍalib di giranin Xodê danî gundê me ser çemê Zoqê li Girê 'Ereba,	Three companies of Ferîq Pasha's army, overwhelmingly powerful, by God, hit our village, on the river Zoqa, at Girê 'Ereba,
Lê belê Xodê zane berê topa dabûne Bekira ser malê me de, gûlê topa dirijin weki mûman û çîra,	Yes, God knows, their shells had a direct hit on Bekira, on our houses, the shells and bullets cascade down like candles and lamps,
Gelek hene şad û nişûdêd wî Miḥemê 'Evdo bavê Saleh siwarê Bozê	There are many, the famous ones, the heroes of Miḥemê 'Evdo, Saleh's father, rider of Bozê,
Ew sê denga gazî dike Dawûdê 'Isa bavê Dawûd, 'Mane tu segmanî mêrî çêbe lep helîne,	He calls three times to Dawûdê 'Isa, Dawûd's father, 'You are a marksman, do the deeds of a man, lift your hand,
Ew desta li mîrata bazin zîva werîne,	Put your hands to the cursed silver ring,[11]

10 The 'red-braids' here seem to be the women. It is unclear whether the men are simply declaring that they will not see their women until after the battle, or are eschewing sexual intercourse until the end of the fighting.

11 The word *bazin* can mean a circle of metal, ring or bracelet; it is uncertain whether he is referring to the trigger or some other part of the gun.

Berê xwe ji kozik û çeperê, Xodê zane 'eskerê Ferîq Paşa megerîne

Don't turn your gaze, God knows, from the trenches and dugouts of Ferîq Pasha's army,'

Aferîme Mihemê 'Evdo siwarê Bozê bavê Saleh,
Barê xwedê bi tana şîrê zirav 'ela êvarê siwarî di hajiwane nav çadira.

I congratulate Mihemê 'Evdo, rider of Bozê, Saleh's father,
By God, with his thin sword alone in the evening twilight, the brave horseman was attacking them among their tents.

5. Lê dayê, lê dayê,
Diyarî min û kûrana Bekira bişewite wa bi kaşa,
Xwedê danî ser çemê Zoqayê li gundê me Girê 'Ereba, sê bêlûkêd giranê ji 'eskerê Ferîq Paşa,
Ew minê dêna xo dayê, bi destê pêyayêd Şingariya kitekitê reşoka mîratêd Hadî Paşa,
Di destê pêyayêd 'eskerê Ferîq Paşa mîratêd topa, Xodê zane dîsa dubarî van reşaşa
Ew minê dênê xwe dayê, binê 'eskerê meşiya li aliya xerbî ṛa gehişte birka 'Êlî Paşa
Belê li aliya şerqê ṛa kete çemê Reşe, gelek hene şad û nişûde xortêd Ûsiva xortêd Mêrka û Bekira,

5. Alas, mother,
Let my region and Bekiran valley burn up, hills and all,
By God, they attacked by the river Zoqa, at our village, Girê 'Ereba, three full companies of Ferîq Pasha's army,
I was looking at it, in the hands of the Sinjari foot-soldiers, the musket-fire of Hadî Pasha's cursed ones,
In the hands of Ferîq Pasha's infantry, the cursed cannon, God knows, again the repeating machine-guns,
I was looking at it, below the soldiers, below the army was marching, on the western side 'Elî Pasha's regiment arrived,
Yes, to the east, where the river Resha is, they are many, there are many, the famous, the heroes, Ûsivan lads, Mêrkan and Bekiran lads,

Ew dibêje,'Gelî bav û bira mêrî çêbin, lep hilînin enişka bi kozika meteresa bikutînin,

He said, 'Dear fathers and brothers, do the deeds of men, raise your hands, elbows to the trenches, strike their positions,

Ew çeqmaqê tifinga rakin fîşeka tê bixînin.
Bela ji pê 'eskerê Ferîq Paşa venagerîn mala saleke sê heyva,
Bi Xodê koç û erebanê hukumetê li çemê Bekira xelas nekin meytan û laşa.'

Raise the bolts of your rifles,[12] load them with cartridges.
May this army of Ferîq Pasha not return home for a year and three months,
By God, may those coaches and carts of the Government at the river Bekiran not finish with their bodies, their corpses.'

6. Bêje lê dayê, lê dayê,
Ketime silsila Çilmêrê diyarî sûke,

6. Say, alas, mother,
I went to the peaks[13] of Chilmêra, near the town,

12 In translating this, I have assumed that the rifles are mostly Mausers or similar; the bolt would be raised and drawn back before the cartridge is inserted.

13 The word *silsila* literally means 'chain' or 'genealogy' but can sometimes mean a mountain range (BR).

Mi dî carê sê bêlûkêd 'eskerê Ferîq Paşa kirine çemê Mêrka, fetilîn wê gêdûkê,
De welê Xwedê zane, gelek hene şad û nişûdêd wî Dawûdê 'Isa bavê Dawûd sê denga gazî dike,
Meḥmûdê Osê, Ḥemo Şêro bavê Seydo û Sifûqê Meto bavê Berces,
Miḥemê 'Evdo bavê Saleh, 'Gelî bav û bira mêrî çêbin, lep hilînin, em ji 'eskerê Ferîq Paşa venabin,

Cema li 'esr û êvarê pêşa 'eskerê Ferîq Paşa bigihe aliya Kirkûkê.'

I saw, when three companies of Ferîq Pasha's army made for the river Mêrka, on the other side of that pass,
By God, there are many, God knows, the famous, the heroes, that Dawûdê 'Isa, Dawûd's father, called out three times,
To Meḥmûdê Osê, Ḥemo Shêro, Seydo's father, and Sifûqê Meto, Berjes' father,
Miḥemê 'Evdo, Saleh's father, 'Dear fathers and brothers, do the deeds of men, raise your hands, we won't let ourselves be routed by Ferîq Pasha's army,
In the evening, let all of Ferîq Pasha's army reach the road to Kirkuk.'

Ferîq Pasha: Lezgîn Seydo

1. Belê e ye
Gula kiçik sê denga gazî dike li beṛiyê Gula mezin,
'De lê lê xwehînge sibê dinya li me bû xopana dara bêjingê,
Ew sibeyê dinya li me bû xopana dara bêjingê,
Belê şad û nişûdê ewe Osê Mecdî kekê Kemêl gelek hene,

Ewê sê denga gazî dike Sifoqê Meto bavê Berces, Miḥemê 'Evdo bavê Saleh, mane Dawûdê 'Isa bavê Dêwêd,
Mane şad û nişûdê xwedê zane evan, ciwanmêra gelek hebûyan,

Ezê temaşe kim Xodê zane ... Bekira ... Xodê danîne
Mi li ber çemê Kersê raserî milkê feqîra, gelî bira bin dara zivingê bira o.

1. Alas, yes,
Little Gulê calls out three times in the wilderness to Big Gulê,
'Oh sister, in the morning my whole world was destroyed like the wood of a a sieve,
This morning my whole world is destroyed, like the wood of a sieve,
Yes, the famous ones, heroes of Osê Mejdî, Kemal's elder brother, there are many,
He is calling three times, to Sifûqê Meto, Berjes' father, Mihemê 'Evdo, Saleh's father, and Dawûdê 'Isa, Dawûd's father,
For me, the famous ones, the heroes, God knows, were these, there were many valiant ones,
I will watch, God knows, the ... Bekiran ... they camped, by God,
I [saw] by the stream of Kersê, above the land of the Feqiran, oh, dear brothers under the shady tree, oh brother.'

2. Li bin dara zivingê
Gelek hene şad û nişûdê Osê Mecdî kekê Kemêl,

Ewe sê denga gazî dike Sifûqê Meto bavê Berces, ew Miḥemê 'Evdo bavê Saleh, Dawûdê 'Isa di Xwedê zane bavê Dêwêd,

2. Under the shady tree,
There are many, the famous ones, the heroes of Osê Mejdî, Kemal's elder brother,
He calls three times to Sifûqê Meto, Berjes' father, Mihemê 'Evdo, Saleh's father, and, God knows, to Dawûdê 'Isa, Dawûd's father,

'Welleh gelî bav û birayê mêrî çêbe, xebatê mêra bikin, dest hilînin

Ew çavê xwe ji 'eskerê û nefir il 'ama 'eskerê Ferîq Paşa mejêkirîn,

Wella destê xwe çexmaqe mîratê bêşetaşa bipelînin,
Ew pişta xo cot cotêd rexta bişidînin, 'erz û 'eyalê Êzîdiya bifikînin,
Belê Xwedê o ava neke mala belûked 'eskerê Ferîq Paşa,
Belê destê me ji 'erz û 'eyalê me qut bûye,
Ew tiştek di destê me da nema gelê bira li xêrî xopanê darê tifingê bira o.'

'By God, dear fathers and brothers, do the deeds of men, struggle like men, raise your hands,
Do not tear those eyes of yours away from the soldiers and massacre of Ferîq Pasha's army,
By God, feel the triggers of your machine guns with your hands,
Tighten both your bandoliers at your backs, liberate the Yezidi kith and kin,
Oh God, don't leave the houses of Ferîq Pasha's companies of soldiers standing,
Yes, our hands have been separated from our kith and kin,
Not a thing remained in our hands, dear brothers, but the destructive wood of our rifles, oh brother.'

3. Wella hay nayê, hay nayê,
De hay nayê, hay nayê, hay nayê,
Wellah Mendikane xayîne çune de xalêtê, çûne rayê,
Ev serê sê rojî Xwedê tamam e, dengê topa û tifingê 'eskerê Ferîq Paşa agirê Xodê berdane dunyayê,

Ev serê sê rojî tamam in Xwedê zanibe Xorkaniya xayîne li fezi'e û şîmeta dînê me nayê
Ezê temaşe kim, serî sê rojî Xodê tamam in,
Ew dengê tifinga 'Elî Aẍa bavê Milḥem ji xopana gêdûka ẍerbî nayê

Mane ezê çi bikim, heke destê bi tenê şeṛê 'Elî be,
Li roja qewamê li miqabilê bêlûkê nizamê wê rojê bira çima deng jê nayê?

3. Alas, oh God,
Alas, no help comes,
God, the Mendikan are treacherous, they went astray, they changed their allegiance,
By God, three full days have now passed, the noise of the cannon and rifles of Ferîq Pasha's army, the fire of God, have lost the world,
Three days have passed, God knows, the Khwerkan are treacherous, no help comes from [those of] our religion,
I will watch, three full days have passed,

That noise of the gun of 'Elî Agha, Milḥem's father, does not come from the cursed pass to the west,
What shall I do if 'Elî has to fight by hand alone?
On the day of action opposite the companies of [Ferîq Pasha's] force, on that day, brother, why does no sound come from him?

4. Mi dî Gula kiçêya
Ko sê denga gazî dike li beṛiyê Gula mezin,
'Lê lê xwehîngê,
Ezê bi diyarê sirta Çilmêra diketim, minê raserî bajarê Şingalê mêzê kir raserî sûkê,

4. I saw Little Gulê,
Who calls out three times in the wilderness to Big Gulê,
'Oh, sister,
I was going to the area just by Chilmêra, I was looking down on the town of Sinjar, over the town centre,

Ew bila Xwede o avaneke mala bêlûkêd 'eskerê Ferîq Paşa,
Ew li bayana sibê da girtine derê geliyê Kûr Bimbarek,
Ew çemê Zêrwa û Bekira, lê lê xwehîngê, vê sibê girtiye qûntara gêdûkê.'

May God not leave the houses of Ferîq Pasha's companies of soldiers standing,
In the dawn of the morning they took the place of the valley of Kur Bimbarek,
That river of Zêrwan and Bekiran, oh sister, this morning, they took the foot of the pass.'

5. De welê
Girtiye qûntara gêdûkê
Ew gelek hene şad û nişûdêd Osê Mecdî kekê Kemêl,
Ew sê denga gazî dike Sifûqê Meto babê Berces Miḥemê 'Evdo bavê Saleh wellê Dawûdê 'Isa bavê Dêwêd,
Mane me ṛe gelî bav û bira mêrî çêbin, xebateke mêra bikin, dest hilînin,
Ew pişta xo cot cotêd rexta bişidînin, destê xo li çekmaqê mîratê bêşetaşe bipelînin,
De belê Xwedê zanibe çavê xwe ji 'esker û nefir il 'ama 'eskerê Ferîq Paşa meşkênînin,
Ewan gulî sorê bi Êzîdiya bifikînin inşela û reḥman ezê 'eskerê Ferîq Paşa xelas bikim,
Mane gelî bira ezê taliyeke mayî berê 'eskerê Ferîq Paşa bidim terefê Kerkûkê bira o.'

5. By God
They took the foot of the pass,
There are many, the famous one, the heroes of Osê Mejdî, Kemal's elder brother,
He calls three times to Sifûqê Meto, Berjes' father, Miḥemê 'Evdo, Saleh's father, by God, Dawûdê 'Isa, Dawûd's father,
'For us, dear fathers and brothers, do the deeds of men, the struggles of men, raise your hands,
Tighten both your bandoliers at your backs, feel the trigger of your cursed machine- guns with your hands,
Yes, God knows, do not turn your eyes from the massacre of Ferîq Pasha's army,
Liberate the red-braids for the Yezidis and by God's mercy I will finish off Ferîq Pasha's soldiers,
Dear brothers, in the end I will drive Ferîq Pasha's army towards Kirkuk, oh brother.'

6. Wella hay nayê, hay nayê, hay nayê, hay nayê,
Ew Mendikaniye xayîne,
Çûne li xalêtê çune rayê,
Ev serê sê rojê Xwedê tamam in
Dengê topan û tifingê 'eskerê Ferîq Paşa agirê Xwede berdane vê dunyayê,
Wellah bi navê xwedê Xwerkanê xayîne fezi'e û şîmeta dînê mi nayê
Ev serê sê rojê Xwedê tamam e dengê tifinga 'Elî Aẍa bavê Milḥem,

6. Alas, oh God, no help comes,
Those Mendikan are treacherous,
They went astray, they changed their allegiance,
By God, three whole days have now passed,
The sound of the cannon and rifles of Ferîq Pasha's army, the fire of God, has lost the world,
Yes, in God's name, the Xwerkan are treacherous, help from our religion does not come,
By God, three days have now passed, the sound of the rifle of 'Elî Agha, father of Milḥem,

E ji wa mîratê xodê zane gêdûkê ẍerbî nayê
Mane ew ezê çi bikim, gelî bira heke destê bi tenê şeṛê 'Elî beye,
Ew li roja qewamê miqabelê dijmina me
Wê rojê bira çima dengê nayê?

From that cursed pass, God knows, in the west, it does not come,
And what shall I do, dear brothers, if 'Elî has to fight with his hands alone?
On the day of action facing our enemy,
This day, brother, why does the sound not come?

7. Wella mi dî Gula kiçik
Ko sê denga gazî dike li beṛiyê Gula mezin
'Lê lê xwehîngê,
O ezê bi diyarê kavlê bavê Reşo ketim belê xwedê zane bi geneka,
Ezê bi diyarê kavlê bavê Reşo ketim vê sibê bi geneka,
Ew bila rebê 'elimê mala bêlûke 'eskerê Ferîq Paşa xwedê o ava neke,
Mi dî di bayana sibê da, girtiye çemê Zêrwan û Bekira ya
Li derê geliyê Kûr Bimbara vê sibê girtî neqeb û navbêna cot cotêd girika bira.'

7. By God, I saw Little Gulê
Who calls out three times in the wilderness to Big Gulê,
'Alas, alas, sister,
Oh, I was near the ruins of Resho's father, God knows, with their green bushes,
I was near the ruins of Resho's father this morning, with their green bushes,
May the Lord of the universe not let the house of Ferîq Pasha's companies of soldiers stand, oh God,
I saw in the dawn of the morning, they have taken the streams of Zêrwan and Bekiran,
At the valley of Kur Bimbarek this morning, they have taken the boundaries, the places between the two hills, brother.'

8. Dê belê
Girtîbû wana naqeb û navbêna cot cotêd girika,
Ewê gelek hene şad û nişûdêd, Xodê zane, Osê Mecdî kekê Kemêl,
Mane sê denga gazî dike Sifûqê Meto bavê Berces, wellah Miḥemê 'Evdo bavê Saleh, Dawûdê 'Isa bavê Dêwêd,
'Ew gelî bav û birayê mêrî çêbin, xebatê mêra bikin, dest hilînin,
Ew pişta xo cot cotêd rexta bişidînin, destê xwe cekmaqê mîratê bêşetaşe bipelînin.'

8. Alas, yes,
They had taken those boundaries, the places between the two hills,
They are many, God knows, the famous ones, the heroes, of Osê Mejdî, Kemal's elder brother,
He calls out three times, to Sifûqê Meto, Berjes' father, oh God, Miḥemê 'Evdo, Saleh's father, and Dawûdê 'Isa, Dawûd's father,
'Dear fathers and brothers, do the deeds of men, the struggles of men, raise your hands,
Tighten both bandoliers at your backs, feel the triggers of your cursed machine-guns with your hands.'

9. 'Dê belê,
Xwedê zanibe, çavê xwe ji 'esker nefir il 'ama 'eskerê Ferîq Paşa meşinîne,

9. 'Yes,
God knows, do not let your eyes move from the massacre of Ferîq Pasha's soldiers,

Wellah gulî sorê Êzdiya bifikînin inşela û reḥman ezê 'eskerê Ferîq Paşa xelas bikim,'
Mane gelek hene şad û nişûdê Osê Mecdî kekê Kemêl,
Dibêje şeṛê 'esiriya bi êvarê derê geliya Kûr Bimbarek
Ew şeṛê giran ketî ser milê Mîrza koçeka bira o.

By God, liberate the red-braids of the Yezidis, by God's mercy I will finish off Ferîq Pasha's army,'
There are many, famous ones and heroes of Osê Mejdî, Kemal's elder brother,
He says there is a battle in the evening, at the valley of Kur Bimbarek,
A grievous battle fell upon the people of Kochek Mîrza, oh, brother.

10. Belê
Gula kiçik sê denga gazî dike li beṛiyê Gula mezin
'De lê lê xwehînge vê sibêkê
Ezê bi diyarê çemê Zêrwan û Bekiran berê geliyê Kûr Bimbara ketim, vê sibê bişewite wa bi kaşa,
Mane rebê 'elimê ava neke mala bêlûkek 'eskerê Ferîq Paşa,

Li bayana sibê da, girtiye derê geliyê Kûr Bimbara, çemê Zêrwan û Bekiran,

Mi dî li bayana sibê, bû gumînê topa, bû lekelekê xopanê van reşeşa,

Li destê segmanê malêd êzdiya dabû reqîne xopanê kitekita bêşetaşa,

Ew gelek hene şad û nişûdê Osê Mecdî keke Kemêl,

Sê denga gazî dike Sifûqê Meto bavê Berces,
Wellah Miḥemê 'Evdo bavê Saleh siwarê Bozê,
Ev Dawûdê 'Isa bavê Dêwêd
"Gelî bav û bira, mêrî çêbin, xebatê mêra bikin, dest hilînin,

Ew piṣta xo bi cot-cotêd rexta bişidînin destê xo çeqmaqe mîratê bêşetaşa bipelînin."'

10. Yes,
Little Gulê calls out three times in the desert to Big Gulê,
'Alas, sister, this morning,
I was going to the river Zêrwan and Bekiran, to the valley of Kur Bimbarek, this morning may it all burn up, hills and all,
May the Lord of the universe not leave the houses of a single company of Ferîq Pasha's soldiers standing,
At the dawn of the morning, they captured the valley of Kur Bimbarek, the stream of Zêrwan and Bekiran,
I saw in the dawn of the morning there was the whining of shells, the ruinous firing of automatic rifles,
In the hands of the marksmen from the Yezidi houses, the lethal firing, the crack-crack of machine-guns,
They are many, the famous ones, the heroes of Osê Mejdî, Kemal's elder brother,
Sifoqê Meto, Berjes' father, cries out three times,
By God, to Miḥemê 'Evdo, Saleḥ's father, rider of Bozê,
That Dawûdê 'Isa, father of Dawûd,
"Dear fathers and brothers, do the deeds of men, the struggle of men, raise your hands,
Tighten both bandoliers behind you, feel the triggers of your cursed machine-guns with your hands."'

11. De belê
'Erz o 'eyalê Êzîdiya bifikînin û ezê . . .,
Wellah bi navê Xwedê inşela û reḥman, ezê 'eskerê Ferîq Paşa xelas bikim,

11. Oh yes,
Liberate the Yezidi kith and kin, and I . . .,
By God, in God's name, by his mercy, I will put an end to Ferîq Pasha's army,

Mane ezê bikim sê şeva sê roja
Li derê geliyê Kûr Bimbarek çemê Zêrwan û Bekiran,
Bi tirimbêl û salonêd ḥukumetê a xelas nekin mîratê meytan û laşa bira o.

I will see to it that for three nights and three days,
At the valley of Kur Bimbarek, at the river Zêrwan and Bekiran,
The government, with its cars, its vans, won't have finished [taking away] the cursed corpses and bodies, oh brother.'

12. Wella hay nayê,
De hay nayê, hay nayê, hay nayê, hay nayê,
Ew Mendikaniya xayîne, çûne de xalêtê çûne rayê,
Ev serê sê rojî Xwedê tamam in, xwedê zanibe, dengê topan û tifingê
Ê 'eskerê Ferîq Paşa û agirê Xodê berdane dunyayê.

12. By God, alas,
Alas, no help comes
Those Mendikan are treacherous, they went astray, they changed their opinion,
Three days have now passed, God knows, the sound of the cannon and rifles
Of Ferîq Pasha's army and the fire of God have lost the world.

13. Welle, bi navê Xwedê, Xorkaniya xayîn e, fezi'e û şîmeta dînê me nayê
Ezê çi bikim, serê sê rojî Xwedê tamam e, dengê tifinga 'Elî Ax̆a bavê Milḥem,
Ew ji wê xopanê gêdûkê bi Xodê x̆erbî nayê
Mane ezê çi bikim heke destê bi tenê şeṛê 'Elî beye
Ew li roja qewamê miqabelê dijminê me
Vê rojê çima deng jê nayê bira o.'

13. By God, the Xwerkan in God's name are treacherous, help does not come from our own religion,
What shall I do, three days have now passed by God, the sound of the gun of 'Elî Agha, Milḥem's father,
From the cursed pass, by God, in the West, it doesn't come,
What shall I do if 'Elî must fight by hand alone?
Alas, the day of action, facing our enemy,
On this day why does the sound not come from him, oh brother?'

Ferîq Pasha: Pîr Micho

1. Hay nayê, hay nayê, hay nayê, hay nayê,
Dilê min bû tara bêjingê,
Belê mi berê xo dayê yêd wekî Sifûqê Meto bavê Berces, Miḥemê 'Evdo bavê Saleh Ḥemo Şêro bavê Seydo,
Bi runiştine li bin dara zivingê
'Destê me ji 'erz û 'eyalê me qetiya
Li pêşiya me şeṛ û taliyê me fermaneke girane,
Di destê me de nema ji xênî xopana dara tifingê.'

Alas, help doesn't come,
1. My heart became the hoop of a sieve,
Yes, I saw those [heroes] like Sifûqê Meto, Berjes' father, Miḥemê 'Evdo, Saleh's father, Hemo Shêro, Seydo's father,
They were sitting under the shady tree
'Our hands have been separated from our kith and kin,
In front of us, battle and behind us, a grievous persecution,
In our hands, there is no more than the lethal wood of the rifle.'

2. Hay nayê ...
Gula kiçik bang dike Gula mezin
'Lê xwehingê rabim biçime serê çiyayê Şingalê,
Serbanê Çilmêra pêşberî sûkê,

Xodê o ava neke mala 'eskerê Feriq Paşa
Xîvet û çadirê xwe vegirtine gundêd gêdûkê
Osê Mecdî sê denga gazî dike Sifûqê Meto bavê Berces, Miḥemê 'Evdo bavê Saleḥ, Hemo Şêro bave Seydo, "Gelî bav û bira mêrî çêbin destî xebatekî mêra bikin,
Çavê xwe ji 'eskerê Tirka neşkenînin,
Destê xwe li çeqmaqî bipelînin,
Îzna Xodê emê weke dem û heywanê[14] berî 'eskerê Ferîq Paşa bidine xopana Kerkukê."'

2. Help doesn't come...
Little Gulê calls Big Gulê
'Oh, sister, let me up and go to the top of Mount Sinjar,
The peak of Chilmêra, looking out over the town,
Oh God, don't leave the houses of Ferîq Pasha's army standing,
They have pitched their tents at the villages at the pass,
Osê Mejdî calls three times to Sifûqê Meto, Berjes' father, Miḥemê 'Evdo, Saleh's father, Hemo Shêro, Seydo's father, "Dear fathers and brothers, do the deeds of men, begin the work of men,
Don't take your eyes off the Turkish army,
Feel your triggers with your hands,
If God permits, we will drive Ferîq Pasha's army to destruction in Kirkuk, as [we did] in time gone by."'

3. Kavlê bavê Ḥemo gelek e,
Xodê o ava neke mala Ferîq Paşa

Xîvet û çadir vegirtine li girê Derikê li girê gêdûkê yekayeke

Şad û nişûdêd Osê Mecdî kekê Kemêl gelek hene
Sê denga gazî dike Sifûqê Meto bavê Berces, Miḥemê 'Evdo bavê Saleh, Hemo Şêro bavê Seydo, 'Gelî bav û bira mêrî çêbin, dest bi xebatekî mêra bikin',
Destê xo li çekmaqê tifinga bipelînin,

Li pêşiya malê me şeṛ û li taliya me fermaneke girane
Îzna Xodê û Êzîdê Sor emê berê 'eskerê Ferîq Paşa bînê xopanê Diyarbekir.'

3. The ruins of Ḥemo's father are many,
Oh God, don't leave the house of Ferîq Pasha standing,
They have pitched their tents, both at Dêrik hill and the hill by the pass, one by one,
The famous ones, the heroes of Osê Mejdi, Kemal's older brother, there are many,
Sifûqê Meto, Berjes' father, calls three times to Miḥemê 'Evdo, Saleḥ's father, Ḥemo Shêro, Seydo's father, 'Dear fathers and brothers, do the deeds of men, begin the work of men,
Feel the triggers of your rifles with your hands,
Before our houses is war, behind us is a grievous persecution,
If God and Êzîdê Sor[15] permit, we will drive Ferîq Pasha's army to ruinous Diyarbekir.'

4. Dîsa Xoreka tu şeṛî nekir
Dengê tifingêd Ferîq Paşa li xortêd Êzîdiya bûye şekir,

4. Again the Khwerkan didn't fight at all,
The sound of Ferîq Pasha's guns was sugar-sweet to the young Yezidis,

14 Thus KJR.
15 Presumably a holy figure, but otherwise unknown.

Şad û nişûdêd Osê Mecdî kekê Kemêl gelek hene,

Sê denga gazî dike Sifûqê Meto bavê Berces, Miḥemê ʿEvdo bavê Saleh, Hemo Şêro bavê Seydo, 'Gelî bav û bira, mêrî çêbin dest bi xebatekî mêra bikin,
Destê xo li çeqmaqê tifinga bipelînin,

Li pêşiya malê me şeṛ û li taliya me fermaneke girane
Îzna Xodê û Êzîdê Sor emê berê 'eskerê Ferîq Paşa binê xopanê Diyarbekir . . .'

The famous ones, the heroes of Osê Mejdi, Kemal's older brother, there are many,
Sifûqê Meto, Berjes' father, calls three times to Miḥemê ʿEvdo, Saleḥ's father, Ḥemo Shêro, Seydo's father, 'Dear fathers and brothers, do the deeds of men, begin the work of men,
Feel the triggers of your rifles with your hands,
In front of our houses is war and behind us a grievous persecution,
If God and Êzîdê Sor permit, we will drive Ferîq Pasha's army to ruined Diyarbekir . . .'

DAWÛDÊ DAWÛD

Dawûdê Dawûd by ʿEmerê Dawûd

From Silêman and Jindî 1979: 185–9; footnotes have been incorporated into the text in square brackets:

The notes below on the life and work of Dawûde Dawûd were spoken by the tongue of his son, 'Emerê Dawûd, when he was 55 years old, and written by the hand of Khelîlê Jindî in the village of 'Eyn Sifni, on 7 October 1977.

Dawûdê Dawûd bi dû şeṛa dijî înglîziya ṛabû, yê 'ewil, wekî me gotî, li sala 1925–1926. Hoya serekî ew bû serokêd Êzdiya – bi teḥrîka înglîz – bûne dû tay (beş). Hindek nokerêd înglîz bûn û bi ḥukmê wan dirazî bûn, mîna Seʿîd Begê, mîrê Êzdiyayê wî demî ḥukumeta înglîz eve kir heta ku ev serokina êk li êkî bidet û hemû pêkve lawaz bin û ew bişêt bête ser ḥaziriyê. 'Emerê Dawûd digot, 'Têtе bîra min mûçexorêd ferensî li Sûriya dihatin û pare dînan û didane serokêd hindek êla, û bextê wan pê dikiṛî û razî kirin ku 'erdê Singarê pêxine ser xaka Sûriya.' Belê 'Emer dibêjit, 'Babê min qayil nebû pare ji wan hilgirt û daxwaziya wan qebul ket. Got, "Şingar parçeke ji 'erdê Îraqê." Ango welat peristina xo diyar kir. Her hosa bi ḥukmê înglîz razî nedibû.'

Dawûde Dawûd fought two battles in rebellion against the English. The first, as we have said, was in 1925–6. While he was one of the leaders, the leadership of the Yezidis, at the instigation of the English, split into two factions. Some were servants of the English and were contented with their rule, like Seʿîd Beg, the Yezidi Mîr at that time; the English government did this so that this would set leaders one against another and everyone would be weakened together, and it would be able to dominate. 'Emerê Dawûd said, 'I recall that French agents came from Syria and offered money and gave it to the heads of various tribes, and bought their loyalty and made them agree that the territory of Sinjar be annexed to the land of Syria.' Well, 'Emer says, 'my father was not willing to take money from them and agree to their wish. He said, "Sinjar is part of the country of Iraq." So he made his patriotism clear. But he remained unhappy with English rule.'

'Van egera êk û dû girtin û ḥêcet bo Înglîz çêbû pajone ser Dawûdê Dawûd. Ṛabû Şêx 'Icîl şêxê êla Şemeriya teḥrîk kirin ku biçit 'erdê Ezdiyêd Şingarê jê bistînit. Dawûd ev serşoriye qebûl nekir û bersîngê wan girt. Ḥukumeta Înglîz nekire nemerdî, hêzeke mezin ji lêşker û top û ṭeyarêd xo şandine ser gundêd Dawûdê Dawûd. [Ev hêze ligel 'Erebêd Şêx 'Icîl]. Şeṛekî mezin rûda û zilamêd Dawûd dû ṭeyarêd înglîzî êxandin. Êk jê li gundê Mêrka keft u dû efserêd biritanî têda hatine sotin. Ya dûwê li gundê Zêrwa tiveng lêdan û ço li gundê Tel Alşor [gundeke dikefte ser gundê Ḥerdan, li ser tixobê Til 'Efr û Şingarê. Mêrka û Zêrwa dû gundêd Dawûdê Dawûd in.] Keft, belê kes di vê 'eyarê da nehate kuştin. Ṭeyara sêyê şiya qortal ket.'

'These conditions set one person against another and made it necessary for the English to attack Dawûde Dawûd. Up came Sheykh 'Ajîl, sheykh of the Shammar tribe, whom they incited to go to the Yezidi territory in Sinjar and take it from them. Dawûde Dawûd did not agree to this plan and confronted them. The English government did not hesitate to act and sent a big force of their soldiers and bombs and aeroplanes against the villages of Dawûdê Dawûd [note: this force was with Sheykh 'Ajîl's Arabs]. A big battle broke out and Dawûd's men shot down two English planes. One of them fell on the village of Mêrkan and two British officers inside were burnt to death. The other was hit by gunfire at the village of Zêrwan and went as far as the village of Tel Alşor [a village by the village of Ḥerdan, on the border of Tel 'Afar and Sinjar. Mêrkan and Zêrwan were two of Dawûd's villages]. It fell, but nobody inside this plane was killed. A third plane was able to make it to safety.'

'Serbazêd înglîzî gehiştine gundî û ya destê wan gehiştinê kir. Her ji kuştina pîremêr û jin u zaroka, heta talan kirin û şewitandina gunda. Bi ṛastî firmaneke bêmeded û yeman bû ji miletê êzdiya ṛa.'

'The English soldiers reached the village and took control over it. Everywhere they killed old men, women and children, until the villages were plundered and burned. It really was a terrible persecution for the Yezidi people.'

'Dawûdê Dawûd girtin û bo maweya 3 sala dûr êxistine parêzgeha Naṣiriye sê salêd xo bi derdeserî û nexoşî birine ser. Piştî hingî destûriya wî dan bête Şingarê. Bo maweya 6 manga lêma û neî kirine qeza Şêxan (Êsifinê) û ço gundê Êsiya [gundeke bi 10–12 km dikeftine ṛojavayê Êsifinê]. Sê sal li wê derê jî ṛabartin û li sala 1932 vegeṛiya Zêrwa ya gundêd xo.'

'Dawûde Dawûd was arrested and for a period of three years was exiled to the prison of Naṣiriyya, three years which brought bitterness and misery on him. After that they gave him permission to go to Sinjar. For a period of six months he stayed and they confined him to the Sheykhan area, ('Eyn Sifni) and he went to the village of Êsiyan [a village some 10–12km west of 'Eyn Sifni]. For three years he remained there and in 1932 returned to Zêrwan, one of his villages.'

'Hêşta Dawûdî bêhna xo venedayî Înglîz hatin daxwaziya 'eskeriyê ji Êzdiya kirin, ew jî li sala 1935 bû.'

'Dawûd had still not had time to draw breath when the English came and wanted to make the Yezidis do military service; that was also in 1935.'

'Dawûdî got, "Heke êla Şemer 'eskerî da, em di amadeyne", çonke wî zanî (Şemer) nadin. Nexoş û neḥezêd Êzdiya delîvê xo dîtin û ḥêcet bo dagîrkerêd bogen çêbû siyaseta xo ya pîs bi destê koneperest û nokerêd xo bi cî bînit. Ṛabûn lêşker şandine ser Şingarê û li Êzdiya dan. Gelek ji herdû ciya hatin kuştin.'

'Dawûd said "If the Shammar tribe give some of their men, we will send some", because he knew that the Shammar wouldn't give them. The disaffected and the enemies of the Yezidis saw their chance, and the occupiers needed to implement their dirty policies by using reactionaries and lackeys of theirs. Up they came and sent soldiers against Sinjar and attacked the Yezidis. Many from both places were killed.'

'Wê gavê ḥukumeta înglîz 7 kes li sêdarê dan û 1500 kes kêşane dadgehêd 'orfî. ['Emerê Dawûd navê pênc kesa ji vanêd sêdarê dayîn gotin ew jî evne bun: Bedel Ḥeso 'Isa – Silêmanê Meḥmûdê Osê – Bercesê Ḥisênê Osê – Qasimê 'Eliyê Ado – Ḥeciyê 'Ebdî]. Hemû hatine ḥukm kirin, bigire her ji 15 sala û heta bigehite ḥukmê heta hetayî, li zêndan û bendxanêd parêzgehêd Kirbila û Be'qûbe û Rimadî û Naṣiriye, belav kirin.'

'At that time the English government hanged 7 people and sent 1500 people to the criminal courts. ['Emerê Dawûd mentioned the names of five people they hanged, which were as follows: Bedel Ḥeso 'Isa, Silêmanê Meḥmûdê Osê, Bercesê Ḥisênê Osê, Qasimê 'Eliyê Ado, and Ḥeciyê 'Ebdî.] They all came and and were given sentences which all ranged from 15 years to life, and were scattered throughout the prisons, in the cells of jails in Kerbela and Ba'quba and Rimadi and Naṣiriyya.'

'Dawûdê Dawûd û herdû kurêd xo ('Emer û Hadî) li gel 100 peyadara ṛevîne Sûriya. Mendûbê ferensî li wê derê ṣalox û xeber ji ḥukumeta Birîtanya, li Îraqê şandin ku li van kesa xoş bin. Belê daxwaziya wan bi cî nehat.'

'Dawûde Dawûd and both his sons ['Emer and Hadî] with 100 supporters fled to Syria. The French authorities there, on word and information from the British government, sent a message to Iraq that they would treat those people well. But their wish did not come to anything.'

'Çaxê şoreşa Reşîd 'Elî al-Gilanî li sêyî Nîsana 1941 bi serkeftî û ḥukumeteke nîştimanî pêkhênayî, Dawûdê Dawûd vegeṛiyaye. Belê piştî Înglîz şiyayî vê ḥukumeta niştimanî bişkînit û careke dî dest û darê Îraqê bêxte jêr destê xo, asin bi ṣarî jenîn!'

'At the time of the revolution of Rashid 'Ali al-Gilani on the third (sic) of April 1941, with the victory and the setting up of a national and all-party government, Dawûdê Dawûd returned. But after the English were able to break that national government, and to bring the Iraqi power once more under their control, the iron grew cold.'

'Miṣerefê Mûsil Se'dî al-Qizaz şande pê Dawûdê Dawûd û Şêx Xelef û bextê xo dayê çu lê neket. Wî demî jî Esma'îl Ḥeqî Resûl qaîmeqamê Şingarê bû. . . . .'

'The prefect of Mosul, Sa'di al-Qizaz, sent a message to Dawûde Dawûd and Sheykh Khelef and gave his word nothing would happen to them. At that time Asma'il Haqi Rasul was Qaimaqam of Sinjar . . .'

'Belê çu cara baweriya mirovî li çîna koneperest û derebeg û dagirkera neêt. Ne şeref heye, ne bext û bawerî jî heye. Ser û binê wan ẍedire! Xodan ziman û peyvêd hilûne. Dîn û îmana wan pareye!!'

'But when people trust the class of old-fashioned people and feudal lords and occupiers it never comes to anything. There is neither honour, not fortune nor trust. From head to toe they are treachery! Their tongues and their words are smooth. Money is their faith and their religion!'

'Demê dadgeha Dawûdê Dawûd û Şêx Xelef hatine danan, çu li ser Şêx Xelef derneêxistin û berdan. Belê xefik û torêd qaîm di rêka Dawûdî da vedabûn, ku berê wî dane bendîxanêya Mûsil. Gelek pêneço di bendîxanêda 'emrê Xodê kir.' Wekî kûṛê wî jê digot li ṣala 1954 bû. piştî 70 û hindik ṣal 'emer kirîn.

'When the case against Dawûde Dawûd and Sheykh Khelef came to court, no charges were brought out against Sheykh Khelef and he was left alone. But they had set strong traps and snares for Dawûd, so that they could send him to Mosul prison. Not long afterwards he died in prison.' According to his son that was in 1954. Therefore he had lived for seventy years and a bit.

[Description of massacre of Yezidis by Muslims in Mosul; a Yezidi eyewitness was sheltered by the family of his *kerîf*].

Di ser vê hemûkê ṛa Dawûdê Dawûd mirovekî xodan xîret û bext bû. Serşoṛî û nexoşî, çucara, qebûl nekir. Her hosa piyawekî dîndar û ṛêya ola xo bû. Digotin peyva derew di devî ṛa dernedikeft û nediviya guh lêbit. Axiftina gotiba jî diviya dû ta nebit û bête cî.

Besides all this, Dawûdê Dawûd was a man of passion and honour. He never agreed to vice and wickedness. In every way he was a religious man, following his faith. They say he never let a wicked lying word pass his lips and would not permit himself to hear one. If he had said something, it had to be done immediately, without his repeating it.

[This is illustrated by an anecdote describing his anger towards a man who had sworn at a Yezidi.]

Dawudê Dawûd: Silo Koro (Jelîl 1985: 221)

1. Lê, lê, lê dayê, lê, lê, lê dayê,
Şêrînê digo, 'Memo, lawo, pejna Memê min nayê,
Bira serê kewê sorî sosinî jêkin,
Bigeṛênin li devê dayrê qehwocaẍê bi Beẍdaye,
Bira navê kuştina Memo bela bibe li dinyayê,
Reşoyê Qulo xêrê nebîne şeṛ jê nayê,

1. Alas, oh mother, alas, alas,
Shêrîn said, 'Memo, my lad, the figure of my Memo doesn't come to me,
Let them pluck off the head of the partridge, red as an iris,
Let them bring it as far as the office of the head of barracks in Baghdad.
Let the news of the killing of Memo become a disaster in the world.
May Resho Qulo not see good fortune, there is no fighting from him,

Ḥisênê Berces kiçûk û mezinê çiyayê
Şengalê anîne ṛayê,
Ezê çi bikim, berê xortê cana dane
sefera Kerbelayê,
Berê Dawûdê Dawûd, bavê Hadî, keke
'Eyşanê, ketiye sefera ser Ḥilayê.'

Ḥuseyn Berjes made the great and the small
of Mount Sinjar change their opinion,
What shall I do? He sent our handsome
lads off to Kerbela,[16]
Dawûdê Dawûd, Hadi's father, 'Eyshan's
elder brother, made the journey to Hillah.'

2. De nayê, de nayê,
Şêrînê digo, 'Ezê hawar dikim, hawar
nayê,
Hawar heye, lê hindad ji meṛa nayê,

Ez çi bikim qublit û şemalê çiyayê
Şengalê ṭemam xayînin,
Kesek di hawar û hindada Dawûdê
Dawûd, bavê Hadî, keke Eyşanê, li
min nayê.'

2. Alas, alas, it doesn't come,
Shêrîn said, 'I am calling for help, help
doesn't come,
There is help,[17] but real help doesn't come
to us,
What shall I do? The South and the North
of Mount Sinjar are full of treachery.
No-one comes to me with real help for
Dawûdê Dawûd, Hadi's father, Eyshan's
elder brother.'

3. Lê lê lê dayê, lê lê lê dayê,
Lê lê lê dayê, lê lê lê dayê, geliya
Bekira, li gaza Çilmêrê, navsera çiyayê
Şengalê, ji xema dilê miṛa li Kûrebere,

Me qaleke giran danîbû li navsera
ciyayê Şengalê Kûrebere,
Me dî 'eskerê Şêx 'Isa efendî baş
qumandarê dewletê Ḥisên Fewzî Paşa
bi 'emrê melik Ẋazî, hate ser kozik û
nawçê Memo, bi gotina û bi galgala sê
dibarî ba xebera,

Şêrînê sê denga gazî kire, 'Wudêmê
Ezo, Ḥisênkê Inizê, Silêmanê
Meḥmûd, bavê mino, dest hilînin,
Destê xwe li qebdê xencera bişidînin,

Xûna narincî bi 'erdê da biṛijînin,
Çevê xwe ji belûk 'eskerê Şêrîfo
neşkênînin,
Şad û şihûdê Silêmanê Meḥmûd gelek
hene,
Ewî li ḥucuma 'ewilî xudiyê tamatîkê
daye ber xencera.'

3. Alas, alas, mother,
Alas, mother, the valley of Bekiran, in the
district of Chilmêra, in the middle of
Mount Sinjar, for the sadness of my heart,
at Kurebere,[18]
We made a great noise in the middle of
Mount Sinjar, at Kûrebere,
We saw the soldiers of Sheykh 'Isa
Effendi, commander-in-chief of the coun-
try of Ḥuseyn Fewzî Pasha, in the time of
king Ghazi; he came to the trenches where
Memo was, he talked evil talk with bad
words.
Shêrîn shouted out three times, 'Wudêmê
Ezo, Ḥisênkê Inizê, Silêmanê Meḥmûd,
oh my father, raise your hands,
Tighten your hands round the hilt of your
daggers,
Spill the orange blood on the ground,
Don't let Sherifo's companies of soldiers
out of your sight.
The famous ones, the heroes of Silemanê
Mehmûd, there are many,
In the first attack he ran the man with the
automatic rifle through with his dagger.'

16 Because of the ergative construction and variations in local usage, it is unclear whether this should be interpreted as 'they went'.

17 The word *hawar* can mean either 'help' or 'a cry for help'; I have opted for the former here because it is used in this sense at the end of the previous line.

18 A place in Sinjar (KJR).

4. De nayê, de nayê,
Şêrînê digo, 'Ezê hawar dikim, hawar nayê,
Hawar heye, lê hindad ji me ṛa nayê,
Ez çi bikim, qublit û şemalê çiyayê Şengalê ṭemam xayînin,
Kesek di hawar û hindada Dawûdê Dawûd bavê Hadî kekê Eyşanê li min nayê.'

4. Oh, it doesn't come, it doesn't come,
Shêrîn said 'I am calling for help, help doesn't come,
There is help, but real help doesn't come to me.
What shall I do? The South and the North of Mount Sinjar are full of treachery.
No-one comes to me with real help for Dawûdê Dawûd, Hadi's father, Eyshan's elder brother.'

5. Lê, lê, lê dayê, lê, lê, lê dayê,
Şêrînê digo, 'Memo lawo, şeṛeke qewimî li dara geliyê Bekira, li gaza Çilemêri, li navsera çiyayê Şengalê,
Ji xema dilê min û te ṛa li wî banî,
Me qaleke giran danîbû li navsera çiyayê Şengalê li wî banî,
Mi dî 'eskerê Şêx 'Isa Efendî, baş qumandarê dewletê Ḥusêîn Foucê Paşa bi 'emrê melik Ẍazî, li kozik û çeperê Memo, bi hewa kete banî,
Giṛegiṛa midiṛi'a, dengê reşaş û bêlafiṛa dinya tev hilanî,
Şêrînê digo, 'Memo lawo, pejna Memê min nayê,
Ez nizanim Memê mi kanî.'
Memê digo, 'Yadê, ezî vame,
Li pêşiya bêlûk 'eskerê Şerîfo ṛawestame,
Wexta mi dest davîte desgîra tivingê, derpa 'ewil mi lêdabû, şifêrê bêlafira bi çengekî,
Mi nehîşt ew teyara ḥerbî bi xêr û silamet bi hewa keve banî.'

5. Alas, alas mother, alas mother,
Shêrîn said, 'Memo, my lad, a battle happened at the wood in Bekiran valley, in the district of Chilmêra, in the middle of Mount Sinjar,
To the pain of your heart and mine in this high place,
We made a great noise in the middle of Mount Sinjar, in this high place,
We saw the soldiers of Sheykh 'Isa Effendi, the commander-in-chief of the country of Ḥuseyn Fewzî Pasha by command of king Ghazi, at Memo's trenches and dugouts, they flew overhead.'
The firing of Mausers, the noise of automatic rifles and aircraft stirred up the world,
Shêrîn said, 'Memo, young man, the figure of my Memo doesn't come to me,
I don't know where my Memo is.'
Memo said, 'Oh mother, I'm here,
I have stopped in front of the company of Shêrifo's soldiers,
When I put my hand to the grip of my gun, my first shot hit the pilot of the plane in the arm.
I didn't allow that warplane to fly over in peace.'

6. Lê, lê, lê dayê, lê, lê, lê dayê
Şêrînê digo,'Memo lawo, şeṛeke qewimî li dara geliyê Bekira, li gaza Çilemêrî, li navsera çiyayê Şengalê, ji xema dilê mi ṛa, li kenarê vê hewayê,
Me qaleke giran danîbû li navsera çiyayê Şengalê li kenarê vê hewayê.

6. Alas, alas, oh mother,
Shêrîn was saying, 'Memo, my lad, a battle happened at the wood in Bekiran valley, in the district of Chilmêra, in the middle of Mount Sinjar, to the sadness of my heart, at the edge of the sky,
We made a great noise in the midst of Mount Sinjar at the edge of the sky.

Mi dî 'eskerê Şêx 'Isa efendî, başqumandarê dewletê, Ḥisên Foûcê Paşa bi 'emrê melik Ẍazî, li kozik û nawçê Memo hat û bi sê erîşa hela dayê.

We saw the army of Sheykh 'Isa Effendi, commander-in-chief of the state, Ḥuseyn Fewzî Pasha in the time of king Ghazi, come to the trenches, the place where Memo was, and with three attacks he dissolved them.

Dengê reşaş û tematîka agir berdane vê dinyayê,
Ezê hawar dikim hawar heye, lê hindad ji me ṛa nayê,
Ḥeyfa mi tê wê yekê destê xortê cana li darê kelemçê dan
Ferza Ezîdîna, lê ew jî qismek ji me kurdane
Berê wana dane ber textê melik Ẍazî, dayra meḥkema vê Beẍdaê.

The sound of machine guns and automatics set this world on fire,
I call for help, there is help, but it doesn't come for me.
I am sad, that they put our handsome lads in handcuffs,
They bind the Yezidis, but this is also our fate as Kurds,
They sent them[19] before the throne of King Ghazi, the headquarters of the judges in Baghdad.'

7. De nayê, de nayê,
Şêrînê digo, 'Ezê hawar dikim, hawar nayê,
Hawar heye, lê hindad ji me ṛa nayê,

7. Oh, it doesn't come, it doesn't come,
Shêrîn said, 'I am calling for help, help doesn't come,
There is help, but real help doesn't come for me,

Ez çi bikim, qublit û şemalê çiyayê Şengalê ṭemam xayînin,
Kesek di hawar û hindada Dawûdê Dawûd, bavê Hadî, kekê 'Eyşanê li min nayê'.

What shall I do? The South and North of Sinjar are full of treachery,
No-one comes to me with real help for Dawûdê Dawûd, Hadi's father, Eyshan's elder brother'.

Dawûdê Dawûd: "Pîr Qewwal"

1. Lê dayê, lê dayê, lê dayê, lê dayê, lê dayê, lê dayê, lê dayê, lê dayê, lê dayê,
Şêrinê bi sê denga gazî dike, 'Memo, lo lawo bejna Memê min nayê,

1. Alas, mother,
Shêrîn calls three times, 'Memo, oh young man, the figure of my Memo doesn't come,

Wê serê kewê sorî sosinî jêkin vê derê ne ocax li yê wê xodayê vê beẍdayê

They will pluck off the head of the wild partridge, of the lily, in that place, that barracks in Baghdad,

Hele dayê hele dayê
Hele dayê ez çi kim sala berê vê salê û Êzdiyêd çiyayê xayînin,

Alas mother,
What can I do? For the past year, the Yezidis of the mountain have been treacherous,

Hawara Dawûdê Dawûd bavê Hadî kekê Eyşanê o.'

Get help for Dawûdê Dawûd, Hadi's father, Eyshan's elder brother, oh.'

19 See Silo 1: 8 for a similar construction.

2. Lê dayê, lê dayê, lê dayê, lê dayê, lê dayê, lê dayê, lê dayê, lê dayê, lê dayê,
Şêrîne sê denga gazî dike Reşoyê Qulo sê deng jê nayê,
'Ḥisênê Berces xêrê bike xêrê nebînetê, kiçik û mezinêd êzdiya çiyayê Şingalê ayîne rayê

2. Alas, mother, alas, alas, mother, Alas, mother, alas, alas,
Shêrîn shouted out three calls to Resho Qulo, three calls do not come from him,
'May Ḥuseyn Berjes not see good fortune even if he does good, he made the great and small of the Sinjari Yezidis change their opinion,

Berê xorte ciwane dayê sefere Kerbeleyê
Berê Daûdê Dêwûd bavê Hadî kekê Eyşanê dayê seferê ser Ḥeleyî

He sent the handsome lads on the journey to Kerbela,
He sent Dawûdê Dawûd, Hadi's father, Eyshanê's elder brother, on journey to Hillah.

Hele daê hele daê hele daê ez çi kim sala berê vê salê Êzîdiyêd çiyayê xayîn in, hawara Daûdê Dêwûd bavê Hadî kekê Eyşanê.'

Alas, mother, alas, mother, alas, What shall I do? For the past year, the Yezidis of the mountain have been treacherous, get help for Dawûdê Dawûd, Hadi's father, Eyshan's elder brother.'

3. 'Ax lê dayê,
Berê şêrek û qaleke giran çêbû ... li derê geliyê Bekira li gaza Çilemêra li hewayê,
Berê şeṛek û qalekê giran çêbû li derê geliyê Bekira li gaza Çilemêra ji xema dilê min û te ṛe dîsanekê li hewayê

3. 'Oh, mother,
Once, a battle and a great noise took place ... at Bekiran valley, at the peak of Chilmêra in the air,
Once, a battle and a great noise took place at Bekiran valley, at the peak of Chilmêra, to my sorrow and yours again, in the air,

Belê Xodê ceza bide 'eskerê 'emerê Gezî Ḥisên effendî Qoçe Paşa,

May God punish the soldiers who fought for Hisên Effendi Qoçe Pasha in the time of Ghazi,

Hişyar û şêre Dawûdê Dêwûd bavê Hadî kekê Êyşanê digo 'Memo ev deşta xwediyê ...,'

He is watchful and lionhearted, Dawûdê Dawûd, Hadi's father, Eyshan's elder brother, he said, 'Memo, that plain is a place of ...,'

Dawûdê Dêwûd bi sê denga gazî dike 'Ûdêmê Ḥezo Ḥesoke Hemzî Silemanê Mehmûd, 'Bavê me, mêrî çêbikin bixebitin
Vê sibê hûnê dest hilînin ... mêra bikujin xwîna narincî ber 'erdê weşînin,
Destê xwe li qebdê xencera bişidînin,

Dawûdê Dawûd calls out three times to Ûdêmê Ḥezo, Ḥesokê Hemzî, Silêmanê Meḥmûd, 'Oh you fathers of ours, do the work of men, keep struggling
This morning you will raise your hand, ... kill men, make the orange blood pour forth on the earth,
Squeeze the handle of your daggers in your hands,

Çavê xwe ji bêlûkê 'eskera, nizama Înglîzî bişkînin,
Bira vê sibêkê dîsayê,
Em dest bi kiçik û mezinê Êzdiyê çiyayê Şingalê bikin,

[Don't take] your eye from the companies of soldiers, break the English force,
This morning again let it happen,
We will begin with the great and small of the Yezidis of Mount Sinjar,

... textê 'emrê Gezî bergehê wê Bex̌dayê ...'

... the throne in the time of Ghazi ... the view of Baghdad ...'

4. Helê dayê helê dayê
Helê dayê ez çi kim sala berê vê salê û Êzdiyêd çiyayê xayînin
Hawara Dawûdê Dêwûd bavê Hadî kekê Eyşanê ê.

4. Alas, mother, alas, alas,
What can I do? The past year, the Yezidis of the mountain are treacherous.
Get help for Dawûdê Dawûd, Hadi's father, Eyshan's elder brother, oh.

DERWÊSHÊ 'EVDÎ

Derwêshê 'Evdî: Israel Ohanyan (Jelîl 1978 I: 279–90)

Bavê Dewrêş 'Evdî bû. Dewrêş hê tinebû. 'Evdî şivanê Zor Temir Paşayê milî bû. Ḥafirê Gêsî û 'Ecîl Birahîm – ew şêxê ḥezar û pênsid Gêsa bûn. Zor Temir Paşayê Milî ax̌ê Kîka û Mila bû. Kîka û Mila kurd bûn. Gêsa 'ereb bûn.

The father of Derwêsh was 'Evdî. Derwêsh was still not born. 'Evdî was the shepherd of Zor Temer Pasha of the Milan. Hafir Gêsî and 'Ajîl Brahîm were the sheykhs of one thousand five hundred of the Gêsî. The Kîkan and Milan were Kurdish. The Gêsî were Arabs.

Ṛojekê Gêsa hev û dinê civiyan. Ḥafirê Gêsî, 'Ecîl Brahîm go, 'Emê nijdakê bavêjine ser Kîka û Mila. 'Emê konê Zor Temer Paşa bidine ber şûra'. Ewî 'eşîra xwe hilanî û ser konê Zor Temer Paşa va girt, sed mêrê 'ereba jê koşt. Zor Temer Paşa ṛabû ṛeviya. 'Evdî li miḥîna Zor Temer Paşa siwar bû, şûrê xwe hilanî û kete nav neyara. Bû çingînê şûra, bû terqînê mertala. Ev ḥezar siwarê Gêsa ji ber 'Evdê ṛeviyan. 'Evdê sed mêr ji wan kuşt û hate malê, ji hespê peya bû. Hingê kêfa Zor Temer Paşa zeḥf zeḥf ji 'Evdî ṛa hat, çima ko Zor Temer Paşa ji ber neyara xilas bû.

One day the Gêsî all gathered together. Ḥafir Gêsî and 'Ajîl Brahîm said, 'We will send out a raiding party against the Kîkan and Milan. We will put the camp of Zor Temer Pasha to the sword'. He gathered up his tribe and attacked the camp of Zor Temer Pasha, the Arabs killed a hundred of their men. Zor Temer Pasha upped and fled. 'Evdî rode the mare of Zor Temer Pasha, raised his sword and fell upon the enemy. There was the clashing of swords, the ringing of shields. Those thousand Gêsa warriors ran away from 'Evdî. 'Evdî killed a hundred of their men, came home, and got off his horse. From then Zor Temer Pasha's heart went out to 'Evdî, because Zor Temer Pasha had been delivered from his enemies.

Zor Temer Paşa 'Evdî zewicand. Sala wî qediya Xudê kuṛek dayê. Zor Temer Paşa navê wî danî Dewrêşê 'Evdî.

Zor Temer Pasha found a wife for 'Evdî. A year passed for him, God gave him a son. Zor Temer Pasha gave him the name Derwêshê 'Evdî.

Zor Temer Paşa gelekî ji vî kuṛkî û ji bavê wî ḥiz dike, weke birayê xwe ji wan ḥiz dike. Sal û zeman ketine nav. Dewrêş mezin bû, ʿemrê wî bû bîst û pênc sal. Piçek mal û halê wan çê bû. ʿEvdê ji ber Zor Temer Paşa derket. ʿEdûle, qîza Zor Temer Paşa, ew jî qîze, gellek delale, di dilê dê bavê xweda gellek ʿezîze. Dewrêşê ʿEvdî, ew hê ji ʿEdûlê jî delaltire. Dilê wî û ʿEdûlê[20] heye. ʿEvdê konê xwe bar kir û ji ba Zor Temer Paşa çû û konê xwe li beṛiyê vegirt.

Zor Temer Pasha loved this boy and his father very much, he loved them as if they were his brothers. Time passed and years went by. Dewrêş grew up, he was twenty-five years old. Their house and their life had got a little better. ʿEvdî did well from Zor Temer Pasha. ʿEdûle, the daughter of Zor Temer Pasha was unmarried, she was very lovely, she was very dear to the hearts of her mother and father. Dewrêşê ʿEvdî was even more lovely than ʿEdûle. He and ʿEdulê were in love. ʿEvdî packed up his tent and went from Zor Temer Pasha's place and set up camp in the desert.

ʿElî û Bozan herdû birayê ʿEvdêne, Seʿdûn jî birayê Dewrêşe, ev herdu malê han ji hev naqetin, tev êzdîne. ʿEvdî extiyar bû, ʿemrê wî bû nod salî. Zêdeyî Dewrêş û Seʿdûn zaṛoyê wî tine bûn.

ʿElî and Bozan were both brothers of ʿEvdî, Seʿdûn was a brother of Dewrêş too; these two houses were never broken apart and were both Yezidi. ʿEvdî was old, his age was ninety. Apart from Dewrêş and Seʿdûn he had no children.

1. Dilê mi liyane,
ʿErdê beṛiyê ʿerdekî dûzî bêpîvane,

1. My heart is longing,
The land of the desert is a measureless flat land,

Hezar û pênsid siwarê Gêsa li hev civiyane,
Çûne dîwana girane,
Li ber xo danîne Qurana ʿezîmşane,

One thousand five hundred Gêsa warriors gathered together,
They went to a big guest-hall,
They set down before themselves the Qurʿan of exalted rank,

Dibê, ʿEmê ḥicûmeke mezin bavêjin ser Kîkan û Milane,
Ḥicûma ʿewil, emê bavêjinê ser kozê qîz û bukê wane,
Ḥicûma didûwa, emê bibine ser biṛê qîz û xortê Kîkan û Milane,

And said 'We will launch a great attack against the Kîkan and Milan,
The first attack, we will launch on the sheep-pens of their girls and brides,
The second attack, we will make on the herds of the girls and lads of the Kîkan and Milan,

Ḥicûma sisiya, emê konê Zor Temir Paşa bidine devê şûrane,
Ji berê da em dijminê bav û kalane.'

The third attack, we will put the camp of Zor Temer Pasha to the sword,
In the past we have been enemies of their fathers and elders.'

Mektûbekê nivisandin, mektûb qasî cerîdane,
Dane destê du ḥeb xortane,
Go, ʿBibin û heṛine dîwana Zor Temir Paşane,

They wrote a letter, a letter as long as a newspaper,
Gave it into the hand of two young men,
They said, 'Take it and go to the guest-hall of Zor Temer Pasha,

20 One would expect *dilê wî li ʿEdûlê heye*, 'he was in love with ʿEdûlê' but Jelîl's wording may reflect local usage.

Bêbextî di nava meda ne xûyane.'	Treachery is never seen amongst us'.
Dibê evan herdu xorta siwar bûn û meşiyane,[21]	These two young men mounted and rode,
Berê xo dane oda Zor Temir Paşayê Milane,	They went towards the guest-halls of Zor Temer Pasha of the Milan,
Çûne devê deriyê odê sekinîn û mektûb dane destane,	They went through the door into the room, stopped and gave the letter into [his] hands,
Ev herdu xort vegeṛiyane nava Gêsane,	These two young men returned among the Gêsa,
Zor Temer Paşa ṛûdinê û mektûbê dixwêyîne,	Zor Temer Pasha sat down and read the letter,
Destê xwe li çoka xwe dixîne,	He struck his knee with his hand,
Stêrkê xwe dibarîne,	He let his tears flow,
Dibê, "Evdî jî ji ba mi çû, kes qewata min tinîne.'	Said, "Evdî too has gone away from me, I have no power'.
2. Liyane, liyane, liyane,	2. My heart is longing, longing,
Zor Temer Paşa gazî kir giregir, fêriz û pelewanê Kîkan û Milane,	Zor Temer Pasha called the big, the brave, the champions of the Kîkan and Milan,
Temam di oda giran da li hev civiyane,	All of them gathered together in the great room,
Tev ji nava xwe ṛazîne,	Together they were proud of themselves,
Filan ibn filane,	So and so, son of such and such,
Qelûnê wan temama destê wane,	All of them with pipes in their hands,
'Ebbayê basrayî li nava milê wane,	Cloaks from Basra round their shoulders,
Şûrê wan tev girêdayiye li kêlekê wane,	Their swords bound at their sides,
Titûnê dikişînin, ode bûye toz û dûmane,	They were smoking tobacco, the room was full of dust and smoke,
Zor Temer Paşa hêja dageṛî nava wane,	The esteemed Zor Temer Pasha moved amongst them,
Mektûba neyara bi destane.	The enemies' letter in his hands.
Mektûb deranî, mektûbê dixwêyîne,	He opened out the letter, he read it out,
Go, 'Gelî Kîkano, gelî Milano,	He said, 'Dear men of the Kîkan and Milan,
Gelî fêrizno, gelî pêlewanîno,	Dear brave ones and champions,
Ûn baş bala xwe bidinê vê mektûba hano.'	You take a good look at this letter of theirs.'
Zor Temer Paşa mektûbê dixwêyîne,	Zor Temer Pasha read out the letter,
Dibê, 'Dilê min liyane, liyane, liyane,	He said, 'My heart is longing, longing, longing,
'Erdê beṛiyê 'erdekî dûze, bêpîvane,	The land of the desert is a flat, measureless land,
Ḥezar û pênsid siwarê Gêsa têda li hev civiyane,	One thousand five hundred Gêsan warriors gathered together in it,

21 The word *dibê* or *divê*, which occurs several times in the text, literally means '[the original poet] says' or 'they say'.

Kişiyane dîwana girane,	They drew together in a great guest-hall,
'Ecîl Birahîm milûkê wane,	'Ajîl Brahîm is their king,
Ḥafirê Gêsî bêyreqdarê wane,	Ḥafir Gêsî, their standard-bearer,
Li ber xo danîne qurana 'ezîmşane,	They set down before themselves the Qur'an, of exalted rank,
Teva sond dixwar bi 'ezîmşane,	Together they swore an oath by the exalted rank,
Teva sond dixwar bi vê qurana hane,	Together they swore an oath by this Qur'an, like this,
"Emê ḥicûmek bidinê ser Kîka û ser Milane,	"We will make an attack on the Kîkan and Milan,
Ḥicûma 'ewil, wê bavêjinê ser kozê qîz û bukê we Kîka û we Milane,	The first attack, we will launch on the pens of the girls and brides of you Kîkan and you Milan,
Ḥicûma didûwa, ê şûr berde qîz û xortane,	The second attack, put to the sword the girls and lads,
Ḥicûma sisiya, ê konê Zor Temir Paşa bide devê şûrane."	The third attack, put the camp of Zor Temer Pasha to the sword."
Gelî mêrxasa, înca şeṛ girane.'	Brave people, this time it is a heavy war.'
3. Dibê, ev fêriz û pelewanê hanê,	3. He spoke, and these brave men and champions of theirs,
Simbêlê wan melûl bûn,	Their moustaches were drooping,
Serê simbêla kete ser lêvane,	Their moustaches drooped down over their lips,
Me'dê xwe kirin, weke jinebiyane,	They scowled like widows,
Weke çelê genim, 'erd bi darka kolane,	They dug into the ground with their sticks, as if it were a pit for burying wheat,
Di ber xo da hêdî hêdî giriyane,	For themselves they slowly wept,
Yeko yeko ṛabûn, derketin ji oda Zor Temer Paşayê Milane.	One by one they rose, and left the guest-room of Zor Temer Pasha of the Milan.
4. 'Edûlê hate odê sekinî, go, 'Zor Temer Paşa, bavo, dilê min liyane,	4. Edûlê came into the room, stopped and said, 'Zor Temer Pasha, father, my heart is longing,
Qe tu nizanî, heye Dewrêşê 'Evdî, lawikê Êzîdxane?	Do you not know that there is Derwêshê 'Evdî, the lad of the Yezidi religion?
Ewe, kû dibe qesasê ḥezar pênsid siwarê Gêsane,	It is he who can be the killer of one thousand five hundred Gêsa warriors,
Ewe, kû konê te xilas dike ji devê şûrane,	It is he who can deliver your camp from the mouth of their swords,
Dewrêşê di nava pelewana da gellekî navgirane.'	Derwêsh is much renowned amongst the champions.'
Zor Temer Paşa dibê, "Edûlê, de ṛabe, mektûbekê binivisîne, ji Dewrêşê 'Evdî ṛa, lawkê êzîd ṛa bişîne.'	Zor Temer Pasha said, "Edûlê, get on, write a message, and send it to Derwêshê 'Evdî, the Yezidi lad.'

5.ʿEdûlê ṛadibe mektûbekê dinivisîne,
Dide destê xortekî û zû dişêyîne,
Dewrêş li ser mêrgekî sekiniye,
Hevsarê Hidman bi destane û Hidman diçêrîne.
Dewrêş mektûbê ji destê vî xortî digre û dixwêyîne,
Mektûbê maçû dike û ser eniya xwe datîne,
Li Hidman siwar dibe û dixarîne,
Xo bi malê digihîne,
Ko vaye bavê wî, ʿElî û Bozan û Seʿdûn tev ṛûniştîne.
Sekinî mektûbê ji wan ṛa dixwêyîne,
Go, ʿEvdî bavo, dilê min liyane,
ʿErdê beṛiyê ʿerdekî dûzî bêpîvane,
Ḥezar û pênsid siwarê Gêsa têda li hev civiyane,
Tev çûne dîwana girane,
ʿEcîl Birahîm milûkê wane,
Ḥafirê Gêsî bêyreqdarê wane,
Li ber xo danîne qurana ʿezîmşane,
Teva sond dixwar bi ʿezîmşane,
Teva sond dixwar bi vê qurana hane,
"Em û Kîka û Mila neyarê bav û kalane,
Emê ḥicûmeke mezin bavêjine ser Kîka û Milane,
Ḥicûma ʿewil, li ser kozê qîz û bukane,
Ḥicûma didûwa, emê şûr berdine qîz û xortane,
Ḥicûma sisiya, ê konê Zor Temir Paşa bide devê şûrane."
Mektûb hate dîwana Zor Temer Paşayê Milane,
Zor Temer Paşa mektûbê dixwêyîne,

5. ʿEdûlê got up, wrote a message,
Handed it to a lad, and sent it swiftly,
Derwêsh was lingering in a pasture,
Hidman's halter was in his hands as he let Hidman graze.
Derwêsh took the message from this young lad's hand and read it,[22]
He kissed the message and pressed it to his forehead,
Mounted on Hidman and galloped off,
Took himself home,
There were his father, ʿElî and Bozan and Seʿdûn, sitting together.
He stopped and read out the message to them,
He said, "Evdî, father, my heart is longing,
The land of the desert is a flat measureless land,
One thousand five hundred Gêsa warriors gathered together there,
They came together to a great guest-hall,
ʿAjîl Brahîm is their king,
Ḥafir Gêsî is their standard-bearer,
They set down before themselves the Qurʿan, the power of highest heaven,
Together they swore an oath by the power of highest heaven,
Together they swore an oath by this Qurʿan of theirs,
"We and the Kîkan and Milan are enemies since our ancestors' time,
We will launch a great attack on the Kîkan and Milan,
The first attack, against the pens of their girls and brides,
The second attack, we will put to the sword their girls and lads,
The third attack, we will put the camp of Zor Temer Pasha to the sword."
A message came to the guest-hall of Zor Temer Pasha of the Milan,
Zor Temer Pasha read out the message,

22 This is the only variant which ascribes literacy to Derwêsh; the Sinjari songs do not often ascribe literacy to their protagonists; it is tempting to credit this detail to the non-Yezidi provenance of this telling, though there is no hard evidence.

Fîncana qawê li ser destê ‘Edûlê datîne,
‘Edûlê fîncana qawê li ser tepiska zêrîn datîne,
Li nava dîwana Kîka û Mila digeṛîne,
“Heçî kesê fîncana qawê ji ser destê min hilîne,
Ewê min mar ke, ê ḥeyfa bavê min hilîne.”’

He put a cup of coffee into the hand of ‘Edûlê,
Edûlê set down the cup of coffee on a golden tray,
She wandered around the guest-hall of the Kîkan and Milan,
“Whoever lifts this cup of coffee from my hand,
He shall marry me, and take vengeance for my father.”’

6. Dibê, ‘Bavo, dilê min liyane, liyane,
Tu bide min ‘Elî û Bozane,
Tu bide min Seʿdûnê birane,
Ezim, ko heṛim fîncanê hilînim ji ser destê ‘Edûla qîza Zor Temer Paşayê Milane,
Ezim, diqelînim ḥezar û ḥevsid siwarê Gêsane,
Ezim, konê Zor Temer Paşa xilas bikim ji devê şûrane.
Bavo, Zor Temer Paşa emekdare,
Emekê wî li ber çevê min xûyane.’

6. He said, ‘Father, my heart is longing, longing,
You give me ‘Elî and Bozan,
You give me my brother Seʿdûn,
I’ll do it, I will go and take the cup from the hand of ‘Edûlê, daughter of Zor Temer Pasha of the Milan,
I will roast one thousand five hundred Gêsa warriors,
I will deliver the camp of Zor Temer Pasha from the (mouth of the) swords.
Father, Zor Temer Pasha is righteous,
His righteousness is clear to my eyes.’

7. Dibê, ‘Evdî giriya û stêr ji çevê bavê wî bariyane,
Go, ‘Weyî weyî li min û vî bextî hane,
Lawo, sebir bike, sebir ji ba Xudane,
Ezê du xebera ji kuṛê xwe ṛa bêjim, bala xwe bide vê xebera hane.’
Go, ‘Lawo, ‘emrê min hijde salî bû, ez şivanê mala Zor Temer Paşayê Milame,
Carekê dîsa li ser serê wî ṛabû fermaneke girane,
Kîka, Mila ji ber Gêsa ṛeviyane,
Ez ṛabûm siwar bûm li miḥîna Zor Temer Paşa Milane,
Mi şûr girêda, mertal avîte zendane,
Ez dageṛiyame nava neyarane.
Dibe çingînê şûra, terqînê mertalane,’
Go, ‘Lawo, min sed ji wan kuştin û tev ji ber bavê te ṛeviyane,

7. They say, ‘Evdî wept and tears trickled down from the father’s eye,
He said, ‘Alas, alas for me and that honour of theirs,
Lad, be patient, patience belongs to God,
I will say two words to my son, pay attention to these words.’
He said, ‘Lad, when I was eighteen years old, I was the shepherd of the family of Zor Temer Pasha of the Milan,
Another time again there was a death sentence passed on him,
The Kîkan and Milan fled from the Gêsan,
I got up and rode the mare of Zor Temer Pasha of the Milan,
I strapped on my sword, tossed aside my shield from my forearms,
I fell upon the enemy.
There was the clashing of swords, the ringing of shields,’
He said, ‘Lad, I killed a hundred of them and they all fled from your father,

Min konê Zor Temer Paşa xilas kir ji destê neyarane,
Paşî Zor Temer Paşa çi got? Go, "Evdê êzdiye, li çiyayê Şengalê dibe dizê kerane."
Tu ji ya bavê xo bikî, Zor Temer Paşa bêbexte, emekḥerame.'
Dewrêş dibê, 'Bavo, dilê min liyane, liyane,
Sûretê 'Edûla Zor Temer Paşa li ber çevê min xûyane,
Ez bextê teda, tu dilê min neşkênî ji boy vî şeṛê hane,
Tu bide min ʿElî û Bozane,
Tu bide min Seʿdûnê birane,
Emê siwar bibin li hespane,
Heṛine dîwana Zor Temer Paşa Milane,
Emê binheṛin ṛay, şêwr û tekbîra wane.'

I delivered the camp of Zor Temer Pasha from the hand of the enemy,
Afterwards what did Zor Temer Pasha say? He said, "ʿEvdî is a Yezidi, on Sinjar mountain he is a donkey-thief."
You take it from your father, Zor Temer Pasha is treacherous and dishonourable'.
Derwêsh said, 'Father, my heart is longing, longing,
The image of ʿEdûlê, child of Zor Temer Pasha, appears before my eyes,
I throw myself on your mercy, do not break my heart over this battle,
You give me ʿElî and Bozan,
You give me Seʿdûn my brother,
We will ride on our horses,
We'll go to the guest-hall of Zor Temer Pasha of the Milan,
We will find out their views, their counsels and their thoughts.'

8. Dibê, Dewrêş ṛabû ji piyane,
Cilê zirî û mizirî kişande xwe, siwar bû li Hidmane,
Xatir xwest ji dê û bavane,
Go, 'Dao, bavo, çûn bi destê mine, hatin bi destê Xudane.'

8. They say, Derwêsh rose to his feet,
He put on his armour and mounted on Hidman,
Said goodbye to his mother and father,
He said, 'Mother, father, I am leaving by my own will, I will return by God's will.'

9. Bi Dewrêş ṛa siwar bû ʿElî û Bozan, Seʿdûnê birane,
Ev herçar derketin, berê xo dane dîwana Zor Temer Paşayê Milane.
Giregir fêriz û pelewanê Kîka û Mila di dîwana Zor Temer Paşa da li hev civiyane.
Dibê, Dewrêş nêzîk bû devê derê dîwana wane,
Hidman çev bi miḥîna ket, bû ḥîşîna Hidmane,
Alê dîwanê se kirin ḥîşîna Hidmane,

Gotin, 'Ev Dewrêşê ʿEvdî hate dîwana girane'.
Dewrêş û ʿElî û Bozan û Seʿdûnê bira peya bûn ji hespane,
Kişiyane dîwana girane,
Tev ji ber Dewrêş ṛa ṛabûn û sekinîn ji piyane.

9. ʿElî and Bozan, and Seʿdûn his brother rode with Derwêsh,
All four rode out and made for the guest-hall of Zor Temer Pasha of the Milan.
The big, the brave and the champions of the Kîkan and Milan were gathered in the guest-hall of Zor Temer Pasha.
They say, Derwêsh drew near to the door of their guest-hall,
Hidman's eye fell on a mare, there was a loud neigh from Hidman,
The people in the guest-hall heard the neighing of Hidman,
They said, 'This is Derwêshê ʿEvdî who has come to the great guest-hall.'
Dewrêş and ʿElî and Bozan and Seʿdûn his brother got down from their horses,
Drew near to the great guest-hall,
Everyone got up from respect for Derwêsh and stayed on their feet.

Dewrêş ṛûniştit li ser doşeka ḥerba girane,	Derwêsh sat down on the cushion of great battles,[23]
Li teniṣta wî ṛûniştit ʿElî û Bozan û Seʿdûnê birane.	By his side sat ʿElî and Bozan and Seʿdûn his brother.
ʿEdûlê se kir, ko Dewrêş hate dîwana girane,	ʿEdûlê saw that Derwêsh had come into the great hall,
Fîncana qawê danî ser destane,	She took a cup of coffee in her hand,
Anî geṛand li nava fêriz û pelewanê Kîkan û Milane,	She carried it around among the brave and the champions of the Kîkan and Milan,
Çû sekinî li ber Dewrêş, vî fêriz û pelewanê hane,	She came up to Derwêsh, this brave man, this champion, and stopped,
Dewrêş ṛabû piya, fîncana qawê hilanî ser destane,	Derwêsh rose to his feet, took up the cup of coffee in his hands,
Qawe danî ser dev û lêvane,	Held the cup to his mouth, his lips,
Di nava odêda devê xo xiste ḥinarê rûyê ʿEdûlê û ṛamûsane.	In the middle of the room, he put his mouth to ʿEdûlê's cheek, lovely as a pomegranate, and kissed her.
10. Dewrêş ṛabû derket ji oda girane,	10. Dewrêş got up, left the great hall,
Pêṛa ṛabûn ʿElî û Bozane û Seʿdûnê birane,	After him ʿElî, Bozan and Seʿdûn his brother arose,
Derketin, siwar bûn li hespane,	Went out, got up on their horses,
Şûr û mertalê wan li milê wane,	Their swords and shields at their shoulders,
Bînana Ezrahîl û Cebrahîl, ko dageṛin ji ezmane.	Like ʿEzraʾîl and Jibraʾîl, who rule from the sky.
Zor Temer Paşa gazî kir, 'Ûsib efendî, tu jî heṛe bigihîje wane.'	Zor Temer Pasha called, 'Yusif Effendi, you go too and catch up with them.'
Gazî kir li ʿElî û li Silêmane,	He called to ʿElî and to Silêman,
Ew jî di fêriz û pelewanê navgirane,	They too were among the famous ones, the brave and the champions,
Go, 'Hûn herdû jî heṛin bigihîjine wane.'	He said, 'You two go as well and catch up with them.'
Paşî bavê Dewrêş û diya ʿElî û Bozane	Afterwards the father of Derwêsh and the mother of ʿElî and Bozan
Hatine mala Zor Temer Paşayê Milane,	Came to the house of Zor Temer Pasha of the Milan
Xo avîtine ser dest û piyê 'Edûla Zor Temer Paşayê Milane.	They flung themselves at the hands and feet of ʿEdûlê, child of Zor Temer Pasha of the Milan.
Go, 'Em ketine bextê te û Xudane,	They said, 'We have come to appeal to your conscience and to God,
Tu heṛî pêşiya Dewrêş, destê xo bavêjî ḥevsarê Hidmane,	You go after Derwêsh, put your hand on the bridle of Hidman,
Tu bêjî, "Diya te û bavê te extiyarin, kesek xweyî û xudanê we nemane,	You tell him, "Your mother and your father are old, they have no-one left of their own to take care of them,

23 Jelîl's note: whoever sits in this place must take the coffee-cup from ʿEdûlê and go to war.

Tu bidî Seʿdûn û ‘Eliyê birayê Bozane,
Bavê te guneye, mala we bêxweyî û bêxudane."'

You give back Seʿdûn and ‘Elî the brother of Bozan,
Your father is wretched, your house is without owner and master."'

11. ‘Edûlê çû pêşiya Dewrêş, destê xo avîte ḥevsarê Hidmane,
Go, ‘Dewrêş, ez ketime bextê te û Xudane,
Mala we mişemire, bêxweyî maye,
Tu bidi ‘Elîyê birayê Bozane û Seʿdûnê birane.'
Dewrêş go, "Edûlê, bese ji van te‘n û niçane,
Ez nadim ‘Elî û Seʿdûnê birane,
Ê gelek kûçikê wa Kîka û Mila hene,
Wê kenê xwe mi bikin û wê bidin hilobiyane.'

11. ‘Edûlê went to Derwêsh, laid her hand on the bridle of Hidman,
She said, ‘Derwêsh, I have come to appeal to your conscience and to God,
Your house is desolate, it is without a master,
You give back ‘Elî the brother of Bozan and Seʿdûn your brother'.
Dewrêş said, "Edûlê, enough of this reproach and hissing,
I won't give ‘Elî and Seʿdûn my brother,
There are many dogs among those Kîkan and Milan,
They will smile at me and give me their contempt.'

12. Dibê Dewrêş serê xwe ji ‘Edûlêṛa nimiz kir,
‘Edûlê serê jêṛa bilind kir,
Dewrêş devê xwe xiste ḥinarê ṛûyane,
Dibê nava Kîka û Mila da bû çîṛe çîṛe ṛamûsane.

12. They say, Derwêsh bent down his head towards ‘Edûle,
‘Edûlê lifted her head up towards him,
Derwêsh put his mouth to her lips as lovely as pomegranates,
They say, amongst the Kîkan and Milan there was the sound of kisses.

13. Dewrêş berda serê Hidmane,
Û berê xwe da serê ṛê û dirbane.
Dewrêş gazî kir, ‘Gelî birano, gelî hevalno,
Ji berêda kuştin ṛiya mêrane,
Meriv têye kuştin, namûsa xo nade destê neyarane,
Dilqewî bin, bi emrê Xudane.'
Û bi hevra meşiyane.

13. Derwêsh gave Hidman his head,
And turned towards the road,
Derwêsh called, ‘My brothers, my comrades,
Killing has long since been the way of men.
When a person is killed he gives none of his honour to his enemies,
Be stout-hearted, by God's will.'
And together they rode on.

14. Dibê, ji efendimê xwe ṛa bêjim:
Beṛî beṛîstan, çolî çolîstan,
Havîn çû, ma zivistan,
Serê Dewrêşê ‘Evdî û her pênc hevalê wî hêja têkeve şeṛ û qewxê giran.
Dewrêşê ‘Evdî, ‘Elî û Bozan û Seʿdûnê bira,
‘Elî û Silêman û Ûsib katibê wan, peya bûn ji hespan,

14. Let me say about this gentleman of mine:
The dry desert, the tilled fields,
Summer went, and winter settled,
Dewrêşê ‘Evdî and all five of his dear friends came to war, to terrible screaming,
Dewrêşê ‘Evdî, ‘Elî and Bozan and Seʿdûn his brother,
‘Elî and Silêman and Yusif their scribe, dismounted from their horses,

Û li ser kaniyê ji xwe ṛa ṛûniştin,	And sat down together by a stream,
Xarina xwe xarin, hespê xwe çêrandin,	They ate their food and pastured their horses,
Dewrêş gazî kir, 'Gelî hevala,	Derwêsh called, 'My comrades,
Ûn li vir bin, ezê heṛim binhêṛim û temaşê kim,	You stay here, I will go to see and spy out,
Çika ev koma van neyara li kuê derêne, ṛaste anî derewe.'	Where these tents of our enemies are, whether it is true or false.'
15. Dibê, heval man, Dewrêşê 'Evdî hespê xwe siwar bû û meşiya,	15. They say, the comrades stayed, and Dewrêşê 'Evdî sat on his horse and walked away,
Çar seḥeta ew ṛê çûye,	He made his way for four hours,
Bala xwe dayê, ko ḥezar kon vegirtiye.	And then saw a thousand pitched tents.
Çar ḥeb qîz hatine sergîna, Dewrêş ji wan pirsiye,	Four girls were coming to dry dung, Derwêsh questioned them,
Go, 'Ev konê han konê kiye?'	Saying 'Whose tents are these?'
Qîzika lê nihêrt û tirsiyan,	The girls looked and him and were afraid,
Gotin, 'Tu neyarî? Îşê te li vir çiye?'	They said, 'Are you an enemy? What is your business here?'
Go, 'Ez ne neyarim, du devê min hinda bûne,	He said, 'I am not an enemy, two camels of mine are lost,
Gelo we devê min nedîtiye?'	Have you by some chance seen my camels?'
Herçar keçika got, kûṛ, û giriya,	All four maidens wept bitterly
Û Dewrêş pey wan çûye.	And Derwêsh went after them.
Ev herçar kecik çûn ketine konê şêxê wan û qîrîn li malê kiriye,	These four maidens rushed to the tent of their sheykh and screamed out inside the house,
Go, 'Siwarekî vaye li pey me hatiye.'	They said, 'A horseman is here, he has followed us.'
Dewrêş hat devê derê kon sekinî,	Derwêsh came to the opening of the tent and stopped,
Kalekî extiyar di bin konda bû,	An old man was inside the tent,
Ev kalê han ṛabû û çû pêşiyê.	This old man rose and came forward.
Dewrêş go, 'Apo, du devê min hinda bûne, we ne diye?'	Derwêsh said, 'Uncle, two camels of mine are lost, have you seen them?
Gava kal Dewrêş nihêrtiye,	When the old man looked at Derwêsh,
Dewrêş nas nekiriye,	He did not know Derwêsh,
Bes Hidman nas kiriye,	He only knew Hidman,
Ewî û bavê Dewrêş bi hev ṛa hevaltî kiriye,	He and Derwêsh's father had become comrades,
Miḥîna 'Evdê hêja li bîra wiye,	He could still remember 'Evdî's splendid mare,
Zane, ko Hidman jî ji wî ṭerziye.	He knew that Hidman too was from that stock.[24]

24 cf. Ps. *ṭarz*, 'form'.

Kal go, 'Xorto, tu ne Dewrêşê 'Evdiyî? Tu ji mi ṛa bêje bi ṛastiye, Tu derewa dikî, tu ne li deva digeṛî,	The old man said, 'Lad, are you not Derwêshê 'Evdî? You tell me truly, You are lying, you are not looking for camels,
Tucar mi te nedîtiye, Tu gelekî bi xezebî, te cilê hesin xwe kiriye, Te tasa hesin ser serê xwe daniye,	Never have I seen you, You are full of anger, you have clad yourself in clothes of iron, You have put an iron helmet on your head,
Û te şûr û mertalê xwe girêdaye, Ji apê xweṛa bêje, binhêṛe, îşê te çiye?'	And girded yourself with sword and shield, Come, tell your uncle, what are you here for?'
Dewrêş go, 'Apo, ezê ji teṛa bêjim bi ṛastiye,	Derwêsh said, 'Uncle, I will tell you truly,
Di nava me û Gêsa da neyartiye, Ez hatime, ko komê bibînim, koma wan li kuê derêye.' Go, 'Lawo, tu xortekî gelekî ḥeyfî,	Between us and the Gêsan is hatred, I have come to see their camp, to see where their tents are'. He said, 'Lad, you are a vengeful young man,
Min û bavê te, me bi ḥev ṛa hevaltî kiriye, Bila min bike, tu mekeve vî şeṛiye,	I and your father, we became comrades together, Take my advice, do not involve yourself in this war,
Em Misilmanin û tu Êzdiye, Û heq û ḥesabê te li ṛiḥê te çiye?	We are Muslims and you are Yezidi, And what use is your justice, your old scores, to your soul?
Ji me geṛe, di nava me û mala Zor Temer Paşa da neyartiye.' Dewrêş go, 'Apo, erê, biṛa ez Êzdîme,	Turn away from us, the hatred is between us and the house of Zor Temer Pasha'. Derwêsh said, 'Uncle, yes, indeed I am Yezidi,
Bes ez eşîra Zor Temer Paşayê milîme!	But I am of the tribe of Zor Temer Pasha of the Milan!
Min nan û avê wî zeḥf xariye.'	I have eaten and drunk with him so many times.'
Evî kalî gote Dewrês, go, 'Lawo, înca ezê te ṛa bêjim bi ṛastiye, Ḥezar siwar tevî Ḥafirê Gêsî, 'Ecîl Birahîm li girê Leylanê, li gola Xatûniyê sekiniye, Lawo, ez ketime bextê te Xudê da, tu xo bernedî vî agiriye.' Dewrêş go, 'Apo, bi Xudê, ez hatime ji bona vî agiriye.'	This old man spoke to Derwêsh and said, 'Lad, this time I will tell you truly, One thousand warriors with Hafir Gêsî and 'Ajîl Brahîm are camped on the hill of Leylan, at the lake of Khatûnî, Lad, I am falling on your mercy, by God, do not lose yourself in this fire'. Derwêsh said, 'Uncle, by God, I have come for this fire.'
16. Dewrêş xatir ji kalê xast û vegeriya, Hate ser kaniyê, ba hevala ṛûniştiye,	16. Derwêsh said goodbye to the old man and returned, He came to the spring and sat down with his comrades,

Go, 'Gelî hevala, ez çûm, mi seh kiriye,
Karê xwe bikin, em ṛabin, weke şêra,
bi hevṛa heṛine vî şeṛiye.'

17. Bi hevṛa ṛabûn û li hespa siwar bûn,
Û li ser ṛiya girê Leylaniyê û gola Xatûniyê kar bûn,
Û bi nêzîk bûn, û bi hev ḥesiya bûn,

Şirîḥet û qanîn li nava wan bû,
'Ecîl Birahîm şêxê wan bû,
Ḥafirê Gêsî beyreqa şeṛ hilda bû,

Ṣeḥet yek qirarê wan bû,
Ṣehet yek temam bû.
Dewrêş û Se'dûnê bira,
Û 'Elî û Bozan û 'Elî û Silêman,
Ûsiv katibê wan, şûr ji kalan kişandin, ketine nav neyara,
Bû çingîna şûra, bû terqînê mertala, bû ḥişînê hespa û li hev dabû,

Mêr têne kuştin bi seda û xûn ṛijiya bû,
Ji neyara dusid hate kuştin, ji Zor Temer Paşa kuştî 'Elî û Silêman bû.

Şeṛ sekinî, bîna xwe berda bû,

Ṛabûne ser xwe, dîsa li hev dabû,
Bû çingînê şûra, bû ḥîşînê hespa, bû terqînê mertala, dê dev ji ewledê xwe berda bû,
Hingî ko şeṛ giran bû.
Ji ḥeyşsid siwarî hate kuştin çarsid, çarsid mabû.
Bi van siwara ṛa hate kuştin Se'dûnê bira bû.
Dewrêş û 'Elî û Bozan mabû,
Ûsiv, başkatibê wan, sekinî bû li dera habû,
Ûsiv dinhêre, mêraniya Dewrêş çawa bû,
Dinivîsîne, û li ber çevê wi xuya bû,
Careke dinê şeṛ giran bû,
Dewrêş û 'Elî û Bozan ketine nava van her çarsid siwarê habû.

He said, 'Dear friends, I went, I found out, let us do our work, let us get up, like lions let us go to this battle'.

17. They arose together and mounted on their horses,
And made off down the road to the hill of Leylan and the lake of Khatûnî,
And when they were near, and they perceived them together,
Shari'a and law ruled among them,
'Ajîl Brahîm was their sheykh,
Ḥafir Gêsî was holding aloft their standard of war,
At one o'clock they made their decision,
At one o'clock it happened.
Derwêsh and Se'dûn his brother,
And 'Elî and Bozan and 'Elî and Silêman,
Yusif, their scribe, drew their swords from their scabbards, and fell upon the enemy,
There was the clashing of swords, the ringing of shields, the neighing of horses, and they came together,
Men were killed in their hundreds and blood flowed,
Of the enemy, two hundred were killed, of Zor Temer Pasha's men 'Elî and Silêman were killed.
The battle stopped, the fighters had lost their breath,
They retreated, and again rushed together,
There was the clashing of swords, the neighing of horses, the ringing of shields, mothers lost their children,
The battle was so great at that time.
Of eight hundred warriors, four hundred had been killed, four hundred remained.
With these warriors Se'dûn, Derwêsh's brother was killed.
Derwêsh and 'Elî and Bozan remained,
Yusif, their chief scribe, had stopped and was at that place,
Yusif could see how valiant Derwêsh was,
He wrote, and before his eyes it was clear,
One more time the battle was heavy,
Derwêsh and 'Elî and Bozan fell upon those four hundred warriors.

18. Wey lo, wey lo, wey lo, wey lo,
Dibê, Derwêş bînaya melkemotê kulê,
Bînaya Ezrahîl û Cebrahîl tirs û hêbet xiste nava xelqê,
Bû çingînê şûra, bû ḥîşînê hespa, bû terqînê mertala, û ji sibê ḥeta êvarê li hev dabû,
Dewrêş sêsid siwar kuştin, sed siwar ji wan mabû,
'Ecîl Birahîm, Ḥafirê Gêsî hêja saẍ bûn.
Bi van siwara ṛa hate kuştin û 'Elî û Bozan bûn.

18. Oh, alas,
They say, Derwêsh was like an angel of death, of suffering,
Like 'Ezra'il and Jibra'îl he drove fear and awe among the people,
There was the clashing of swords, the neighing of horses, the ringing of shields, and from morning till night they fought each other,
Derwêsh killed three hundred warriors, one hundred of them remained,
'Ajîl Brahîm, and Hafir Gêsî were still unharmed,
With these warriors 'Elî and Bozan were also killed.

19. Liyane, liyane, liyane, liyane,
Şeṛê Dewrêş şeṛekî girane,
Dewrêş siwar bû li Hidmane,
Du mûyê melkemota nav çevane,
Şûr kişand ji kalane,
Ḥicûm da Hafirê Gêsî û 'Ecîl Birahîm, şêxê wane.
Bû çingînê şûra, bû ḥîşînê hespa, bû terqînê mertala,
Dewrêş mêra dikuje, wan ser piştê hespa berdane,
Pêncî ji wan kuşt, pêncî û Ḥafirê Gêsî û 'Ecîl Birahîm mane,
Divê, serê Dewrêşê 'Evdî, lawkê êzdî, hêja kete şeṛ û deqê girane,
Lingê Hidman kete qulê cird û mişkane,
Lingê Hidman şkestin ji herdû çokane,
Dewrêş qulibî, kete ser piştane,
Ḥafirê Gêsî û 'Ecîl Birahîm, şêxê wane,
Û vî pêncî siwarê han ajotine ser laşê Dewrêşê 'Evdî, siwarê Hidmane,
Ji hespa peya bûn, wî dane ber şûrane.

19. Longing, longing,
The battle of Derwêsh was a great battle,
Derwêsh was riding on Hidman,
Two hairs of the angel of death between his eyes,
He drew his sword from its scabbard,
Attacked Hafirê Gêsî and 'Ajîl Birahîm, their sheykh.
There was the clashing of swords, the neighing of horses, the ringing of shields,
Derwêsh killed the warriors, he knocked them from their horses,
He killed fifty of them, fifty and Ḥafirê Gêsî and 'Ajîl Brahîm remained,
They say, Dewrêshê 'Evdî, the Yezidi lad, again rushed into battle and into the heaviest fighting,
Hidman's leg fell into a rat or mouse hole,
Hidman's legs broke at both knees,
Derwêsh toppled, fell on his back,
Ḥafir Gêsî and 'Ajîl Birahim, their sheykh,
and these fifty warriors of theirs fell upon the body of Dewrêşê 'Evdî, rider of Hidman,
They leaped down from their horses and put him to the sword.

20. Wey lo, wey lo, wey lo, wey lo,
Ûsiv başkatib hate dîwana Zor Temer Paşayê Milane,

20. Alas, alas, alas, alas,
Yusif the chief scribe came to the hall of Zor Temer Pasha of the Milan,

Go, 'A ji te ṛa mêraniya Dewrêş ber çevê we xuyane.'

He said, 'Here you are, the heroism of Derwêsh is clear before your eyes'.

21. 'Edûlê sekinî û kuştina Dewrêş bihîst, û bi ser ḥinarê ṛûyê xweva giriya. Xelqê go, 'Heqê wê heye bigrî'. Înca 'Edûlê kilam avîte ser Dewrêşê 'Evdî.

21. Edûlê stopped and heard of the killing of Derwêsh and wept, her cheeks red as pomegranates. The people said, 'She is right to weep for him'. 'Edûlê raised a song about Dewrêşê 'Evdî.

22. 'Edûlê dibê, 'Herê delalo, herê delalo, lo, lo, lo delêl,
Siwarê mala bavê min ji mal siwar bûn, germa vê havînê,

22. 'Edûlê said, 'My dearest, alas, oh, my beloved,
The warriors of my father's house rode out from home, in the heat of this summer,

Pêşiya selefê siwara kete çiyayê 'Evdil 'Ezîzê,
Nîvê siwara ma li girê Leylaniyê, gola Xatûniyê,
Paşiya siwara ma li qiraçê Mêrdînê,

The first warriors in the group went to the mountain of 'Evdil 'Ezîz,
The middle of the group was at the hill of Leylan, the lake of Khatûniyê,
The last warriors remained at the plain of Mardin,

Gelî Kîkan û gelî Milano,
Heçî kesê, ko ciwaba Dewrêşê 'Evdî, siwarê Hidman, lawkê êzîdî, delalê malê, xêmê binê beṛiyê, ji nava ḥezar û pênsid siwarê Gêsa ji miṛa bîne,

Dear people of the Kîkan and Milan,
Whoever brings me news of Derwêshê 'Evdî, rider of Hidman, the Yezidi lad, beloved of our home, whose tent is in the desert, from among the one thousand five hundred warriors of the Gêsan,

Ezê bidimê çar aşê bavê min li ber ava Misêrbînê,
Hege bi herçar aşa qayîl nebe, ezê bidimê de ḥeb caniyê bavê min hene, kiḥêlin, 'eslîne, ezê bidim bi ṛiḥînê,

I will give him four of my father's mills on the banks of the water of Nusaybin,
And if he is not satisfied with all four mills, I will give him ten of my father's colts, thoroughbreds, of pure stock, I will give them as insurance,

Çar qesr û qonaxê bavê min hene, ezê bidimê li bajarê Misêrbînê,
Eger herçar qesr û qonaxa qayîl nebe, ezê di ser da bidimê ḥezar û pênsid zêṛê osmanlî ji xizînê.'

My father has four fortresses and mansions in Nusaybin town, I will give them,
If he is not satisfied with all four fortresses and mansions, I will give him in addition one thousand five hundred Osmanli gold pieces from the treasury.'

23. 'De bajo, de bajo, ṛêdûro, de bajo,
Hesp betiliyo, de bajo,
Kîskê te qulo, titûna te ṛijiyao, de bajo,
'Eba ser milê te sê tixto,
Li te bû belao, de bajo,

23. 'Drive on, drive on, you whose road is long, drive on,
You whose horse is weary, drive on,
You whose pouch is empty, whose tobacco has poured away, drive on,
You whose back is clad in a robe of three layers,
You whom calamity has befallen, drive on,

Malê me wane, serê çît û berçîtê Zor Temer Paşayê milî ji teva xuyane,

There are our houses, you can see the kerchiefs and turbans of Zor Temer Pasha of the Milan among them,

Sîng û berê min ji teṛa mêrg û çîmane.'

My breasts are pasture and meadow for you.'

24. 'Heṛê-lo, delal, heṛê-lo, delal, heṛê-lo, delal,
Beṛiya Ḥamûdê beṛiyake ṛaste, çîqa li mi dûze,
Pozê kela Mêrdînê li serda xare û serda xûze,
'Edûlê gazî dike, 'Gelî Kîkano, gelî Milano, ḥeçî kesê ciwabekî xêrê ji alê delalê malê, Dewrêşê 'Evdî, lawkê êzîdî ji xêmê binê beṛiyê, ji nava ḥezar û pênsid siwarê Gêsa ji miṛa bîne, ezê bidimê malê diniyayê, ḥezar û pênsid zêṛê di altûze.

24. 'Alas, my beloved, alas, my beloved,
The desert of Ḥamûd is a true desert, how measureless it is to me,
The top of the fortress of Mardin is bent and hunchbacked,'
'Edûlê called, 'People of the Kîkan, people of the Milan, whoever brings good news from the dear one of my house, Derwêshê 'Evdî, the Yezidi lad, from the tent in the desert, from among a thousand five hundred Gêsan warriors, I will give him worldly goods, one thousand five hundred pieces of pure gold,

Herê lo, delal, li min avîtiye stêrka sibê, stêra ṛecilxêre.

Alas my dear one, the morning star, the star of daybreak, has been taken from me.

Delêlî malê, Dewrêşê 'Evdî, lawkê êzîdî, siware li Hidmanî nêre,

The darling of the house, Dewrêşê 'Evdî, the Yezidi lad, rider of Hidman the stallion,

Hate devê derê Zor Temir Paşayê Milî, min lingê xwe lêda li şim û mesê zêṛe,

He came to the door of Zor Temer Pasha of the Milan, I struck my leg against candles and golden tables,

Bi meşa kevokî, hêdi-hêdî ez çûme pêşiyê, min destê xwe avîte li ḥevsare Hidmanê nêre,
Mi go, lo, lo, lo, delêl, ez nizanim, te ne şeṛe û te ne xêre,
Delêl xeyîdî, bi mi ṛa xeber nade bi sere zimêne,
Mi go, lo, lo, lo, delêl, ez te nadim bi Ḥemmê,
bi Kinê, bi herdu fêriz û pêlewana, ko li xêmê binê beṛiyê ji kuştinê, ji malê 'alemê nabin têre,

With little bird's steps, I slowly went forward, put my hand on the bridle of Hidman the stallion,
I said, alas, alas, alas, my dear one, I don't know, you have neither evil left nor good,
The beloved one was angry, he did not reply with his tongue,
I said, 'Oh, my dear, I wouldn't give you up for Ḥemmê,
for Kinê, for those two brave men and champions, that even in the tent in the desert are not sated from killing, from the wealth of the world.

Ez te nadim bi kuṛê Birahîm Paşa ji mala zengo zêṛe,
Ez te nadim bi kuṛê Bedirxan Begê, mîrê Bota ji maleke del û têre.'

I wouldn't give you for the son of Brahîm Pasha whose house is golden with wealth,
I wouldn't give you up for the son of Bedirkhan Beg, the Emir of Botan, from a house brave and full [of riches].'

25. 'Lo, lo, lo, lo, lo, delêl,
Ez te nadim bi sultanê dînê Êzîdxanê,

Ku li çiyayê Şengalê îsal ḥezar û pênsid salê wan qediyayê, quruşekî wan negihîştiye destê dewletê, neketiye kassa xundkêre.

Delêl xeyîdiye, bi miṛa xeber nade serê zimêne,
Mi go, lo, lo, lo, delêl, te goştê min ḥeland, teyê hestiyê min ṛizand, bala xwe bidê tilî pêçiyê minî zerî zeytûnî, bînana mom û şima diḥelin, bi enîşka milê miva bû bizmêre.'

25. 'Alas, alas, my beloved,
I would not give you for the son of the Sultan of the Yezidis,
Who on Mount Sinjar this year one thousand five hundred years have passed, but not a penny of theirs has reached the hand of the Ottoman sultan, nor fallen into the coffers of the Shah.
My dear one was angry, he did not reply to me with his tongue,
I said, alas, my dear, you have dissolved my flesh, you have withered me to the bone, look, my fingers and toes, olive-yellow, are dissolving like wax or candles, nails pierce my elbow and shoulder.'

26. 'Lo, lo, delêl, ji bîna tilî pêciyê min teyra serê xwe deraniye ji hêlînê, me ṛa serê xwe deraniye ji qulê dîwêre,

Ezê ṛabim, xilxalê lingê xwe bişkênim, ji Hidman ṛa bikime cotekî nêle,

Ezê xizêma pozê xwe derxim, jê ṛa bikim hûr bizmêre,
Ezê keziyê xwe bibiṛim, ji Hidman ṛa bikim gulik û ṛîşî û du hevsêre,

Ji îro peyda, wê berê te têkeve binê beṛiyê, nava ḥezar û pênsid siwarê Gêsa, xelqê bibêje, "Ev siwarê hanê çiqa bi ḥizne, çîqa bi delale û çi bi cemêle".'

26. 'Alas, alas, my dear, from the smell of my fingers and toes the birds have put their heads out of the nest, snakes have put their heads out from the hole in the wall,
I will get up, I will break the anklet on my leg, I will make for Hidman a new harness,
I will pull the jewel from my nose, I will make from it fine nails,
I will cut my braid, I will make for Hidman a saddle-cloth and tassels and two bridles,
From today onward, when you go to the desert, among one thousand five hundred Gêsa warriors, the people will say, "That warrior, how good he is, how beloved, how beautiful".'

27. Heṛê lo, delal, heṛê lo, delal, heṛê lo, delal,
De bajo, ṛêdûro, de bajo,
Ji hevala mao, de bajo,

Kîskê te qulo, titûna te ṛijiyao, de bajo.

'Ebakê te sê tixto,
Li ser milê te bû belao, de bajo,
Malê me wane, serê çît û bercîtê konê Zor Temer Paşa ji teva xuyane,

Derdê min derdekî girane.'

27. Alas, my beloved one,
Drive on, you whose road is long, drive on,
You who have stayed back from your comrades, drive on,
You whose pouch is empty, whose tobacco is poured out, drive on,
You whose cloak has three layers,
You whom calamity has befallen, drive on,
There are our houses, you can see the kerchiefs and the turbans of the the tents of Zor Temer Pasha among them,
My pain is a grievous pain.'

'Edûlê sekinî kêrik li zikê xwe da ji boy xatirê Dewrêşê lawkê êzîdî, siwarê Hidmane.

'Edûlê stopped, stabbed a knife into her belly for the sake of Derwêsh the Yezidi lad, rider of Hidman.

Derwêshê 'Evdî: 'Egîtê Têjir (I) (Jelîl 1978 I: 295–8)

1. Mîro go, 'Kuro, cot qewaz, ṛabin pêye,
Gazî Dewrêşê 'Evdî kin, bira bê yalê dîwanxanêye!'

1. Mîr said 'Boy, you two bodyguards, get to your feet,
Call Derwêshê 'Evdî, let him come to the side of the guest-hall!'

2. Wexta Dewrêş hate yalê dîwanêye,
Mîr go, 'Dewrêşo lawo, min ṛa bêje rastiyêye,
Çika ṛojê oẍirmê giran, ṛeqe ṛeqe darê darṛima, firxînê me'negiya, nalînê şêr û 'erfûta, ḥawe ḥawê lawê kurmanca, mêr beranberî çend mêra dertêye?'

2. When Derwêsh came to the side of the guest-hall,
Mîr said, 'Derwêsh lad, tell me the truth,
On the day of heavy destiny, with the crashing of wood on wood, the waggons and horses, the wailing of lionhearts and heroes, the shouting of young Kurmanji lads, how many men can a man face?

3. Dewrêş go, 'Serê mîrê xwe kim, bi ṛastiyêye,
Ṛojê oẍirmê giran, wexta ṛeqe ṛeqe darê darṛîma, firxînê me'negiya, nalînê şêr û 'erfûta, ḥawe ḥawê lawê kurmanca, çiqas merî çê be ancax mêr beranberî mêr dertêye'.'

3. Derwêsh said, 'I swear on the head of my king, truly,
On the day of heavy destiny, with the crashing of wood on wood, the waggons and horses, the wailing of lionhearts and heroes, the shouting of young Kurmanji lads, how brave a man would be if he were to come out to face another man.'

4. Mîr got, 'Kuṛo, cot qewaz, ṛabin pêye!
Nigê Dewrêş bavne qeydêye!
Stiyê wî bikine lelêye!
Sivê van çaxa ezê berê Dewrêş bidime ḥevsêye!'

4. Mîr said, 'Boy, you two bodyguards, get to your feet!
Bind the foot of Derwêshê 'Evdî with fetters!
Put his neck in the stocks!
In the morning I will put him into prison!'

5. 'Edla qîz hate biniya dîwanêye,
Lênihêṛî, nigê Dewrêş qeydêye,
Stiyê Dewrêş lelêye,
Mîrê sibê wî bişîne ḥevsêye.

5. The girl 'Edûlê came into the guest-hall,
She saw it all, Derwêsh's foot in the fetters,
His neck in the stocks,
That in the morning the Mîr would put him in prison.

'Edlê go, 'Mîr xwedê mala te xirab ke, te çima nigê vî şêrî avîtiye qeydê, stiyê wî kiriye lelêye?

'Edûlê said, 'Mîr, may God ruin your house, why have you put this lion's foot in fetters, and his neck in the stocks?

Texmîna min, evî şêrî te ṛa fire kiriye sînorê der û dinêye.'

My guess is that this lion has broadened the borders of the world for you.'

6. Mîr go, 'Kuṛo, ewê forqê bivin yalê malê,
Nigê Dewrêş derxin ji qeydê,
Stiyê wî derxin ji lelê, bira heṛe malê,
Emê sivê heṛine beṛiya Sucetê, serê baẍê Misrê,
Kêfê, eşqê, nêçîrê'.

6. Mîr said, 'Boy, take this group to the side of the house,
Take Derwêsh's foot from the fetters,
Take his neck from the stocks, let him come to the house,
In the morning we will go to the wilderness of Sujet, by the Egyptian garden,
For joy, for friendship, for hunting.'

7. Siva bû, sara sivêye,
Cot qewaz ṛabûne ser kulekêye,
Gotin, 'Dewrêş lawo, mîr te dixaze kêfê, eşqê, nêçîrêye.'

7. It was morning, the cool of morning,
The two servants went to the suffering one,
They said, 'Derwêsh lad, the Mîr wants you for joy, for friendship, for hunting.'

8. Dewrêş ṛabû pêye,
'Etman kişand ji ṭewlêye,
Lê kir zînê dewêye,
Cot tejî avîte merezêye,
Go, 'Yala, ya, Xwedêye'.

8. Derwêsh rose to his feet,
Drew 'Etman from his stall,
Put a saddle on his back,
Loosed two greyhounds into the fields,
Cried, 'Yallah! God is great'.

9. Ewî meriva ajotin serê baẍê Misrêye.
Mîr û Dewrêşva ajotin serê baẍê Misrê, ser kaniya Sucetêye,
Mîr go, 'Dewrêş lawo, dilê mîrê te vêsbê kivavek goştê kara xezalê dibêye'.
Dewrêş go, 'Mîro, Xwedê mala te xirav ke, me'niya te, me'niya duh, sibêye,
Vî qîṛê xiṛî xalî kivava goştê kara xezalê te ṛa ku bêye?'
Xeber devê Dewrêşê 'Evdî, lawkê êzdîda, lênihêṛî, komek karê xezala pevketine, jêla têne,
Dewrêş banzda ser pişta 'Etmêye,
Nav dest û piyê 'Etmêda, bû nalîna kara xezalêye.
Dewrêş gopal avîtê, xezal da orta zînê 'Etmêye,
Anî serê kaniyêye,
Go, 'Mîro, han teṛa him şîve, him teştêye.'

9. Those people drove to the Egyptian garden.
Mîr and Derwêsh drove to the Egyptian garden, by the stream of Sujet,
Mîr said 'Derwêsh lad, the heart of your Mîr this morning wants a steak of the meat of a young gazelle'.
Derwêsh said, 'Mîr, may God ruin your house, when you speak of yesterday, you mean tomorrow,
What is the use of this querulous shouting about the meat of a young gazelle?'
The word was in the mouth of Derwêshê 'Evdî, the Yezidi lad, he saw a herd of young gazelles had arrived, and were coming up above,
Derwêsh sprang up on the back of 'Etman,
Between the hoofs of 'Etman, was the crying of a young gazelle.
Derwêsh threw aside his staff, lifted the gazelle into 'Etman's saddle,
Carried it to the bank of the stream,
Said, 'Mîr, this is both dinner and breakfast for you.'

Mîr xaribû kivavek goştê kara xezalêye,
Qapût kişande ser xwe, ser kaniyê kete xewnê û xewêye.

The Mîr ate a steak of the meat of the young gazelle,
Drew his cloak over himself, and fell into sleep and dreams by the stream.

10. Wextekê Dewrêş dîna xwe dide, jêrê, beṛiyêye,
Lênihêṛî, ḥesavê qirş û qalê 'erdê, hesavê mijê ḥezar ḥevsid mêrê Ḥesenayê Cerdê, wê pev ketine, jêla têne,
Dewrêş go, 'Mîro, ṛave bibîne 'ecebê'.

10. At one moment Derwêsh was looking down at the desert,
He looked and saw all sorts of branches and specks of earth, all sorts of cloud made by seventeen hundred men of the Ḥesenê Jerdan, all together, coming up,
Derwêsh said, 'Mîr, wake up and see a strange sight'.

11. Mîr go, 'Dewrêş lawo, bike bilezîne,
Mîrê xwe ji van dera biṛevîne,
Îzna xwedê, sivê vî çaxî, ezê dîwana gişka 'erdekî, ser textê xwe bivînim.'

11. Mîr said, 'Derwêsh lad, make haste,
Take your Mîr away from this place,
If God wills it, this time tomorrow, I will sit on my throne and see that my guest-hall is my whole land.'

12. Dewrêş go, 'Mîro, tu mîrtiyê te nakeve, ez heme Dewrêşe dînim,
Ezê kefenê xwe li ser pişta 'Etmayê bişidînim,
Yan ezê serê ḥezar ḥevsid mêrî bifirînim,
Yan ezê guliyê qîz û bûkê Kîkan û Mila darekê derê konê ṛeş bixemilînim'.

12. Derwêsh said, 'Mîr, do not lose your royal dignity, I am still mad Derwêsh,
I will pack my own shroud on the back of 'Etman,
Either I will vanquish seventeen hundred men,
Or I will decorate the tree by your black tent with the braids of the daughters and brides of the Kîkan and Milan.'[25]

13. Ew Dewrêşe, Dewrêşê dîne,
Kefenê xwe li ser pişta 'Etmê dişidîne,

Zengiyê li 'Etmê dixiṛîne,
Li siyarê cerdê diqîṛîne,
Çenga ser çengada vedigeṛîne,
Teng û qûşa lê diqetîne,
Berdidê, dadixe ser şiherê Bîrê.

Qîz û bûkê şeherê Bîrê ṛadivin temaşê,

Divê, 'Hela lêbinêṛin, tê bêjî, melkemotê mêrê kulêye.'
Qîzek dibê, 'Bira xwedê bide siḥetê, mêrekî tenê peşmûdê kir aqas siyarê cerdêye.'

13. He was Derwêsh, mad Derwêsh,
He packed his own shroud on the back of 'Etman,
Kicked at the stirrups of 'Etman,
He screamed at the Jerdan horsemen,
He pushed them back hand over hand,
Tore off their saddle and crupper,
Let go, and set them down at the town of Bîrê.
The daughters and brides of the town of Bîrê came up to look,
They said, 'Look at this, you would say it is the angel of death, the sorrow of men,'
One girl said, 'May God preserve us, one man alone has had such an effect on so many horsemen of the Jerdan.'

25 A reference to the custom, still practised by Yezidi women, of cutting off braids in honour of the dead.

14. Were delal, hey delal, delal, delal, hey delal,
Delalo deliko, biçûko, 'efato, bi mendiko,
Xweyê ṛima donzde moviko,
Ber dilê xelqê da netuyî, netişto,

Ber dilê min 'evdalê usane, nola ḥinarek, ḥinara Aleşgirê bêdendiko.

'Edlayê digo, 'Wekî minê koma bav û bira şerm nekira,
Minê 'erebî biqîṛanda, unizî bilûbanda,
Minê bigota, ez ne kîkîme, ne milîme,

Ez berdilka Dewrêşê 'Evdî, lawkê êzdîme.

14. Come beloved, oh beloved,

My love, dear heart, young one, brave one, clever one,
You whose spear has twelve sections,
You who are nothing to the hearts of people,
But for my heart, a servant's heart, you are like a pomegranate, a seedless pomegranate of Eleshkirt.
'Edûlê said, 'If I had not shamed my father and brothers,
I would have screamed in Arabic, I would have cried in Turkish,
I would have said, I do not belong to the Kîkan, I do not belong to the Milan,
I am the lover of Derwêshê 'Evdî, the Yezidi lad.'

SECTION B

Stories and Songs of Love

DERWÊSHÊ ʿEVDÎ: MEḤMÛDÊ ʿELIYÊ TEMO (JELÎL 1978 I: 292–4)

1. Wey delal, wey delal, wey delal, wey delal, wey delal,	1. Alas, alas my love,
Ber dilê ʿevdalî xwedê da, tiyo netişteko,	You who are nothing to the heart of any servant of God,
Ber dilê min ʿevdala xwedê da, hinarî deşta Bêlacûkê, xurê kalan û pîran bêḥeb û bêdendiko,	But to me, a servant of God, you are a pomegranate of the plain of Bêlajuk, food of the grandfathers and grandmothers, flawless with no seeds,
De divê, misînê qawê ser darî darçiniya dekelijî,	They say, a pot of coffee was simmering over cinnamon-wood,
Ezê çûme yalê dîwanê, dîwanê ṭijî,	I was going to the side of the guest-hall, the hall was full,
Ezê çûme yalê malê, malê ṭijî,	I was going to the side of the house, the house was full,
Ezê çûme yalê odexanê, şêst pênc pêlewan têda ṛûniştî,	I went to the side of the guest-hall, sixty-five champions were sitting in it,
Wexta min ça û qawe digeṛandî, xema min meʿrûma xwedê nîbû,	When I was taking round the tea and coffee, I felt no sorrow, God's poor one,
Wexta ezê diçûme tûşa Dewrêşê ʿEvdî, lewandê şevê, lawkê êzdî,	When I was face to face with Derwêshê ʿEvdî, the reckless one of the night, the Yezidi lad,
Nizam kerbyana bû, şermana bû, yanê tirsan bû, çevê min ṛeşêve dihatin, tilî pêçiyê min diḥejiyan, çokê min dilerizîn, minê niqitka qawê ṛijandibû ser ʿeba Dewrêşê ʿEvdî.	I don't know whether from sorrow, from shame, or from fear, my eyes became dark, my fingers trembled, my knees shook, I spilt a drop of coffee on the cloak of Derwêshê ʿEvdî.
Wey delal, wey delal, wey delal, wey delal, wey delal,	Alas, beloved,
Ezê pey Dewrêşê ʿEvdî, lawkê êzdî ṛa, nabêjim, ʿtu delalî.ʾ	After Derwêshê Evdî, the Yezidi lad, I will say to no-one, ʿYou are my love.ʾ

2. Divê, navê kapêk pol pere cem min tinebû,
Minê destê xwe bire nava sîng û berê xwe, zêrekî diha dîtibû xercê şeherê bavê minî ḥevt sala bû,
Minê hildabû, ezê çûme dikanê van ‘etara,
Minê go, dikançiyo, ha, dikançiyo, minê niqitka qawê ṛijandiye ser ‘eba Dewrêşê ‘Evdî,
Minê hildabû ḥevt qalib sabûne, teşt û sîtile, ezê çûme ber çemê Payê vê mîrayê,
Çemê Payê mîrayê ava çil çar kaniya bû.
Ava çîl çar kaniya mi çikiya bû,
Tilî pêçiyê min maşiya bû,
Ḥevt qalib sabûna min ḥeliya bû,
Teşt û sîtilê min qul bibû,
Hela hê niqitka qawê ser ‘eba Dewrêşê ‘Evdî neçûbû.
Wey delal, wey delal, wey delal, wey delal, wey delal,
Ezê pey Dewrêşê ‘Evdî, lawkê Êzdiya ṛa, navê mêra naynime ser xwe.

2. At this time I had no money about me,
I put my hand on my breast inside my clothes, I saw a piece of gold there – my father’s going-to-town money for seven years,
I took it out, I went to the shop of those grocers,
I said, shopkeeper, shopkeeper, I spilt a drop of coffee on the cloak of Derwêshê ‘Evdî,
I took seven cakes of soap, a bowl and a cauldron, I went to the Pa, that river of kings,
The river Pa, of kings had the waters of forty four streams.
The waters of forty-four streams dried up for me,
My fingers were swollen,
I wore away seven cakes of soap,
My bowl and cauldron had holes in them,
But still the drop of coffee on the cloak of Derwêshê ‘Evdî had not gone.
Alas beloved, alas,
After Derwêshê ‘Evdî I will not link the name of any men with my own.

3. Divê, bahare, heyamê êlê derketinê,
Mala me kevn bûne, kêç ketinê,
Ḥevt kuṛapê mine ber girtinê,
Kalebavê mine ber mirinê,
Pîredayka mine ber şûştinê,
Ḥerçik çevê min çevê Dewrêşê ‘Evdî dikeve, minê tirê, gişte xweşe ṛû akara dinê.
Wey delal, wey delal, wey delal, wey delal, wey delal,
Ezê pey Dewrêşê ‘Evdî, navêjim, ‘tu delalî’.

3. It is spring, the time for the family to come outside,
Our houses have grown old, the fleas have come out,
Seven of my cousins are about to be arrested,
My father’s father is about to die,
My mother’s mother is about to be washed,[26]
Whenever my eye falls on the eye of Derwêshê ‘Evdî, it seems to me, all is lovely on the face of the world.
Alas beloved, alas,
After Derwêshê ‘Evdî, I will say to no-one ‘You are my love’.

4. Mîr go, ‘Gelî qewaza, ṛabin pêye,

4. Mîr said; ‘You attendants, get to your feet,

26 i.e. for burial.

Heṛin, bêjin Dewrêşê 'Evdî, bê, mîr te dixwaze ji dîwanêye.'

Go, say to Derwêshê 'Evdî, come, the Mîr wants you in the guest-hall.'

5. Cotê qewaza ṛabûn pêye,
Çûn go, 'Dewrêşê 'Evdî, mîr te dixwaze ji dîwanêye!'
Dewrêş hat go, 'Mîr, te çi dibêye?'

5. The two attendants got to their feet,
Went and said, 'Derwêshê 'Evdî, the Mîr wants you in the guest-hall!'
Derwêsh came and said, 'Mîr, what do you desire?'

Mîr go, 'Dewrêşo, dilê min dibêye,

Mîr said, 'Derwêsh, my heart desires [to know],

Wexta li xamê jêrin dibe qîṛîna kuṛê kurmanca, noṛîna me'negiya, şingîna kose misiriya, wexta xûn davê zenguê me'negiyane, gelo wî çaxî, mêr beremberî çend mêraye?'

When in the deepest misery comes the crying of the Kurmanji boys, the neighing of horses, the rattle of Mausers, when blood flows from the stirrups of the horses, at that time, how many men can a man face?'

6. Dewrêş go, 'Mîr, dilê min dibêye,
Wexta xamê jêrin dive qîṛîniya kuṛê kurmanca, noṛîna me'negiya, şingîna kose misiriya, wexta xûn davê zenguê me'negiyane, ancax, mêr beremberî mêr dertêye.'

6. Derwêsh said, 'Mîr, my heart says,
When in the deepest misery comes the crying of the Kurmanji boys, the neighing of horses, the rattle of Mausers, when blood flows from the stirrups of the horses, at that time, then a true man comes out to face men.'

Mîr got, 'Gelî qewaza, ṛabin pêye!
Destê Dewrêşê 'Evdî lêxin lêlêye!
Stuyê wî lêxin kelemçêye!
Linge wî lêxin qeydêye!
Milê Dewrêşê 'Evdî bigrin, bavêjin kela zîndanêye!'
Wey delal, ezê pey Dewrêşê 'Evdî, lewandê şevê, lawkê êzdî ṛa, kesekî ṛa navêjim, 'tu delalî'.

Mîr said, 'Servants, get to your feet,
Put the hand of Derwêshê 'Evdî in fetters,
Put his neck in chains!
Put his leg in the stocks!
Take Derwêshê 'Evdî's people, and throw them into the prison fortress!'
Alas my love, after Derwêshê 'Evdî, the reckless one of the night, the Yezidi lad, I will say to no-one, 'You are my love'.

7. Dewrêş go, 'Mîr, ezê wî kim îlahiye,

7. Derwêsh said, 'Mîr, I will do what God orders,

Ezê gava ṛavim pêye, ezê te temem kim sêsid û şest û şêş mêrê di ṛimêye.'

When I get to my feet, I will be equal to three hundred and sixty-six men for you with my spear.'

Mîr go, 'Dewrêşo, dilê min dibêye kivava kara karxezalêye.'
Dewrêş go, 'Mîro, dilê min dibêye,
Dilê te ne kivava kara karxezalêye,

Mîr said, 'Derwêsh, my heart wishes[27] for a kebab of the meat of a young gazelle,
Derwêsh said, 'Mîr, my heart says,
Your heart does not wish for a kebab of the meat of a young gazelle,

Tu dixwazî min bişînî pêşiya ḥezar ḥevsid mêrê 'eskerê 'Emerê Unise, min hatî xezêye.'

You want to send me to face one thousand seven hundred fighting men of 'Emerê Ûnise, you have come to me as my fate.'

27 The performer seems to be playing on the ambiguity of *dibêye*.

Wey delal, ezê pey Dewrêşê 'Evdî, lewandê şevê, lawkê êzdî ṛa, kesekî ṛa navêjim, 'tu delalî'.

Alas my love, after Derwêshê 'Evdî, the reckless one of the night, the Yezidi lad, I will say to no-one 'You are my love'.

DERWÊSHÊ 'EVDÎ: 'EGÎTÊ TÊJIR (II) (JELÎL 1978 I: 294–5)

1. Mîro, dilê min yane, yane,
Keko, dilê min yane, yane,
Ez fêza xwe da dinhêṛim – zozanê Kîkan û Milane,
Vêsbê derê konê bavê min 'evdalê, lev civiyane,
Gişkî filanî bêvane, gişkî navî bi nîşane,
Şivqelnê gêlazê destê wane,
Gişk kuṛê ax̌a û begane,
Ez bala xwe didimê Dewreşê 'Evdî, şêx 'Evdî, lawkê êzdî, ne navdane,
Delalo delal, delalo delal.

1. Oh King, my heart is longing, longing,
Brother, my heart is longing, longing,
I am looking at my own place – the *zozan* of the Kîkan and Milan,
This morning the place of my father's tent is destitute, among the crowds,
Everybody, so and so and such and such, all the ones with famous names,
Cherrywood pipes in their hands,
All the sons of Aghas and Begs,
I give my attention to Derwêsh Sheykh 'Evdî, the Yezidi lad, who is not amongst them,
Oh my beloved.

2. Ez çûme dîwanê, dîwane tijî,
Çûme qawexanê, misînê qawê ser darêd darçîna di qij qijî,
Minê misînê qawê hilanîbû, dîwana mala bavê xwe bela kiribû, nizanim, ji ḥub û ḥizkirinê çilka qawê ser 'eba Dewrêşê 'Evdî, delalê min da, ṛijî bû.
Were delal, hey delal, delal, hey delal.

2. I went to the guest-hall, the guest-hall was full,
I went to the coffee-room, the coffee pot was singing on cinnamon-twigs,
I lifted up the jug of coffee, made a blunder in the guest-hall of my father's house, I don't know [how], from love, a drop of coffee spilled on the cloak of Derwêshê 'Evdî, my beloved.
Come my dear one, my love.

3. Min zêrek serê xwe qetandibû,
Da siyarekî ji sivik siyara,
Min got, 'Siyaro, tu xwe kî, bi navê xwedê kî,
Tê ji bajarê Ṛiḥayê ḥevt qalib sabûna ṛeqê min ṛa bînî.

3. I broke away a gold piece from my headdress,
I gave it to one of the gentlemen,
I said 'Go, go in God's name, like the gentleman you are,
Bring me seven cakes of hard soap from the town of Urfa.'

4. Were delal, hey delal,
Çevê minê xalî navin ji av û hêsirê zelal.

4. Come my beloved,
My eyes will not be free from the clear water of tears.

5. Bihar bû, ṛeqe ṛeqe 'ewra bû,
Guṛe guṛe çema bû,
Çemê Mûradê donzde movika, ḥevt çeviya bû,

5. It was spring, the clouds were thundering,
The rivers were babbling along,
The river Murad had twelve sections, seven curves,

Çemê Mûradê li min çikiya,
Ḥevt qalib sabûn destê min da maşiya,

Tilî pêçiyê min weriya,
'Eba Dewrêşê 'Evdî, delalê dilê min, qawê da ma,
De were delal, hey delal, delal hey delal.

The river of Murad dried up for me,
Seven cakes of soap wore away in my hand,
My fingers were swollen,
The coffee was still in the cloak of Derwêshê 'Evdî, the beloved of my heart,
Come, my dear, my beloved.

6. Dewreşo qurba, bihare, ḥeyamê derketinê,
Xan manê mala bavê min 'evdalê, germ bûne, kêç ketinê,

Ḥevt birê min, wekî heṛine ber kuştinê,

Kalebavê min ber şûştinê,
Pîrediya min ber mirinê,
Wexta çevê min çevê Dewrêşê Evdî, ḥûtê binê beṛiyê, qeremanî Sindî, dikeve, min tirê, ḥemû saẍin li ṛûbara dinê.
Were delal, hey delal, delal hey delal.

6. Oh Derwêsh, may I be your sacrifice, it is spring, the time for going out,
The buildings of the house of my father, God's servant, have grown warm, the fleas have come to them,
If seven of my brothers are about to be killed
My grandfather is about to be washed
My grandmother is about to die
When my eye falls on the eye of Derwêshê 'Evdî, giant of the desert, hero of Sindî, to me it seems that all is well in spite of the world.
Come beloved, oh beloved.

BESA KHELÎL (COLLECTED BY DR KHELÎL JINDÎ RASHOW IN SHEYKHAN DURING THE 1970S)

1. Lê lê dayê,
Min kiḥêla serê ṭewlayê,

Min ẍezala serê şewlayê,
Min tifinga bergirê dev gundayê,
Belê xodê dizane min sûnda xwarî xirabe dayê,
Wey lê lê, li min poşmane dayê.

1. O mother,
I am the thoroughbred filly, the best in the stable,
I am the gazelle, the best in the grasslands,
I am the gun defending the village,
Yes, God knows, the oath I swore[28] is ruined, mother,
O mother, I feel bitter.

2. Lê lê dayê,
Ew Besê bang dike, Lo lo Brahîmo!
Tiliya min li çava keto wer wenakê!
Xodê zane ez keçika xelkê me,
Gava li gera nêva mala, li kolana,

Çavê min li êkî weke Welatê Beḥrî, kekê Perîşanê, ji mala Miḥemed Begî, Cizîrê Botî, biketa,

2. O mother,
Besê cries, 'Ibrahim! I put my fingers in your eyes like this!
God knows I am a normal girl,
On my way between the houses, in the alleys,
If my eye had fallen on someone like Welatê Behrî, Perîşan's elder brother, from the house of Miḥemed Beg of Jezîre Botan,

28 This refers to a private commitment to her lover, made before her marriage (KJR).

Ez li kolana, li ber ra bimeşim, xo liba kim,
Belê, xodê zane, ez li ber destê şêxan û mela,
Ezê xo ji Birahîmkê Temo, bi sê telaqa xo telaq kim,
de lo lo, de lo lo,
ax de lê lê li min poşmane dayê.

I would walk after him in the alley and make myself beautiful,
Yes, God knows, in front of the sheykhs and mullas,
I would divorce myself from Ibrahim Temo, by saying 'I divorce you' three times,
Oh,
Alas, alas, mother, I feel bitter.

3. De lê lê dayê,
Ew Besa bang dike, dibêje,
Le lê Ḥitê, Nurê, sibḥanellaḥ ji bejin û balîna min re,
Xodê zanibe nav û navkêla min qendîle
Taxê sîng û berê min nebûne befra çiyayê Elegezê li ber hêlima bayê gure,
Belê xozika min li wî xortî be, xortê nûhatî,
Malekî zorî zav hebe,
Taxim û sîngê Besê bikiṛe ji canê xo re,
de lo lo, de lo lo
ax de lê lê, li min poşmanê dayê.

3. O mother,
Besa is calling, she says:
Oh Ḥitê, Nurê, oh God, my height, my figure,
May God know my waist is slim as a candle,
My breasts are like the snow on Mount Alagöz, in the blast of the strong wind,
Yes, my wish would be for that young lad, the lad who has just come,
He would have a house full of riches
He would buy Besê's breasts for his dear self,
Oh,
Alas, alas, mother, I feel bitter.

4. De lê lê dayê,
Ew Besê bang dike dibêje,
Lê le Ḥitê Nurê, sibhane Ellah xelk ji min ṛedibêje bi şêranî, Besê xoka Nurê,
De xodê zane nav û navkêla min qendîle,
Taxê sîng û berê min nebûne çiṛa şîre,
Ew şah û biskê min kara ẍezala nebûne têla tembûrê,
Belê dayk û babê min xêrê bikin, xêrê nebînin,
Çawa ez nedame êkî wekî Beḥrî, kekê Perîşanê, ji mala Miḥemed Begê Cizîrê Botî, ṭenga canê min re,
Çawa ez dame Birahîmkê Temo,
Sîwarê bergirê, xodanê kûrkê qetiyayî,
Ew qeraşê aşê Nisebînê,
Ew dinya û 'alem jê ṛe dibêjin, 'Nan hijmêre ber tenurê',

4. De lê lê dayê
Besê is calling, she says:
Oh, Ḥitê, Nurê, by God, people say to me, 'You are very lovely, Besê, Nurê's sister, God knows my waist is slim as a candle,
My breasts are like a drop of milk,
With my hair, my fringe, I am like a young gazelle, like the neck of a lute,
Yes, if my father and mother do good, let them not see any benefit,
How could they not give me to a man like Behrî, Perîşan's elder brother, from the house of Miḥemed Beg of Jezîre Botan, the one nearest to my heart,
How could they give me to Ibrahim Temo,
Who rides a mule, who owns an old cloak,
He works the mill at Nusaybin,
The whole world says, 'He counts the loaves as they come out of the oven,'[29]

29 i.e. he is mean.

de lo lo, de lo lo
ax de lê li min poşmanê dayê.

Oh,
Alas, alas, mother, I feel bitter.

5. Lê lê dayê
Ew Besê bang dike, dibêje,
Lê lê Ḥitê Nurê, dinya û ‘alem ji min ṛe dibêjin, navê min Besa Xelîle,
Belê nav û navkêla min nebûne qendîle,
Taxim û sîng û berê min nebûne çiṛa şîre,
Ew dayk û babê min xêrê bikin, xêrê nebînin,
Çawa ez nedame êkî wekî Apê Beḥrî, kekê Perîşanê, ji mala Miḥemed Begê Cizîrê Botî, tenga canê min re,
Çawa ez dame Birahîmkê Temo,
Sîwarê bergirê, xodanê kûrkê qetiyayî,
Ew qeraşê aşê Nisebînê,
Mêrê sê jinaye,
Erê dema şev hate nîvanekî şevê,
Li ber sîng û berê Besê razaye,
Erê xodê zane mînayî gayê pîre.
De lo lo, de lo lo
ax de lê lê li min poşmanê dayê.

5. De lê lê dayê
Besê is calling, she says:
Oh, Ḥitê, Nurê, the whole world is saying to me, my name is Besa Khelîl,
Yes, my waist is like a candle,
My breasts are like a drop of milk,
If that mother and father of mine do good, let them not see any benefit,
How could they not give me to a man like Uncle Behrî, Perîşan's elder brother, from the house of Miḥemed Beg of Jezîre Botan, the one nearest to my heart,
How could they give me to Ibrahim Temo,
Who rides a mule, who owns an old cloak?
He works the mill at Nusaybin,
He is a man with three wives,
Yes, when the middle of the night came,
He slept on the breast of Besê,
Yes, God knows, just like an old ox.
Oh,
Alas, alas, mother, I feel bitter.

6. Eman, belê ezê dibêjim Besa minê
Te çav reşê, te çav xûmrî,
Eve çend roje tu ji ḥisabê mêrê xirab tu dihonîji, tu dikey bimirî,
Erê rabe tu destê xo li nêv destê min ke,
Ezê te birevînime ser sînorê wî gawirî,
De eman wayê, eman wayê, torîn wayê.

6. Pity me, yes, I say, o my Besê,
With dark eyes, with brown eyes,
For days now you have been fretting because of your vile husband, it will be the death of you,
Come on, get up, put your hand in mine,
I will take you away over the border to the Christian place,
Oh pity me, oh, so beautiful.

7. Belê dayê Besê bang dike, dibêje,
‘Qurban herçar malê li gelî de,
Belê xodê dizane lawikê min xencer girêda li ser saye sipîde,
Erê qurban tu ẍema mexo, minê cotê memika ji te ṛe kedî kirine,
De eman were, torîn were.

7. Oh yes, Besê is calling, she says, ‘I am your sacrifice, there are four houses in the valley,
God knows, my young lad has a dagger bound onto his white clothes,
No, do not be sad, I have been taming both my breasts for you,
Pity me, come, beautiful one.

Erê xodê zane lawikê min tolaze, çav li dere,
Belê sîng û berê min nebûne zozana Şerefedînê, befre li sere.

Yes, God knows, my young lad is handsome, he looks at other girls,
Yes, my breast is like the *zozan* of Sherefedîn with snow on it.

8. Eman Besa minê, diyarî min û gundê Nuredînê,
Ew rişeşeke baranê girte qontara çiyayê Qerqelînê,
Belê çawa, kê dîbe, kê bînabe, ji nîşev û paşve ew kûndekî şkêrê, hat û bifire ser hêlîna gogeçînê?

8. Pity me, my Besê, in my region, the village of Nuredîn,
The patter of the rain came over the foot of Mount Qerqelîn,
But whoever might have seen it, whoever might not, how after midnight did that owl of the rubbish-dump come and fly to the nest of the kestrel?

De eman wayê, torîn wayê,
Belê xodê dizane, Besa min stêreke, sêsed û şeşt û şeş ẍezale,
Belê gundî û xelkîno, loma meken,
Xewa min ber ḥemêza mêrê xirab nayê.

De eman wayê, torîn wayê,
Yes, God knows, my Besê is a star, she is three hundred and sixty six gazelles,
Yes, you people of the village, don't blame me,
I can't sleep while her vile husband embraces her.

9. Belê Besê bang dike, dibêje,
'Qurban, bejna min zirave, kûlilka nava bendêre,
Ew kirasekî di ber bejna min kara ẍezala daye,
Erê xode dizane medrumê gewre,
Serê memika têre dabû dere,
Erê herçî xortê nuhatî di ber bejna Besê de razê,
Di dilê xo de, li vê dinyayê nahêlî, ne tu kûle, ne tu kesere,
De eman wayê, torîn wayê.

9. Yes, Besê is calling, she says, 'I am your sacrifice, my figure is slim, a poppy in the fields,
This dress is covering a figure like a young gazelle,
Yes, God knows, a grey dress,
You can just see the points of my nipples,
Yes, whichever young man sleeps next to Besê's body,
In his heart, he will forget all pain, all sorrow in this world',
Pity me, beautiful one.

10. Eman Besê, ezê dibînim stêreke hilatî ji kinarê Werşîta,
Ew bila şewqê neda ba bejn û balîna kêsim ẍezala, gerden çîta,
Erê ji xêra navê Xodêre ...

10. O Besê, I see a star has risen from the direction of Wershîta,
Let the light not shine on your height, your slender figure like a gazelle, your neck like fine gauze,
Yes, in God's name ...

KHERABO!

(Collected amongst the Omerî by 'Tawûsparêz' (Roger Lescot) (*Hawar* 38, Year 10, 22 January 1942, 604–6)

1. Xerabo, Xerabo, weleh û bileh, tu xerab î.

1. Bad boy, bad boy, my God, you're a real bad 'un.

Tu bix̌alix̌alê, bi gotinê çênabî.	You won't let yourself be touched by my wheedling and talking.
Malê te pir e, ji canê te ṛe 'edabo!	Your wealth is great, may it be a torment to you!
Qama te kin e, hemberî taximê memikê mi nabo!	Your height is small, you didn't come up to my breasts!
Şevê Kanûna dirêj in, tu ji ber serê min ranabo!	December nights are long, don't leave my side!
Belkî debara te dibe, ebûra min di mala bavê mi de nabo!	Perhaps you might have a livelihood in my father's house, but there is no living for me!
2. Xirabo, weleh, tu xerab î.	2. Bad boy, you really are wicked.
Tuê ji dinyayê, ji 'alemê xirabtir î.	You're worse than the world, worse than the universe.
Tu ji koma pismamê mi çêtir î.	You're better than my cousin's crowd.
Serê memikê mi, rebena Xwedê, mînayî tiriyê Çêlikê Eliyê Remo, di çax û benga xwe de dekemilî.	My nipples, poor one of God that I am, are like the grapes of Chêlikê 'Eliyê Remo,[30] when they are mature on the vine.
Serê memikê mi, rebena Xwedê, mîna Qesrê Pirota, serê Miḥela Meşkîna avakirî.	My nipples, poor one of God that I am, are like Pirota Castle, which dominates the district of Meshkîna.[31]
3. Xerabo, dîno, havîn e, xweş havîn e.	3. Bad boy, mad boy, it's summer, lovely summer,
Nanê cehîn e û dewê tirşîn e.	The bread is made of barley, the drinking yoghurt is tart.
Serax û binraxa min û xelkê delal 'ebakî şalîn e.	The mattress and blanket for me and my dear one is a cloak of silk.
Heçî derdê dila ne dî be, bila nebîne!	Whoever has not known pain in his heart, let him not see!
Tu rabe, ji mi ṛe gwîzaneke berbera bîne!	Get up, bring me a barber's razor!
Ezê serê memikê xwe biçipilînim, ji kala ṛe bikim taştê, ji xorta ṛe bikim firavînê.	I will cut my nipple off, I will make it into breakfast for the old men, lunch for the young men,
Bazê dilê min rojika rojiya se meha digire, bila êvarê pê fitara xwe bişkênîne.	My hawk has been fasting for three months longer than Ramadan, let him break his fast and feast in the evening.
4. Xerabo, xerabê dînê,[32] te mîka xwe daye bi bizinê,	4. Bad boy, bad and mad, you gave up your lamb for a nanny-goat,
Te gula xwe daye bi sosinê.	You gave up your rose for an iris.

30 Lescot's note: an Omerî village.
31 Lescot's note: a district of Mardin.
32 Thus Lescot; however, the wording is likely to be *xerabê dinê* 'the world's worst', which fits better with the internal rhyme scheme.

Te berê xwe dayê qetlê û sêpayê zinê.	You are rushing towards slaughter and the gallows of adultery.
Ez û Xerabê bi tenê şevê nîvê şeva li zikaka biniya mala li hev runiştin.	Alone with my bad boy at midnight, I used to sit in the street, below the houses.
Me gilîkê xwe pev kirin û gazindê xwe dihiştin,	We exchanged our complaints and let our reproaches go,
Kundê şkêra, wawîke ber devê çema, li halê min û bejna zirav diponiştin,	The owl on the heap of stones, the jackal by the river, nodded their heads sadly, full of pity for me and my slim one,
Mirîkê gorê di mezela, ê go îsal hezar û pênc sed sal mirî bûn, kefenê xwe li cemcûmê serê xwe gerandin, li ser qebrê xwe rûniştin,	The dead in the graves, who have been dead fifteen hundred years, wound their shrouds around their skulls and sat on their tombs,
Li halê min û bejna zirav diponiştin.	Nodded their heads sadly, full of pity for me and my slim one.
Ez bi te ṛe dost bûm, tu bi mi ṛe dijmin bûyî.	I was a friend to you, you were an enemy to me.
Tu li paş xanîka li min dikelistî, te derbek bi tifingê berda mi, ez dikuştim.	You were spying behind my house, you fired your gun at me, you killed me.
Şevê nîvê şeva, te bi destê tola jina xwe girt, û ez li ber dîwara dihiştim.	At dead of night, taking your cursed wife by the hand, you left me alone.
5. Xerabo, dîno, mi bihîstî tu zewicî, te ji xwe ṛe yek dixwestî.	5. Bad boy, mad boy, I've heard you have married, you've asked for a girl's hand.
Heke ji mi çêtir be, bila li te helal be, li wî canî, ya na, ezê tu nifra li te nakim, tu dûrîdest î.	If she is worth more than I, may God consent to your marriage. If not, I will curse you no longer – you are not available to me!
Xwedê teala bike, Rebî, goştê canê te bihele, li hewa bimîne komek hestî,	May God let your body dissolve with nothing left of you but a bunch of bones exposed to all weathers,
Tu kwîr bibî, têkevî ber vî destî!	May you go blind and fall into my hands!
6. Xerabo, dîno, tu zewicî, te yek anî,	6. Bad boy, mad boy, you've married, you've wedded a girl.
Heke ji min çêtir be, bila li te helal be, li wî canî.	If she is worth more than I, may God consent to your marriage!
Ya na, Xwedê teala bike, Rebî, li canê te keve derdek, tu nebînî tu dermanî.	If not, may God let your body be struck with a sickness without a cure!
Ezê serê sibêhê rabim, bi destê te bigirim, te bikişînim wî cebanî.	I'll get up early and drag you by the hand to the cemetery.
7. Xerabo, Xerabo! Xwedê teala bike, Rebî, heçi ji Xerabê min ṛe bêje 'Tu xerabo'	7. Bad boy, bad boy! By God, may God grant, whoever says to my bad boy 'you bad boy',
Bila karîn û warîna zarokê nêr tu care di mala wan de nabo!	May there never be the cries of a boy-child in their house!

Bila sed olçek genimê sor li binê beṛiya Mêrdînê biçîne, li şwîne bila qerezîwana reş nabo!

If they sow a hundred measures[33] of red wheat down in the desert of Mardin, let there be no black buckwheat in their plot of land!

Êmayî, bila kuliyê par û pêrar lê rabo!

For the rest, let the locusts of last year and the year attack it!

Bila salekê bîne ser bênderê, gêre bike û bidêre, ew ji jê ṛe bi ka bo!

Let them spend a year on the harvest, let them thresh and scatter, let it become straw for them!

Kulmek zadê ji wan ṛe saî nabo!

May not a fistful of grain be pure!

8. Heçî ji Xerabê mi ṛe bêje: 'Tu baş î, tu pir qenc î', Xwedê teala bike, Rebî, kulmek garîsê li pişta mala biçîne,

8. Whoever says to my Badboy, 'You are good, you're very handsome', may God grant, my God, if they sow a fistful of millet behind the house,

Li şwînê sed olçek genimê sor hilîne;

Let a hundred measures of red wheat grow up on their plot of land;

Bi ofara binî qîza şêxkî, aẍakî ji xwe ṛe bîne;

With the grain left on the threshing floor let him marry the daughter of a sheykh or an agha;

Zikata malê vê salê bide min û bazê dila, emê pê daweta xwe li dar xînin.

Let him give me and my hawk the house's alms[34] for this year, we'll have enough for our wedding.

Min dî bazê dilê xwe bar dike, berê xwe dide aşê mala Hecî Şemdîn e.

I saw my hawk, he loads up his beasts and heads for the mill of Hajî Shemdîn's house.

Tu li wê newalê timam bigere, tu li heft seriya bigere, tu çavkî di wan de nabîne.
Mi dî mîrata çapê li arvanê bazê dilê min dixîne.
Heft çap û nîva ji arvanê bazê dilê mi hiltîne.
Daweta min û Xerabê bi tenê sala vê salê nêv cî li dar dimîne.

Walk the complete length of this valley, wander up seven peaks, you won't see a single spring.[35]
I saw, the miller measures out the flour of my hawk.
He draws out seven and a half bushels from my hawk.[36]
My wedding to Badboy alone will not happen this year.

9. Xerabê mi xeyidî ji gundiya, ji maliya.
Mi dî da ser rêka Omeriya,
Minê digo, 'Ezê rabim, ban kim heval û hogir û hemşeriya,
Bila herin, xelkê delal vegerînin bi kef û eşq û laqirdiya,

9. My bad boy fell out with the people from the village, with those nearby,
I saw him out on the Omeriyan road,
I said 'I'll up and call my friends and allies and fellow-townsmen,
Let them go, let them fetch my dear one with joy and love and talk,

33 Lescot's note: an olchak equals approximately 60 kilos.
34 Lescot's note: this refers to the alms compulsory under Islam, called *zekat*.
35 Lescot says that this line must be addressed to the mill owner.
36 The miller is paid with a share of the grain.

Bila Xwedê teala biqedîne miradê miradxwaza û dilketiya,
Bila miradê min û Xerabê mi bimîne heya koçerê me vegerin ji deşta Mûşê, rûnin akinciya.

Let God grant the desire of those who yearn and of lovers,
Even if the desire of me and my bad boy has to wait until our nomads return from the plain of Muş to settle down.

10. Xerabo, dîno, Xerabê xelkê,
Te bejin ziravo, bi terha benikê,
Dilkê min û bejna zirav di hev hebû çi kula go ketiye mala xelkê.

10. Bad boy, mad boy, cruel one,
You who are slim as a tether of muslin,
My heart and my slim one endured together all the sorrows that befall people.

Xerabo, dîno,
mala bavê keleşgewra mi li wê çivê, li wê ewcê, li wê zikakê, li wê fitlekê,
Te meşqazê, meşqetikê, meşordekê,

Bad boy, mad boy,
the house of of my fair girl's father is at this corner, on this street, at this curve.[37]
You who move as gracefully as the wild geese and ducks, as the partridge of the wilderness,

Heçiyê xortê go bi çavê xwe dî û bi dilê xwe zewicî, ewê sê roj û sê şevê xwe kuştine ji dinyayê, ji qocê felekê.

Whichever young man married according to his own heart, after looking at his beloved, would subtract three days and nights from his life, for destiny.

11. Xerabo, dîno, bila li te be, li wî dilî,
Bila li mala hezar û heft sed bavê te be, li wê sewdanê, li wî aqilî.

11. Bad boy, mad boy, may disaster be upon you, upon your heart,
May disaster be upon your one thousand seven hundred ancestors, on your love, on your sanity!

Çewa te dev ji mi, kihêla serê tewla berda, tuê li bergîla şix̆ulê Rismiliya û Qibaliya dihesilî?
Mi ji te ṛe ne go, 'Di meha biharê, bergîla li şwîna kihêla metewilî!'

How did you give me up, the best thoroughbred mare in the stable, for that nag of Rishmili and Qibali stock?[38]
Didn't I say to you 'In spring, you must not harness old nags instead of thoroughbreds?'

Li xûşka mezin binêr, dû ṛe xûşka biçûk ji xwe ṛe werî.
Lawiko, dîno, ezê çi bikim? Sala vê salê, ez bi mêr im, tu bi jin î.

Look at the elder sister before you marry the younger.
Oh lad, crazy boy, what shall I do? This very year, I have a husband, you have a wife.

Kul û kederê te gelek in, şak berdane ser vî dilî.
Kul û kederê ji bîra nakim, heya axê mezelan, kêlê di kevirî.

The griefs and sorrows you have caused are many, they tear at my heart.
I won't forget the grief and sorrow, until [I am in] the dust of the grave, under the tombstone.

Kul û kederê te pir bûne, tucar dernakevin ji vî dilî.

Your grief and sorrows were great, they will never leave this heart.

37 The young man is now speaking, though there has been no obvious stanza or other break
38 Lescot's note: the Rishmilan and Qibaliyan inhabit two villages on the outskirts of Mardin. They are much despised by their neighbours.

Xelkê digo, 'Keleşgewra te esmer û genimgwîn e.'[39]
Bi xelkê teḥl e û bi nevsa mi şêrîn e.
Tu rabe, serê xwe di kulek û şibakê qesrê ṛe biderxîne!
Bila sira bayê Qerejdaẍê li ser şêbiskê te ê şê xîne!
Bi ser henarkê rûkê rastê te vegerîne.

People used to say, 'Your beloved is brown and dark.'
She is bitter to others, to me she is sweet.
You stand up, put your head through the window of the building!
Let the breeze of the wind of Qerezhdakh blow on your fair curls,
And blow them back against your right cheek.

Ez dikim herim welatê ẍerîb û ẍurbetê, tu kanî ramîsanekê bi mi de, ji boẍaza qirikê, ji xanûmanê gerdenê,
Bila kederê ramîsanê te keçikê li welatê ẍerîb û ẍurbetê di dilê mi de nemîne.

I'm about to go to a strange and desolate land, let me take a kiss from your throat, your neck,
Oh young girl, see to it that when I am in a strange land, I will not have the regret of not having kissed you in my heart.

Wexta Ezraîl dakeve, rûhê mi distîne,

Wê gavê, bila diwanzde mîkweta zêdî heqê mi li mi xîne,
Bila heqê ramîsanê keleşgewra mi ji mi hilîne!

When 'Ezra'îl comes down and takes my soul,
Then, let him give me twelve hammer blows more than I deserve,[40]
To make me pay for the kiss of my lovely girl!

12. Xerabo, Xerabo, Xerabo! Wey li minê, wey li minê, wey li minê,
Çewa îro hatiye cewaba nexêr e, ji mi keçikê re.
Digo, 'Delalê dilê te li welatê ẍerîb û ẍurbetê nexweş e, nexweşekî li ber mirinê.'
Ezê ji komê pismama ne wêrim herim serekî bidimê.
Xwezî ji xêra Xwedê re, ezê bîstekekê li tenişta Xerabê xwe runiştama, meye li hevûdu helal bikira heqê ramîsana, malîfeta derdê dilketinê!
Geli gundî û malîno, car û cîrano, hûnê bi qedrê Xwedê kin, mala Xerabê mi ziyareteke pir evzel e, hûnê bi destê min bigirin û mi bibîne.

12. Bad boy, bad boy, bad boy! alas, alas for me,
The bad news has just come to me, poor girl that I am.
It said, 'The one your heart loves is sick in a strange and desolate land, a sickness unto death.'
I dare not go from my cousins' tent to see him.
I wish by God's blessings I were sitting a while by the side of my bad boy, we would pay our debts in kisses, the cure for the pain of love!
People of our village, neighbours by the love of God, my Badboy's house is a very holy shrine, you must take me by the hand and lead me there.

13. Çi darika di bexçê mala bavê mi de bû, ji gula, ji beybûna xemilandî,

Xerabê mi rahiştî hejkî, lêxisti, timam diweşandî.

13. Whatever trees were in the garden of my father's house, adorned with roses, with camomiles,
My Badboy held up a branch, struck, finally scattered them,

39 The young man is again speaking.

40 Lescot's note: according to Muslim belief, 'Ezra'îl the angel of death, strikes the dead soul to make him admit his sins.

Bê lome be, çewa dostikek mero gelik î bedew hebe,	Let him be without blame, as long as he has such a beautiful friend,
Li çiyayekî mîna çiyayê Omeriya be,	On a mountain like the mountain of the Omeriyan,
Mero dev jê berde, dil pêkeve erebekê, li binê beṛiya jêrî, û lêvdeqandî!	Let him leave, to fall in love with an Arab of the plain below, with tattooed lips.
14. Xerabo, wile, tu Xerabo,	14. Bad boy, my God, you're bad,
Malê te pir e, ji canê te ṛe edabo!	Your wealth is great, may it torment you!
Tu bi şêxkî diwanzde elmî bo,	If you were a Sheykh learned in twelve sciences,
Sed werdê te di bêrîka mi de bo	And if I had one hundred of your charms in my pocket
Qenyatiya dilê mi bi te nabo!	My heart would not be more satisfied with you!

SECTION C

Songs of Grief and Lamentation

EYŞA BALÊ (Collected by Khelîl Jindî Rashow)

1. Yaman hevalê, yaman hevalê, yaman hevalê, rabe,
Yaman hevalê, hevaleke min li vê dinyayê,
Navê xelkekî minî delal 'Eyşanê
Bejna zirave ji tayekî gulan û reş riḥane,
Kesk dike li bax̌a û li bax̌estane,
Xelkekî minî delale
Nesax̌î bê hale,
Mededî yamane.
Geriyam li eqlîma û li şehrestana
Li doktor û hakîma
Li dûbarî van dermana
Yaman hevalê!

1. Oh help, my love, my love, wake up,
Oh help, my love, the one I love most in this world,
My dear one's name is 'Eyshê,
She is slim as a rose branch, as the dark basil,
Growing green in the garden, in the orchard,
She is my dear, my beloved,
She is grievously sick,
She desperately needs help.
I searched the corners of the world, the cities
For doctors, for scholars,
Searching again for those remedies,
Oh help me, oh my love!

2. Herçi mirina xelkekî minî delal nebihîstî,
Şêr û heywana cî û mekan xo berdane
Rojê li nîvro girtî meclis û dîwana
Mêr û melika selawat ji mirina 'Eyşê vedane
Ḥûriya li ezmanê heftê kef kutane
Quling li zozana dageriyana

2. Who has not heard of the death of my beloved?
The lions, the wild beasts have left their places, their homes,
The council-chambers and courts are closed at midday,
Men and angels pay respects at 'Eyshê's death,
The Houris of the seven heavens have been clapping their hands,
The cranes have come down from the *zozan*,

Xezalêd binê beṛiyê mendehoş bûne,
Berê xo dane zozane,
Ew jî heywanêd Xodê bûn
Hizna xelkekî minî delal kêşane

Yaman hevalê!

The gazelles in the desert are shocked,
They have left for the *zozan*,
They also were God's wild creatures
[Who] have shown their sadness for my dear one
Oh help, oh my love!

3. Dar û berê geliyê Sikane bi ser min û xelkê delal vereşiyane
Mijeke 'ezîma giran girtiye devê geliyan û baniyane,
Wextê herdû çavêd belek keftine ber firwarê,
Min dîbû xişîna tok û mandel û zêr xizêma zêrî zere,
Min dî xelkekî minî delalî hogan herdû çavêd reş û belek ji mirinê ṛe wergîrane
Min dî hêviyê kitkitê û cotcot cinazê xelkekî minî delalî li hevûdû geṛane
Hûn pê bizanin xelkekî minî delal bêhalî nexoşi mededî yemane
Wê li me bite mêvane

3. The trees and stones of Sikan[41] valley rained down on me and my dear one,
A dark, heavy fog closed the mouth of the valleys and the heights,
When her two dark eyes began to close in death,
I saw, there was a gentle tinkling of her necklace, her gold nosering, yellow gold,
I saw my dear one, my precious one, close both her lovely dark eyes in death,
I saw hope turn away, little by little, from the body of my beloved one,
You would know then that my beloved, my love is mortally sick, she needs a remedy,
Let her become a guest to us.

4. Yaman hevalê, yaman hevalê, yaman hevalê,
Çendî şahiyekê mezin li serê gundê me dibeste
Xelkekî minî delaliyê, nesaẍe,
Bêhalî mededî yamane
Ezê bîstekê herime li bala wê bikim qestê,
Ez nebûm hecacekî tesbî û wekaz li destê
Dinya dem û heywanêd Xodê bûn, wextê herdû çavêd reş û belek keftine ber ferwarê,
Mi dî, bûwe xoşîne tok û mendel û zer xezane zêrî zer, bi ser xalekî gerdenê boẍazê qirkê de şkeste,
Yaman hevalê, yaman hevalê, yaman hevalê.

4. Oh help, help my love, my love,
How much happiness there has been above our village!
My beloved one, my love, is sick,
Mortally sick, she needs a remedy,
I will go and sit by her a while, I will make it my aim,
I was like a pilgrim with prayer-beads, staff in hand,
The world stood still when both her lovely dark eyes began to close in death,
I saw, there was a gentle tinkling of her necklace, her gold nosering, yellow gold, it broke over her neck, her breast,
Oh help, help my love.

5. Yaman hevalê, yaman hevalê, yaman hevalê,
Bila nehate bayekî herdeme, bayekî Samsûnê, bayekî şkêra,

5. Oh my love, my love, my love,
If only that constant wind had not blown, the wind of Samsun, of the mountains,

41 Yezidi informants were uncertain of the whereabouts of this place, but thought it was 'somewhere in Turkey'.

Bila nedabe li gerdena Eyşa Balê heta kimyonekî zêra,	If only it had not blown on the neck of 'Eysa Balê, on her pure[42] gold,
Dinya dem û heywanêd xodê ne, herdem bi demê re, herdem bi wextê re,	This world and its centuries belong to God, every period, every time in its own time,
Dinya nemabû ji Aḥmedê lawê Tirkî re	This world didn't last for Aḥmed the young Turk,
Dinya nemabû ji Boz Begê lawê pîre	It didn't last for Boz Beg, the old woman's son,
Dinya nemabû ji 'Elî Şêr, şêrê Xodê re	It didn't last for 'Elî Shêr, the lion of God,[43]
Neh xelatî reb'l alemîn ji ezmana nazîlî 'erdê Xodê bûn,	The Lord of the Universe gave nine gifts to God's earth,
Sê jê hatibû jê re,	Three of them came to him,
Serê heft salî tamam şeṛ dikir bi kafirêd berî bedlê re,	For seven years he made war with the pagans in his time,
Yaman hevalê, yaman hevalê, yaman hevalê!	Oh help, help my love, my love!
6. Dinya nemabu ji Noşê Rawan re,	6. This world didn't last for Anushîrwan,
Dinya nemabu ji Cimcimê Siltan re,	This world didn't last for Sultan Skull,[44]
Dinya nemabu ji êkî wekî Hemze Pehlewan re	This world didn't last for someone like Hemze the Champion,
Dinya nemabu ji Rustemê Zalê re	This world didn't last for Rustem Zal,
Dinya nemabu ji 'Aşik Xerîb û Şa Sinemî ṛa,	This world didn't last for 'Ashik Gherib and Shah Sinem,[45]
Dinya nemabu ji Mem û Zînê re,	This world didn't last for Mem and Zîn,
Dinya nemabu ji Siyabend û Xecê re,	This world didn't last for Siyabend and Khej,
Dinya nemabu ji Mecnûn û Lêlê re,	This world didn't last for Mejnûn and Leylê
Dinya nemabu ji Silêman pêxember û Belqîz Xatûnê re,	This world didn't last for the prophet Solomon and the Queen of Sheba,
Kerem û êradêt barî te'ale hebûn vêre,	He had God's blessings and bounty here,
Kerem û êradêt ala te'ale ketine serî re,	God's blessings and bounty were bestowed on him,
Firiya, nava ezman û erdê re,	He flew between heaven and earth,
Min dî azmanê Xodê jêre kind bû,	I saw God's heaven came down to him
'Erdê Xode jêre bilind bû,	God's earth rose up to him

42 Literally 'cumin', a very valuable kind of gold.

43 'Ali, the fourth caliph of Islam, Mohammed's cousin.

44 This is one of a number of folkloric kings, such as Alexander, who tried to avoid death. A Yezidi *çîrok* tells that Jesus and Simeon came across a skull in the desert, and conversed with it. It had belonged to the great pagan Sultan Jimjim who had eventually died, despite his efforts to the contrary. He had first been sent to Hell but was rescued by the Cow to whom he had prayed (PGK, personal communication).

45 Shah Sinem and Kherîb are two lovers known in oral tradition, like the couples in the next two lines.

Ez bi xulamê 'Eyşa Balê bim,
Xodanê bist û çar gustîlî zer, xizemêd zerîzêre,
Wextê herdû çavêd reş û belek keftine ber ferwarê,
Min dîtî bû xişîna tok û mendel û zer xezanê zêrîzere,
Xelkekî minî delal herdû çavêd reş û belek wergeran ji mirinê re.
Ezê ḥeyf û mixabina bixwazim ji nabiyêt 'omedê,
Ezê sundxworî tobadarim piştî xelkekî xoyî delalî hoganî mîmbaşa keçkan û bûka
Çucar û çucar li gerê govendê, li guhê dîlanê …

May I be the servant of 'Eysha Balê,
Owner of twenty-four yellow rings, nose-rings of yellow gold,
When both her lovely dark eyes began to close in death,
I saw, there was a rustling of her necklace, her gold nosering, yellow gold,
My lovely one, her two lovely dark eyes passed over into death.
I will ask for condolences from prophets of the nations,
I have sworn an oath, a solemn vow, after my dear one, my precious love, commander of the cohorts of girls and brides,
Never, never, in the circle of the dance, at the side of the dancing…

EXAMPLES OF LAMENT: MRS. R.

1. Ey yetîm sed ḥeyf û mixabin	1. Oh orphan, a hundred pities and regrets,
Ey yetîm li derî kolana bimînin	Oh orphan, let them remain at the street door,
Dane ṣoban û êvara	Morning and evening, they talked
Serî êhsînê wî li ber taq û dîwara	By the walls and the doorways about his good deeds,
Vê sibê çavêd wan nesekinin.	This morning, let their eyes not rest [from crying].
2. Kuştiye çolê sed ḥeyf û mixabinê	2. He is killed in the wilderness, a hundred pities and regrets,
Xelkê cihêl çu li biyanêt avêtî bin,	Young people went, to be cast away to a foreign place,
Lo lo birîndaro tu ji birînêd xo tu çawanî?	Oh wounded one, what state have your wounds left you in?
3. Sed ḥeyf û mixabin xelqê nezewicî li cîhê talî werin de …	3. A hundred pities and regrets, that unmarried people come to the final place …
4. Xelqê dema xo nexwarî,	4. A person who did not live out their time,
Xelqê kuçikokê dinya nedîtî …	A little one who did not see the world …

SONGS OF MOURNING: ḤIZRETA ḤESO

Performed at mourning for 'Etarê Şero, Tbilisi 1975. The following are a selection from those published in Jelîl 1978 I: 490–503. I have renumbered them for easy reference within this study; they are separate songs rather than stanzas of a single song.

1. Şevê payîzane dirêjin,
Şarûr ṛûniştiye, bilbilê ḥalê dilê miṛa dibêjin,
Emê kerbê birînê birîndara, hinek keṛin, hinek gêjin.

1. The nights of autumn are long,
The song-thrush has settled, the nightingale tells the condition of my heart,
We [feel] the pain of the wounded ones' injuries, some are deaf, some are dazed.
(Jelîl 1978 I: 490).

2. Dayka dergûşê ji mala bavê berjêr bûye,
Cotek karê xezala li wê dûye,
Diya dergûşê çawa ji mal û mêra kûvî bûye.

2. The mother of the babe[46] came down from the father's house,
Two young gazelles behind her,
The mother of the babe, how wild and distant from home, from men she has become.
(Jelîl 1978 I: 490).

3. Gulî ṛeşê, gulî alê,
Ṛave neynikê bîne, serê xwe girêde, heṛe dewatê mala xalê,
Go, 'Feleka min min dixapîne, ṛoja çûyî îdî nayê.'

3. Black braid, red braid,
Get up, fetch a mirror and do your hair, go to a feast at your uncle's house,
She said, 'My fate is cheating me, yesterday will not come again.'
(Jelîl 1978 I: 490).

4. Çemo, çemê Payê,
Çem çikiyaye deng jê nayê,
Xazî xêra mala xwedêṛa, xortê ṭûre, dîsa mîna hêmanê berê, kêleka dayka xwe ṛûnişta, dîsa jêṛa bigota, 'Dayê,'

Feleka min min dixapîne, mi ṛa nayê ṛayê.

4. Oh river, great river Pa,[47]
The river has dried up, it makes no sound,
If only the joy of the house, by God, the lovely lad,[48] would again do as he did before, [if only] he would sit by the side of his mother, and say again to her 'Mother',
My fate is cheating me, it does not go according to my wishes.
(Jelîl 1978 I: 490).

5. Emê heṛine mala birazavê,

Emê bêjin, 'Birazavê bira, ḥina xortê ṭûre nevêje avê,
Ḥeyfa min nayê girtina mêra, kuştina şêra, ḥeyfa min tê wê ḥeyfê, wekî jina wî ziviṛî mala bavê.'

5. We will go to the house of the best man,
We will say, 'Best man, brother, do not cast the lovely lad into the water yet,
I do not grieve at the capture of men, the killing of lionhearts, I grieve at this grief, that his wife has turned back to her father's house.'
(Jelîl 1978 I: 490).

46 literally 'mother of the cradle'.

47 River Pa, the 'kingly river' (Jelîl 1978 II: 424). Location unknown, though one Badinani suggested it was in the Jezîre area, which would be consistent with other traditions in Jelîl's collection.

48 I am following Rudenko's translation of this word, which was not known to my Sheykhani informants.

6. Kela girtiya çî mezine,
Ṭop lêkeve serobine,
Ça xortê minî ṭûre navda nîne?

6. The fortress of the prisoners is so big,
A cannon is hitting it above and below,
How can my lovely lad not be among them?
(Jelîl 1978 I: 491).

7. Kela girtiya serê çiya,
Dûkî zirav lê kişiya,
Minê bala xwe dayê xortê ṭûre pêşiya cendirma, ziravê dilê diya wî diqetiya.

7. The fortress of the prisoners [is] at the top of the mountain,
A thin line of smoke rises from it,
I looked for the lovely lad before the police-station, the frail heart of his mother snapped.
(Jelîl 1978 I: 491).

8. Sazbendo, sazî derda,
Qasekî sazê xwe bîne xarda,
Têlê vî sazbendî şê û şêbiskê kewaniyanin, simêlê malxiya sosinîne, xazî xêra mala xudêṛa, dil-cegerê mi xeverda.

8. Saz player, teller of pains,
Bring down your saz for a moment,
The strings of this saz player are like the chestnut-hair and braids of women, the moustache of the heads of families are like irises; if only the joy of the house, by God, my heart and liver, would speak.
(Jelîl 1978 I: 492).

9. Simêleke sore bi sosinî,
Êleke giran ber derê mala bavê xortê ṭûre disekinî,
Werin bala xwe bidine min vê yekê, tê bêjî, simêla xortê ṭûre axê goṛada ḥine kirî.

9. A moustache is red as an iris,
A great clan has halted before the house of the lovely lad's father,
Come, give me your attention for this, you will say, the moustache of the lovely lad is hennaed with the earth of the grave.
(Jelîl 1978 I: 493).

10. Kavla Ṭilbîsê nîveka dinê,
Kûçe tengin, ṛê naçinê,
Nizanim, kê çaveke nevxêrê meṛa aniye, go, 'Xortê ṭûre, ketiye ber mirinê.'

10. The ruins of Tbilisi are half the world,
The alleys are narrow, the roads do not go anywhere,
I don't know who brought the bad news to us, they said, 'The lovely lad, he has fallen down dead.'
(Jelîl 1978 I: 493).

11. Me bariye berfa hûre,
Orṭa mala zeva û xezûrda bûye masûre,
Nizanim, xezûrê vî xortî çi jêṛa gotiye, zeva xeyîdiye, naçe mala xezûre.

11. A fine snow rained down on us,
Between the house of the bridegroom and father in law there was a difficulty,[49]
I do not known what the father in law of this young man said to him, the bride-groom is offended, he is not going to the house of the father in law.
(Jelîl 1978 I: 494).

49 The meaning of *masûre* remains obscure; Izoli's definition, 'bobbin', seems unlikely here.

12. Xerîbî ne ṭu kare,
Forma ṛojê: bi ḥesavê, bi defterî, bi jimare,
Wexta xerîbê xelqê xerîbiyê tên, xerîbê me xerîbiyêda dimînin mîna kulekeke pey keriyane.

12. There is no profit in exile,
The rule of the day: by accounting, by copybooks, by numbers,
When other people's exiles come back from exile, our exiles remain in exile like a lame sheep straggling behind the flocks.
(Jelîl 1978 I: 497).

13. Xerîba xudême,
Cûcûka sibême,
Ber peṛê ṛoême,
Mêvanê qebrême.

13. I am the exile of God,
I am the bird of the morning,
I am flying in the sunlight,[50]
I am the guest of the grave.
(Jelîl 1978 I: 498).

14. Stêra sibê lêda,
Birê p̣işta xûşkê girêda,
Go, 'Îdî ez nayêm ṭixûbê weda,
Nizanim, şevekê mi bivînî di xewnêda.'

14. The morning star had set,
The brother fastened his sister's belt,
He said, 'Henceforth I shall not come to visit you,
I don't know, one night you may see me in a dream.'
(Jelîl 1978 I: 499).

15. Xerîbê min pak veṛêkin,
Deste kincê zevatiyê lêkin,
Ax û berê giran şakin.

15. Send off my exile clean and tidy,
Put a bridegroom's outfit on him,
Let the dust and heavy earth rejoice.
(Jelîl 1978 I: 499).

16. Malka xerîba min ne vire,
Ber çemê Xêmûre,
Berf bariye, kulî hûre.

16. The home of my exiled one is not here,
It is by the river Khabûr,
The snow has fallen, in tiny flakes.
(Jelîl 1978 I: 500).

17. Çiya gotê çiya,
Go, 'Ka xelqê li van ciya?'
Me go, 'Birîndarin, nexaşin, ṭapa wan ṭinene, meyê şandiye bilindciya, gelo kî êlêra dageriya?'

17. Mountain said to mountain,
'Where are the people in this place?'
We said, 'They are wounded, they are sick, they have no presence, we sent him out to the high places, but which clan did he come down with?'
(Jelîl 1978 I: 500).

18. Emê çi bikin xwe vî dilê şkestî,
Emê gula biçinin, têkine destî,

18. What shall we do with these broken hearts of ours?
We will pluck flowers, put them in his hands,

50 Thus KJR.

Sivê her kesekê ser mezelê xwe bela be, gelo mezelê xerîba maye li kî destî?

In the morning let each one be at her grave, but who is looking after the grave of the exiled ones?

(Jelîl 1978 I: 501).

19. Dilê min dibêye,
Şevê payîza dirêjin, diçin têye,

Berê malxê mala, xortê ṭûre, daykê dergûşa, kewaniyê mala, dane welatê xerîbiyêye.

19. My heart is longing,
The autumn nights are long, they go, they come,
The head of the house, the lovely lads, the mothers of the babes, the mistresses of the houses, have gone to the land of exiles.

(Jelîl 1978 I: 501).

20. Xemê gote Xeydê,
Emê heṛin çiyayê Antanoskê, çiyangê seydê,
Xortê ṭûre kire gazî, 'Ezê destê dê û bavê xwe nakevim, ḥeta ṛojek ṛoja şeva 'eydê.'

20. Sadness said to Anger,
We will go to Antanosk mountain, a mountain of hunting,
The lovely lad called out, 'I will not be in the hands of my mother and father until the eve of 'Eyd.'

(Jelîl 1978 I: 503).

Notes to Chapters 1–6

NOTES TO CHAPTER ONE

1 The 'Dîwan' of Melayê Jezîrî 'the mullah of Jezîre' (1570–1640), the first work of literature in Kurmanji, was heavily imitative of Persian and Arabic religious poetry. Ehmedê Khanî (1650–1707) based his love epic *Mem and Zîn* on the Kurmanji oral epic *Memê Alan*.

2 Statistics compiled in the early years of the Republic (after the elimination of the more literate Armenians from these provinces) showed that Diyarbakir, Erzurum and Maraş, for instance, had less than 4% total literacy, by comparison with 39.4% for the *vilayet* of Istanbul. Of course, it is unclear from the source (Turkish Official Papers 1928, cited in Georgeon 1995: 170) what degree and type of functional literacy is assumed.

3 A middle-aged Botani man described his experience of such schooling to me in 1998. See Zînar 1998 for details of the education they gave.

4 e.g. 'Literacy . . . is absolutely necessary for the development not only of science but also of history, philosophy, explicative understanding of literature and of any art, and indeed for the explanation of language (including oral speech) itself.' (Ong 1982: 15).

5 During fieldwork I encountered several individuals who wore verses of the Qur'an as talismans; amongst the Yezidis, amulets more often consisted of magical symbols written by authoritative sheykhs.

6 Evliya Çelebi's improbable description of the skills of Abdal Khan Bitlisi, no doubt founded on a real reputation as a patron of arts and sciences (Dankoff 1990: 93–109) is an early witness. According to Čejpek (1968: 652–3) court-narrators of popular genres in the Shah of Iran's household were also relatively well-read. In the smaller Kurdish courts one might not expect the same degree of education, but there would have been a similar mix of oral and literary genre.

7 Nikitine (1956: 258) comments on the role of oral tradition in glorifying the élite classes, a feature criticised by Vilchevsky; he notes that both the élite and the masses listened to the same forms of oral tradition. Literacy amongst tribal leaders at the end of the Ottoman empire was mixed – Soane gives the Southern Kurdish example of Taha Beg, who wrote poetry and enjoyed Persian literature (1926: 228), but Driver (1919: 30) reports that Ibrahim Pasha Milli's son Mehmud Bey, whose home was at Viranshehir, now in Turkey, was illiterate, though he admired literacy.

8 This is a very contentious question; the number of Zaza speakers who claim a distinct identity from Kurmanji-speaking Kurds seems to be very small. For further discussion of questions of identity see van Bruinessen 1994: 29–37; for language see Paul 1998, MacKenzie 1966.
9 See especially Jelîl 1978, which contains many such instances.
10 Vilchevsky, quoted by Nikitine (1956: 255) and Bois (1986: 481).
11 Mukri is not a Kurmanji dialect but shares various features with Kurmanji; the collection contains many traditions also found in Kurmanji.
12 Published by Kamuran and Jeladet Bedir Khan, 1932–45, various locations.
13 For non-Kurdish expression of this, see Bois 1946: *passim* and Nikitine 1956: 259–71.
14 For the role of oral tradition in educating the people about the past see Jelīl 1985: 5–6, 13. Proverbs are often called *gotinên pêşîyan* 'sayings of the forefathers' and are one of the most commonly collected genres. Jelîl (1985: Introduction) refers several times to the *xizne* 'treasure' of Kurdish folklore.
15 As an example of the smaller-scale efforts, the Iraqi Kurdish folklorist Haji Jafar Haris remembered working as one of a team of young teachers, who visited remote villages and collected variant forms of oral traditions such as love songs (interview, Berlin 1998).
16 Exceptions include: Mann's description of Rahman, his informant, and of the training of bards (Mann. 1906 vol. 1: XXVII–XXX), and MacKenzie's introductions to regional sections (MacKenzie 1990 vol. 2).
17 Spies 1972 lists examples from a specific collection giving correspondences with Aarne and Thompson's motif-index; Marzolph 1984 has Kurdish examples.
18 For more detail on Kurdish broadcasting see Hassanpour 1996, 1998.
19 In Ba'drê, two young literate Yezidis, Mr. C. and a friend, complained that the version of *Mem û Zîn* told by an illiterate village elder was unsatisfactory because it did not agree with versions broadcast on the radio.

NOTES TO CHAPTER TWO

1 Such rules may be waived, in exceptional cases, by senior Yezidi authorities. I am indebted to Professor Philip Kreyenbroek and Dr. Khalil Jindî Rashow (KJR) for this information.
2 Thus Layard, Badger, Drower, Edmonds and Kreyenbroek. Lescot (1938) includes both Syrian and Sinjari Yezidis in his study, but his section on Sinjar concentrates more on history and tribal politics than on religion.
3 By this term I mean both Yezidi religion and other aspects of culture, which are closely intertwined in traditional communities.
4 Meiselas (1997: 36) gives a Caucasian Yezidi's account of his father asking for and receiving his mother, who was Armenian, in marriage. He does not present this as a particularly unusual event.
5 According to an oral tradition from the Mardin area, reported by a Syrian Orthodox Christian now in Germany, and as yet unpublished, a Christian leader early this century offered his daughter to whoever would kill an enemy; a Yezidi overheard this and did so. The leader was appalled at the prospect of his daughter marrying a Yezidi, but the Yezidi insisted that if the Christian did not keep his word, he would have to kill him too. The daughter feared for her father and gave herself to the Yezidi. They remained in the area and their children grew up [apparently Yezidi] close to both communities. I am indebted to Dr. Andrew Palmer for this information.

6 Isma'îl Beg, cousin of Mîr 'Elî Beg, attempted to exploit this by living there. He tried to increase his own power-base by gaining control of the Transcaucasian *senjaq*, and by issuing guidance to the Transcaucasian Yezidis in the 1908 document (see later in this chapter).
7 Dr. Rashow has supplied me with some information on collectivisation from a Yezidi source, the periodical *Lalêsh*, (1999 no. 11: 56–61), which lists the destroyed villages and collectives in both Sheykhan and Sinjar.
8 Both terms have similar extended meanings – 'chief', 'religious leader', in Arabic and Kurdish respectively. See Kreyenbroek 1995: 131–2 for a discussion, and the suggestion that the term 'sheykh' refers to the descendants of the companions of Sheykh 'Adī ibn Musāfir.
9 This seems to have been an individual choice. He was apparently the only eunuch in the entire Yezidi community, and studies made of the Yezidis give no hint of this being the case with any earlier Baba Chawûsh.
10 Elopement, which will be discussed more fully in Chapter Five, brings shame on the woman's family. Such sentiments were clearly socially appropriate, but cannot be dismissed as mere posturing. Although no Yezidi-Muslim elopements took place during my stay, 'honour killings' of various sorts had certainly happened within the last decade in the Muslim community in Iraqi Kurdistan.
11 Se'îd Beg (d. 1944) is said to have had 16 wives, according to members of the Mîr's family living in Ba'dre, whom I interviewed in August 1992. However, his grandson Se'îd Teḥsîn Beg had one wife.
12 'Heaven is my witness, that in all my travels I have never seen such courageous youths and pugnacious warriors as these.' (Dankoff 1990: 213). The longest list of Yezidi tribes fighting for the Khan is given as: Khalitî, Chekvanî, Bapirî, Jûlovî, Temanî, Mervanî, Beddî, Tatekî, Gevarî, Gevashî, Bezikî, Mudikî, Kanekhî (Dankoff 1990: 207). Members of the Rozhikî also participated, and are said in Melek Ahmed Pasha's abusive letter to the Khan to be his Yezidi kinsmen (*ibid*: 175).
13 I am indebted to Dr. Andrew Palmer for information on his as yet unpublished research.
14 Drower's sympathetic book, which is ahead of its time in the emphasis it places on the Yezidis' own accounts, gives instances where beliefs and practices as explained to her differ from those recorded by Lescot (1941: 24, 179, 180). Interestingly, she concurs strongly with Lescot on one point (*ibid*: 24): 'M. Roger Lescot . . . complains mildly that the list of the seven [Holy Beings] varied with every person he questioned. I corroborate this. The truth is that on this subject, as on others, the Yezidis are beautifully vague.'
15 For Melek Tawus' ambivalent status and his links with Satan, see Kreyenbroek 1995: 3, 60–1, 149–2.
16 One of the earliest documents clearly emanating from the Yezidi community is the 1872 petition to the Ottoman government requesting exemption from military service, and, to achieve that end, it cited many traditions and taboos which might be incompatible with service in the Ottoman army (Guest 1993: 122).
17 A *kerîf* is a type of sponsor, like a godfather, at a Yezidi boy's circumcision, and remains linked to the family thereafter; many are Muslims. As Kreyenbroek points out (1995: 136–7), families bound by the relationship must not intermarry for seven generations, and a *kerîf* is usually chosen from a group with whom intermarriage is not possible. The Yezidi discourse on Islam has clearly evolved and changed over many years; the present hostility should be seen in the context of the massacres of the second half of the nineteenth century and the early twentieth century.

18 Kreyenbroek (1995: 149) considers it much more likely that it arises from the homonym *khas* referring to the incarnation of a holy being.

19 The theological texts of the Syrian Orthodox Church, particularly the mystical lyric of St. Ephrem, suffered from similar misinterpretation and scorn by Western scholars; for an example, see Wright 1887.

20 'La Commission du *Journal asiatique* n'a pas cru devoir s'opposer à l'insertion de cette notice, malgré ses lacunes et la puerilité de certains détails', Introduction, Siouffi 1882. (Kreyenbroek's translation, 1995: 6).

21 I need hardly add that the occasions I attended were conducted with great propriety; the control of sexuality exercised by the rigid caste system, rules on endogamy, and concepts of 'pure' birth, would hardly seem compatible with orgies. In Layard's account of his visit to the shrine of Lalêsh in 1846 (1849: 270–308), he comments that the Yezidis did not indulge in the orgies attributed to them.

22 I heard these accusations from many people in Dihok in 1992. To take some specific examples, one Chaldaean man of late middle age, who had done business with Yezidis for many years, firmly believed these points; a third-generation Muslim of Yezidi origins, well-read and locally acknowledged to be an expert on Yezidism, insisted that the accounts of orgies were true.

23 A poster carrying the message 'if there is such a people as the Kurds, then the Yezidis are the most original (*aslîtirîn*) Kurds' and attributing it to Mr. Barzani was photographed in Dihok in April 1992 by Mrs. M. Kreyenbroek.

24 It is fair to say that, whilst Sheykh Adi can be said to have founded the sect, the people who became known as 'Yezidis' retained many of their pre-Islamic beliefs and practices.

25 For images of various traditional Yezidi costumes, see Lescot 1938, Guest 1993, Meiselas 1997: 34–9, 167.

26 One may compare the discourses of the Christians, who prefer to trace descent from ancient Assyrian emperors rather than from the Aramaeans, who boasted numerous small kingdoms and a highly developed culture.

27 The author of this book also declared himself the paramount prince of all Yezidis, a claim which would be disputed by many. It is unfortunate that many attempts to argue an ancient Iranian origin for the Yezidis have cited unconvincing evidence such as spurious word derivations; more reliable evidence does exist, but its identification and interpretation requires a degree of specialist expertise and knowledge of various religions.

28 This idea was not new in the early 1990s; according to Edmonds (1967: 67) the young Teḥsîn Beg was lionised in 1944 by Kurdish intellectuals in Baghdad who saw him as 'the head of a community that had preserved its "Kurdishness" to an exceptional degree'.

29 Evidence of other ancient Iranian religions is scanty and scattered; Kreyenbroek (1992, 1995) bases much of his argument for a non-Zoroastrian past for Kurdish religions on myth and cosmogony.

30 I am indebted to Dr. Khalil Jindî Rashow for this information.

31 Nobody stated that the caste system was an innovation introduced by Sheykh Adi and not part of the little-known ancient Yezidism, despite the opinion of some intellectuals that he had brought the sheykhs with him and that the pîrs were a more ancient group.

32 A *ferman* was an official decree; in Kurdish generally it has, over time, come to mean a hostile decree resulting in persecution.

33 For accounts of this incident I am indebted to Nawzat Beskfî, a relation of Silêmanê Mistê and to 'Abdilaḥad Hormoz Khoshaba, whose father-in-law arrested Silêman after he had become an outlaw.

34 KJR, personal communication, October 1999.
35 Badger (1852: 115) points out that, even if they had written books, they could not make use of them. However, he wrongly discounts the possibility of a corpus of oral religious texts.
36 KJR, personal communications, 1999.
37 This concept of a book or collection of information existing somewhere but being unavailable is surprisingly widespread; cf. Shryock 1997: 189, where Bedouin told him of an elderly tribesman (probably a myth) who had a book of poems containing important traditions which others had forgotten, so that they were not lost.
38 He uses *naskirin*, the verb for knowing people rather than facts.

NOTES TO CHAPTER THREE

1 For example, a well-known story tells how Sheykh Adi brought forth water from Zemzem at Mecca in the Lalêsh valley by striking a rock with his stick. It is still considered to be holy water. Stories also recount how the Yezidis came to occupy the valley; a Christian monastery existed there, and by performing miracles, Sheykh Adi persuaded the monks of his claim. Both these traditions were referred to by various informants, young and old, at festivals in 1992.
2 Allegedly this was because he and his large following posed a threat to the Atabeg of Mosul, Badr al-Dīn Lu'lu' (Guest 1993: 19–21; Kreyenbroek 1995: 31).
3 There is confusion in the written sources over which of the two 'Adīs brought the 'Adawiyya order to Lalêsh; oral tradition has chosen to opt for the first and more prestigious 'Adī, the founder of the order. This increases the status of Lalêsh, and as Kreyenbroek notes (1995: 31) it may well be true.
4 This is most memorably explained by Edmonds (1967: 6) 'For people who believe in the transmigration of souls what appear to us to be the most appalling inconsistencies and anachronisms present no difficulty whatever: it is as silly to say that Shaykh X and Shaykh Y whose appearances on earth seem to have been separated by one or more centuries, or even the archangel Gabriel and Shaykh Sajadin, cannot be "the same" as to try to make out that Mr. Jones who was seen last night in tails, white waistcoat and decorations cannot be the same as Mr. Jones who was seen the day before in a lounge suit or last summer in shorts and an open shirt.'
5 For instance, Sheykh Shems is sometimes identified with Jesus, and Yazīd b. Mu'āwiyya, a figure venerated by the Yezidis, is sometimes identified with Sheykh Adi.
6 Gelê 'Elî Beg is a gorge on the road to Diyana, through which part of the 'Hamilton Highway' was built (Hamilton 1937: *passim*). It is some distance from Yezidi territory, but locals also associate it with this Yezidi figure. The Blind Mîr's campaign against the Yezidis had been provoked by 'Elî Beg's murder of the Kurdish chieftain 'Elî Agha, whose relations had appealed to the Mîr of Rawanduz for redress (Guest 1993: 68–69).
7 For example, Mr. H. thought *Derwêşê 'Evdî* was 700 years old; it is probably about 150 years old (see next chapter). A murîd family with many educated members discussed its age in one meeting; they knew it was more recent than *Êzdî Mîrza*, but had no idea that the difference was more than one and a half centuries.
8 Many sheykhs and pîrs were not knowledgeable enough about their religion to give religious instruction to their murîds, but continued to receive alms and to perform necessary duties such as funeral rites (Kreyenbroek 1995: 125ff).

Sheykhs in theory have an obligation to offer protection and, where necessary, financial assistance to their murîds (Edmonds 1967: 7), but the extent of this seems to vary a great deal; many murîds are more prosperous than their sheykhs.

9 See Kreyenbroek (1995: 38, 44 n. 96) for the probable derivation of the names from ʻAdnānī and Qaḥtanī, used by North and South Arabian tribes respectively.

10 This traced principal lines of descent as far back as the fourteenth century, and listed branches after 1700. It was the only such detailed example I saw. The owner said that before literacy, such information was passed orally from parents to children.

11 The Hawerî tribe members questioned, all of whom were at least middle-aged, all mentioned Ḥesen Hawerî, who was much less well-known to other tribes. It is not clear how much knowledge younger generations had of this figure.

12 For a summary see Ben-Amos 1976: Introduction.

13 The breadth of this term is noted by Grima: 'the word . . ., although it varies slightly in meaning throughout the Muslim world, is commonly used to refer to folktales, fairy tales, legends and romances.' (1992: 29). However, she also notes that within the Paxtun community the term can denote gossip or personal experience narratives (*ibid.:* 246). If this latter usage exists among the Yezidis, who were apparently more forthcoming about personal experiences than the Paxtun, it was not found.

14 This scheme is perhaps more satisfactory than that proposed by Jelîl; almost all the *stran* are 'historical' by definition as most deal with events older than living memory. The songs about war are no more 'historical' than the love songs, whose protagonists are figures from history. However, they do enjoy higher status than the love songs.

15 This may well be a usage peculiar to Northern Iraqi Yezidis; it was certainly not encountered amongst the other communities in Badinan, who always used *şîn*. In conventional written Kurdish the term *dîrok* means 'history'.

16 The pronunciation seemed to vary between *peste* and *beste*. For this terminology, cf. J. Bedir Khan, 1932: 11, where a genre *beste* is defined as 'les chansons plus lourdes' with the same few words repeated and prolonged to such an extent as to be hardly recognisable. (This is one technique used in the Yezidi *stran* proper.) However, a rather light-hearted *peste* is consistent with the remark of Ms. F, a young Muslim woman from Dihok who described them as 'silly songs where the words don't really make sense'.

17 Figures from Kurdish legend such as Khej and Siyabend did appear in *stran* about love, but they were in a minority; it was also quite possible that members of the older generation at least believed that they had existed.

18 Personal communication, 1996.

19 The long narrative is called *beyt* in most Sorani areas and some Kurmanji areas, such as Badinan (*pace* Chyet 1991: 80).

20 The range of meanings associated with this term will be discussed in Chapter 6.

21 There seems to be no special Kurmanji word distinguishing the form *cante fable*, or alternating prose and verse, from verse narrative. However, it certainly exists in Kurdish, either with or without lyrical passages, and it may be a misunderstanding of this form which led to views of it as imperfectly remembered performance, and to Nikitine's extraordinary hypothesis that the long narratives evolved from the joining together of a succession of lyrics (1947–50: 47).

22 The words which rhyme at the ends of the lines usually have their stress on the penultimate syllable in both narrative and lyric. The many varieties in rhyme-scheme make it difficult to draw up fixed definitions of stanza (cf. Mann *loc. cit*).

23 'Cigerxwîn' (1988: 111) complains that many contemporary *stran* are padded out with such words.

24 The most famous *stranbêj*, including Lezgîn Seydo, Kheyro and his father Khelef Elias, and Qarpal Sinjarî, are all murîds. Feqîr Khidir, another murîd, is also well-known. Sheykh Derwêsh, Pîr Micho, and his father Pîr Giro, are among the best-known non-murîds.

25 The term *dîlok* was used by women at Khanek during the Yezidi New Year celebrations in April 1992. Rudenko (1982:14) has *dilok* and derives it from *dil* 'heart'; this derivation seems unlikely, especially in the light of the Badinani usages *dîlok/dîrok*, but may be an indicator of local perceptions of the emotional charge of the genre.

26 Muslim Kurds do indeed make physical gestures; I have observed Barzani Muslims pulling roughly at their hair, though they did not strike their chests as the Yezidis did; according to Dr. Shukriya Rasool, some Muslim Kurdish tribes also strike themselves. She also attests that some Kurdish Muslims, including the Hamawand and Dizayî tribes, tear hair out and leave it at the grave. The practice of a bereaved woman cutting some of her hair off is known widely in Kurdistan; a well-known curse directed at a woman is 'may God cut her hair', i.e. 'may she be bereaved'. (Yezidis hang their braids over the grave in a line, and one of the more affecting sights of their graveyards is a row of sun-bleached braids blowing gently in the breeze.)

27 The only exception to these strict rules of appropriate social context for laments which I encountered during fieldwork was the willingness of the Barzani women of Qosh Tepe to lament for their menfolk who had been taken away by Iraqi government forces ten years previously (Allison 1996: 42–4). However, they constitute an exceptional case; it was unclear how much opportunity they had had for overt lamentation while the area where they lived was under government control, and many of them seemed reluctant to accept that their relations were really dead. The fact that the 'disappearance' of their menfolk had remained unresolved for so long, and their abduction in such a large number, seemed (hardly surprisingly) to have produced an unusually lengthy period of deep mourning for the whole community.

28 The songs were recorded during mourning for 'Etarê Shero, who died in Yerevan in 1974. The recording was made in Tbilisi in September 1975 (Jelîl 1978 I: 44, II: 502).

29 One middle-aged murîd from Dêrebûn, Mrs. S., sang a short part of a rhythmic song which accompanied the grinding of grain and knew part of the same song in neo-Aramaic as sung by her Christian neighbours in her former village. She said she could not remember the song in full, and had forgotten the other work songs as it was so long since she had sung them.

30 *Şerm* has a wide range of meaning, from mild social embarrassment to stronger shame; it usually denotes a sense of shame which is socially appropriate, and is often used of female behaviour. It does not mean 'shame' in the sense of a great disgrace, which is denoted by *'eyb*.

31 It was the 'sacred' or 'legendary' history which was usually used by the propagandists of the 1960s and 1970s to emphasise links between Yezidis and Arabs.

NOTES TO CHAPTER FOUR

1 The first steps were taken towards allotting (Islamic) *waqf* status to the shrine, but this was never completed and it was restored to Mîr 'Elî Beg in 1907 (Fuccaro 1999: 140).

2 He was not killed in this engagement, but later, avenging a theft of animals by a rival Simoqan clan, the 'Elî Jermkan. Ironically perhaps, in the battle recalled in this song, he is fighting alongside the 'Elî Jermkan chief.
3 It is not clear why Mala Khalitî villages appear to be allied to clans of the Simoqan in this song; presumably it reflected the state of local politics at the time. Lescot contrasts the Simoqan nomads with the Jenewîyan, whose high incidence of feuds he attributes to their settled lifestyle; the Simoqan feuded less with neighbours, he says, because they did not live permanently by them (1938: 179–80).
4 Both these words mean 'family' though according to Izoli's dictionary, they can have the figurative meaning 'honour and virtue'. However, Yezidis have assured me that a more literal meaning is required here. The English phrase 'kith and kin' is usually used without strict emphasis on the distinction between the two categories and seems the most natural way of rendering the Kurdish device of using two words into English.
5 Other anachronisms used in the songs include *reşaş* 'automatic rifle' ("Kheyro" 7: 4; Kheyro Khelef 5: 5; and *bêşetaş*, 'machine gun' ("Qarpal" 8: 5; Lezgîn 2: 6, 5: 6, 8: 6, 10: 8, 13).
6 In fact, Kheyro Khelef also adds Ḥemo to his list of heroes, but rather unobtrusively, and only once in one of his latter stanzas (6: 5); it was very unlike the clear references made by Pîr Micho, and may even have been a 'slip of the tongue'. Various Yezidis who listened to the recording with me did not remark on it.
7 Occasionally a singer would pause within a stanza; I have only noted this as a break between stanzas if the pause contained melody rather than rhythmic repetition of a chord, or in the case of "Qarpal" whose musical accompaniment was minimal, if the pause was relatively long.
8 Either of the latter two examples, of course, could refer to Gula mezin, 'Big' Gulê.
9 Edmonds, who had met him, continues: '[Dawûd was] nearly always the first in trouble . . . How far this was due to real wickedness and how far due to the fact that his enemy . . . had been recognized as Chief of the Mountain and to certain genuine grievances in connexion with his lands I cannot now presume to judge.' He cites Dawûd as one of the four dominant figures in Sinjar during his time in Iraq.
10 I have rendered these by square brackets in my own transcriptions in Part II.
11 It is interesting that this telling assumes literacy.
12 The rest of Derwêsh's speech to his father is a repetition of the contents of the message from the Gêsan, but the offering of 'Edûlê's hand which could have been mentioned during the scene in the guest-house (stanza 3) is new.
13 Another published example is the Yezidi song *Şeṛê Xalita* 'The battle of the Khalitan' as quoted in *Hawar* (Lescot 1944), which repeats the names of the protagonists and locations in the same way.
14 One reads accounts of certain communities teaching their history to their children by taking them around the area and showing them important sites; certainly in my own fieldwork experience, people (not only Yezidis) have taught me about past events in the same way. In the Yezidi community, the Lalêsh valley in particular is full of important little places, each of which is linked to meaningful past events and figures of religious significance.
15 One might just as easily argue that if such lack of specific identification of 'observers' is tolerated in performance of old songs, it could also be tolerated in new compositions – so it might be 'original' anyway.

16 Another common element contributing to the negative portrayal of battle is the frequent use of such words as *mîrat* 'cursed' and *xopan* 'ruined'. The area is seen as sullied by the battle. Such terms are used both by named observers and by narrators.
17 Indeed, the *stranbêj* Mr. B., whom I asked about it, considered that it should not have been called *Dawûd* at all. Nevertheless, that name was used for this song by a dealer in Dihok and by Jelîlê Jelîl, so I have retained it.
18 For widespread Sinjari opposition to Mîr Se'îd Beg, see Fuccaro 1999: 143–7.
19 See Fuccaro 1999: 86 for details of RAF procedures. British policy of using air control in the colonies has recently been the subject of historical reevaluation and media attention in the UK.
20 For the development of the discourse relating to minorities in the context of Iraqi nation-building, see Fuccaro 1999: 132–65.
21 This is in contrast with Kurdish folktale and legend, where women can be warriors (e.g. Bedir Khan and Falgairolle 1938: *passim*). Of course, the lack of female warriors in the *stran* is in keeping with the genre's basis in historical fact; fighting women have been rare in Iraqi Kurdistan, especially among the Yezidis. There are songs where women express the wish to fight alongside the men; such sentiments gain their resonance from the fact that this would be crossing normal gender boundaries.

NOTES TO CHAPTER FIVE

1 Homosexuality, hardly surprisingly, proved a difficult and embarrassing area of questioning, on which I made little progress. It was acknowledged to exist, as a practice rather than as a state of being, but always associated with other groups. Whereas women in particular had no qualms about making jokes about impotence, for instance, they never referred to homosexuality in my hearing. It is certainly true that in Kurdistan, as in Europe, many young men migrate to large cities (usually outside Kurdistan) in search of a 'scene'.

Since relationships in general between the sexes in Kurdish society are governed by different types of constraint from same-sex relationships, perhaps one should not expect similar idioms where homosexuality was concerned. It is conceivable that the loving descriptions of young men put in the mouths of women and girls in the *stran* might mask homoerotic feelings, but no informants ever gave a hint to me of such feelings on the part of singers and poets (on whose private lives they could sometimes be quite voluble).
2 Since then, she has pursued her career and remains unmarried.
3 According to Yalçin-Heckmann, in the context of Muslim Kurds in Hakkari, 'when what should be kept private becomes public in such a way, the expressed female decision is underplayed, disguised, and manipulated by men by emphasizing how cunning the man or 'loose' the woman was' (1991: 248).
4 See Kreyenbroek 1995: 148 for the similarity of this attitude to Zoroastrian belief.
5 It should perhaps be said that if a Muslim girl were to elope with a Yezidi man, Muslims would be likely to feel a similar repugnance as they regard Yezidis as ritually impure. They would undoubtedly also view the elopement as a challenge to the supremacy of Islam. However, although the degree of outrage might be similar, the type of grievance would be different, because of the dynamics of power between the communities.
6 Mîr Teḥsin Beg has also acknowledged the problems associated with attempts to force young people into marriage, and has counselled the Yezidis in the diaspora

against this during a conference in Oldenburg in 1997. He also forbids the taking of bride-price.

7 Amongst young urban Kurds, especially those of the diaspora, these terms are less likely to denote a romantic or sexual relationship.

8 Other tellings of the story of Derwêsh in the Caucasus show other preoccupations. Bois (1959: 278) cites an example of *Dervîshê 'Awdî*, collected, or possibly, composed using folkloric models as inspiration, by Jasimê Jelîl, where the focus is on social class; his fatal battle is a test to prove himself worthy of marrying the daughter of a beg. Here she is called Meyran, daughter of 'Timur Beg the handsome'.

9 Ereb Şemo (1989: 94) describes autumn as a time when lovers exchanged confidences and gifts and recalled the carefree days of summer when they had had the freedom to be alone together.

10 I am grateful to Dr. Maria O'Shea and Mr. Nasir Rezazî for this information.

11 It is unclear whether this refers to sexual intercourse taking place during their secret assignation, or whether it is simply the news of his marriage which is a terrible blow to her.

12 There is anecdotal evidence, from reliable sources, of honour killings being committed by women at Qosh Tepe, a community of Kurdish Muslim women whose men were removed by Iraqi government forces. Some of the younger women who were raped by members of the security forces were later killed by women in their families.

13 This is, of course, an Islamic law, but it clearly has meaning in the Yezidi context as well.

NOTES TO CHAPTER SIX

1 However, it is also fair to say that a shortcoming of many anthropological studies of discourses on various subjects is the lack of detailed attention paid to genre, an issue which is considered here.

2 This fascinating book shows how Paxtun women place emphasis on emotions deemed acceptable by their social group and suppress unacceptable ones. Grima also describes how feelings are expressed in their social context.

3 A further study of the subject by Dr. Shukriya Rasool of the University of Salahaddin awaits publication, and other researchers are working on the laments of the Kurdish Jews.

4 For an account of such a visit to a Yezidi family, see Murad 1993: 189–91.

5 I am grateful to Mrs. Fawziya Rahman for this information.

6 I am grateful to Dr. Khelil Jindî Rashow for this information.

7 The literal meaning of *kimyon* is 'cumin'; here, according to Mrs. Hayat Rashow, it means a particularly pure gold.

8 I am grateful to Dr. Vardan Voskanyan for this information.

9 In Kurdish this has various other meanings corresponding to 'disappointed' 'annoyed' and 'disturbed'. It is a bitter rather than gentle emotion, but is used to describe reactions to everyday disappointments as well as to catastrophe.

10 The phrase 'seeing the world' *dinya dîtin*, clearly implies marriage in this context, according to Yezidi informants.

11 Of course, religious rituals and texts do exist in association with death among the Yezidis; at funerals, *qewls*, or religious texts, would be recited by qewwals (Kreyenbroek 1995: 161). The secular nature of the women's lament will be described later in this chapter. By contrast, Dr. Shukriya Rasool has evidence of some use of religious material among the laments of some Kurdish Muslims,

sometimes even with musical accompaniment, though many Muslims consider laments (and sometimes music as well) to be offensive to God.

12 Bois (1966:115) quotes Lescot's comments on this genre thus: 'At first sight the *peyîzok* does not seem to be much different from other compositions inspired by the sentiment of love . . . [but] it is the background and the natural setting . . . which gives it its peculiar tonality. Each verse begins with a brief glance at the autumn landscape whose melancholy inspires in the poet gloomy thoughts . . . Winter approaches . . . Gone are the carefree days.'

13 For the association of sickness with bereavement in a Bedouin community, see Abu Lughod 1986: 202.

14 The phrase *dayka dergûşê* 'mother of the babe', in a geographical area where one would expect *dîya dergûşê*, in accordance with local dialect, is particularly noticeable; *dîya* occurs in many other songs.

15 It was noted in Chapter 3 that Yezidi women cut off their braids for close relatives who die young or tragically in wars or accidents. The custom of attaching scraps of cloth to trees or to saints' graves is common to Yezidis, Muslims and Christians in the region.

16 It is not clear whether these were groups of women from the same household or from the same paternal clan. This lamentation seemed to be practised equally by members of all castes.

17 It is one of my great regrets, and a shortcoming of this work, that my limited access to the collectives meant that it was not possible to interview Mrs. J. later to explain all the unclear references in her lament. Certainly the distress of the participants precluded such an interview on the day itself.

18 According to Fawziya Rahman, Kurdish Muslim widows who are lamenting may refer to their husbands by a variety of different titles; the underlying principle is that a woman's husband means everything to her. Sometimes this is spelt out in such sentiments as 'you are my brother, my father . . .' etc.

Appendix: Informants and Performers

The notes below give a few relevant details of performers and of those people who gave particularly helpful interviews or other guidance during my fieldwork. They are intended to give the reader an outline of the range of living 'sources' used for this book. Where possible these details include gender, tribe, caste or religious group, age, and educational status. Not all these details were available in every case. Unless otherwise indicated, all are Yezidis. Most interviews took place in Badinan in spring, summer and autumn 1992. Their approximate ages are given as for the date when they spoke to me. In the case of the performers recorded by Jelîl, who were already elderly in 1978, it is quite likely that many are no longer alive. Unable to verify this, I have continued to speak of them in the present tense, as Jelîl's book does. They are listed in alphabetical order, in order of first name (or pseudonym), except where they prefer to use family names as surnames in the European manner.

Such brief summaries hardly do justice to the knowledge of these people, nor to their kindness. Many welcomed me into their houses, where their wives, sisters and daughters prepared meals at short notice, and several family members gave me useful information. Behind each listed individual is a group of others who contributed in many ways, offering practical help, making suggestions, and often taking interviews in unexpected and fruitful directions.

Mr A., middle-aged, literate *stranbêj*. In Ba'drê he performed a variety of *stran* to illustrate his classification of them.

'Abdilaḥad Hormoz Khoshaba, male, Chaldaean (Church Uniate with Rome) Christian, 60s, semi-literate. I lodged with his family for much of my stay. A native of the Dihok area, he had kept a general store for many years in the town and made many contacts in the area. His mother tongue was neo-Aramaic, but he knew the Kurdish language and community well.

Mr B., middle-aged *stranbêj*. Gave a great deal of information about the tradition of the *stranbêj* and about specific songs.

'Eydo Baba Sheykh, 30s, educated, sheykh. His father had been Baba Sheykh, one of the most important Yezidi religious figures, and his brother was a prominent PUK martyr. Sheykh 'Eydo himself is an authority on Yezidi traditions, both religious and folkloric.

Miriam Baba Sheykh, 20s, educated to degree level. She supplied useful information about women's traditions and provided many contacts and hospitality during interviews.

Mr C., murîd, 30s, educated. He had been a KDP *pêşmerge* before the 1991 uprising. His family lived in Ba'drê; he provided introductions to various members of the community.

Sheykh Derwêsh, 70s, Yezidi Sinjari *stranbêj*.

Mr E., murîd, 50s, Hakarî tribe, illiterate. He was born and bred in Ba'drê; he performed a prose narrative of *Mem and Zîn*.

'Elî Lezgîn, male, *stranbêj*.

Ms F., Muslim, late teens, educated. A school-leaver with excellent English, she summarised many of the *stran* and translated during some of the visits made to Muslim villages.

Feqîr Khidir, murîd. Sinjari *stranbêj*.

Ms G., murîd, 20s, educated. The daughter of a teacher, and one of the few Yezidi women with a university degree, she found time from her other work to provide introductions in the community, and to translate on visits to Khanek and Lalêsh.

Pîr Giro, male, 90s, Sinjari *stranbêj*.

Mr H., murîd, 80s, Qa'îdî, illiterate. Originally from Sînê, a destroyed village near the Shari'e collective village. He was very knowledgeable; in former years, he had been able to sing *stran*, which he had learned from listening to the *stranbêj* Sheykh Nader Khetarî when he was in his twenties, though he did not have formal instruction. By 1992, he no longer sang, but was able to tell historical traditions as prose narrative.

Ḥeso Nermo, male, murîd, 30s, Qa'idî. His family lived in Dihok but had come from the Shari'a collective. He provided many introductions to his family and to others.

Ḥisên Omerî, male, Muslim *stranbêj*.

Ḥizret Ḥeso, female, 'semi-literate'. She was born in 1920 and lives in Tbilisi. Her husband and brother have passed away. Ḥizret lightens the load on her heart with songs. She knows many songs, and has a high, clear voice. In Tbilisi bereaved families always ask her to come and sing songs of lament (Jelîl 1978 II: 502).

Mrs I. and Mrs D., murîd, 50s, Dina, illiterate. Both women remembered their lives in their former village (Kebertû, near the Khanek collective, now demolished) well, and described the onerous work they used to do there, as well as the performance of traditional songs and stories by women. Mrs D. had been well known in her village for her sewing skills; Mrs I. had been a village midwife.

Îsraêl Ohanyan (Îsê Vartê), male, Armenian, illiterate. He was born in 1910 in the village of Ḥiznemîre, near Diyarbakir, Turkey. He speaks excellent Kurdish; he spent his childhood and young adulthood among the Reshkotan, a Kurdish tribe. When he was eighteen his family moved to Qamishli in Syria. He knows many Kurdish songs and tales, and learned from the singers Yahoyê Ḥejî Mohammed and Mistê Quto. All his songs are Reshkotan songs. In 1966 he moved from Syria to Soviet Armenia (Jelîl 1978 II: 505–6).

Mrs J., Yezidi, 30s. She is a widow with a young son, and locally known for her expertise in performing 'personal' laments.

'Jerdo', (pseudonym), male, probably a Sinjari Yezidi *stranbêj*. No further information available.

Sheykh K., male, 60s, Hawerî, illiterate. He lived in Khanek; not only did he tell me some oral traditions, such as the story of Ḥesen Hawerî, himself; he also provided some very useful contacts, and his house was the location of many of the interviews carried out in that collective village.

Ms K., 20s, Hawerî, illiterate. Ms K., daughter of Sheykh K., had been married but had separated from her husband, and was once more living at her parents' home in Khanek.

Kheyro Khelef, male, murîd, c.40s. Sinjari *stranbêj*.

Pîr Khidir Silêman, male, 40s, educated. Originally from the Sheykhan area, Pîr Khidir studied Kurdish and Persian at university. With Khelîl Jindî, a fellow student, he published the Yezidi religious poems. He followed this with two further books, one on Yezidi village life and the other on Sheykhan. He provided a great deal of information and support during fieldwork.

Khodêda Abû Azad, murîd, c. 40s, Sheykhani *stranbêj*.

Sheykh L., male, Hawerî, 70s. He was *micewer* (headman) of a Yezidi village near Dihok, but was born in Zêdava, Turkey, and came to Iraq after the Second World War. During our interview he gave a description of the semi-nomadic life his tribe once led.

Lezgîn Seydo, male, murîd, 40s, Sinjari *stranbêj*.

Mr M., caste unknown, 50s, Mêrkan tribe (Sinjari). He had been living in Ba'adrê for some years after being on the run, accused of murder. He reminisced about Dawûdê Dawûd.

Meḥmûd 'Elîyê Temo, male, Shemsanî sheykh, literate. He was born in 1923 in the village of Dîhan, near Talîn in Armenia, and still lives in Armenia. He learned his songs from his brother Ḥesen (Jelîl 1978 II: 504).

Meḥmûd 'Eydo, male, murîd, 30s, educated. A Sheykhani, he had lived in Sweden for some years and returned to Iraq to marry. He provided various Yezidi and other contacts.

Pîr Micho, male, pîr, 40s, Sinjari *stranbêj*. Son of Pîr Giro.

Mr N., murîd, 70s, illiterate. He told several *çîrok* during our interview in Ba'drê in August 1992 and gave some fascinating information on folk belief.

Mr P., murîd, Qa'idî, 50s. He described his lineage and the history of his area during a visit to his house in Shari'e in July 1992.

Qarpal Sinjari, male, murîd, Sinjari *stranbêj*. Qarpal died in 1992.

'Pîr Qewwal' (pseudonym), male, Sinjari *stranbêj* related to Pîr Giro.

Mrs R., Hakarî, murîd, 50s, illiterate. Originally from the Arabic-speaking area of Ba'shîqe and Beḥzan, she grew up in Ba'drê, where she worked in the fields for the house of the Mîr, Teḥsin Beg. Mrs R. is a well-known performer of laments for the dead, and gave a great deal of information about the genre.

Fawziya Rahman, female, Sinjari Muslim, c. 50, educated. She has lived in London for most of the past twenty years or so, but was brought up in Sinjar, and knew many Yezidi families. She gave information on traditional love songs and on women's lament. Interviewed in London, May 1996.

Dr Shukriya Rasool, female, Sorani, c. 50. Dr Shukriya completed her Ph.D in Kurdish folklore in the former Soviet Union, and now teaches at the University of Salahaddîn in Erbil. She is an acknowledged expert on lament and readily shared her expertise. She has completed a study of the subject, which, to my knowledge, remains unpublished due to the situation in Iraqi Kurdistan.

Dr Khelîl Jindî Rashow, male, Adani sheykh, 40s, educated. Dr Rashow is an authority on Yezidi folklore, and co-published the Yezidi religious poems, or *qewls*, in 1979, which caused consternation among some Yezidi religious authorities. He now researches at the University of Göttingen.

Riza 'Elî, male, Yezidi. He was born in Armenia in 1920. His parents escaped from persecution in the Van area. He learned his songs from his maternal uncle, Ahmed Shewêsh (Jelîl 1978 II: 506–7).

Mrs S., (now deceased), murîd, 50s, Hawerî, illiterate. She was formerly from the village of Dêrebûn (near Pêsh Khabûr, by the Syrian border); she had left it some twenty-five years previously and was living in the Khanek collective. She remembered many details of her former life, such as work songs, and performed several examples, interspersed with many jokes!

Sargîs Bozoyan, male, Armenian, illiterate. He was born in 1901 in the village of Kozê near Artêş in Turkey. He speaks very good Kurdish; his father, Martîros Barêyan, was the *dengbêj* of 'Elî Ḥesen Agha. He lives in Armenia (Jelîl 1978 II: 499).

Ibrahim Sheykhani, male, sheykh (Adani), 30s, educated, brother-in-law of Dr Rashow. He came to London in his late teens, and trained as a hairdresser. He maintains a lively interest in Yezidi music, and has a large collection of cassettes and videos. Interviewed in London, January 1996.

Silo Koro, male, *stranbêj* living in Syria. He was born in 1921 in Syria. An early childhood illness left him blind. He is extremely well known; Jelîl comments on his wide repertoire – he knew both the lyrical *stran* and the long narrative *destan* – his great stamina for singing, and his prodigious memory (Jelîl 1985: 301–2).

Mr Y., an elderly *stranbêj*, was interviewed about *stran* and his learning of his craft.

Bibliography

Aarne, A.A. and Thompson, S. (1961) *The Types of the Folk-Tale: a Classification and Bibliography*, 2nd revision, Helsinki.

Abrahams, R. (1976) 'The Complex Relations of Simple Forms', in Ben-Amos, pp. 193–214.

Abu-Lughod, L. (1986) *Veiled Sentiments: Honor and Poetry in a Bedouin Society*, Berkeley.

—— and Lutz, C.A. (1990) *Language and the Politics of Emotion*, Cambridge.

Ahmad, S.S. (1975) *The Yazidis: their Life and Beliefs*, Miami.

Allison, F.C. (1995) 'Kurden' in *Enzyklopädie des Märchens*, Band 8: 635–647, Berlin.

—— (1996) 'Old and New Oral Traditions in Badinan', in Kreyenbroek and Allison, pp. 29–47.

Amindarov, A. (1994) *Kurdish-English/English-Kurdish Dictionary*, New York.

Anastase Marie, Père (1911) 'La découverte récente des deux livres sacrés des Yézidis', *Anthropos* VI, pp. 1–39.

Anon. (Turkish Government publications) (1928) *Population de la Turquie par vilayet et cazas par villes et par villages, d'après la recensement du 28 octobre 1927*, Ankara.

Atiyeh, G.N. (ed.) (1995) *The Book in the Islamic World: the written word and communication in the Middle East*, Albany.

Azîzan, H., see Bedir Khan, J.

Badger, G.P. (1852) *The Nestorians and their Rituals*, 2 vols, London.

Bedir Khan, J., and Lescot, R. (1970) *Grammaire kurde (dialecte kurmandji)*, Paris.

Bakayev, Č. see Beko.

Beko, Ch. (1957) *Kurdsko-Russkii Slovar*, Moscow.

Bakhtin, M.M. ed. tr. C. Emerson and M. Holquist (1986) *Speech Genres and Other Late Essays*, Austin, Texas.

Bascom, W.R. (1965) 'The forms of folklore: prose narratives', *JAF* 78, pp. 3–20.

Basset, R. (1924) *Mille et une contes arabes*, Paris.

Bauman, R. (1977) *Verbal Art as Performance*, Prospect Heights.

—— (1983) 'The field study of folklore in context', in Dorson, pp. 362–7.

—— and Briggs, C.L. (1990) 'Poetics and Performance as Critical Perspectives on Language and Social Life', *ARA* 19, pp. 59–88.

—— and Sherzer, J. (eds) (1974) *Explorations in the Ethnography of Speaking*, London, 2nd ed. 1989.

Bedir Khan, J. (1932) 'Le Folklore kurde', *Hawar* 3, pp. 9–11.
—— 'Herekol Azîzan' (1933) 'Besna', *Hawar* 22, pp. 5–7.
—— and Lescot, R., (1970) *Grammaire kurde (dialecte kurmandji)*, Paris.
Bedir Khan, K. (1938) 'La Femme kurde', *Hawar* 19, pp. 294–6.
—— and Falgairolle, A. (1938) *Le roi du Kurdistan*, Paris.
Ben-Amos, D. (ed.) (1976) *Folklore Genres*, Austin, Texas.
Bittner, M. (1913) *Die Heiligen Bücher der Jeziden oder Teufelsanbeter: (Kurdisch und Arabisch)*, Denkschriften der kaiserlichen Akademie der Wissenschaften in Wien, Phil.-Hist., Klasse, Band LV, Vienna.
Blackburn, S.H. (1988) *Singing of Birth and Death: texts in performance*, Philadelphia.
Blau, J. (1965) *Dictionnaire kurde-français-anglais*, Correspondance d'Orient 9, Brussels.
—— (1975) *Le kurde de 'Amādiya et de Djabal Sindjār; analyse linguistique, textes folkloriques, glossaires*, Travaux de l'Institut d'Études iraniennes de l'Université de la Sorbonne nouvelle 8, Paris.
—— (1989) 'Le kurde' in *Compendium Linguarum Iranicarum*, Wiesbaden, pp. 327–35.
—— (1996) 'Kurdish Written Literature', in Kreyenbroek and Allison, pp. 20–28.
Blum, S. and Hassanpour, A. (1996) ' "The Morning of freedom rose up": Kurdish popular song and the exigencies of cultural survival,' *Popular Music*, vol. 15/3, pp. 325–43.
Bois, T. (1946) *L'âme des Kurdes à la lumière de leur folklore*, Cahiers de l'Est 5 and 6, Beirut.
—— (1955) 'Un Coup d' oeil sur la litterature kurde', *Al-Machriq* 49, pp. 69–112.
—— (1959) 'Poètes et troubadours au pays des Soviets', *Al-Machriq* 53, pp. 266–99.
—— (1961) 'Les Yézidis: essai historique et sociologique sur leur origine religieuse', *Al-Machriq* LV fasc. I, pp. 109–28; fasc. II, pp. 191–242.
—— (1966) *The Kurds*, Beirut.
—— (1986) 'Kurds and Kurdistan' in *Encyclopaedia of Islam*, Tome V, Leiden, pp. 438–86.
Bozarslan, H. (ed.) (1994) *Les Kurdes et les États*, Peuples Méditerannéens no. 68–69.
Brauer, E. and Patai, R. (1993) *The Jews of Kurdistan*, Detroit.
van Bruinessen, M. (1992) *Agha, Shaikh and State*, 2nd ed., London.
—— (1994) 'Nationalisme kurde et ethnicités intra-kurdes' in Bozarslan, pp. 11–37.
—— (1998) 'Shifting National and Ethnic Identities: The Kurds in Turkey and the European Diaspora' in *JMMA* vol. 18 no. 1.
—— (2000) 'Les Kurdes, États et tribus', *Études kurdes*, Paris, pp. 9–31.
—— and Blau, J. (eds) (1988) *Islam des Kurdes*, Les Annales del l'Autre Islam no. 5, Paris.
Browne, J.G. (1932) *The Iraq Levies 1915–1932*, London.
Čejpek, J. (1968) 'Iranian Folk Literature', in Rypka, pp. 607–710.
Celîl, see Jelîl.
Chadwick, H.M and N.K. (1932–40) *The Growth of Literature*, 3 vols, Cambridge.
Chaliand, G. (ed) (1980) *People Without a Country*, London.
Charmoy, F.B. (ed.) (tr.) (1868, 1870, 1873, 1875), *Chèref-Nâmeh ou Fastes de la Nation Kourde; par Chèref-oudîne, Prince de Bidlîs, dans l'Iïalèt d'Ärzeroûme*, 4 vols, St. Petersburg.
Chol, Isma'il Beg (1934) *The Yezidis: Past and Present*, Beirut.
Chol, Emir Muawwiyah (1983) *To Us Spoke Zarathustra*, Paris.
Christensen, D. (1963) 'Tanzlieder der Hakkâri-Kurden,' *Jahrbuch für musikalische Volks- und Völkerkunde* 1, pp. 1–47.

—— (1975) 'Ein Tanzlied der Hakkari-Kurden und seine Varianten', *Baessler-Archiv* XXIII, pp. 195–215.
Chyet, M. (1991) *And a Thornbush Sprang Between Them: Studies on Mem û Zîn, a Kurdish Romance*, Ph.D. thesis, University of California at Berkeley.
'Cigerxwîn' (Şêxmus Ḥisên) (1988) *Folklora Kurdî*, Stockholm.
Cindî, see Jindî.
Coakley, J.F. (1992) *The Church of the East and the Church of England: a History of the Archbishop of Canterbury's Assyrian Mission*, Oxford.
Connelly, B. (1986) *Arabic Folk Epic and Identity*, Berkeley.
Coulthard, M. (1977) *An Introduction to Discourse Analysis*, London, 2nd ed. 1985.
Dakhlia, J. (1990) *L'oubli de la cité*, Paris.
Dankoff, R. (1990) *Evliya Çelebi in Bitlis: the relevant section of the Seyahat-name, edited with translation, commentary and introduction*, Leiden.
Deshen, S. and Zenner, W.P. (eds) (1982) *Jewish Societies in the Middle East: Community, Culture and Authority*, Washington.
Dirr, A. (1917–18) 'Einiges über die Yeziden', *Anthropos* 12/13, pp. 558–74.
Dorleijn, M. (1996) *The Decay of Ergativity in Kurmanji: language internal or contact induced?*, Tilburg.
Dorson, R.M. (1983) *Handbook of American Folklore*, Bloomington, Indiana.
Driver, G.R. (British Government Publications) (1919) *Kurdistan and the Kurdish Tribes*, Mount Carmel.
—— (1922) 'An Account of the Religion of the Yazidi Kurds', *BSOAS*, pp. 197–213.
Drower, E.S. (1941) *Peacock Angel*, London.
Drushinina E.S. (1959) *Kurdskie skazki*, Moscow.
Dundes, A. (1964) 'Texture, text and context', *Southern Folklore Quarterly* 28, pp. 251–65, repr. Bloomington, Indiana, 1980 in his *Interpreting Folklore*, pp. 20–32.
—— (1966) 'Metafolklore and Oral Literary Criticism', *The Monist* 50, pp. 505–16.
Edmonds, C.J. (1967) *A Pilgrimage to Lalish*, London.
Elliot, M. (1996) *'Independent Iraq': the Monarchy and British Influence, 1941–1958*, Library of Modern Middle East Studies 11, London and New York.
Ellow, P. (1920) *Assyrian, Kurdish and Yezidis, Indexed Grammar and Vocabulary with a few grammatical notes*, Baghdad.
Empson, R.H.W. (1928), *The Cult of the Peacock Angel*, London.
Evliya Çelebi (ed. Cevdet *et al.*) (1896–1938) *Seyahat-name*, Istanbul.
Feitelson, D. (1959) 'Aspects of the Social Life of Kurdish Jews', *Jewish Journal of Sociology* 2, pp. 201–216, repr. in Deshen and Zenner 1982, pp. 251–72.
Fentress, J., and Wickham, C.J. (1992) *Social Memory*, Oxford.
Finnegan, R. (1976) 'What is Oral Literature Anyway? Comments in the light of some African and other comparative evidence', in Stolz and Shannon, pp. 127–76.
—— (1977) *Oral Poetry – its Nature, Significance and Social Context*, Cambridge, 2nd ed. Bloomington, Indiana 1991.
—— (1990) 'What is Orality – if Anything?', *BMGS* 14, pp. 130–149.
—— (1992) *Oral Traditions and the Verbal Arts*, London.
Firat, M.Ş. (1961) *Doğu Illeri ve Varto Tarihi (The History of Varto and the Eastern Provinces)*, Ankara.
Frank, R. (1911) *Scheich 'Adî, der grosse Heilige der Jezîdîs*, Berlin.
Fuccaro, N. (1993) 'A 17th century travel account on the Yazidis: implications for a socio-religious history', *AION* 53, fasc. 3, pp. 241–53.
—— (1997) 'Ethnicity, State Formation, and conscription in postcolonial Iraq: the case of the Yazidi Kurds of Jabal Sinjar', *IJMES* 29, pp. 559–80.

—— (1999) *The Other Kurds: Yazidis in Colonial Iraq*, London.
Furlani, G. (1930) *Testi Religiosi dei Yezidi*, Testi e Documenti per la Storia delle Religioni 3, Bologna.
Georgeon, F. (1995) 'Lire et écrire à la fin de l'Empire ottoman: quelques remarques introductives,' *REMMM* 75–76/1–2, pp. 169–179.
Goody, J. (1977) *The Domestication of the Savage Mind*, Cambridge.
—— (1987) *The Interface between the Written and the Oral*, Cambridge.
—— (1996) 'Questions of Interface in Turkey,' *REMMM* 75–76/1–2, pp. 11–16.
Grima, B. (1992) *The Performance of Emotion among Paxtun Women*, Modern Middle East Series no. 17, Austin, Texas.
Grothe, H. (1911–12) *Meine Vorderasienexpedition 1906 und 1907*, 2 vols, Leipzig.
Guest, J.S. (1993) *Survival Among the Kurds: A History of the Yezidis*, London.
Guidi, M. (1932a) 'Origine dei Yazidi e Storia Religiosa dell'Islam e del Dualismo', *RSO* 12, pp. 266–300.
—— (1932b) 'Nuove Ricerche sui Yazidi', *RSO* 12, pp. 377–427.
Hamilton, A.M. (1937) *Road through Kurdistan*, London.
Hansen, H.H. (1961) *The Kurdish Woman's Life: Field Research in a Muslim Society, Iraq*, Nationalmuseets Skrifter, Etnografisk Roekke VII, Copenhagen.
Hassanpour, A. (1983) 'Bayt' in Yarshater vol. 4, pp. 11–12.
—— (1992) *Nationalism and Language in Kurdistan, 1918–1985*, San Francisco.
—— (1996a) 'The Creation of Kurdish Media Culture', in Kreyenbroek and Allison, pp. 48–84.
—— (1996b) 'Dimdim' in *Encyclopaedia Iranica* vol. VII, New York, pp. 404–5.
—— (1998) 'Satellite footprints as national borders: MED-TV and the extra-territoriality of state sovereignty', *JMMA* vol. 18, no. 1, pp. 53–72.
Havelock, E.A. (1978) 'The alphabetization of Homer' in Havelock and Herschell, pp. 3–21.
—— and Herschell, J.F. (eds.) *Communication Arts in the Ancient World*, New York.
Henige, D.P. (1974) *The Chronology of Oral Tradition*, Oxford.
—— (1982) *Oral Historiography*, London.
Hinnells, J. (ed.) (1994) *Studies in Mithraism*, Rome.
Hymes, D.H. (1974) *Foundations in Sociolinguistics: an Ethnographic Approach*, Philadelphia.
Izoli, D. (1992) *Ferhenga Kurdî-Tirkî, Türkçe-Kürtçe*, Istanbul.
Jaba, A. (1860) *Recueil de notices et de récits kurdes servant à la connaissance de la langue*, St. Petersburg.
—— A. (1879) *Dictionnaire kurde-français*, St. Petersburg.
al-Jabiri, K.F. (1981) *Social Change among the Yezidis in Northern Iraq*, D. Phil thesis, Oxford.
Jardine, R.F. (1922) *Bahdinan Kurmancî, a Grammar of the Kurmanji of the Kurds of Mosul Division and Surrounding Districts of Kurdistan*, Baghdad.
Jelîl, J(elîl) (1985) *Zargotina K'urdê Suriayê (Folklore of the Kurds of Syria)*, Yerevan.
Jelîl, J(emîla) (1973–86) *Kurdskie Narodnye Pesni i Instrumental'nye Melodii, (Kurdish Traditional Folk Songs and Instrumental Melodies)*, 2 vols, Moscow, vol. 1 repr. Stockholm 1982.
Jelîl, O. (1960) *Kurdskii Geroičeskii epos 'Zlatorukii Khan'*, Moscow.
—— translit. S. Mustafa and A.K. Muhammad (1977) *Stranê Zargotina Kurdayê Tariqîyê (Historical Songs from Kurdish Folklore)*, Baghdad.
—— and Jelîl, J(elîl) (1978) *Zargotina K'urda (Kurdish Folklore)*, Moscow.
Jindî, H. (ed.) (1957) *Folklora Kurmancîê*, Yerevan.

—— (1962) *Kurdskie epičeskie pesni-skazy (Kurdish epic songs-tales)*, Moscow.
—— (1972) *K'lamêd cimaet'a k'ördaye lîrîkîe (Lyrical Songs of the Kurdish Community)* Yerevan.
Kreyenbroek, P.G. (1992) 'Mithra and Ahreman, Binyāmīn and Malak Ṭāwūs: Traces of an Ancient Myth in the Cosmogonies of Two Modern Sects', in Gignoux (ed.) *Recurrent Patterns in Iranian Religion, StIr* Cahier 11, pp. 57–79.
—— (1994) 'Mithra and Ahreman in Iranian cosmogonies' in Hinnells, pp. 173–82.
—— (1995) *Yezidism – Its Background, Observances and Textual Tradition*, Lewiston, New York.
—— (1998) 'On the Study of Some Heterodox Sects in Kurdistan', in van Bruinessen and Blau, pp. 163–84.
—— and Allison, F.C. (eds) (1996) *Kurdish Culture and Identity*, London.
—— and Sperl, S. (eds) (1992) *The Kurds: an Overview*, London.
Kurdo, Q. (1960) *Kurdsko-Ruskii Slovar*, Moscow.
Kurdoyev, K, see Kurdo.
Layard, A.H. (1849) *Nineveh and its Remains*, 2 vols, London.
—— (1853) *Discoveries in the Ruins of Nineveh and Babylon*, London.
Lerch, P. (1857–8) *Forschungen über die Kurden und die iranischen Nordchaldäer I-II*, St. Petersburg, repr. Amsterdam 1979.
Lescot, R. (1936) 'Quelques Publications Récentes sur les Yézidis', *Bulletin d'Études Orientales* 6, pp. 103–8.
—— (1938) *Enquête sur les Yézidis de Syrie et du Djebel Sindjar*, Beirut.
—— (1940–42) *Textes kurdes*, vol. I Paris, vol. II Beirut.
—— 'Tawûsparêz' (1942) 'Xarabo', Hawar 38, pp. 604–8, repr. in Wikander 1959, p. 80ff.
—— 'Tawûsparêz' (1943) 'Le mariage chez les Kurdes', *Hawar* 52, pp. 764–8.
—— 'Tawûsparêz' (1944) 'Chansons', *Hawar* 54, pp. 783–4.
Lindisfarne, N. (1991) 'Romantic Love and Illicit Sex: the Middle Eastern Case', unpublished paper held in SOAS library.
Lord, A.B. (1960) *The Singer of Tales*, Cambridge, Mass.
Luria, A.R. (1976) *Cognitive Development: Its Cultural and Social Foundations*, Cambridge, Mass.
McDowall, D. (1996) *A Modern History of the Kurds*, London.
MacKenzie, D.N. (1961–2) *Kurdish Dialect Studies*, 2 vols, London, repr. London 1990.
—— (1962) 'The Origins of Kurdish' *Transactions of the Philological Society*, pp. 68–86.
—— (1963) 'Pseudoprotokurtica', *BSOAS* 26, pp. 170–3.
—— (1966) *The Dialect of Awroman (Hawrāmān-ī-Luhōn): Grammatical sketch, texts and vocabulary*, Historisk-filosofiske Skrifter udgivet af det Kongelige Danske Videnskabernes Selskab, Bind 4, nr. 3, Copenhagen.
Makas, H. (1900, 1926) *Kurdische Texte im Kurmānǰí-Dialekte aus der Gegend von Märdin*, Leningrad.
Mann, O. (1906, 1909) *Die Mundart der Mukri-Kurden*, 2 vols, Berlin.
Marzolph, U. (1984) *Typologie des persischen Volksmärchens*, Beirut.
—— (1998) 'What is folklore good for? On dealing with undesirable cultural expression', *JFR* 35, no. 1, pp. 5–16.
Meiselas, S. (1997) *Kurdistan in the Shadow of History*, New York.
Menzel, T. (1911–12) 'Ein Beitrag zur Kenntniss der Yeziden' in Grothe, vol. I, pp. 89–211.
Middle East Watch (1993) *The Anfal Campaign in Iraqi Kurdistan*, New York.

Millingen, F. (1870) *Wild Life among the Koords*, London.
Mills, M.A. (1990) *Oral Narrative in Afghanistan: the Individual in Tradition*, New York.
—— (1991) *Rhetorics and Politics in Afghan Traditional Storytelling*, Philadelphia.
Muhawi, I. and Kanaana, S. (1989) *Speak, Bird, Speak Again*, Berkeley.
Murad, J.E. (1993) *The Sacred Poems of the Yazidis: An Anthropological Approach*, Ph.D. thesis, University of California at Los Angeles.
Nasr, S.H. (1995) 'Oral Transmission and the Book in Islamic Education', in Atiyeh, pp. 57–70.
Nau, F. and Tfinkdji, J. (1915–17) 'Receuil de textes et de documents sur les Yézidis', *ROC*, 2nd series, vol. 20, pp. 142–200, 225–75.
Nazdar, M. (1980) *The Kurds in Syria*, in Chaliand, pp. 211–217.
Nezan, K. (1980) 'The Kurds under the Ottoman Empire' and 'Kurdistan in Turkey' in Chaliand, pp. 19–46, 47–106.
Nikitine, B. (1929) 'Quelques Fables kurdes d'animaux', *Folklore*, XL, pp. 228–44.
—— (1947–50) 'La Poesie Lyrique Kurde', *L'Ethnographie* 45, pp. 39–53.
—— (1956) *Les Kurdes: Étude Sociologique et Historique*, Paris, repr. 1978.
—— and E.B. Soane (1923) 'Kurdish Stories from my collection', *BSOS* IV, pp. 121–38.
Noel, E. (1921) 'The Character of the Kurds as illustrated by their proverbs and popular sayings', *BSOS* I, pp. 79–90.
O'Shea, M.T. (1996) 'Kurdish Costume: Regional Diversity and Divergence', in Kreyenbroek and Allison, pp. 135–55.
Omar, F. (1992) *Kurdisch-Deutsches Wörterbuch (Kurmancî), Ferhenga Kurdî-Elmanî*, Berlin.
Ong, W.J. (1982) *Orality and Literacy: the Technologizing of the Word*, London and New York.
Parry, A. (ed.) (1971) *The Making of Homeric Verse: The Collected Papers of Milman Parry*, Oxford.
Paul, L. (1998) *Zazaki: Grammatik und Versuch einer Dialektologie*, Wiesbaden.
Perwer, Ş. (1990) *Çîroka Newrozê*, Uppsala.
Pitt-Rivers, J. (1977) *The Fate of Shechem, or The Politics of Sex: Essays in the Anthropology of the Mediterranean*, Cambridge.
Portelli, A. (1991) *The Death of Luigi Trastulli and Other Stories*, New York.
Prym, E. and Socin, A. (1887, 1890) *Kurdische Sammlungen, Erzählungen und Lieder in den Dialekten des Ṭûr 'Abdîn und von Bohtan*, 2 vols, St. Petersburg.
—— (1890) *Übersetzung*, St. Petersburg.
Rasul, I.M. (1979) *A Study in Kurdish Folkloric Literature*, Suleymaniye.
Reynolds, D.F. (1995) *Heroic poets, poetic heroes: the ethnography of performance in an Arabic oral epic tradition*, Ithaca.
Ritter, H. (1976) 'Kurmāncī-Texte aus dem Ṭūr 'Abdīn', *Oriens* 25–6, pp. 1–37.
Rizgar, B. (1993) *Kurdish-English, English-Kurdish Dictionary*, London.
Rohat (1995) *Li Kurdistanê Hêzeke Nuh: Jinên Kurd*, Stockholm.
Rosenberg, D.V. (1990) 'Language in the discourse of the emotions', in Abu-Lughod and Lutz, pp. 162–85.
Rudenko, M.B. (1982) *Kurdskaya Obryadovaya Poeziya*, Moscow.
Rypka, J. (1968) *History of Iranian Literature*, Dordrecht.
Sabar, Y. (1982) *The Folk Literature of the Kurdistani Jews*, New Haven.
Said, E.W. (1993) *Culture and Imperialism*, London.
Scribner, S. and Cole, M. (1981) *The Psychology of Literacy*, Cambridge, Mass.
Shryock, A. (1997) *Nationalism and the Genealogical Imagination: oral history and textual authority in tribal Jordan*, Berkeley.

Silêman, Kh. (1985) *Gundiyatî*, Baghdad.
—— and Jindi, Kh. (1979) *Êzdiyatî: liber Roşnaya Hindek Têkstêd Aînî Êzdiyan*, Baghdad, repr. 1995 in Latin script.
Siouffi, N. (1882) 'Notice sur la secte des Yézidis', *JA*, ser. 7, vol. 19, pp. 252–68.
—— (1885) 'Notice sur le Chéikh 'Adi et la Secte des Yézidis', *JA*, ser. 8, vol. 5, pp. 78–100.
Slyomovics, S. (1987) *The Merchant of Art: An Egyptian Hilali Oral Epic Poet in Performance*, Berkeley.
Spies, O. (1973) 'Kurdische Märchen im Rahmen der orientalisch vergleichenden Märchenkunde', *Fabula* 14, Heft 3, pp. 205–17.
Stolz, B.A., and Shannon, R.S. (eds) (1976) *Oral Literature and the Formula*, Ann Arbor.
Soane, E.B. (1913) *Grammar of the Kurmanji or Kurdish Language*, London.
—— (1926) *To Mesopotamia and Kurdistan in Disguise*, 2nd ed., London.
'Stranvan', (1933) 'Lawiqo!', *Hawar* 19, p. 3.
Street, B.V. (1984) *Literacy in theory and practice*, Cambridge Studies in Oral and Literate Culture 9, Cambridge.
Sykes, M. (1915) *The Caliphs' Last Heritage*, London.
Şemo, E. (1983) *Dimdim*, Stockholm.
—— (1989) *Şivanê kurd/Le berger kurde*, Paris.
Tatsumura, A. (1980) 'Music and Culture of the Kurds,' *Senri Ethnological Studies* V, pp. 75–93.
'Tawûsparêz', see Lescot, R.
Thomas, R. (1992) *Literacy and Orality in Ancient Greece*, Cambridge.
Tonkin, E. (1991) *Narrating our Pasts: the Social Construction of Oral History*, Cambridge Studies in Oral and Literate Culture 22, Cambridge.
Uzun, M. (1991) *Rojekê ji rojên Evdalê Zeynikê*, Stockholm.
—— (1992) *Destpêka Edebiyata Kurdî*, Ankara.
Vansina, J. (1985) *Oral Tradition as History*, London.
Wikander, S. (1959) *Recueil de textes kourmandji*, Uppsala.
Wright, W. (1887) 'Syriac literature' in *Encyclopaedia Britannica* vol. 22, 11th ed., repr. London 1894 as *A Short History of Syriac Literature*.
Yalçin-Heckmann, L. (1991) *Tribe and Kinship among the Kurds*, Frankfurt.
Zinar, Z. (1998) 'Medrese Education in Kurdistan,' in van Bruinessen and Blau, pp. 39–58.

Index

Aarne, A. A. and Thompson, S., 282
Abdal Khan Bitlisi, 33, 39, 281, 283
'Abdilaḥad Hormoz Khoshaba, 284
Abrahams, R., 63
Abu Lughod, L., 5, 135, 137, 168, 291
Adani sheykhs, 46, 47, 48, 55, 56, 286
'Adawiyya order, 56
'Adi b. Musāfir, 40, 41, 283, 185
agha, 66
Ahmad, S.S., 3
'Ahmed the young Turk', 174
'Ajîl Birahîm, 119, 123, 239–55
Alagöz, Mount, 153, 264
Alevis, 37
Alexander (the Great), 13, 71, 175
'Ali, caliph, *see* 'Elî Shêr
Allison, F.C., 13, 197, 287
Amadiya, 66, 69
Anastase Marie, Père, 47
Anfal campaign, 29–30
Anushîrwan, 174, 275
Antanosk, mountain, 182–3, 280
arabesk, 136
Armenia, 5
'Ashik Gherîb, 66, 72, 174–5, 275
Asma'īl Haqī Rasul, 233
'Assyrians' *see* Christians
Azîzan, H., see Bedir Khan, J.

Ba'ath party, 37, 50, 57, 131
Baba Chawûsh, 31, 140, 283
Baba Sheykh, 140, 149
Baba Sheykh, 'Eydo, 20
Badger, G. P., 16, 36, 40, 282, 285
Badinan, 7, 37, 45, 67, 68, 72, 80, 84, 130, 133, 136, 139, 148, 150, 154, 167–99 *passim*, 214, 286, 287
Ba'drê, 20, 27, 29, 37, 52, 59, 69, 71, 72, 74, 75, 104, 177–87, 283
Ba'shîqe, 75
Bakayev, Č. see Beko.
Bakhtin, M.M., 61, 63
Barzani,
  Mes'ud, 17, 18, 38, 134, 284
  Mulla Mustafa, 134, 169
  tribe, 30, 76, 186, 190, 196, 287
Battles, 112–20
Bauman, R., 21, 23, 25
bav, *see* clan
Bavê Behjet, 115
Bayezîd Beg, 40
Bedir Khan, J., 14n., 65, 163, 150–1, 282, 286
Bedir Khan, K., 14n., 282, 289
Bedirkhan Beg, 161, 253
beg, 65
Behlûl, 71
Bezanê, 75
Bekiran, 90, 106, 113, 114, 215–31, 234–9
Bêlajuk, plain of, 152, 259–62
Belqîz, Queen of Sheba, 174–5, 275
Ben-Amos, D., 61, 63, 286
Berjes, son of Sifûqê Meto, 90–101 *passim*, 215–231 *passim*
Besa Khelîl, 136, 150–51, 151–61, 163–5, 263–6
Besna, *see* Besa Khelîl
beste, *see peste*
beyt, 66, 67, 68, 286

Bilbilo, 152
Bîrê, 120
Biroyê Sherqî, 45, 78, 80, 81, 202
Bîrê, 257
Bîsharê Cheto, 118, 129
Bitlisi, Abdal Khan, *see* Abdal Khan Bitlisi
  Sheref Khan *see* Sheref Khan Bitlisi
Blackburn, S.H., 24
Blau, J., 7, 16, 47, 66, 72
blood-feud, 86
Blum, S., 15
Bois, T., 15, 78, 176, 282, 290–1
Book, the
  People of, 26–52,
  religions of, 10, 25, 33, 35
  Yezidi status, 44
Boz Beg, 174
Brahîm Pasha, 160, 253
Brauer, E., 16
Briggs, C.L., 21, 25
British mandate, 36, 46, 55, 103, 128, 130, 231–4
Browne, J.G., 103
van Bruinessen, M., 7, 10, 281–2

çantefable, 66, 286
Čejpek, J., 281.
Çelebi, *see* Evliya Çelebi
Celîl, see Jelîl.
Chaldeaeans, *see* Christians
Chêlikê 'Eliyê Remo, 155, 267
Chilmêra, 93, 107, 113, 115–6, 215–231 *passim*, 234–9
Chol, *see* Mîr of the Yezidis
Christensen, D., 15
Christianity, 56
Christians, 28, 32, 34, 37, 43, 44, 101, 102, 103, 130, 137, 139, 205, 284, 291
  attitudes towards Yezidis, 282
  Chaldaean, 284
  Church of the East, 11
  Syrian Orthodox, 11, 284
  Yezidi attitudes towards, 35
Chyet, M., 15, 67, 286
'Cigerxwîn' (Şêxmus Ḥisên), 115, 118, 156, 287
Cindî, see Jindî.
çîrok, 64, 71–2, 82, 84, 171, 275
çîrokbêj, 71
Ciwan Hajo, 209
clan, 28, 45
Cole, M., *see* Scribner, S.
Conflict, portrayals of, 86–134
  tribal resolutions of, 86
Coulthard, M., 12

Daḥḥam al Hadi, 103
Dakhlia, J., 53
dancing, 65, 69, 70, 84 *see also peste*
Dankoff, R., 283
Daseni, 43
Dawûdê Dawûd, 51, 73, 94, 101–7, 126–8, 131, 169, 202, 288
  theme and *stran* of, 25, 80, 87, 101–7, 112–3, 114, 117, 125–6, 133–4, 201, 207–8, 231–9, 289
Dawûdê 'Isa, 90–101 *passim*, 215–231 *passim*
Death, Loss and Lamentation, 167–99
  vocabulary associated with death, 169
dengbêj, 68, 71, 78, 81, 136, 170
Dêrebûn, 27, 42, 287
Derwêshê 'Evdi, 19, 51, 54, 78, 142
Derwêshê 'Evdi traditions, 62, 71, 81–2, 87, 118–126, 131, 132, 201, 204, 290
  coffee motif, 110, 145–8
  narratives, 108–12, 118–124, 165, 205, 239–58
  lyrics, 136, 151–62, 163, 259–63
destan, dastan, 67, 80 *see also beyt*
'devil-worship', *see* Slanders
Dihok, 19, 27, 28, 30, 37, 39, 43, 45, 66, 68, 83, 141, 284, 286, 289
dîlok, 75, 287, *see also şîn*
Dimdim, see Khanê Lepzêrîn
Dimli (language), 11, 282
Dimlî (tribe), *see* qewwals
Dina, Dinayî, 43, 79
dîrok, 65, 286 *see also şîn*
dîv, 13
Dorleijn, M., 12
Doskî, 45
Driver, G.R., 48, 281
Drower, E.S., 282–3
Dundes, A., 21, 61, 63
Durrani, 138, 141

Edmonds, C.J., 44, 87, 101, 102, 104, 284, 285, 288
'Ebdelleh Beg stran, 98, 221

'Edûlê, 78, 108–12, 118–124, 132, 133, 136, 142, 154–62, 165, 204, 239–58, 288
'Edûlê and 'Emer Agha, 153
'Edûlê and Genj Khelîl, 160, 162
'Egîtê Têjir, 108–12, 119, 124, 131, 145–50, 151–62, 163, 205, 255–8, 262–3
Ehmed Ferman Kîkî, 150–62
Ehmedê Khani, 6, 281
'Eldîna, 86, 128
'Elî Agha, 90–101 *passim*, 117, 215–231 *passim*, 285–12, 119–126, 239–55
'Elî and Meryem, 142, 144
'Elî and Suleyman, 118, 239–55
'Elî Beg, 57, 283, 285, 287
'Elî Jermkan, 90, 288
'Elî Pasha, 114, 215–231
'Elî Pismamo, 162
'Elî Shêr, 174–5, 275
Elliot, M., 130
'Emerê Dawûd, 104–5, 126–8, 129, 130–32, 133–4, 213, 231–9
'Emerê Ûnisê, 146, 261
emirs
as patrons of the arts, 10–11
time of, 55
Empson, R.H.W., 101, 102
epic, 63
epithalamia, 78
Erbil, 28
'Evdî, 109–12, 120–22, 131, 239–5
Esmerê, 152, 153
ethnography of speaking, 22–3
'Etarê Shero, 177, 187, 276, 287
'Etman, *see* Hidman
Evliya Çelebi, 33, 36, 39, 281
'Eyn Sifni, 27, 28, 231, 232
'Eysha Balê, 118, 171–5, 183, 273–6
Êzdî Mîrza, 46, 51, 57, 59, 71, 201, 285
Êzdîna Mîr, 56
Êzîdê Sor, 230
Ezra'îl, 124, 246, 251, 271

Fakhr al-Dn, 56
Faroq Beg, 69
'Faroq's father', 192
Fawziya Rahman, 140, 169, 196, 290, 291
Fayṣal, King, 113
Feqîr Hejî, 140
Feqîr Khidir, 69, 81, 287
feqîrs, 30
Feqîran, 28, 31, 101, 215–31
'Ferîq Pasha', 28, 45, 114, 129, 206
theme and *stran* of, 70, 80, 81, 87–101, 105, 107, 112, 113–7, 118, 133–4, 144, 202–8, 207, 215–31 *see also stran* of war
constituent elements, 88–90
heroes, 124–5
variation of original, 90–94
artistry in performance, 94–101
ferman, 44, 129, 130, 205, 284
Festivals, 22, 37, 285
New Year, 75, 76, 176, 187–99
Finnegan, R., 8, 12, 23, 62
Firat, M. Ş, 6
folklor, see folklore
folklore
and metafolklore, 63
future of, 208–10
Orientalist views, 5
local attitudes to, 16, 20, 52, 69, 82, 83, 84, 167, 202
political uses and significance, 6, 16, 18, 209–10
folk-tale, 60, 71
Fuccaro, N., 101–4 *passim*, 127–32, 200, 287, 289

Gabriel, *see* Jibra'îl
gazelles, 132, 145, 146, 151–2, 154, 173, 184, 192 *see also* landscape and nature imagery
Gelavêj, 142
genealogies, 10, 40, 55, 58–9, 139–40, 286
genre, 60–85
and status, 19
and function, 53–4, 87
and gender, 77–80
definitions, 61–2
George, Margaret, 164
Georgeon, F., 281
Gêsan, 109–12, 119–24, 159, 160, 170, 239–55, 288
Ghazi, King, 106, 107, 113, 234–9
Girê 'Ereba, 90–101 *passim*, 113, 114, 215–231 *passim*
Giro, Pîr, 81, 105, 148, 152, 156, 160, 162, 171, 287
Goldenhand, see *Khanê Lepzêrîn*

Goody, J., 10
government, 92, 103–4, 114
  representations of, 87, 126–7, 130
  resistance to, 45–6, 86–134 *passim*
Grima, B., 5, 135, 164, 168, 180, 286, 290
Guest, J.S., 16, 87–8, 101, 137, 163, 283, 284, 285
Guidi, M., 40
Gula kiçik ('Little' Gulê) 90–101 *passim*, 115–17, 204, 215–231 *passim*
Gula mezin ('Big' Gulê) 90–101 *passim*, 116, 215–231 *passim*, 288
Gulistan, wife of Şivan Perwer, 142
Gulîzera 'Etar, 79, 187

Habbabat, 90, 101
Ḥafir Gêsî, 119, 123, 239–55
Hajo, Ciwan, 68
Halabja, 117
Halîma, 156
Hamilton, A.M., 285
Hansen, H.H., 136
Ḥasan al-Basrī, 56
Ḥasan Hawerî, 201, 286
Haskan, 103
Hassanpour, A., 15, 282
Havelock, E. A., 8
Hawerî, 42, 50, 71, 79, 286
Ḥemo Shêro, 28, 88, 94, 101–4 *passim*, 128, 130, 131, 134, 202, 224, 229–31, 288
Hemze the Champion, 174–5, 275
Henige, D.P., 58
Ḥesen Sinjarî, 161
Ḥesenî, 111
Ḥesokê Hemzî, 106
Heverkan, 26, 27, 35
Ḥezo, 78, 81
Hidman, 110, 119, 159, 170, 239–55, 255–8
Ḥikmat Sulayman, 104
Ḥisên Omerî, 124
Ḥisênê Elkê, 201
Ḥisênkê Inîzê, 234–9
Ḥisênê Jerdan, 257
Ḥizreta Ḥeso, 77, 177–87, 195–9, 276–80
homosexuality, 136, 289
Ḥuseyn Berjes, 105, 234–9
'Ḥuseyn Effendi Qoche Pasha', 234–9
Ḥuseyn Fewzî Pasha, 107, 234–9
Hymns, see *qewls*

Ibrahim Pasha Millî, 45, 80, 88, 108, 281
Ibrahim Temo, 155, 157, 163, 263–6
'Isa Derwêsh, 150
Islam, 56
Isma'îl Beg, 48–9, 283
Israel Ohanyan, 78, 108–12, 118–9, 120–23, 131–2, 142, 146, 148, 154–62, 170, 205, 239–55
Izoli, D., 217, 278, 288

Jaba, A., 14, 78
al-Jabiri, K.F., 3
'Jacobites', *see* Christians
Ja'far Pasha al 'Askerî, 103
jash, 46, 202
Jelîl, Jasim, 210, 290
Jelîl, Jelîl, 13–16, 19, 49, 76, 82, 104–7, 144–50, 177–99, 214, 286, 289
Jelîl, Jemîla, 15
Jelîl, O., 13—16, 19, 49, 76, 132, 144–50, 177–99, 207, 214, 286
Jenewiyan, 90, 288
Jerdan, 111, 124
'Jerdo', 88–101, 115–16, 218–9
Jews, 11, 44, 137, 149
Jezîre Botan, 5, 39, 265, 277
Jibra'îl, 124, 246, 251
'Jigerkhwîn' see 'Cigerxwîn'
Jindî, H. 15, 170, 171
Jindî, Kh. *see* Rashow, Kh.
jinn, 13, 59, 141

Kamal, Y., 210
KDP (Kurdish Democratic Party), 17, 37, 38
KDPI (Kurdish Democratic Party – Iran), 163
Kemal, Pîr, 90–101 *passim*, 215–231 *passim*
Kênê, 143
kerafet, 35, 45, 200, 234, 283
Khabûr, 147, 279
Khanê Lepzêrîn, 13, 19, 66, 67, 111, 120, 132, 205, 210
Khanek, 20, 27, 29, 30, 37, 42, 44, 50, 52, 71, 74, 79, 83, 137, 177, 187, 194, 195
khas, 56–7, 58–9, 284

Khasse, 35
Khej and Siyabend, 13, 67, 136, 142, 151, 174–5, 275, 286
Khelef Elias, 81, 287
Kherabo!, 143–4, 151–62, 163, 213, 266–72
'Kheyro', 88–101, 116, 117, 125, 219–21, 288
Kheyro Khelef, 69, 81, 88–101, 113, 114, 116, 117, 125, 129, 140, 144, 156, 158, 162, 208, 287, 288
Khidir Elias, 13
Khidir Feqîr, 152, 153, 158, 162
Khodêda Abu Azad, 69
Khodêda, son of Ḥemo Shêro, 102
Khwerkan, 90, 117, 126, 202, 215–31
Kiçê, 81
Kida Ûso, 79
Kîkan, 110, 111, 121, 145, 148, 150–51, 160, 162, 239–58, 259–63
Kochek Mîrza, 29, 31, 88, 215–31
kocheks, 31
Komela, 163
Koroğlî, 13
kotel ceremony, 156, 162, 169–70
Kreyenbroek, P.G., 3, 4, 16, 26–52 *passim*, 55, 56–7, 149, 174, 187, 215, 275, 282–6, 289, 290
Kurdish autonomous zone, 17–21, 27, 28, 31, 37–8, 50, 82
Kurdoyev, K, see Kurdo.
Kurmanji, 5–6, 25, 61, 69, 75, 133, 153, 281, 286
  alphabets and writing systems, xi-xii, 7, 213–4
  as adjective, 132, 261
  education and official status, 6–7
  subdialectal differences, 39, 83, 92, 104–5, 291
  genre and register, 63–4, 70–75

Lalêsh, 17, 20, 26, 28, 51, 56, 88, 171, 284, 285, 288
landscape and nature imagery, 16
  animals, 111, 151, 157, 172–5
  birds, 105, 152, 157, 181, 209
  flowers, 105, 152–3, 172, 209
  fruit, 145, 152, 153
  gardens, 111, 172–3
  mountains, 154, 182–3, 186
Lavijê Pîrê, 171, 175
lawik, *see stran*
Lawkê Simoqî, 152
Layard, A. H., 16, 33, 35, 36, 40, 282, 284
legend, 59–60, 63, 67, 71, 85
Lerch, P., 14
Lescot, R., 16, 36, 40, 56, 78, 86, 102, 126, 137, 143, 152, 156, 213, 266–72, 282–3, 288, 291
Leyla and Majnun, *Leylê and Mejnûn*, 13, 158, 174–5, 275
Lezgîn Seydo, 69, 81, 88–101, 115, 116, 117, 153, 162, 213, 224–9, 287, 288
Lindisfarne, N., 138, 141
literacy, 281
  definitions, 9
  for divination, protection and cures, 10, 48
  in Kurmanji, 7–12
  taboo on, 3, 47
  in Yezidi context, 46–52
Lord, A.B., 8, 9, 12
Love as theme, 135–66
  vocabulary, 142
Luria, A. R., 9
Lutz, C.A., 168
lyrical song, 63, 64–70 *see also stran*

MacDowall, D., 6
MacKenzie, D.N., 163, 282
Makas, H., 14, 16, 78
maktab, *see medrese*
mal, *see* clan
Mala Khalitî, 90, 128, 288
Mann, O., 14, 282, 286
marriage
  and love, 136–41
  endogamy, 31–3, 162, 165, 204
  elopement, 32, 138, 140, 142–3, 149, 150, 165, 283, 289
  'honour killing', 283
  intermarriage, 32
  polygamy, 32, 136
Marzolph, U., 6, 282
massacres, 35, 45, 234, 283
  Yezidi fears of violence, 44
Matrano, see *'Elî and Meryem*
Mayan Khatun, 163
medrese or Qur'anic school, 8, 10
Meḥmûdê 'Eliyê Temo, 144–50, 152–62, 163, 259–62

Meḥmûdê Osê, 224
Meiselas, S., 282, 284
Melayê Jezîrî, 6, 281
Melek Tawus, 34, 35, 51, 55, 149, 150, 215, 283
Mem and Zîn, 13, 66, 67, 71, 72, 75, 82, 120, 136, 149, 174–5, 275, 281, 282
Mem Shivan, *see* Khanek
  shrine of, 193–4
Memê Alan, *see Mem and Zîn*
Memo, son of Shêrîn, 105–7, 113, 234–9, 117, 171, 234–9
Mendikan, 116, 126, 202, 215–32
meqam, 64
mêranî, *see stran* of war
Mêrkan tribe, 88, 90, 104, 114, 223
  village, 103
mêrxasî, *see stran* of war
meshạbet, 34
Meshkîna, 155
Micho, Pîr, 69, 81, 88–101, 105, 113, 116, 117, 124, 142, 161, 206, 287
Miḥemê 'Elî Agha, 116, 117, 215–31, *see also* 'Elî Agha
Miḥemê 'Evdo, 90–101 *passim*, 124–5, 215–231 *passim*
Milan, 26, 27, 45, 108, 110, 120–23, 145, 148, 150–51, 160, 163, 237–58, 259–63
military service, 103–4, 232
  Petition of 1872, 48, 88, 283
Mills, M.A., 5, 24, 71, 131
'Mîr' in oral traditions, 111–12, 120, 131–2, 145, 146, 149, 152, 255–8, 259–62
Mîr of the Yezidis, 27, 28, 29, 30, 31, 32, 34, 38, 46, 69, 88, 126, 140, 284
Mîrza Mohammed, 79
mitirb, 65, 68
Mr A., 65, 170
Mr B., 52, 57, 65, 67, 69, 83, 90, 115, 204, 206, 288
Mr C., 282
Mr E., 71, 75
Mr H., 51, 54, 57, 72, 74, 285
Mr N., 59, 72
Mr P., 43
Mr Y., 67
Mrs J., 189–99, 291–99, 276
Mrs S., 52, 287
Ms F., 286
Ms K., 189–90, 192
Mu'āwiya, Prince, 41
Muhawi, I., 5
mujama'at, *see* villages
Mullah Nasruddin, *see* Nasruddin Hoca
  Murad, river, 145, 262–3
Murad, J.E., 3, 176, 196–8, 290
murîd caste, 30, 32, 43, 52, 68, 72, 287
Music, 291
  studies of, 15
  accompaniment to song, 66, 70, 96
  instruments, 68, 69, 188
  of lamentation, 77
Muslims, 43, 47, 101, 136, 137, 139, 205, 208, 291
  control of Lalêsh shrine, 88, 287
  Yezidi attitudes to, 19, 20, 32, 35, 37, 43, 44, 46, 57, 88, 140, 283
  Yezidi alliances with, 45, 88, 128, 143, 149, 289
  oral traditions about, 66, 122, 123
  informants, 69, 73, 195–6, 290
Mûsqoran, 90
Myth, 36, 40, 60

namûs, 126, 135–9, 141, 162, 163, 165
narrative
  family history, 58–9, 82–3
  poetry and song 63, 64–70, 108, *see also beyt*
  prose, 70–75, 82–3
  Kurdish terminology, 67, 71
Nasr, S.H., 10, 46
Nasruddin Hoca, 6, 13
Nazdar, M., 7
'Nestorians' *see* Christians
Newroz, 6
Nezanê, 162
Nikitine, B, 15, 67, 124, 125, 129, 131, 133, 281, 282, 286

O'Shea, M.T., 290
Omeriyan, 143, 266, 269, 272
Ong, W.J., 8, 281
oral formulaic analysis, 12
oral tradition, 3, 208–10
  anachronisms, 93
  chronological and generic frameworks, 53–85
  decline in Kurmanji, 9
  definitions, and status, 9–10

academic studies and collections, 14–16
popular interest and collection, 19, 84
secular traditions, 50–52
composition and transmission, 80–83
status and value, 85, 87
orality
in Kurmanji, 5, 7–12
and subversion, 5
definitions, 8–9
in Yezidi context, 46–52
and Islam, 10, 46
Osê Mejdî, 89–101 *passim*, 215–231 *passim*

Pa, 'river of kings', 145, 259–62, 277
Palmer, A., 282, 283
Patai, R., 16
Parry, M., 12
Paul, L., 282
Peacock Angel, see Melek Tawus
performance, 4
definitions, 23
and text, 23–15
environments, 52, 69, 76–7, 83, 131, 161
stance and techniques, 70, 74
audience reactions, 70, 84, 98–101, 191–2
Perwer, Ṣivan, 68, 117, 136, 142, 209
peste, 65, 67, 69, 70, 84, 286
pêşmerge, 136, 164, 167, 169
pîr caste, 30, 32, 77, 195, 285
Pirota Castle, 155, 267
'Pîr Qewwal', 105–7, 117, 133, 237–9
Pitê, 158, 162
Pitt-Rivers, J., 141
PKK (Kurdish Workers' Party), 41, 163
Place-names (non-local) in oral tradition, 159
Baghdad, 106, 147, 159, 234–9
Basra, 147
Damascus, 147, 159
Diyarbakir 96, 215–231
Eleshkirt, 258
Hillah, 105, 113, 232–9
Kirkuk 96, 98, 215–231
Kerbela, 105, 113, 232–9
Malatya, 154
Mardin, 154, 252, 253, 267, 269
Muş, 270
Nusaybin, 160, 252, 264
Tbilisi, 278
Urfa, 262
Van, 143
Zînar, 154
Prophets
Adam, 48
Abraham, 13, 48, 59
Muhammad, 13, 40
Noah, 48
Solomon, 13, 59, 71, 72, 174–5, 275
Prym, E., 16
PUK (Patriotic Union of Kurdistan), 17, 37, 38

'Qarpal', 88–101, 113, 115, 117, 215–8, 288
Qarpal Sinjari, 69, 89, 141, 287
Qasim Ḥeso, 66
Qasim Meyro, 81
Qasim Shesho, 86, 115, 202
Qatani sheykhs, 58, 286
Qerezhdakh, 271
Qerqelîn, 266
qesse, 64, 74, 79, 205
qewls, 4, 34, 55, 84, 201, 290
qewwals, 31, 50, 66, 149, 165, 188
Qibali, 270
Qîran, 103
qub, 42

Ramadan, 155, 266
Rashid 'Ali al-Gilani, 104, 233
Rashow, H., 181, 290
Rashow, Kh. Jindî, 16, 47, 49, 104–5, 126–8, 169, 171–5, 213–4, 215–39 *passim*, 263–6, 273–6, 279, 282–5, 290
Rasool, Sh., 75, 198, 287, 290
Rasul, I. M., 67
Razazi, N., 68, 290
Reshkotan, 109
Resho Qulo, 105, 126, 128, 234–9
Resho and Khansê, 158
Resho û Chawîsh, 129
'Resho's father', 215–31
Reynolds, D. F., 5
Rishmili, 270
Ritter, H., 16
Rohat, 164
Rosenberg, D.V., 167

Rudenko, M. B., 168–99 *passim*, 277
Rustem Zal, 79, 174–5, 275

Sabar, Y., 16
'Sacred Books'
  Mesefa Resh, 47, 48, 55
  Kitêba Jilwe, 47, 48, 55
Sa'di al-Qizaz, 127, 130, 233
Ṣakhr Abū 'l Barakat, 56
Samsun, 274
Sarkis Bozoyan, 147–8, 156, 159, 161
Scribner, S., 8–9
Se'dûn, 109–12, 119–24, 239–55
Se'îd Beg, 126, 128, 137, 140, 231, 283, 289
Selimê Mistê, *see* Silêmanê Mistê
Şemo, E., 290
senjaq, 34, 283
Senem, 147
serpêhatî, 74
separateness, *see* Yezidism
Şerê mala Şeşo, 81, 86, 204
Sêvê, 156
Seyahat-name, 33
Seydo, son of Ḥemo Shêro, 94
Shah 'Abbas, 13, 175
Shah-name, 6
Shah Sinem, 174–5, 275
shame, 287
Shammar, 103, 149, 232–3
Sharaf al-Dîn, 56
Shari'e, 20, 29, 43, 51, 52, 54, 58, 59, 71, 74
Shemsani sheykhs, 58
Sheref Khan Bitlisi, 33, 40
Sherefedîn, 154
Sheref-name, 33
Sherifo, 107, 234–9
Shêrîn, mother of Memo, 105–7, 113, 117, 234–9, 133, 170, 171, 207, 234–9
Sheykh Adi
  ambivalence towards, 41
  holy being, 27, 34, 40, 47, 56, 57, 58, 60, 85, 171, 284, 285
  shrine of, 28, 37, 287
Sheykh 'Ajîl, 127, 130, 232
sheykh caste, 30, 32, 41, 77, 195, 283, 285
Sheykh Derwêsh, 81, 287
Sheykh Fekhr el-Dîn, 56
Sheykh Ḥasan, 56
Sheykh Ḥesen, 46, 56, 58
Sheykh 'Isa Effendi, 106, 234–9
Sheykh K., 44, 50, 137, 139
Sheykh Khelef, 103, 127, 130, 233–4
Sheykh Khidir, 103
Sheykh Mend, 58
Sheykh Naṣr el-Dîn, 56
Sheykh Sejadîn, 56
Sheykh Shems el-Dîn, 56, 58
Sheykhan, 26–52 *passim*, 57, 66, 69, 78, 80–81, 83, 88, 94, 113, 140, 150, 151, 171, 177, 181, 201, 205, 206, 207, 232, 283
Sheykhmus, 81, 158
Shryock, A., 5, 73, 84, 285
Sifûq Agha, 88, 90
Sifûqê Meto, 90–101 *passim*, 215–31 *passim*
Silêman, companion of Derwêshê 'Evdî, 109–12
Silêman, Kh., 16, 20, 49, 89, 94, 126, 141, 144, 148–50, 163, 171, 189, 204, 206, 213–4, 231–4
Silêman Beg, 108
Silêman Khershênî, 153
Silêmanê Meḥmûd, 106, 234–9
Silêmanê Mistê, 45, 202, 284
Silo Koro, 105–7, 113, 117, 133, 234–7
Simêl, 43, 130
Sîmurg, 13
Sikan, 274
Simoqan, 90, 288
ṣîn, 13, 64, 75–77, 168, 171, 175–99
  as duty, 195–9
  composition and transmission, 80, 83, 84
  Muslim laments, 75–6, 191
  performers, 76–7
  'personal', 175–6, 187–99, 203
  semi-professional, 177–87, 195–9
ṣîn imagery, 180–87, *see also* landscape and nature imagery
  desirability of deceased, 194–5, 196–9
  place and mood, 182–3
  sickness and wounding, 183–4, 189, 193–5
  wedding motifs, 181–2, 186–7
  estrangement, see *ẍerîb*
Sinjar, 4, 20, 24, 26–52 *passim*, 65, 66, 67, 69, 78, 80–82, 83, 86, 88, 90–101 *passim*, 104–7 *passim*,

113, 121, 126, 127, 128, 130, 133, 140, 148, 151, 158, 161, 171, 201, 204, 205, 206, 209, 215–231 *passim*, 232–3, 234–9, 245, 254, 283, 288–9
Siouffi, N., 40, 284
Sipan, Mount, 142
şi'r, 67, 178
slanders
  'devil-worship', 3, 26, 37
  no washing, 37
  orgies, 37
Slyomovics, S., 5
snakes, 58
Soane, E.B., 281
social context, 21–23
Socin, A., 16
Sodalê, 143, 152, 159
Sorani, 6, 69, 75, 153, 198, 286
  official status in Iraq, 7
stran, 12, 23, 73, 78, 79, 203–8
  composition and transmission, 80–82
  definitions, 65–8
  folkloric songs, 64, 65
  historical songs, 65, 176, 286
  love songs, 45, 65, 67
  status, 83
stran of grief, 65, 167, 171–5, 198 *see also* landscape and nature imagery
  doctors in, 172
stran of love, 141–66, *see also* landscape and nature imagery
  antiphonal songs, 141
  breasts, 153–6
  musical instruments, 153
  representation of women, 136, 151–62, 163–6
  sexually explicit, 135
  sickness, 158–9
stran of war, 65, 86–101, 104–7, 148
  battles, 112–20, 133–4, 203
  martial heroes, 120–8, 133–4
  villains, 128–32
  women as observers, 115–8
stranbêj, 20, 24, 51, 65, 66, 67, 68–70, 78, 81–3, 84, 89–101, 105–7, 115, 140–62 *passim*, 201–9
'Stranvan', 152
Street, B.V., 9–10
Sultan Êzdî, 90–101 *passim*, 215–231 *passim*
Sultan of the Yezidis, 161
Sultan Skull, 174–5, 275

Talabani, Jalal, 17, 18, 38
Tatsumura, A., 15
Tazhi, *see* qewwals
taziye, 25, 76, 169, 178, 189, 196–8
ṭawusgeṛan, 34
'Tawûsparêz', see Lescot, R.
Tbilisi, 17, 25, 77
Teḥsîn Beg, 40, 49–50, 284, 289–90
television, 9, 19, 52
Temer Pasha, 124
Teref, 86
Texts and translations, 213–80
Thomas, R., 8
ṭiwaf, 42, 69
Tur Abdin, 27, 34, 68

Ûdemê Ḥezo, 106, 238, see also Wudemê Ḥezo
'Umar Wahbī Pasha, 28, 87–8, 102 *see also* 'Ferîq Pasha'
Ummayyad, 41
Ûsivan, 113, 114, 223
Uzun, M., 78, 81

Vilchevsky, 13 n., 131, 281, 282
villages, 75, 141, 154
  collectivisation, 9, 29–30, 44, 52, 283
  nostalgia for, 18, 42
  political significance in Kurdish identity, 18, 203
  recall of, 59
  depicted in oral tradition, 136, 144, 162
Voskanyan, V., 290

Wansa, Princess, 137, 139
welat (homeland), 200, 209
Welatê Behri, 263–6
Wêranshehir (Viranşehir), 108, 281
Wershîta, 266
'Widow's Lament', 187–99
women's lament, 63 *see also shîn*
work songs, 78
Wright, W., 284
Wudemê Ezo, 234–9

x̌erîbî, 170–99 *passim*, *see also stran* of grief

Yalçin-Heckmann, L., 136, 138, 165, 289
Yazīd b. Mu'āwiya, 215, 285
Yerevan, 17
Yezidi, *passim*
folkloric status, 26, 38
diaspora, 43, 75, 140
discourses of identity, 3, 36, 38–42, 52, 85, 200
in the Caucasus, 27, 41, 43, 48, 52, 66, 75, 77, 108, 111, 132, 149–50, 168, 177, 210, 282
in Syria, 27
material culture, 39–40
Yezidi historical discourses, 43–46, 51
ages and epochs, 54–5
and legend, 59, 287
chronology, 54–60
anxiety over persecution, 44–45
feeling of disinheritance, 43
preservation of knowledge, 44
resistance to outside authority, 45
presentation of united front, 46
unpredictability of government, 46
Yezidi periodicals
Dengê Êzîdiya, 49
Lalêsh, 49
Roj, 49
Yezidi women,
access to, 19–20
Yezidism, 4, 25, 149
and relations with others, 26–52
caste system, 26, 30–31, 58, 284
debate on origins, 36, 38, 40–41
outsider views, 33–36, 37, 38
purity, notions of 5, 32, 34, 43, 44, 50, 127–8, 133–4, 139–41
orthopraxy, 34, 35, 49
reincarnation, 56–7
taboos, 26, 32, 35, 39, 42
veneration of holy earth, 37
Yusif, scribe of Zor Temer Pasha, 119, 239–55
Yusif and Zuleikha, 13

Zakho, 27, 28, 192
Zargotina K'urda, 65, 66, 67, 71, 79, 80, 81, 108–112, 115, 144–50, 152–62, 177–87, 195–9, 214, 239–58, 259–63, 276–80, 282, 286
Zaza, *see* Dimli
Zembilfirosh, 79
Zerîfka Osê, 90–101 *passim*, 115–17, 215–231 *passim*
Zêrwan, 103, 113, 215–31, 232
Zinar, Z., 281
Ziravê, 158
Zor Temer Pasha, 108–12, 118, 120–123, 131, 148, 161, 239–55
Zoroastrianism, 41
zozan, 154, 174, 191, 200, 209, 273–4
see also landscape and nature imagery